Religion, Power, and the Rise of Shinto in Early Modern Japan

Bloomsbury Shinto Studies

Series editor: Fabio Rambelli

The Shinto tradition is an essential component of Japanese religious culture. In addition to indigenous elements, it contains aspects mediated from Buddhism, Daoism, Confucianism, and, in more recent times, Western religious culture as well—plus, various forms of hybridization among all of these different traditions. Despite its cultural and historical importance, Shinto Studies have failed to attract wide attention partly due to the lingering effects of Japanese ultranationalist propaganda during World War II that made use of aspects of Shinto. The Series makes available to a broad audience a number of important academic works that help dispel widespread misconceptions, according to which Shinto is intrinsically related to Japanese nationalism and constitutes the essence of Japanese culture. By putting such stereotypes into perspective, the series promotes further research and understanding of what is still an underdeveloped field.

Mountain Mandalas: Shugendo in Kyushu, Allan G. Grapard
The Origin of Modern Shinto in Japan: The Vanquished Gods of Izumo, Yijiang Zhong
The Sea and the Sacred in Japan, edited by Fabio Rambelli
Shinto, Nature and Ideology in Contemporary Japan, Aike P. Rots
A Social History of the Ise Shrines, Mark Teeuwen and John Breen

Religion, Power, and the Rise of Shinto in Early Modern Japan

Edited by Stefan Köck, Brigitte Pickl-Kolaczia, and Bernhard Scheid

BLOOMSBURY ACADEMIC
Bloomsbury Publishing Plc
50 Bedford Square, London, WC1B 3DP, UK
1385 Broadway, New York, NY 10018, USA
29 Earlsfort Terrace, Dublin 2, Ireland

BLOOMSBURY, BLOOMSBURY ACADEMIC and the Diana logo are trademarks of
Bloomsbury Publishing Plc

First published in Great Britain 2021
Paperback edition published 2023

Copyright © Stefan Köck, Brigitte Pickl-Kolaczia, Bernhard Scheid and contributors, 2021

Stefan Köck, Brigitte Pickl-Kolaczia and Bernhard Scheid have asserted their right under the Copyright, Designs and Patents Act, 1988, to be identified as Editor of this work.

Cover design: Ben Anslow
Cover image: Yoshida Shrine in Mito City © Brigitte Pickl-Kolaczia, 2018

All rights reserved. No part of this publication may be reproduced or transmitted in any form or by any means, electronic or mechanical, including photocopying, recording, or any information storage or retrieval system, without prior permission in writing from the publishers.

Bloomsbury Publishing Plc does not have any control over, or responsibility for, any third-party websites referred to or in this book. All internet addresses given in this book were correct at the time of going to press. The author and publisher regret any inconvenience caused if addresses have changed or sites have ceased to exist, but can accept no responsibility for any such changes.

A catalogue record for this book is available from the British Library.

Library of Congress Control Number: 2021930421.

ISBN: HB: 978-1-3501-8106-9
PB: 978-1-3502-3186-3
ePDF: 978-1-3501-8107-6
eBook: 978-1-3501-8108-3

Series: Bloomsbury Shinto Studies

Typeset by RefineCatch Limited, Bungay, Suffolk

To find out more about our authors and books, visit www.bloomsbury.com and sign up for our newsletters

Contents

List of Illustrations	vii
Preface	ix
Editorial Conventions	xi

Introduction: Tokugawa Religious Orthopraxy and the Phenomenon of Domain Shinto   *Bernhard Scheid*   1

Part One   Tokugawa Orthopraxy

1 Anti-Christian Temple Certification (*terauke*) in Early Modern Japan: Establishment, Practice, and Challenges   *Nam-lin Hur*   21

2 Ieyasu's Posthumous Title and the Tokugawa Discourse on "Divine Country"   *Sonehara Satoshi*   33

Part Two   Unwanted Religious Groups

3 Anti-Christian Measures in Nagasaki During the Early Edo Period (1614–44)   *Carla Tronu*   47

4 When the Lotus Went Underground: The Nichiren Buddhist Fujufuse Movement and Its Early Modern Persecution   *Jacqueline I. Stone*   61

5 "Deviant Practices" and "Strange Acts": Late Tokugawa Judicial Perspectives on Heteropraxy   *Kate Wildman Nakai*   75

Part Three   Intellectual Challenges

6 Shinto as a Quasi-Confucian Ideology   *Inoue Tomokatsu*   91

7 Buddhist-Confucian Polemics and the Position of Shinto   *W. J. Boot*   103

8 Ikeda Mitsumasa and Confucian Ritual   *James McMullen*   117

9 Calendars and Graves: Shibukawa Harumi's Criticism of Hoshina Masayuki and Yamazaki Ansai   *Hayashi Makoto*   133

Part Four Institutional Challenges

10 Shinto in the 1660s and 1670s: The *Shrine Clauses* of 1665 as an Expression of Domain Shinto   *Mark Teeuwen*   151

11 Domain Shinto and *shintō-uke* in Okayama-han   *Stefan Köck*   163

12 "*Kami* is *kami*, Buddha is Buddha": Religious Policies in Mito Domain in the Later Seventeenth Century   *Brigitte Pickl-Kolaczia*   177

13 Shinto Priests and the Yoshida in Izumi Province   *Yannick Bardy*   191

14 Competing Claims for the Faith and Affiliation of Shrine Priests: The Shirakawa, Yoshida, and Hirata Atsutane   *Anne Walthall*   203

Notes   217
References   247
List of Contributors   267
Index   269

Illustrations

List of Figures

0.1	Tokugawa-related protagonists of Domain Shinto.	12
1.1	Non-Christian temple certificate (*terauke shōmon*).	26
1.2.a–c	Census register of sectarian inspection (*shūmon ninbetsuchō*).	28–9
2.1	Tokugawa Ieyasu as Tōshōgū Divinity (*Tōshōgū goshin'ei*).	38
2.2	Eulogy by Tokugawa Iemitsu, twenty-first commemoration of the death of Ieyasu, 1636.	40
7.1	Portrait of Hayashi Razan.	105
8.1	Ikeda Mitsumasa.	118
8.2	Ikeda tombs at Waidani.	122
9.1	Pacifying stone on the grave of Hoshina Masayuki.	141
9.2	Shinto-style vessel (*ohoto*) for a coffin.	141
9.3	Turtle stone commemorating the life of Hoshina Masayuki.	142
9.4	Votive tablet of Yamazaki Ansai (Suikasha).	143
9.5	The grave of Shibukawa Harumi.	146

List of Maps

3.1–4	Major religious institutions in the Nagasaki region during the sixteenth and seventeenth centuries.	52
13.1	Ōiseki Shrine and Kasuga Shrine in Izumi province.	196
14.1	Hirata-affiliated Hachiman shrines in Mikawa province.	213

List of Tables

11.1	Buddhist temples and clergy in Okayama-han.	170
11.2	Persecution and religious affiliation.	170
12.1	Temples and temple reductions by founding period and sect.	181
12.2	Measures against Hachiman shrines as of 1696.	186

Preface

Religious control was a key issue for the Tokugawa regime. Its most prominent policy was probably the introduction of a legal system that compelled all Japanese to have their religious affiliation certified by a Buddhist temple. However, regarding Buddhist institutions as the sole means used to control religious activity would mean ignoring the plurality and diversity of the religio-political challenges in the early modern period and the various ways they were tackled.

In 2016, the editors of this volume began to investigate a non-Buddhist variety of religious control, namely *shintō-uke*, certification of religious affiliation via Shinto shrines. This involved a research project focusing on two domains—Okayama and Mito—where forms of precisely this phenomenon occurred in the mid-seventeenth century. In order to better understand this specific type of religious control, it soon became clear that we needed to take a step back to view the bigger picture. This motivated us to organize a conference in order to explore the agents, guidelines, and obstacles that shaped religious policies of Tokugawa Japan at various levels: *bakufu*, *han*, and local village; head temples and rural temples; shrines ancient and new; patrons of Shinto; and thinkers with various intellectual backgrounds. Fortunately, we managed to assemble a number of leading scholars working on these questions, as well as a group of up-and-coming specialists, at a conference entitled "Control, repression, and tolerance in early modern Japanese religion," which took place at the Austrian Academy of Sciences, Vienna, from October 31 to November 3, 2018. We benefited immensely from discussing and rethinking our approaches with the other participants, and hope that the present volume will communicate these insights to a wider readership. Our gratitude includes Prof. Dr. Katja Triplett, the only conference participant who unfortunately was prevented from providing a contribution for this publication.

We wish to thank Prof. Dr. Birgit Kellner and the Institute for the Cultural and Intellectual History of Asia (IKGA) for providing the funds for the above-mentioned conference, and the Austrian Science Fund (FWF) for supporting the project "Shinto-uke: religious control via Shinto shrines" (P 29231-G24). Our thanks also go to our student assistants Leonora Pillhofer, Natalie Schnauder, and Benedikt Weiser for their valuable support before and during the conference. Finally, we would like to mention that the conference and this volume contributed to the successful application for a follow-up project on "Domain Shinto" in early modern Japan, again sponsored by the Austrian Science Fund (P 33097-G).

With regard to the completion of this volume, our thanks are due first and foremost to the participants of the conference and their untiring efforts to elaborate on their contributions and answer all our questions in the publication's editorial process. In terms of idiomatic expression, the chapters of this volume (most of them written by non-native English speakers) profited from the experienced eye of Cynthia Peck-

Preface

Kubaczek from the IKGA. In addition, we would like to thank the staff of Bloomsbury for their professional guidance and Lisa Carden for her careful copy-editing. Finally, we are grateful to Dr. Niels van Steenpaal for organizing an image of Hayashi Razan in COVID19-ridden Kyoto, Prof. Dr. Masanobu Higashino for some last-minute checks of manuscripts in the Ikeda Family Archive of Okayama University, and an anonymous peer reviewer for a most supportive evaluation of this volume.

Stefan Köck, Brigitte Pickl-Kolaczia, Bernhard Scheid
Vienna, Oktober 2020

Editorial Conventions

This volume is dedicated to historical analysis rather than to source editions. For this reason, a number of standardizations and simplifications have been applied to the primary material.

Names

The names of Japanese historical figures follow Japanese lexical conventions. Honorary titles, by which such figures were often identified in their times, have been replaced by personal names, also in direct quotes from the sources.

All names, including *ex post* designations of religious groups, are capitalized and in regular type. However, a name (e.g., Fujufuse) can be rendered in italics (*fujufuse*), when referring to the concept that gave the respective group its name.

Dates

As a general rule, dates following traditional Japanese era names (*nengō*) are translated into the corresponding year of the Common Era (CE): 1613 represents Keichō 18 (year eighteen of the Keichō era). In order to maintain consistency with primary sources, however, months and days follow the traditional Japanese counting, which was four to eight weeks behind corresponding CE dates. For instance, 1613/1/1 (read "1613, first month, first day") corresponds to February 20, 1613. Consequently, a mechanical translation from *nengō* to CE fails when applied to dates of the last two months of the pre-modern Japanese calendar. In such cases, Japanese and CE dates are both given: Keichō 18/12/1 (January 10, 1614). Intercalary months according to the traditional lunisolar calendar are indicated by a small "i" (1816/i8/17).

Periodization

- Premodern Japan (before 1868)
    - Ancient period, sixth–eighth century.
    - Classical period, eighth–twelfth century.
        - Nara period, 712–795
        - Heian period, 795–1185
    - Medieval period, twelfth–sixteenth century.
        - Kamakura period, 1185–1336

Editorial Conventions

- Muromachi period, 1336–1573
- Sengoku period, 1467–1590
- Early modern (Edo/Tokugawa) period, 1600–1867

Offices and Titles

Common offices and titles are usually translated into English (followed by the Japanese term in brackets), except for terms that have already found entry into the English vocabulary such as tenno (emperor), shogun (military ruler), or daimyo (regional lord).

Translation Issues

Our translations of primary-source material quoted in chapters originally written in Japanese follows the adaptation into modern Japanese by our Japanese contributors rather than the original texts in classical Japanese or Chinese.

Introduction

Tokugawa Religious Orthopraxy and the Phenomenon of Domain Shinto

Bernhard Scheid

After its military establishment in 1600, the Tokugawa regime invested unprecedented efforts in the creation of a stable feudal hierarchy headed by the shogun. Controlling and channeling religious faith was a key objective of the regime, since autonomous religious institutions as they had existed in medieval Japan were conceived as a potential threat to Tokugawa hegemony. In retrospect, this new concern with religion had started already during the military re-unification of Japan under Oda Nobunaga 織田信長 (1534–82) and Toyotomi Hideyoshi 豊臣秀吉 (1537–98), who forcefully subdued monastic institutions such as Mt. Hiei 比叡山 and theocratic communities under the command of Honganji 本願寺, the head temple of the Amidist Ikkō 一向 sect. Tokugawa Ieyasu 徳川家康 (1543–1616) continued this "taming of Buddhism" by political means when he began issuing laws pertaining to Buddhist temples, thereby establishing a set of officially acknowledged sects. These were the first steps taken by the Tokugawa to remove the medieval military legacy of Buddhist institutions and to impose upon them the duty to pray for the peace and prosperity of the new shogun's regime.[1]

Christianity, which had spread all over Japan in the later sixteenth century, was seen as a religion with even more dangerous potential than certain Buddhist sects. When Ieyasu decided to outlaw it, Buddhist institutions became instrumental in fighting the "pernicious creed" (*jakyō* 邪教) and turned into an important stabilizing factor for the *pax* Tokugawa. Thus, anti-Christianity formed something like an *ex negativo* definition of Tokugawa religious orthopraxy.

After Ieyasu's death in 1616, his deification and enshrinement as a native deity became the basis for a corresponding "positive" practice that added a sacred aura to the ruling dynasty. The "rise of Shinto" addressed in the title of this volume, however, was not only due to Ieyasu's deification. It was also supported by a number of leading regional lords (daimyo) under the sway of Neo-Confucian intellectuals who had developed a distinctly anti-Buddhist discourse.

The complex dynamics of religious politics—the taming of Buddhism and the repression of Christianity—and new intellectual trends—the Neo-Confucian critique of Buddhism and the mapping of a non-Buddhist national legacy, which was called

"Shinto"—are the thematic framework of this collection of essays. Particular emphasis is given to the restructuring of religious institutions during the Kanbun era (1661–73), which occurred almost simultaneously in a number of domains and resulted in local separations of Shinto shrines and Buddhist temples. This phenomenon, which we propose calling "Domain Shinto" or *hanryō shintō* 藩領神道, leads us back to the research project that gave rise to this volume and within which the editors are still working.[2] The basic motivation for creating this volume has been the editors' desire to elucidate the context from which Domain Shinto emerged, and to outline its impact on Shinto history. These questions are discussed in more detail in the second part of this introduction.

Religious Orthopraxy and its Challenges: The Chapters within This Volume

The volume starts (Part 1) with the question why and how anti-Christianity and ruler deification became the two poles of Tokugawa orthopraxy. It proceeds (Part 2) with asking how the Tokugawa regime dealt with unwanted religious groups, and goes on (Part 3) to investigate why many intellectuals looked for alternatives to Buddhism in the guise of Confucianism and Shinto. The final chapters (Part 4) analyze how these new concepts led to Shinto-focused religious reforms by individual daimyo and to a gradual "Shintoization" of shrines at the local level.

Part 1: Orthopraxy

The first chapter by Nam-lin Hur provides a detailed overview of the most significant measure in Tokugawa anti-Christian policy: the requirement to obtain certification of non-Christian status through Buddhist temples (*terauke* 寺請). Hur traces the gradual evolution of this system from the expulsion of European Christians and the banning of their religion in 1614, to the nationwide prescription of *terauke* in 1664. Subsequently, he explains why *terauke* continued even after Christianity was virtually annihilated in the late seventeenth century, and describes the various political and social functions this system took on. This is of central importance for understanding the case studies in Part 4, particularly those that deal with attempts to substitute *terauke* with Shinto certification. Hur concludes his chapter with a short overview of anti-Christianity in the modern period, demonstrating that even during the initial phases of the Meiji government, an attempt was undertaken to continue anti-Christian certification, this time using Shinto shrines.

Sonehara Satoshi, in contrast, addresses the deification of Ieyasu, which he regards as deeply imbued with the idea of Japan as a "divine country" (*shinkoku* 神国). As pointed out in other chapters as well, this concept emerged already in the anti-Christian edicts of Toyotomi Hideyoshi as a positive counter-image to Christianity, and was turned into a kind of manifesto by Ieyasu's advisor Konchiin Sūden 金地院崇伝 (1569–1633), when he drafted an edict against Christianity enacted in Keichō 18/12 (early

1614).³ Sonehara points out that the *shinkoku* concept, even if related literally to the "land of the *kami*" (or the "land of Shinto"), could be read through a Buddhist lens that regarded the divine country of Japan also as a "Buddha land." According to Sonehara, this Buddhist understanding of *shinkoku* assumed quasi-official status when the Tendai 天台 abbot Tenkai 天海 (1536?–1643) deified Tokugawa Ieyasu based on Tenkai's own Buddhist version of Shinto. Ieyasu was thereby ritually transformed into the deity Tōshō Daigongen 東照大権現, an "avatar" (*gongen* 権現) of a buddha in the guise of a *kami*. In the subsequent religious discourse of the Tokugawa elite, Tōshō Daigongen became part of the notion of *shinkoku*, as Sonehara demonstrates through an analysis of eulogies for Ieyasu.

Taken together, both chapters of Part 1 clearly demonstrate that Buddhism was at the core of Tokugawa religious orthopraxy, even if—or rather because—different reasons are given in order to explain this fact. In Sonehara's view, the decision to worship Ieyasu in a Buddhist-Shinto fashion was a major factor for the inclusion of Buddhism in the sacralization of Tokugawa rule. Hur, on the other hand, stresses the importance of Buddhist temples in anti-Christian and, ultimately, everyday ideological control.

Part 2: Unwanted Religious Groups

The chapters of Part 2 provide details on how the Tokugawa actually dealt with "heteropraxy," including not only Christians, but also heterodox Buddhist sects and unwanted folk practitioners. These essays confirm that religious protest was a salient challenge to Tokugawa rule and occurred throughout the entire Tokugawa period.

Carla Tronu discusses the case of Nagasaki, which emerged as the center of Japanese Christianity in the later sixteenth century. Her chapter mentions the first successes of the Christian mission, but focusses on the difficulty of wiping out the foreign religion once it was perceived as "pernicious." In particular, Tronu investigates the reestablishment of traditional religious institutions in Nagasaki, which transformed it from a Christian city into a "normal" Japanese one. The chapter shows that Christian opposition to this political aim continued for decades after Ieyasu's ban of Christianity in 1614, and was subdued not only by force but also by the gradual establishment of a new religious identity in form of temples and shrines. Some of these where strategically placed on former Christian sites, but in general the Christian tendency to build up communities around churches was replaced by the more traditional Japanese pattern of establishing religious institutions on the outside edges of urban communities.

Jacqueline Stone traces the history of the Fujufuse-ha 不受不施派, a subsect of Nichiren 日蓮 Buddhism. This group of radically exclusivist Lotus adherents followed the principle of *fujufuse* 不受不施, "neither receiving [alms] nor giving [prayers]." In practice, they denied religious service to any non-member of their sect. This included even the Tokugawa and all other mundane authorities. Consequently, they were outlawed in the 1660s, in a way similar to the earlier prohibition of Christianity. Stone points out that the principle of *fujufuse* was actually mainstream among late medieval Nichirenists. Thus, the compromise-ready faction of Nichiren Buddhism, which accepted submission to the *bakufu*, had a hard time "converting" its grassroots followers, which in turn led to fierce and brutal infighting within the entire sect. The persecution of the Fujufuse by worldly authorities, on the other hand, demonstrates two things: 1) the determination of the new regime to streamline religious faith according to a new standard of loyalty; and 2) the commitment to antinomian Buddhist teachings by a significant part of the Nichiren tradition.

Kate Wildman Nakai investigates the legal treatment of "deviant" or "strange" religious practices, as it appears in precedents collated by the deliberative council (*hyōjōsho* 評定所), the highest judicial organ of the *bakufu*, in the early nineteenth century. Nakai uses the recommendations for appropriate sentences by this council to arrive at an understanding of what kind of religious beliefs or practices were considered illegal and why. She points out that judicial interpretations did not follow a fixed canon of "orthopraxy," but were situational, putting the emphasis on the status of a delinquent and his or her implicit stance towards the *bakufu*, rather than on what he or she actually did. While most cases deal with individual instances of deceit or fraud and do not give the impression that heterodoxy *per se* was still a pervasive problem in the early nineteenth century, this changed around 1827, when Christianity reappeared in a famous incident in Osaka. In place of the more common "exile to a remote island," in this case the wrongdoers were sentenced to crucifixion. This indicates that Christianity was still the epitome of a "pernicious" religious creed in the late Tokugawa period.

Part 3: Intellectual Challenges

More indirect challenges to the Tokugawa management of religious faith emerged from several interrelated milieus: a new class of scholars and intellectuals interested in (Neo-) Confucianism; a new type of benevolent dictator-daimyo, who envisioned socio-political reforms on the basis of Confucian ideals of rulership; and a surprisingly small stratum of shrine priests who gradually emancipated themselves, at least in some places, from the traditional Buddhist supervision of shrine cults. All of these groups shared a critical view of Buddhism and were at the same time loyal to the ruling regime. This opened a window for the self-sustained development of Shinto. Part 3 of this volume tackles the question of why early Tokugawa Confucianism was particularly interested in "Shinto" as an alternative to Buddhism, and what "Shinto" actually meant from a Confucian perspective.

According to Inoue Tomokatsu, Confucianism became important in Tokugawa Japan as a hallmark of East Asian (or Chinese) civilization, in spite of the institutional hegemony of Buddhism. Confucianism, however, placed little value on martial virtues. Therefore, the Tokugawa's self-perception as "warriors" made it difficult to adopt Confucianism in its entirety. In this situation, Neo-Confucian intellectuals created a new Shinto paradigm, which was largely based on Confucian ideas but was also compatible with "martiality." This was the "quasi-Confucian ideology" that appeared in the seventeenth century in the guise of "Shinto." Inoue relates this intellectual trend to the Shinto reforms of the 1660s, discussed in Part 4. He argues that the comparatively well-known reforms in Aizu 会津藩, Mito 水戸藩, and Okayama 岡山藩 were just the most radical examples of a general political trend to: (1) revive ancient shrines; (2) separate these shrines from Buddhism; and (3) shut down "illicit shrines" (*inshi* 淫祠), that is, syncretic shrines without a historical pedigree. These reforms were not only tolerated but actively pursued by *bakufu* leaders such as Hoshina Masayuki 保科正之 (1611–73). In Inoue's depiction, "quasi-Confucian Shinto" appears as a counter-model to Sonehara's Buddhist Shinto, but the actual relationship between these ideological currents remains open to discussion.

This topic is addressed by W.J. Boot, who asks how Buddhists (still the majority within the intellectual elite) reacted to the anti-Buddhist polemics advanced by Neo-Confucian critics such as Hayashi Razan 林羅山 (1583–1657). In particular, he deals with the Shingon 真言 intellectual Jakuhon 寂本 (1631–1701) and the Ōbaku 黃檗 monk Chōon Dōkai 潮音道海 (1628–95), who paid back Razan's assaults in the same coin. Two texts emerge as important points of reference in these polemic exchanges: Razan's history of Japanese shrines (*Honchō jinja kō* 本朝神社考, published around 1645) and the apocryphal *Taisei kyō* 大成経, alledgedly by Shōtoku Taishi 聖徳太子, which may be described as a lengthy Buddhist version of classical Japanese mythology.[4] Both *Taisei kyō* and Razan's shrine history deal primarily with "Shinto," including national mythology and its traces in contemporary shrine cults. Thus, Shinto played a key role as a kind of token that both Confucians and Buddhists claimed for themselves. The debate was essentially about the question of which side was closer to Shinto. Voices from the Shinto priesthood itself, however, did not take part in this discussion.

James McMullen introduces us to the mentality of Ikeda Mitsumasa 池田光政 (1609–82), daimyo of Okayama and one of the most radical religious reformers of his time. Mitsumasa was originally inspired by Confucian teachings and is thus a perfect example of the ideological trend outlined by Inoue. After an initial interest in the tradition of Shingaku 心学 ("doctrine of the mind") by Nakae Tōju 中江藤樹 (1608–48), focusing on interior cultivation, in his later years Mitsumasa shifted to a more governmental philosophy in the tradition of Zhu Xi 朱熹 (1130–1200). It was only then that Mitsumasa began to imply institutional religious innovations, which focused initially on Confucian rituals as substitutes for Buddhist ancestor worship. We look in vain for a particular commitment to Shinto that might explain Mitsumasa's radical restructuring of Okayama's religious landscape (as described by Stefan Köck in Part 4). According to McMullen, Mitsumasa's personal religious convictions were entirely confined to a Confucian worldview. Mitsumasa's son and successor, however, did not share his predilections and thus most Confucian reforms in Okayama did not stand the test of time.

Hayashi Makoto approaches Confucian Shinto from a more sociological perspective. His chapter first deals with the vital role of what he calls the "salon of Hoshina Masayuki." Masayuki was not only a preeminent daimyo and statesman of the mid-seventeenth century, but also a Confucian intellectual and sponsored learned debates among scholars such as Yamazaki Ansai 山崎闇斎 (1619–82) and the Shinto teacher Yoshikawa Koretaru 吉川惟足 (1616–94). Thus, Masayuki's residence in Edo became a melting pot of Confucian and Shinto ideas, some of which were put into practice by Masayuki in his own domain, Aizu. Among the younger generation of scholars in his salon was Shibukawa Harumi 渋川春海 (1639–1715), who became famous for his calendar reform of 1685. As Hayashi argues, this endeavor was triggered by a belief in a native calendar conceived by Jinmu Tennō 神武天皇, Japan's mythological first emperor, which Harumi tried to recreate. Harumi applied a similar nativist axiom also in his lesser-known attempt to reconstruct original Shinto funerals. In other words, the calendar reform was a product of nativist ideals materializing for the first time in Masayuki's salon. These ideas seem to have foreshadowed a self-contained voice of Shinto as it later emerged in the guise of National Learning (Kokugaku 国学).

Altogether, the chapters of Part 3 illustrate the appeal of Neo-Confucian thought for intellectuals dissatisfied with the traditional prerogatives of Buddhism. At the same time, they hint at the difficulties to challenge Buddhism at an institutional level, especially when it came to funerals. It seems possible that the Confucian interest in Shinto derived in no small part from the pragmatic consideration that it was much easier to substitute Buddhist ritualism by shrine rites than by Chinese ritualism, which lacked a living tradition in Japan.

Part 4: Institutional Challenges

Part 4 lastly arrives at regional temples and shrines and their transformation. From this perspective, the later seventeenth century appears as a laboratory of what we call "Domain Shinto," culminating in the separation of Shinto and Buddhism (*shinbutsu bunri* 神仏分離) in a few provinces, typically led by daimyo interested in Confucian Shinto, as already mentioned by Inoue. In these provinces, the religious landscape was turned upside down by a massive destruction of both unwanted temples and "illicit shrines." The net effect was in most cases a severe reduction of religious structures and only a few older shrines profited from these measures. Most of them took place in the years after the enactment of the first Tokugawa law for shrine priests, the *Shrine Clauses* (*Jinja jōmoku* 神社条目, also known as *Shosha negi kannushi hatto* 諸社禰宜神主法度), of 1665. The close succession of Shinto legislation and Shinto reforms seems to be no coincidence and yet it is still unclear how they related to each other.

The most notable stipulation of the *Shrine Clauses* is the official (yet somewhat ambiguous) acknowledgement of the Yoshida 吉田, a traditional lineage of imperial court priests, as the leading authority in the world of Shinto. According to Mark Teeuwen, however, the *Shrine Clauses* not only strengthened the Yoshida, but also encouraged a general "Shintoization" of shrines, since they credited "Shinto" a status on par with Buddhism—according to some contemporary interpretations at least. This led to the self-empowerment of priests and Shinto-friendly daimyo. Was this Shintoization an intended aim of the *Shrine Clauses*? In order to answer this question, Teeuwen analyzes cases of Shinto-Buddhist separation at well-known shrine-temple complexes, namely Izumo 出雲, Hie 日吉, and Ise 伊勢. While Izumo and Ise were indeed Shintoized through a radical reduction of Buddhist facilities around the shrines, the attempt to disentangle Hie from Buddhism failed. In contrast to Inoue, who mentions these cases as well, Teeuwen does not see a clear-cut ideological pattern at work. Rather, he points to inherent problems of the religious legislation as it took shape in the 1660s: While it seemed to grant a choice of religious affiliation—of course only within the boundaries of accepted religious sects, but including Shinto—the ensuing competition among "brokers of faith" became a problem and urged the government to discourage religious freedom. This may be one reason why the heyday of Domain Shinto ended by the late seventeenth century.

Stefan Köck leads us back to Okayama, analyzing in detail the dramatic religious restructuring measures of daimyo Ikeda Mitsumasa. One year after the *Shrine Clauses*, Mitsumasa reduced the number of shrines in Okayama to one per village and of Buddhist temples by more than 50 percent. In 1667, he introduced a system of religious certification by Shinto shrines (*shintō-uke* 神道請), which was fully established two years later. In this way, Okayama became the first comprehensive example of Domain Shinto, characterized by the separation of shrines and temples, a separate Shinto priesthood, and separate Shinto rites. However, Köck agrees with McMullen that these reforms did not follow a specific masterplan. Rather, each step in the reforms yielded originally unintended results that necessitated increasingly radical reforms. In this process, the persecution of Buddhists, especially Fujufuse Nichiren adherents (mentioned in Part 2), who had a particular stronghold in Okayama, was an important catalyst. Their massive expulsion from Okayama seems to have led to a shortage of Buddhist monks performing the task of *terauke*, which encouraged Mitsumasa to have the populace certificated by shrines. After Mitsumasa left his office in 1672, mandatory *shintō-uke* was discontinued. This was due both to governmental verdict and the lack of enthusiasm for Mitsumasa's reforms by his successors. In the end, however, *shintō-uke* remained an option for shrine priests, who had been generally strengthened by Mitsumasa's reforms. Okayama thus preserved a core of Shinto-friendly innovations that appeared elsewhere only towards the end of the Tokugawa period.

Brigitte Pickl-Kolaczia addresses the equally well-known restructuring of religion in Mito Domain by Tokugawa Mitsukuni 徳川光圀 (1628–1701), which occurred nearly at the same time as the Okayama reforms.[5] In Mito, however, there were surprisingly few shrines, and thus the reduction of the number of temples was the most spectacular outcome. In the end, the "one shrine per village" principle, which existed in both domains, led in Mito to an increase in the number of (acknowledged) Shinto sites. *Shintō-uke*, as well as Shinto funerals were also introduced in Mito, albeit to a much lesser degree than in Okayama, since such innovations were meant for shrine personnel only. Thus, the reforms seem to have been less controversial than in Okayama, which may be one reason why more than one generation of rulers put efforts into continuing them. A distinctive feature of the Mito reforms is the abolishment of Hachiman shrines for reasons that are still open to debate.

As in Okayama, Confucianism played an important role in the religious ritualism of Mito's ruling family and its samurai vassals. The examples of Okayama and Mito thus illustrate what has already become apparent in the chapters of Part 3, namely that the religious reforms by certain leading daimyo of that period were driven by a combination, not always consistent, of Confucianism (including Confucian family rituals) and anti-Buddhism, focusing in particular on criticism of Shinto-Buddhist syncretism.

Yannick Bardy's chapter constitutes a regional and a temporal counterpoint to the above mentioned cases of Domain Shinto. It provides a glimpse into the management of local shrines in the eighteenth century, a time when the majority of Japanese villages had shrines but no professional Shinto clergy. Rather than local daimyo, the Yoshida house in Kyoto and their affiliated priests became points of orientation for village shrines. What did Yoshida affiliation actually mean? As explained in more detail below, the Yoshida sold licenses and a number of religious objects that enhanced the status of the respective local shrine and its community. The only prerequisite in terms of Shinto "dogmatics" was the existence/establishment of a professional priest. Bardy analyzes two cases in Izumi province where such Yoshida licenses played a part in local conflicts: in one case, a priest successfully used a Yoshida license to enhance his own status in relation to his community; in the other case, a family of shrine priests defended their privileged position at a locally important shrine. In both cases, the Yoshida helped confirm the status of the local priest, but their support involved enormous financial burdens. For this reason, Yoshida licenses remained the exception rather than the rule in the context of Edo period shrines. Nevertheless, the practice of licensing priests constituted a nucleus of priestly professionalization.

Anne Walthall revisits the question of shrine priest administration, focusing on the early nineteenth century. This was the time when Kokugaku and, in particular, Hirata Atsutane 平田篤胤 (1776–1843) and his school attracted a growing number of adherents. Kokugaku scholars criticized all syncretic forms of Shinto; from their perspective, this also included Yoshida Shinto. Nevertheless, Atsutane was active as a teacher for the Yoshida as well as their archrival, the Shirakawa 白川, soon after both houses created schools for shrine priests in Edo. Walthall analyzes what motivated Atsutane to cooperate with these two established court priest lineages, as well as why they were interested in him. In addition, she presents a case study of shrine priests in Mikawa province who rejected their traditional affiliations to the Yoshida. This proved surprisingly difficult and the priests were only successful because membership in Atsutane's school provided them with the necessary intellectual weapons. The chapter thus illustrates that local strata of late Edo shrine priests became aware of alternatives to Yoshida Shinto due to Kokugaku. The Yoshida in turn applied new strategies to maintain their monopoly on priestly licenses, which involved cooperation with Kokugaku leaders such as Atsutane.

Domain Shinto

As mentioned above, the editors of this volume propose "Domain Shinto" as a generic term for a range of religious reforms that figure prominently in several of the chapters outlined above. These reforms reached a peak in the Kanbun era (1661–73) and were typically directed or at least supported by strong-minded local lords. Domain Shinto reforms aimed in particular to abolish syncretic phenomena such as Buddhist monks taking over ritual functions at *kami* shrines. As Inoue Tomokatsu argues in this volume and elsewhere, these measures went hand in hand with a new consciousness of "ancient Shinto" conceived as a Japanese moral Way that had existed before the advent of Buddhism. It remains open to debate, however, whether this preoccupation with native traditions and the ensuing criticism of syncretic phenomena should be regarded as the mainstream ideology, as Inoue maintains. The official *gongen* cult of Ieyasu outlined by

Sonehara, for instance, may be taken as a counter example, since this cult was entirely based on a medieval, "syncretic" model of religion, according to which Buddhism managed and supervised all matters related to "Shinto."

In order to add my own observations to this discussion, I would like to draw attention to four prerequisites or constituents of Domain Shinto: (1) the impact of Yoshida Shinto; (2) the legal situation of the 1660s; (3) the agents of Domain Shinto; and (4) daimyo funerals and ancestor cults. These topics are of course mentioned in several chapters of this volume, yet mostly only in passing. Thus, they merit a more detailed introduction here.

Yoshida Shinto

Yoshida Kanetomo 吉田兼倶 (1435–1511), who is today regarded as the founder of Yoshida Shinto, created an important prerequisite for Shinto's independence from Buddhism when he designed specific death rites for himself and his family, thus ignoring the traditional death taboo in Shinto.[6] This enabled Yoshida Shinto to offer non-Buddhist death rites for military rulers, starting with the deification of Sengoku warlord Ōuchi Norihiro 大内教弘 (1420–65) in 1486.[7] In this way, Yoshida deification became an option for military hegemons who strove to strengthen their regime by religious means. While the Yoshida-Ōuchi cult still needs to be studied in detail, the deification of Toyotomi Hideyoshi, which seems to have followed the Ōuchi precedent, is much better documented. It was prearranged by Hideyoshi himself as part of his last will and resulted in the construction of a large shrine in Kyoto in 1599, where Kanetomo's descendant Yoshida Kanemi 吉田兼見 (1535–1610) deified Hideyoshi as Toyokuni Daimyōjin 豊国大明神.

Ieyasu regarded Hideyoshi's shrine with growing suspicion, as it attracted immense popularity among the inhabitants of Kyoto. When he finally extinguished the entire Toyotomi clan in 1614 and 1615, it was only natural to destroy also its spiritual memory in form of the Toyokuni Shrine (Toyokunisha 豊国社). The new pattern of ruler deification, however, seemed all the more desirable for the Tokugawa. Shortly after Ieyasu died in 1616, a first preliminary deification rite was performed for him according to Yoshida Shinto.[8] As Sonehara describes in detail below, however, the ensuing contest between the leading religious advisors of the Tokugawa regime resulted in the decision that Ieyasu's deification should not follow Hideyoshi's too closely. This led to the removal of Yoshida Shinto from Ieyasu's cult. Ieyasu's newly built mausoleum, the Tōshōgū 東照宮 in Nikkō 日光, was monopolized by Tendai Buddhism and over time the highest Shinto ceremonies there were performed by Tendai clerics recruited from the imperial family. Thus, Yoshida Shinto was replaced by Buddhist ritualists, Buddhist icons, Buddhist allusions to imperial ancestor cults,[9] and the conception of Ieyasu as a Shinto avatar of a buddha.

In spite of this setback, the Yoshida continued to benefit from another source of prestige and income, namely a unique trade in semi-official licenses for local shrines with no previous relations to the imperial court. This tradition can also be traced back to Yoshida Kanetomo,[10] but it was not before the sixteenth century that it turned into a full-fledged business activity of the Yoshida family, as described by Bardy.

Yoshida authority on Shinto matters was ultimately based on the Yoshidas' claim of possessing timeless "secrets," which turned them into the leading court priests. These secrets did not consist in a particular Shinto teaching—let alone the critique of Buddhism, for which Kanetomo's theoretical writings are famous today—but were related to ritual initiations and magic objects that the Yoshida traced back to the "Age of the Gods." Even if some intellectuals began to raise doubts regarding the actual existence of such secrets already in the seventeenth century, most figures whom we encounter in this volume believed in them. Shogunal regent Hoshina Masayuki, for instance, seems to have been particularly attracted by the charisma of Yoshida secrets, as discussed below. On the other hand, the term *yuiitsu shintō* 唯一神道, "One-and-only Shinto," which was originally coined as a self-designation of Yoshida Shinto by Kanetomo, developed into a kind of slogan for Shinto independence movements in the early Tokugawa period. As I have argued in detail elsewhere,[11] *yuiitsu shintō* was used by shrine priests in Izumo or Ise among others, who had no relation to the Yoshida at all.

In other words, Yoshida Shinto constituted an important prerequisite for a general "Shintoization" of shrines in the Tokugawa period, but was not identical with and probably not even a major driving force behind Domain Shinto in the seventeenth century. In particular, the criticism of Buddhism, which forms a salient feature of Domain Shinto rhetoric, derives from Confucian intellectuals, as already mentioned. The Yoshida, on the other hand, did not even refrain from licensing Buddhist shrine supervisors (*bettō* 別当), as mentioned in Bardy's chapter. Yet, in contrast to Confucians, the Yoshida impersonated imperial religious legacy (both real and imagined). Even if they were challenged in this capacity by the Shirakawa (as discussed below by Walthall), they remained the dominant link between court ritualism and the outer world of Shinto during the entire early modern period.

The Legal Situation

As mentioned, the most striking reforms of Domain Shinto occurred in the wake of new laws on religious administration. Of particular concern were the decrees of 1664 to install *terauke* on a nationwide scale[12] and the tandem enactment of the *Shrine Clauses* and a new *Law for Temples of all Buddhist Sects* (*Shoshū jiin hatto* 諸宗寺院法度), on 1665/7/11. The *Temple Laws* justified measures against unwanted Buddhist sects, as for instance the Fujufuse branch of Nichiren Buddhism. In line with these regulations, persecution of Fujufuse adherents started in 1666.[13] As explained by Köck, this seems to have turned into a catalyst for the radical switch from *terauke* to *shintō-uke* in Okayama. In Mito, the *terauke* system led to a different treatment of temples according to their religious functions and sources of income. Temples that based their economy on funerals usually possessed a fixed community of "patrons" (*danna* 檀那). These temples turned into the actual hubs of the *terauke* system and were left untouched by the authorities. Temples without *danna* support, on the other hand, usually offered so-called *kitō* 祈祷 services such as healing and fortune-telling to all sorts of clients. Mito closed down mainly temples of this latter category since they were regarded as useless and even dangerous. We can surmise that such criticism was in no small part motivated by economic reasons.

Similar distinctions existed between shrines of traditional pedigree (in particular *shikinaisha* 式内社)[14] and illicit shrines (*inshi*). While the identification of local *shikinaisha* and *inshi* occurred in different domains at different times, the removal of unwanted shrines coincided with the reduction of Buddhist temples shortly after the promulgation of the 1665 laws on temples and shrines, respectively. Thus, the new legal situation obviously encouraged local religious reforms. Nevertheless, as pointed out by Teeuwen, the laws themselves reveal not much more than an appeal for stricter norms, but do not specify what these norms should consist of and how they should be enforced.

The Agents of Domain Shinto

Fig. 0.1 provides an overview of daimyo who are known for reforms that we classify as Domain Shinto. All of them are direct descendants of Tokugawa Ieyasu, most of them of the *gosanke* 御三家 or *shinpan* 親藩 categories,[15] with the notable exception of Okayama's Ikeda Mitsumasa. However, Mitsumasa turned into a Tokugawa relative through adoption and marriage. Incidentally, he and two other protagonists of Domain Shinto related to the Tokugawa—Tokugawa Mitsukuni and Hoshina Masayuki—are conventionally known as the "three illustrious lords" (*san meikun* 三名君) of early Tokugawa Japan.

As noted, these main agents of Domain Shinto were supported by Neo-Confucian advisors, who fostered among other things a much more aggressive form of anti-Buddhism than (for instance) the Yoshida. We are therefore confronted with the confusing situation of Tokugawa self-sacralization in the guise of Ieyasu's *gongen* cult—a Buddhist type of Shinto—on the one hand, and the promotion of Shinto on the basis of Confucian and anti-Buddhist ideas by certain daimyo of the Tokugawa family, on the other hand. This leads to the question of whether the respective daimyo undertook their reforms in the interest of stabilizing Tokugawa rule, or in the interest of their specific branch lineages. Let me approach this question by taking a closer look at the above-mentioned daimyo and *bakufu* leader Hoshina Masayuki.

As can be seen in Fig. 0.1, Hoshina Masayuki was the uncle and tutor of Shogun Ietsuna 徳川家綱 (1641–80, r. 1651–80), who at the tender age of eleven years succeeded his father Iemitsu 徳川家光 (1604–51, r. 1623–51). The position of shogunal tutor turned Masayuki into a *de facto* regent and thus into the most powerful political figure in the government. In the 1650s, he earned fame as an able leader due to his efforts to rebuild Edo after the Meireki fire of 1657 (Meireki 3) and the installation of a water supply system for the city from the Tama River. In his own domain, Aizu, he established a storage system based on ancient Chinese models to prevent famine. As Hayashi points out below, his political thinking was marked by the criticism of martial customs from the Sengoku period, such as keeping members of daimyo families being held hostage in Edo (*daimyō shōnin seido* 大名証人制度) or vassal suicide after the death of their lord (*junshi* 殉死). In other words, Masayuki displayed a talent for successful structural reforms and a longing for a civilized Confucian society. But he had not yet put his mark on religious policies.

After 1660, however, when Masayuki was close to fifty years of age, he shifted his attention towards more intellectual pursuits. It is during this period that Masayuki

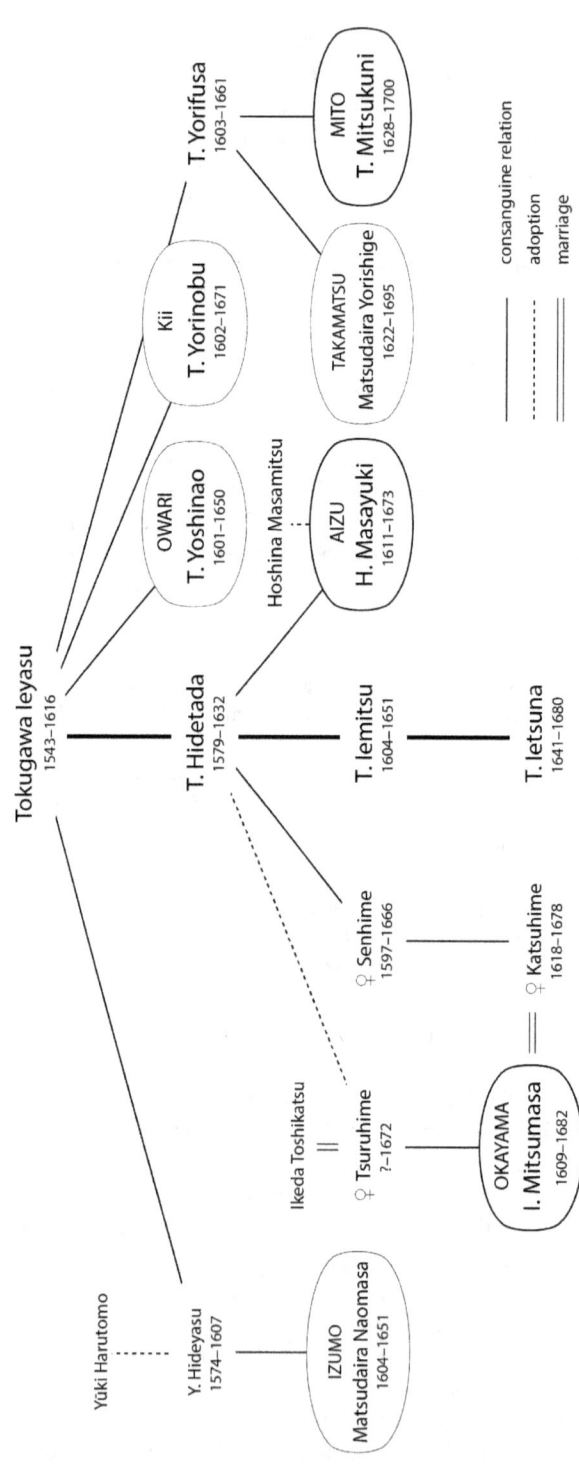

Figure 0.1 Tokugawa-related protagonists of Domain Shinto.

developed a keen interest in Confucianism and Shinto and established an intellectual salon, as detailed in Hayashi's chapter. As regards Shinto, the single most important figure in this salon was the already mentioned Yoshikawa Koretaru. When compared to previous Shinto intellectuals, Koretaru was a most untypical figure, since he was an Edo merchant by birth and profession without any family relations to a particular shrine, let alone to the imperial court. In his search for Japan's "ancient Way," however, he went to Kyoto and met the Yoshida scion Hagiwara Kaneyori 萩原兼従 (1588–1660), the former head priest of Hideyoshi's shrine, who can be regarded as a kind of *éminence grise* of Yoshida Shinto at that time. Strangely enough, the old court priest accepted the Edo merchant not only as a disciple, but also as a suitable "vessel" (*utsuwamono*) for transmitting the deepest secrets of Yoshida Shinto.[16] As mentioned above, the exact nature of these secrets—a written text or an object—is unclear to modern historiography, but their main function was the same in either case: to serve as a token of legitimacy for the head of the Yoshida tradition. The need to find a trustee for these secrets was related to a succession crisis within the Yoshida house at that time. Koretaru was initiated into these Yoshida secrets upon the condition that he return them to the Yoshida house as soon as a new head had been agreed upon. However, he used these tokens to establish himself as a teacher of Shinto for the political elite, starting in 1657 with Tokugawa Yorinobu 徳川頼宣 (1602–71), daimyo of Kishū 紀州藩. At the time, he was already augmenting his secret initiations with a teaching he called "Shinto of the Study of Principles" (*rigaku shintō* 理学神道), a blend of Confucianism and Shinto,[17] probably inspired by Razan's *ritō shinchi shintō* 理当心地神道 ("Shinto of Principles present in the Heart").

After being introduced to Hoshina Masayuki in 1661, Koretaru soon entered his service. Their intellectual and spiritual cooperation involved also other members of Masayuki's salon, in particular his Confucian tutors Hattori Ankyū 服部安休 (1619–81) and Yamazaki Ansai. All of these men were in due course initiated into Koretaru's Yoshida secrets. This break of traditional secrecy rules was a grave offence in the eyes of the entire court in Kyoto, but the status of the beneficiaries made even protests by the emperor futile.

The chronology of Masayuki's Domain Shinto measures in his own domain Aizu starts only after his acquaintance with Koretaru. After a survey of the chronicles of temples and shrines and a search for *shikinaisha* was undertaken in 1664, several *shikinaisha* and other old shrines were rebuilt in 1667. Buddhist elements were removed from many shrines and "illicit shrines" were abolished. In the same year, Aizu introduced a system of registration of religious affiliation at shrines (*jinja aratame* 神社改) comparable to Okyama's *shintō-uke*. In 1672, a list of shrines in Aizu (*Aizu jinja-shi* 会津神社志) was compiled and finally, between 1673 and 1675, Yoshikawa Koretaru and others performed Masayuki's own Shinto funeral and deification.[18]

When comparing these measures to those of other Shinto-friendly domains, we realize that Masayuki was certainly not the first to employ Domain Shinto. Surveys of local shrines, for instance, had been started by his uncle Tokugawa Yoshinao 徳川義直 (1600–50, daimyo of Owari 尾張藩), as early as 1646,[19] and the restructuring of temples and shrines in Mito or Okayama occurred at about the same time or earlier than

Masayuki's. Masayuki, however, differed from his fellow daimyo due to his access to Yoshida secrets, provided by Koretaru. In addition, it is very probable that he was a driving force behind the *Shrine Clauses* of 1665. As I have argued elsewhere, the confirmation of Yoshida prerogatives in this legal document can be explained as compensation for the breach of Yoshida secrets by Koretaru and Masayuki.[20] In addition, both men also helped establish Yoshida Shinto in northeastern Japan, particularly in the domains of Aizu and Tsugaru 津軽藩.[21] But even if the *Shrine Clauses* did not owe their existence to Masayuki's feelings of guilt towards the Yoshida, they were meant and understood as a visible mark of the *bakufu*'s (Masayuki's) interest in Shinto. Since this prompted religious reforms in a number of domains, we may say that Masayuki was indeed a key figure in the establishment of Domain Shinto, even if he was probably not among the pioneers of this trend.

Funerals and Ancestor Cults

Among all the innovations triggered by the cooperation between Hoshina Masayuki and Yoshikawa Koretaru, Masayuki's Shinto funeral and his subsequent deification are particularly noteworthy. While these events are analyzed in detail in Hayashi's chapter, I would like to stress here that Masayuki's funeral met with surprising disapproval by administrators in the *bakufu* and in Masayuki's own domain. A debate regarding this funeral started already a day after his demise in Edo, on Kanbun 12/12/18 (February 4, 1673), between the major ritualist Koretaru and Inaba Masanori 稲葉正則 (1623–96),[22] a senior councilor (*rōjū* 老中) of the *bakufu*. The latter was obviously in a position to disregard Masayuki's last will, which demanded a Shinto funeral without Buddhist interference. Instead, the councilor insisted on the usual sutra readings at a Buddhist temple. According to Koretaru's biography,[23] the councilor advanced the argument that "state affairs must be inclusive and all-encompassing, and this is a state affair (*tenka no hō* 天下の法)."[24] In other words, a *bakufu* leader's funeral had to include Buddhism, no matter what had been the wish of the deceased. This provoked Koretaru to hold a sermon on Shinto that foreshadows crucial nativist arguments familiar to us from one or two hundred years later:

> It goes without saying that Japan is the Land of the Gods (*shinmei no kuni* 神明の国). We are all descendants of the *kami*. Even you, my lord, are a descendant of the *kami*. The Way is the teaching of Amaterasu Ōmikami, but today people continually turn away from the Way of the divine rulers, ignore the feelings of their divine ancestors, and follow an alien teaching. The reason is that no men of true talent have emerged in our Way. Despite generations of wise rulers in the past, the Way remained empty and rotten. Then a leader of wisdom was born, Lord Hoshina, who revived traditional Japanese rites. Appreciation grew and influenced the shogun himself. To help realize his wishes is the right course for a councilor to prove his talent. Would it not be for the merit and benefit of future generations to revive an ailing Way? Should we not offer virtue for posterity, for future generations? If you reject my request, the ancient rites of Japan will never be revived. Is the time not ripe?[25]

While this sermon impressed the councilor, Koretaru had yet another ace up his sleeve, namely a certificate (probably issued by himself) that Hoshina Masayuki had been initiated during his lifetime into the deepest secrets of Yoshida Shinto. According to Koretaru's biography, it was this token of legitimacy that convinced the councilor of the seriousness of Masayuki's wish. He finally granted permission upon the condition that Koretaru would not mention their meeting to any outsider and that he perform the necessary rituals in a modest way.[26] The next day, Masayuki's corpse was carried in a procession from Edo to Aizu, but had to remain unburied for another three months until Masayuki's son and successor came home from Edo to take part in the final ceremonies. It took Koretaru another two years of lobbying to receive permission for the erection of a shrine, Hanitsu Jinja 土津神社, where he deified Masayuki as Hanitsu Reishin 土津霊神. After this precedent had been established, however, all subsequent daimyo of Aizu received Shinto funerals as well. In short, Masayuki's funeral was finally carried out according to his wishes, but was reduced from a "state affair" to a "domain affair." In this sense, Domain Shinto in Aizu resulted in a particular emphasis on Shinto funerals, which superseded the official death rites standardized according to Buddhist norms.

Other protagonists of Domain Shinto such as Tokugawa Yoshinao (daimyo of Owari), Ikeda Mitsumasa, and Tokugawa Mitsukuni exhibited a similar desire for special death rites, but they turned to Confucian ancestor cults. Yoshinao, for instance, requested a Confucian funeral, but when he died in 1650 the government nevertheless conducted a Buddhist sutra recitation.[27] His choice of Confucianism may have been a matter of limited options. Shinto funerals were simply not available without personal links to the Yoshida, at least at the level of official protocol.

On the other hand, Shinto deifications must have existed in daimyo houses outside the Tokugawa family, for instance in Tosa 土佐藩, Kaga 加賀藩 or Sendai 仙台藩, as indicated by Luke Roberts.[28] Early examples such as the deification of Maeda Toshiie 前田利家 (1538–99) or Date Masamune's 伊達政宗 (1567–1636) Ōsaki Hachiman Shrine 大崎八幡宮 in Sendai were probably inspired directly by Hideyoshi's precedent.[29] These cases reveal a widespread desire of local daimyo to be elevated to special posthumous status beyond the usual Buddhist conventions. Under the Tokugawa regime, however, such family cults had to be practiced under the pretext of worshipping a conventional shrine deity such as Hachiman. Ancestor deification was therefore visible and relevant only in an in-house or intra-family context (an *uchi* 内 affair, in Roberts' terms).

The elephant in the room was of course the deification of Tokugawa Ieyasu. It was probably his example that his relatives had in mind for themselves. In their desire for posthumous *kami* status, they strove to strengthen also the status and identity of their branch lineages, while lower-level government officials disparaged such forms of self-aggrandizement and tried to save the privilege of divine status for the founder of the ruling dynasty. Masayuki's case is again a telling example: In 1732, sixty years after his death, his shrine obtained a Daimyōjin title from the Yoshida, the same that was also given to Hideyoshi in 1599. Tokugawa counselors, however, regarded this as a form of disrespect that would confuse the hierarchy in the Tokugawa family pantheon and requested that this title was used only among house retainers but not in formal relations with the *bakufu*.³⁰ This reveals a tension linked to the general dynamics between domains and the central government, the *bakuhan* 幕藩 system. Even if Masayuki had been a key player in both parts of this system, he died as a daimyo and his deification became part of his legacy as a leader of a domain, not of the state.

Conclusion

The above-mentioned characteristics of Domain Shinto can be summarized in the following way: Domain Shinto refers to local Shinto-focused reforms such as the separation of temples and shrines, which reached a peak in the 1660s. These reforms were usually not directly linked to Yoshida Shinto, even though the Yoshida prepared the ground for Domain Shinto and remained an important factor in its background. Equally, the new legislation of 1665 did not contain an explicit order to change the status of Shinto, but obviously provided an excuse to start far-reaching reforms to this end. The agents of Domain Shinto were closely related to the shogun, which indicates that only daimyo of exceptional status were granted some leeway in implementing such religious policies. At first sight, their family ties seem to support the view that their reforms accorded with the official line of the government. On the other hand, we must not overlook the fact that all of these figures were daimyo who ruled their own semi-autonomous domains. As such, they were involved in a constant competition for status and political influence. Even if they cooperated with or were part of the central government, their reforms contained elements detrimental to Tokugawa hegemony, since their tendencies towards self-aggrandizement rivaled the cult of Ieyasu. Buddhism, on the other hand, functioned (among other things) to curtail such tendencies by establishing a certain degree of uniformity through the cultic/funeral practices sanctioned by the Tokugawa government.

In this respect, Domain Shinto owed its existence at least in part to a longing of leading daimyo for a more personalized and autonomous ritualism. The more or less experimental ways to create such ritualism opened a window of opportunity for Shinto to develop into a self-contained religious tradition on par with Buddhism. Since Domain Shinto was dependent on exceptionally determined local rulers, however, its major achievements coincided with their generation.

It remains to be studied in detail what factors contributed to the decline of Domain Shinto reforms after only one or two decades. Personal constellations certainly played a role when the death of Hoshina Masayuki in 1673 re-opened the field for anti-Confucian *bakufu* leaders such as great councilor Sakai Tadakiyo 酒井忠清 (1627–81), who had a direct impact on the re-Buddhification of Okayama.³¹ Yet, these constellations do not explain why there was no subsequent Shinto boom under the pro-Confucian regime of Shogun Tsunayoshi 徳川綱吉 (1646–1709, r. 1680–1709), for instance. Intellectual trends must also be taken into account: Obviously, Domain Shinto was particularly encouraged by a coalition of Confucian and Shinto intellectuals in Masayuki's generation, yet in the next generation, a nativist critique of Confucianism becomes visible as exemplified in this volume by Hayashi's analysis of Shibukawa

Harumi. Thus, Shinto intellectuals stepped out of the shadow of Confucianism, which may have in turned weakened Confucian support of shrine reforms.

In any case, the legacy of Domain Shinto seems to reappear in the later Tokugawa period. In addition to the well-known rise of Kokugaku (documented in Walthall's chapter), Daimyo deifications reemerged in a new way that included commoner participation on the one hand and relations to the tenno on the other,[32] presaging developments of the Meiji-period. In this sense, Domain Shinto was certainly not without consequences. As the issues analyzed in this volume demonstrate, awareness of Shinto increased for both the political and the intellectual elite of Tokugawa Japan, even if Buddhism remained the privileged means of religious control for the state and the general frame of religious orientation for the common people.

Part One

Tokugawa Orthopraxy

1

Anti-Christian Temple Certification (*terauke*) in Early Modern Japan

Establishment, Practice, and Challenges

Nam-lin Hur

Between 1549 and the 1630s, hundreds of Christian missionaries entered Japan, most of them members of the Society of Jesus (Jesuits).[1] They established a community of Christians collectively referred to as Kirishitan 切支丹 (derived from Portuguese *Christão*) that may have reached a total number of followers as high as 760,000 (or about 5 percent of the total population), according to the historian Gonoi Takashi.[2] In the early seventeenth century, however, the Tokugawa regime began purging Christian missionaries and their followers in the name of protecting the "divine country" (*shinkoku* 神国) of Japan. Tens of thousands of Kirishitan were tortured, imprisoned, or executed because of their religious affiliation. The Shimabara rebellion (*Shimabara no ran* 島原の乱) in Kyushu (1637/38) alone claimed the lives of nearly 28,000 people, while another 10,000 to 20,000 were executed.[3]

After having tried various methods within their anti-Christian policy, in the 1660s the Tokugawa regime adopted a system of temple certification (*terauke* 寺請) as a countrywide measure to crack down on Christians. Under this system, Buddhist "temples" (*tera*) were "commissioned" (*uke*) to check and certify that persons affiliated with them were not Christians. Those who failed to obtain a non-Christian certificate from their temple were regarded as Kirishitan and threatened with capital punishment. By the late seventeenth century, the entire population had been subjected to the anti-Christian measure of temple certification. Although Christianity was virtually eliminated at that time, the Tokugawa regime did not give up the system. Instead, national and regional governments alike continued to use it to strengthen their control over the populace.[4]

Despite the importance of this anti-Christian policy as a backbone of Tokugawa governance, scholarship on the *modus operandi* of the system of temple certification is rather lean, fragmented, or localized. Currently, no book-length analysis dedicated to this subject is available in any language—a situation that begs research that combines a variety of related issues into a coherent whole. As an introductory discussion, this chapter examines the overall trajectory of the system of temple certification from its genesis and practice to its demise.

The Establishment of Temple Certification

How and why did Buddhist institutions come to serve as an administrative vehicle for the anti-Christian policy of the Tokugawa regime? Through the leverage of anti-Christianity, Tokugawa Ieyasu 徳川家康 (1543–1616) incorporated Buddhism and Shinto as well as the legacies of the imperial court into the sovereign structure of power politics as it gradually took shape at this time. In particular, the "divine country" banner was juxtaposed with Christianity, which helped Ieyasu establish himself as the supreme defender of Japan. Ieyasu began to demonize Christianity while defining Buddhism as the spiritual pillar of the divine country.[5] Certainly, Tokugawa rule rested primarily upon the military hegemony of the shogunal house. But there was no guarantee that the balance of power between shogun and daimyo (*bakuhan* 幕藩) would stay intact in favor of the former for good. In consolidating the *bakuhan* power structure, Ieyasu mobilized the traditional mode of allegiance and fealty, which consisted of a collective vow of commitment to *kami* and buddhas,[6] against the backdrop of anti-Christianity.[7] Christianity was not presented as simply a source of heterodox teachings; rather, it was styled an enemy of the state, against which all the country's political entities had to unite under the leadership of the Tokugawa.

In the twelfth month of Keichō 18 (January 1614), Ieyasu had his son Hidetada 徳川秀忠 (1579–1632, r. 1605–23) proclaim a statement on the expulsion of Christians.[8] In the first phase of action after the edict, *bakufu* officials rounded up foreign missionaries, along with prominent Kirishitan leaders like the former daimyo Takayama Ukon 高山右近 (1552–1615) and Kibe Pedoro 岐部ペドロ (1587–1639, a Japanese padre ordained by Jesuits in Nagasaki), and expelled them from Japan.[9] Nagasaki and the Kyoto-Osaka area, which had disproportionately high ratios of Kirishitan, soon became the primary targets of the anti-Christian crackdown. In his Kokura domain 小倉藩 in Kyushu, Hosokawa Tadaoki 細川忠興 (1563–1645) conducted one of the earliest examples of Buddhist certification to confirm non-Christian status: first he conducted a census in order to identify Kirishitan, then he forced them to renounce their faith and to obtain a certification from a temple. In this way, he succeeded in "converting" 2,047 Kirishitan to Buddhism by the fourth month of 1614.[10] In Usuki domain 臼杵藩, many Kirishitan were equally forced to associate themselves with Buddhist temples.

The term used to refer to the abandonment of the Kirishitan religion was *korobi* 転び, literally "rolled over," and denoted the switch from Christianity to Buddhism. From 1614 onwards, it gradually became commonplace in Kansai 関西 and Kyushu that Kirishitan, once detected, had to prove their status of *korobi* by obtaining a non-Christian certificate from the Buddhist temple with which they were affiliated. Thus, the enforced association between being non-Kirishitan and being Buddhist began to enter the lives of the early modern Japanese people. At this stage, however, only former Kirishitan needed a Buddhist certificate, not the entire population. For these "rolled over" Kirishitan, a few lines of script on a temple document made the difference between life and death. In this way, Buddhist temples began to exercise the power of non-Christian identification under the government's sanction.

But despite these various anti-Christian measures, Christian missionaries did not stop sneaking into Japan and Japanese converts hardly diminished. From 1614 to 1629, the Jesuits were able to gain more than 20,000 new followers, and the Franciscans acquired more than 26,000 in the Tōhoku 東北 region.¹¹ As a result, the Tokugawa regime cracked down on them with growing brutality. In 1619, fifty-two Kirishitan were burned alive. In the winter of 1623 in Tōhoku, around sixty Kirishitan followers, including a missionary, Diego Carvalho (1578–1624), were arrested, sent to Sendai, and put naked into a cage set up in the midst of a river. After three days of torture and hunger, they all froze to death.¹² Similarly, in 1624 in Akita 秋田藩, the brutal hunting-down of Kirishitan, which was accompanied by the religious inspection of all residents, took thirty-three lives.

In 1628 Mizuno Morinobu 水野守信 (1577–1636), a new Nagasaki magistrate (*Nagasaki bugyō* 長崎奉行), initiated a unique method for identifying Kirishitan: "trampling on Christian images," known as *fumie* 踏絵 or *ebumi* 絵踏み in Japanese. This method entailed forcing the suspect to stamp on an image of the Cross, Christ, or Mother Mary, which many Kirishitan considered to be akin to treading on the face of their own parent. Ward officials (*otona* 乙名) and inquisitors visited residents, forced them to trample on Christian symbols as proof that they were not Kirishitan, and documented the results one by one, trying not to miss the slightest sign of hesitation or embarrassment on the part of the inspectees.¹³ During his three-year term, Mizuno Morinobu brutally executed more than 300 suspected Kirishitan.¹⁴

From 1634 onward, the government under the third shogun Iemitsu 徳川家光 (1604–51, r. 1623–51) began to devise more sophisticated methods for tracking down Christian elements. One of these involved a comprehensive census conducted in Nagasaki in 1634. The extant 1634 Nagasaki document, known as *A Register of Investigation of the Hirado and Yokoseura Ward Residents* (*Hirado-machi Yokoseura-machi ninzū aratame no chō* 平戸町横瀬浦町人数改之帳),¹⁵ shows that Buddhist temples were commissioned to conduct inspections of all ward residents in order to determine their temple affiliation. Unlike the previous register, which was applied to *korobi kirishitan* only, the scope and thoroughness of the 1634 Nagasaki register presaged the coming trend of temple certification. Indeed, from the early 1630s some local domains began to apply temple certification to all residents.

Late in the tenth month of 1637, amid intensifying anti-Christian campaigns, a peasant uprising broke out in Shimabara 島原藩, the domain of Matsukura Katsuie 松倉勝家 (1597–1638). The shogunal government wasted no time in condemning the peasant uprising as a sectarian revolt (*shūmon ikki* 宗門一揆), which meant a Christian-inspired insurrection. In reality, it owed much to the peasants' discontent due to excessive taxes and corvées. The government troops literally exterminated nearly 28,000 people, including women and children.¹⁶ Subsequently, the regime took the Shimabara Rebellion as an opportunity for executing "national" policies for bringing semi-independent local governments, particularly those of *tozama daimyō* 外様大名 (daimyo who had only sworn allegiance to Ieyasu after his victory at Sekigahara 関ヶ原), further into line.¹⁷ Moreover, the Iemitsu government began to impose annual temple certification upon the residents of all shogunal lands. This was modeled after similar (but sporadic) experiments in Kyushu and Kyoto.¹⁸ However, this shogunal measure did not manage to establish temple affiliations for the entire population of the region. There is not even any clear evidence that the system of temple certification was widely implemented across the shogunal heartland, the Kanto region, at this time. Nevertheless, the fact that the government gave serious thought to implementing universal temple certification as a means of eradicating Christian elements is significant.

In 1640, the Tokugawa established an Office of Sectarian Inspection (*shūmon aratameyaku* 宗門改役), headed until 1658 by Inoue Masashige 井上政重 (1585–1661).[19] Inoue played a key role in the development of new ways to eliminate Kirishitan. Instead of threatening them with swords, the gallows, or fire, Inoue switched to inciting voluntary conversion to Buddhism. In order to identify Kirishitan, he believed that relying upon torture alone was not helpful and thus encouraged his officials to investigate each case in detail.[20] In 1642, the shogunal government introduced the five-man group system of controlling Christianity (*goningumi* 五人組), which had been first applied by Sakai Tadakatsu 酒井忠勝 (1587–1662) in his Obama domain 小浜藩. If a Kirishitan was discovered within such a group, then all group members were subject to heavy punishment.[21] This system was to remain in effect throughout the Tokugawa period.

In spite of the local successes of such strategies, Inoue was troubled to find that daimyo rarely coordinated their policies against Kirishitan, thus providing opportunities for Kirishitan to escape persecution. After his initial strategies of both violent and peaceful conversion to Buddhism met with only limited success, Inoue became convinced that temple certification was the most promising method. It had been successful in a number of domains, including Kumamoto 熊本藩, Ōmura 大村藩, Saga 佐賀藩, Hiroshima 広島藩, Kanazawa 金沢藩, Takada 高田藩, Mito 水戸藩, and Yonezawa 米沢藩, as well as in some shogunal lands like Osaka. Due to the relative autonomy of the domain governments and the various sectarian denominations, however, its implementation at the national level was another challenge.

Details of how temple certification should be administered were still to be hammered out, but by the end of Iemitsu's reign, the direction of anti-Christianity seemed to be set. Interestingly, however, the fourth shogun Ietsuna 徳川家綱 (1641–80, r. 1651–80), who succeeded Iemitsu in 1651, initially opted for a soft approach to anti-Christian policy. The advisors of the child shogun, including Hoshina Masayuki 保科正之 (1611–72), pushed for implementing an upgraded reward system and a public awareness campaign, with anti-Christian decrees posted on bulletin boards all over the country.[22]

This soft approach to Christianity soon backfired in 1657, when a large number of Kirishitan were found in Koori village 郡村 in Ōmura domain in Kyushu. In 1658 the government swiftly handed down harsh punishments: 411 were beheaded, twenty were sentenced to life in prison, and seventy-eight died during the investigation. Only ninety-nine were released free of all charges.[23] In the aftermath, Buddhist funerary rites were forced upon all inhabitants of the region and all Kirishitan graves were desecrated, with the bones of the deceased thrown into the sea. This large roundup, commonly known as *Koori kuzure* 郡崩れ (crushing of Koori), was the first of its kind, but it was to be followed by raids in Bungo province (1660). Here, the extensive hunt for underground Kirishitan under the direction of the Nagasaki magistrate lasted more than a decade and resulted in hundreds of further death penalties.[24] Later raids in Owari and Mino (*Nōbi kuzure* 濃尾崩れ, starting in 1661) brought still stricter application of punishment and even longer period of agony.

In 1663 the Ietsuna regime decided to revise the *Laws of Military Households* promulgated by Iemitsu in 1635, adding, for the first time, a strongly worded anti-Christian clause to the country's highest law: "The Kirishitan sect shall be strictly forbidden in all domains and in all places" (Item 19).[25] In the following year, 1664, the government specified this prohibition in a directive delivered to all daimyo and shogunal administrators. The directive contained instructions on religious inspection in the daimyo domains (Item 1), in the shogunal estate (Items 2 and 3), and in the lands of temples and shrines (Item 5), respectively. In the case of daimyo domains, the shogunal government ordered the "installation [of full-time] officials to inspect the vassals of the [daimyo] house and the entire domain residents every year." In the case of shogunal liege vassals (*hatamoto* 旗本), it ordered that "the local lords themselves must be responsible for closely examining their vassals, village heads and elders, and villagers, and, in addition, [they must] prepare the registers of five-man groups each year and be ready to submit them whenever the public authority so instructs."[26] In addition to the task of implementing annual religious inspection, all officials were instructed to "draw up a list of former Kirishitan who have been converted and submit it to Hōjō Awa no Kami (Ujinaga 北条氏長) and Yasuda Wakasa no Kami (Muneyuki 保田宗雪)" (Item 4).[27]

The 1664 directive was truly remarkable in that it provided an overarching framework for the countrywide administration of anti-Christian religious inspection. As far as the matter of Christianity was concerned, all domains, whether they belonged to daimyo, *hatamoto*, or temples and shrines, were now put under the direct supervision of the shogunal government.

The Practice of Temple Certification

By the late seventeenth century, Buddhist temples were taking care of certifying the non-Christian identity of each resident every year. Using these certificates, village or ward officials annually compiled the "register of sectarian inspection" (most commonly called *shūmon aratamechō* 宗門改帳 and *shūshi aratame chō* 宗旨改帳) and submitted it to their superior government office. The register of sectarian inspection was the end point of the evolution of temple certification—all residents of Tokugawa Japan were now registered annually and their non-Kirishitan identity individually checked by the government. Those who were not registered had no place in early modern Japan and could only survive underground.

The inspection by Buddhist monks and the registration by village or ward officials were two separate procedures. Due probably to the sequential link between these two processes, students of Japanese religions and history often fail to differentiate between them, as is seen in the mistake of rendering the term *terauke* (temple certification) as "temple registration." Buddhist temples were never allowed to compile a census register. The responsibility for registering those who were inspected by Buddhist temples belonged exclusively to village or ward officials, not to Buddhist monks.

Initially, the village or ward head was supposed to enter residents into the register of sectarian inspection after they had obtained individual non-Christian certificates from their respective temples (see Figure 1.1). However, this soon gave way to a procedure in which the village or ward head first compiled a register, and then temple heads endorsed the non-Kirishitan status of their affiliated members by putting their stamp under the latters' names. There were several ways to obtain the temple's stamp. In most cases the village or ward official met with the monk, either at the temple or the official's residence, and the monk put his stamp on the register.[28] In some cases, though, Buddhist temples entrusted their stamps to village officials or trusted *danna* 檀那 patrons, so that the latter could execute "temple stamping" in a more flexible manner when needed.[29]

Once two copies of the annual register (the original one, which contained all the necessary stamps, and a duplicate) were completed, the village or ward head submitted the original to the government. The duplicate copy was kept at his office and used as a memorandum for updating any changes during the coming year (e.g., deaths, births, marriages, adoptions, and the like) in red ink. The village or ward head added new information on small, narrow pieces of scrap paper, gluing them at the appropriate place in the register for the upcoming compilation (see Figure 1.2.c). These duplicate copies were kept for years and served as a public reference when authorizing permits for travel, status confirmation, or any other administrative documents.[30] The government offices, on the other hand, were inundated with the original registers of sectarian inspection received every year from every single village and ward under their jurisdiction. It is known that government officials did not really care about verifying

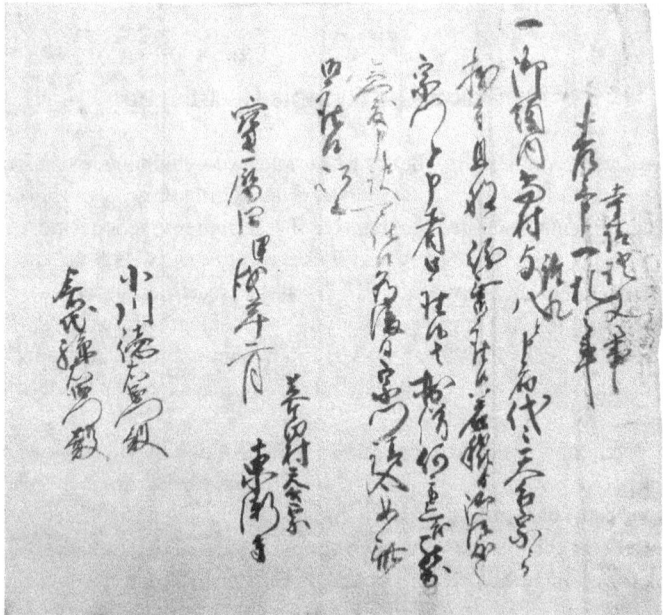

Figure 1.1 Non-Christian temple certificate (*terauke shōmon*). Document issued by the Tenda temple Tōzenji 東漸寺 for its member Yohachi 与八 in Zenda village 善田村 of Shinano province, dated Hōreki 10 (1760)/2.

their contents since it was assumed the wards and villages were Kirishitan-free. Thus, the original registers were usually discarded after three or four years.[31]

Given the patchwork-like structure of governance, the administration of registers of sectarian inspection did not follow the same chain of procedure everywhere, even though local governments were all required to report the results of inspections to the shogunal magistrates of temples and shrines (*jisha bugyō* 寺社奉行). Depending on the administrative type, forwarding the registers fell under the responsibility of various types of officials, who would summarize the inspection results if needed before submitting them to the next higher authority.[32] Moreover, since the shogunal government left much of anti-Christian inspection to the discretion of local governments, the ways in which it was executed and recorded were far from uniform.

It is known that there are only few extant registers of sectarian inspection in some areas of the Tōhoku, Shikoku, and Kyushu regions, and that they are largely missing in Satsuma 薩摩藩 and Tosa 土佐藩. In the case of Chōshū 長州藩, they seem to have been compiled until the mid-eighteenth century, but there are no traces of any later than that.[33] Probably due to high infant mortality, some domains did not record children until they reached a certain age, and even this age limit varied between regions. In spite of the principle of annual registration, some domains conducted it twice a year, some every other year, some once every three years, and some were even more sporadic.[34] In addition, in 1776 the shogunal government suddenly encouraged local administrators to compile registers of inspection according to each Buddhist sect. While registers compiled this way began to emerge in some areas, it is not known how widely this new practice was adopted given the highly complex variations of affiliations between residents and *danna* temples in many villages and wards throughout the country.[35] What varied was not only the manner in which the register of sectarian inspection was compiled, but also its content. Some registers contained more details, such as province of ancestral origin and birth, landholding, occupation, farm animals owned, and so on. Others had additional information, such as about servants or seasonal workers changing households, marriages, and adoptions.[36]

As mentioned above, the annual submission of registers of sectarian inspection was enforced across the whole country, despite the fact that the Kirishitan population had already been more or less wiped out. Accordingly, registers of sectarian inspection began to function more as administrative census registers and became referred to as "census registers of sectarian inspection" (*shūmon ninbetsuchō* 宗門人別帳, *shūmon ninbetsu aratamechō* 宗門人別改帳, or simply *ninbetsuchō* 人別帳).[37] Originally, the term *ninbetsuchō* (also *nayosechō* 名寄帳 or *ninjuchō* 人数帳) referred to census registers that had been drawn from villages since 1591, along with *kenchichō* 検地帳 (cadastral registers), for administrative purposes such as taxation, military recruitment, and the allocation of social status. The *shūmon ninbetsuchō* represented a combination of (anti-Christian) sectarian inspection and administrative census.

This type of register was especially prominent in the shogunal lands from the 1750s and 1760s, when the register of sectarian inspection began to record "landholdings" (*kokudaka* 石高) of each household and the earlier population register was no longer compiled.[38] The merging of these two different types of registers clearly indicates that the system of temple certification was now being used more for administration

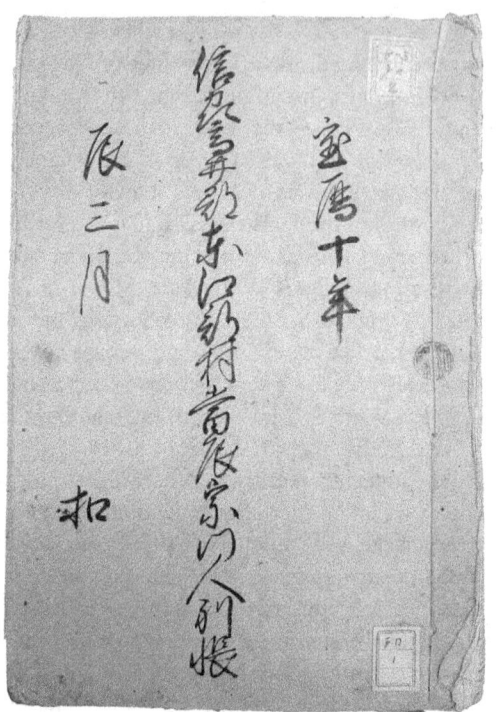
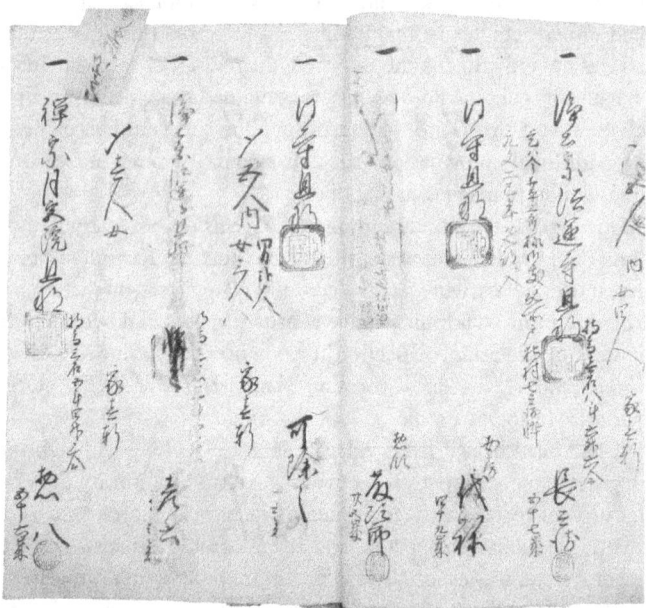

Figure 1.2.a–b Census register of sectarian inspection (*shūmon ninbetsuchō*): a) cover page; b) inner page containing paper slips with new information to be used when updating the document in the following year.

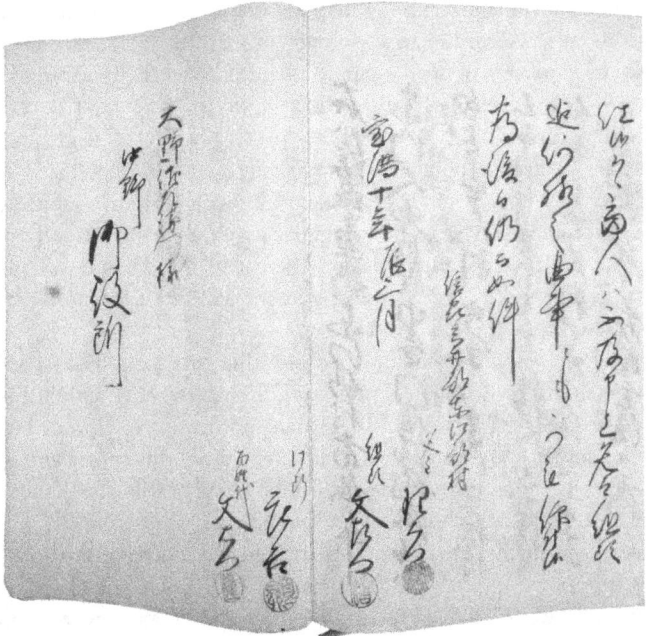

Figure 1.2.c concluding page. Compiled in 1760/2 by the village officials of Higashiebe village 東江部村, Takai district 高井郡 in Shinano province.

purposes than for anti-Christian surveillance.³⁹ Nevertheless, the countrywide chains of order that subjugated the populace, Buddhist temples, village and ward officials, and local governments to the anti-Christian policy were not altered.

Challenges to Temple Certification

At the time when religious certification became standardized countrywide, three domain leaders of anti-Buddhist stance, who were close to the shogunal family—Ikeda Mitsumasa 池田光政 (1609–82) of Okayama 岡山藩, Tokugawa Mitsukuni 徳川光圀 (1628–1701) of Mito, and the above-mentioned Hoshina Masayuki of Aizu 会津藩— introduced programs to diminish Buddhism's pre-eminence. To them, anti-Christianity itself was never a problem: what bothered these Confucian-minded lords was the fact that religious certification was the prerogative of Buddhism. In an attempt to remedy this monopoly, in the late 1660s they launched extensive reforms that involved a considerable retrenching of Buddhist temples (*jiin seiri* 寺院整理).⁴⁰

In Okayama, Ikeda Mitsumasa's critical view of the current Buddhist institutions occasioned the introduction of Confucian-style death rituals⁴¹ and the destruction of temples, especially those affiliated with the Nichiren 日蓮 sects' Fujufuse branch (*Fujufuse-ha* 不受不施派), in 1666/67.⁴² As an even more radical step, he ordered domain residents to obtain their non-Christian certificates from Shinto priests instead of Buddhist monks.[43] According to a government survey conducted in 1669, it appears that more than 95 percent of the domain residents had switched to Shinto certification (*shintō-uke* 神道請, or *shinshoku-uke* 神職請).[44] In 1674, however, Mitsumasa's son and successor, Tsunamasa 池田綱政 (1638–1714), readmitted *terauke* certification. And in 1687, Okayama domain was warned by senior councilor (*rōjū* 老中) Toda Tadamasa 戸田忠昌 (1632–99) that "although Shinto, Confucianism, and Buddhism all provide service to the shogunal house, religious inspection should be unified with temple certification."[45] Soon thereafter, the domain switched back to temple certification and, as a result, its experimental Shinto inspections ceased to exist almost completely.[46]

In the case of the Aizu domain, when Hoshina Masayuki died in 1672, he was buried with a Shinto-style funeral, in line with his general anti-Buddhist stance.[47] He also introduced the possibility of anti-Christian certification by shrines, but soon after his death, the domain government began to retreat from this course and by 1679 had fully reinstalled the system of temple certification, despite strong resistance on the part of the domain's Confucian scholars and Shinto priests.

In Mito, in an attempt to check the privileges provided by shogunal policy for Buddhist institutions, the "temple retrenchment" of Tokugawa Mitsukuni brought about the massive destruction of Buddhist temples. All in all, however, anti-Buddhist critique in Mito was less radical, and *terauke* was replaced only for Shinto priests.[48] This proved more durable than the short-term reforms in Okayama and Aizu.

These cases demonstrate that no sooner had the countrywide system of temple certification been instituted, it was subjected to criticism and even to attempts of rebuff. The reform efforts carried out in these domains, particularly the ones in Mito and Okayama, questioned the rationale of Buddhist religious inspection. But their challenges were all short-lived and unable to destabilize the shogunal policy of temple certification.

In 1773, however, twenty-eight Shinto priests in the Tsuchiura domain 土浦藩 in Kanto joined forces, petitioning the domain magistrate of temples and shrines to allow them to conduct Shinto funerals for themselves and their family members. Their petition soon developed into a group dispute between Buddhist monks and Shinto priests. After several months of consideration, the Tsuchiura domain government decided that Shinto funerals could be allowed under three conditions: (1) consent from the Buddhist monks in the domain; (2) a funeral permit from the Yoshida 吉田 house of Shinto priests; and (3) even if the preceding two conditions were met, Shinto funerals were to be conducted only for the Shinto priest himself and his male successor, but not for any other family members.[49] Obviously, Buddhist temples were not budging an inch, and thus the attempt to implement Shinto funerals was doomed. Nevertheless, the Tsuchiura case spurred the movement for Shinto funerals in other areas as well—a movement that seems to have had at least some effect.[50]

A similar case occurred in 1841, when the Owari government allowed the head priests of Masumida Shrine (Masumida Jinja 真清田神社 the *ichinomiya* 一之宮 of Owari) and Atsuta Shrine (Atsuta Jingū 熱田神宮) to conduct Shinto funerals, provided their *danna* temples consented. Five years later, Atsuta chief priests were exempted from *danna* affiliation and could conduct Shinto funerals among themselves.[51] It is unclear whether the Owari domain government's support of Atsuta Shrine affected the shogunal mandate of temple certification at all, but nonetheless it seemed to signal the dawning of a new age.

Another famous example of a prolonged—and ultimately successful—dispute with Buddhist temples over Shinto funerals occurred in the pro-Shinto Hamada domain 浜田藩 of Iwami. The conflict was triggered by the death of the head priest of Sahimeyama Shrine (Sahimeyama Jinja 佐毘売山神社) in Otone village 乙子村 in 1838.[52] After a group of local priests fought tirelessly for seven years to be released from their *danna* temples so they could conduct their own funerals among themselves, in 1845 the domain office of temples and shrines finally arrived at the following decision: Shinto funerals would be allowed for current priests, their heirs, and former priests, but not for other family members. The requirement of obtaining consent from the *danna* temple, which had been the main issue in this case, was dropped.

In other domains, however, no matter how eagerly Shinto priests sought non-Buddhist funerals, the hurdle of gaining consent from Buddhist temples remained almost insurmountable until the end of the Tokugawa period. *Danna* temples resisted giving up their funerary privileges, which were linked to the right of anti-Christian religious inspection—a privilege that nobody dared to challenge. For this reason, Shinto priests were almost never able to extract themselves from funerary Buddhism, and any exceptional permission for a Shinto funeral was rarely allowed to extend beyond one generation.

The Shinto funeral movement certainly posed a challenge, if not a threat, to the custom of Buddhist funerals. But while it did not threaten the system of anti-Christian temple certification as such, which remained integral to Tokugawa governance, local domain governments had to be cautious when curtailing funerary Buddhism, lest it mistakenly touch the sensitive nerve of shogunal authority. The daimyo domains, which when combined exceeded the size of the shogunal lands by a factor of three, could in theory overrun the shogunal authority with collective action. Thus the central government was most concerned with controlling the country's daimyo through the hierarchical and binding power structure of the *bakuhan* system. The anti-Christian temple certification was a key element reinforcing the operation of the *bakuhan* system and, thus, the central government could not afford to let it be easily compromised.

At least from the 1660s, Buddhist institutions helped the Tokugawa regime bring local domain governments to heel. Buddhist temples, relatively free from the binding principles of *bakuhan* politics, had already penetrated every corner of the country. As the agent for administering anti-Christian certification on a national level, there was, in fact, no better option than Buddhist monks and their institutions. They were well suited to this task not only because of their comprehensive administrative network (which could be mobilized at no extra cost), but also because of their independent and superior status (which gave them supervisory authority over the general populace). The system of temple certification was a key vehicle for the Tokugawa's governance; it had moved far beyond its original rationale as the need to persecute Christian followers.

Epilogue

The system of temple certification began to lose its power as an anti-Buddhist movement spread soon after the Meiji Restoration in 1868. Amid this movement, in 1869/4, the pro-Shinto Meiji government ordered all Shinto priests to conduct Shinto funerals for their family members, effectively freeing them from the bondage of the *danka* system (*danka seido* 檀家制度).[53] At the same time, it encouraged the populace to leave their *danna* temples voluntarily and to switch to Shinto funerals.

A sweeping reform then followed, as the government promulgated a law pertaining to a new system of family registration. With the rationale for establishing "a homogenous national structure for determining the number of households, the size of the population and other census information," in the second month of 1872 local governments were ordered to conduct a census and draw up a register of all residents under their jurisdiction: with recourse to Shinto, not Buddhist certification.[54] This family register, known as the *Jinshin koseki* 壬申戸籍 (*Family Register of the Year of Jinshin* [1872]) system, replaced the previous population register of sectarian inspection, for which Buddhist temples had played a key role for more than two centuries.

The *Jinshin koseki* system introduced a new way of obtaining non-Christian certification, known as *ujiko shirabe* 氏子調 or *ujiko aratame* 氏子改.[55] In this system, the entire population was to be organized into tutelary (*ujiko*) parishes administered by Shinto shrines. Every household was to register its members as parishioners (*ujiko*) at its tutelary shrine, receiving in return protective talismans as proof of their non-Christian identity (at death, the talismans were to be returned to the tutelary shrine). Every six years, at the time of renewing this household registration, officials were to check whether the residents under their jurisdiction still possessed these non-Christian Shinto talismans.[56]

However, government officials soon came to realize that Shinto shrines and priests were not ready to be involved in the important task of a countrywide population registration process, a process still linked to the covert agenda of anti-Christian surveillance.[57] Too many Shinto shrines were without qualified Shinto priests, and too many Shinto priests were themselves in need of reform. The shrine registration in the form of *ujiko shirabe* was abandoned not long after.[58] Thus, religious certification no longer served the Meiji government to suppress Christianity.

On top of that, Western countries had begun to protest Japan's ongoing hostility toward Christianity. Under intense Western pressure, the government advised local governments to refrain from harassing Christians too aggressively. In a situation in which the open suppression of Christianity was no longer viable and Shinto funerals were still alien to most of the populace, the Meiji government opted to switch back to encouraging Buddhist funerals for the populace. The surreptitious anti-Christian strategy, which lacked consistency and only caused confusion, was doomed in light of ongoing Western pressure. In February 1873 the Meiji government gave up: "From now on the existing clauses [concerning the prohibition of Christianity] on public bulletin boards are to be obliterated."[59] This decree brought the prohibition of Christianity to an end. Thus, the system of anti-Christian temple certification became a thing of the past once and for all.

2

Ieyasu's Posthumous Title and the Tokugawa Discourse on "Divine Country"

Sonehara Satoshi[1]
Translation by Bernhard Scheid

This chapter deals with the pre-modern discourse on Japan as a "divine country" (*shinkoku* 神国) and the apotheosis of the first Tokugawa shogun Ieyasu 徳川家康 (1543–1616). While each topic has been extensively researched in Japan as well as in the West,[2] until now they have not been examined in relation to one another. I argue that it is necessary to analyze Ieyasu's apotheosis against the backdrop of the early modern *shinkoku* discourse in order to reveal its religious and political dimensions, and that the event, in turn, shaped the discourse on *shinkoku* with the figure of Ieyasu in divine form being added to it. I demonstrate this in the concluding part of this chapter by analyzing a number of "eulogies" on Ieyasu that have not been studied hitherto.

The Discourse on the "Divine Country" and its Development

The compound *shinkoku*, which is usually translated as "divine country," "land of the gods," or, more specifically, "land of the *kami* (Japanese native deities)," has long been used to signify the uniqueness of Japan. It is usually understood as a nationalist catch phrase that regards the *kami* as protectors of the land, the people, and the state of Japan. According to a widely accepted definition established in the 1950s by scholars such as Tamura Enchō 田村圓澄 (1917–2013) and Kuroda Toshio 黒田俊雄 (1926–93), "divine country" is related to an ideology that includes statements such as "tenno rule, descending from the *kami*, is sacred and everlasting" or "since Japan is a country under divine protection, its sacredness is inviolable."

In the early Tokugawa period, however, a Japanese state in the modern sense, that is, a state based on a unified administrative system, did not yet exist. The term "country" in the *shinkoku* compound was therefore as imaginary and multifarious as the term "divine." Consequently, at that time the claim that Japan was a divine country could convey a number of different subtexts. Starting from this premise, we must consider who used the term *shinkoku* and from which point of interest in order to grasp its meaning.[3]

In the earliest chronicles of Japan, the *Rikkokushi* 六国史, we find the term *shinkoku* only two times, once in the *Nihon shoki* 日本書紀 (720) and once in the *Nihon sandai jitsuroku* 日本三代実録 (901)⁴, both in the context of foreign affairs. All in all, the two examples do not suggest a particular emphasis on the notion of "divine country" in ancient Japan. This changed around 1100, during the "rule of retired emperors" (*insei* 院政). This period witnessed a growing antagonism between the old court nobility and the warrior nobility (*bushi* 武士), which ushered in the foundation of the Kamakura shogunate (1185–1333). At the same time, activists at the court tried to re-establish imperial authority and used the concept of *shinkoku* as its underpinning. In the seventh month of 1123, for instance, Retired Emperor Shirakawa (Shirakawa-in 白河院, 1052–1129), in his capacity as the head of the Tenno house, had an oath (*kishōmon* 起請文) recited in front of the *kami* of the Iwashimizu Hachiman Shrine 石清水八幡宮 that claimed: "Since Japan is a divine country, the promise of the various deities to protect the country will last forever."⁵ This line was declared at a time when the Retired Emperor was facing opposition from among the Buddhist clergy, thus implying the hope that the *kami* would punish such monks. In this case, the "divine" element of "divine country" seems to signify the imperial ancestor deities, while "country" implies the courtly government that had formed around the Retired Emperor. As this government rested on shaky ground, the notion of *shinkoku* became part of a quest for a new order that united the Tenno house, the court nobility, and the elite of the shrine priests.

Around the year 1200, yet another subtext of *shinkoku* emerged. At that time, internal problems—as well as general turmoil in society—forced the warrior nobility to change from confronting the court to cooperating with it. This led to their paying lip service to the court's claim that "Japan is ruled by the tenno, who are all descendants of the *kami*." This alliance was supported by the established schools of Buddhism, in their attempts to repress growing Amidist reform movements, in particular exclusivist *nenbutsu* as it was practiced by Hōnen 法然 (1133–1212) and his followers.⁶ As can be seen in the famous anti-Amidist petition *Kōfukuji sōjō* 興福寺奏状 of 1205, for instance, exclusivist *nenbutsu* was criticized and ultimately outlawed for (among other things) its disregard of the native deities. Conversely, *shinkoku* figured all the more prominently in the religious discourse of the traditional elites. For instance, a message in 1224/5 from the court addressed to the Tendai 天台 headquarter Enryakuji 延暦寺 on Mt. Hiei 比叡山 states: "Since Japan is a divine country, we pay respect to the *kami*, but when we think about their original forms, [we realize that] they are all buddhas."⁷ From this point of view, the "divine" element of *shinkoku* includes *kami* and buddhas, while "country" pertains to the entire people under the combined rule of military and court. This development was enhanced during the Mongol invasions of the late thirteenth century. At that time, temples and shrines competed for government financial support by stressing their efficacy in praying for divine help in the fight against the Mongols. In this way, they used the pressure of danger from abroad to enlarge their spheres of influence. In the course of this process, they spread the consciousness of living in a divine country to wider parts of the society.⁸

The identification of *kami* and buddhas reflects the common worldview of the ruling elites in the medieval period. We must not forget, however, that this identification was structured by the concept of "origin and trace" (*honji suijaku* 本地垂迹), according to which the *kami* were local manifestations or "traces" of the buddhas in their original form.⁹ This Buddho-centric idea implied that the "*kami*" element of *shinkoku* was inferior to the buddhas. Furthermore, it turned the "country" of *shinkoku* into a remote place beyond the border of civilization. Such connotations can even be found in the *Jinnō shōtōki* 神皇正統記 (1343) by Kitabatake Chikafusa 北畠親房 (1293–1354), which is famous for starting with the sentence: "Great Japan is the land of the *kami*."¹⁰ Yet, in spite of being introduced as a divine country, when the author compares Japan to India and China, it appears as nothing more than a cluster of tiny islands in a distant corner of the world. This remoteness of Japan is actually congruent with the *honji suijaku* concept, which led to the common idea that the Japanese were an inferior people who could not be saved by high-level teachings such as Buddhism or Confucianism, but only by Shinto.¹¹

This kind of inferiority complex began to change in the fifteenth century. In his famous "tree metaphor," Yoshida Kanetomo 吉田兼俱 (1435–1511), a prototypical Shinto intellectual of the late medieval period, declared Japanese Shinto as the basis (or the root-and-trunk, *konpon* 根本), Chinese Confucianism as the offshoots (or the branches-and-leaves, *shiyō* 枝葉), and Indian Buddhism as the ephemeral product (or flowers-and-fruits, *kajitsu* 花実) of a tree-like evolution of thought. This model was actually in line with the traditional claim that "the Three Teachings are all the same" (*sankyō itchi* 三教一致). It implied that Buddhism—despite its most sophisticated teachings—was in essence identical with Confucianism and Shinto. Kanetomo insisted, however, that Shinto was the fundament of all other religious teachings. He used this model to turn the priestly traditions of his own Yoshida lineage into a new religious system. We may regard this development as the starting point of a new paradigm of Shinto as it took shape in the early modern period.¹²

In addition, the medieval period gave rise to the idea that the "divine country" of Japan was also a "buddha country" (*bukkoku* 仏国). With the popularization of *honji suijaku*, a pun on the characters 大日本国 spread. Since these characters can be read as "Great Japan" (*Dai-Nihonkoku* 大-日本国) as well as "Dainichi's original country" (*Dainichi honkoku* 大日-本国), they allowed the interpretation that Japan was actually the home of Dainichi Nyorai 大日如来 (Mahāvairocana), the most important Buddha in the teachings of Esoteric Buddhism.¹³ Other theories maintained that Buddhism had declined in India and China while it flourished only in Japan. This led to the ethnocentric claim that the divine country of Japan excelled among all other countries in the world, because it was a Buddha country where Buddha's teachings flourished.¹⁴

Needless to say, the changes in society in the seventeenth century that ushered in the early modern period created yet another kind of subtext of "divine country." Put simply, early modern *shinkoku* discourse included the claim that Japan was both a land of the buddhas *and* a land of the *kami*. This discourse was shaped by the political decision to suppress Christianity (after a first phase of tolerance in the sixteenth century) and the ensuing aim to base the authority of the government on Buddhism and Shinto. As pointed out by Inoue Tomokatsu in this volume, Japan differed from China and Korea in this respect, since in those countries Neo-Confucianism became the dominant political ideology: in early modern Japan, Shinto played a new role in the cult of the first two rulers, Toyotomi Hideyoshi and Tokugawa Ieyasu, who were deified as *kami* after their deaths. Buddhism, on the other hand, became the principal agent of anti-Christian ideological control. In due course, the Tokugawa decided to force the entire populace into becoming members or "donors" (*danka* 檀家) of Buddhist temples, which led to the so-called *danka* system (*danka seido* 檀家制度), centered on Buddhist funerary services.[15] As Hayashi Makoto has argued, funerary Buddhism (*sōsai bukkyō* 葬祭仏教) took over the same function in early modern Japan as Neo-Confucianism did in China and Korea.[16]

The *shinkoku* Discourse of the "Holders of the Realm"

Among the unifiers of early modern Japan—Oda Nobunaga 織田信長 (1534?–82), Toyotomi Hideyoshi 豊臣秀吉 (1537?–98), and Tokugawa Ieyasu—Hideyoshi is famous for regarding Japan as a "divine country." Ieyasu followed his example. Why did these "holders of the realm" (*tenkabito* 天下人) put so much emphasis on *shinkoku*? According to recent studies, the reason lies in their rivalry with Western countries, in particular with Portugal and Spain.[17] As is commonly known, the sixteenth century witnessed the expansion of Western powers to East Asia, where they conducted trade and Christian missionary work. Initially, traders and local lords in Western Japan welcomed them warmly, and even Oda Nobunaga showed them his favor. Traditional elites such as the imperial court and the Buddhist clergy, however, treated Europeans with suspicion from the very beginning, and tried to suppress their influence. This was probably due to the potential of Christianity to obstruct their long-standing privileges. Since the court and the Buddhists were the main proponents of the idea that Japan was a divine country until the end of the medieval period (i.e., the fifteenth and sixteenth centuries), the opposition of these groups to Western culture crystallized in the dichotomy of *shinkoku* ideology and Christianity.[18]

As we can easily imagine, the mere fact that Europeans were invading virtually every country on earth raised fear among those who were critical of Western powers. Hideyoshi was initially pro-European, but news of the detrimental effects of "the bible and the gun" in South America and elsewhere put him more and more on his guard. In particular, Hideyoshi was appalled by the flourishing trade in Japanese slaves and called to account Christian proselytizers (who actually cooperated with slave traders) for this business.[19] In a memorandum (*oboe* 覚) of 1587/6/18, which was addressed to the missionaries and consisted of eleven items, Hideyoshi stipulated among other things that it was forbidden to sell Japanese as slaves in China, Southeast Asia or Korea, or to sell slaves in Japan (item 10).[20] Moreover, Hideyoshi regarded Western military strength with growing suspicion. In 1586, the Jesuit vice-provincial superior Gaspar Coelho (1530–90) proposed supporting Hideyoshi's campaign against Kyushu with warships from the Portuguese trade posts Manila and Goa. One year later, when Hideyoshi took up temporary residence in Hakata (present-day Fukuoka in Kyushu), Coelho showed him a warship armed with large canons that had been built in Nagasaki. These demonstrations of military strength raised Hideyoshi's apprehension of a European invasion in Japan,[21] which is probably the reason why he issued his famous *Edict on the Expulsion of Padres* (*Bateren tsuihō rei* バテレン追放令) on 1587/6/19. It stipulates that missionaries are not allowed to spread the demonic teaching of Christianity in Japan, because Japan is a "divine country."[22]

The same notion comes up again in Hideyoshi's letter to the viceroy of the Indies (the Portuguese governor of Goa) of 1591/7/25, which rejects Christianity on the basis of *shinkoku* in combination with the alleged unity of the Three Teachings, Shinto, Confucianism, and Buddhism:

> Ours is a divine country and the Divine (*shin* 神) is mind (*shin* 心). [...] Thus, the Divine is the root and trunk (*konpon*) of all existence. This Divine is spoken of by Buddhism in India, Confucianism in China, and Shinto in Japan. To know Shinto is to know Buddhism as well as Confucianism."[23]

According to this letter, Japanese orthodoxy consists of the Three Teachings, which all derive from the *kami*, understood here as a fundamental divine essence. This echoes the above-mentioned tree metaphor of Yoshida Shinto 吉田神道, which had in fact a direct influence on Hideyoshi. Christianity, however, does not share the common principles of the Three Teachings, as Hideyoshi goes on to argue. Therefore, it must not be propagated in Japan.

Two years after Hideyoshi's death in 1598/8, victory in the battle of Sekigahara (1600/9) turned Ieyasu into the new "holder of the realm." While he repeated Hideyoshi's decrees against Christianity, he did not enforce them strictly[24] since he was interested in the profits gained from trade with European countries. In the last years of his life, however, scandals such as the Okamoto Daihachi incident 岡本大八事件 of 1612, which revealed conspiracies among Christian members of Ieyasu's personal retinue, reinforced Ieyasu's suspicions against Western powers. This led to Ieyasu's *Edict against Christianity* (*Hai kirishitan no fumi* 排吉利支丹文), issued in the twelfth month of Keichō 18 (Jan. 1614).[25] In this edict we read:

> Japan is the land of the gods and the land of the buddhas. The gods are hallowed here and the buddhas revered, the way of benevolence and righteousness (*ningi no michi* 仁義の道, i.e. Confucianism) is followed assiduously."[26]

Again, the notion of *shinkoku* is combined with the unity of the Three Teachings (Shinto, Confucianism, and Buddhism), which are then juxtaposed in opposition to Christianity. At the same time, "land of the gods" (*shinkoku*) and "land of the buddhas" are both used as epithets for Japan. This combination clearly reveals the religious ideals of power holders at the beginning of Tokugawa rule.

The Significance of Ieyasu's Divine Title

After the death of Tokugawa Ieyasu in 1616, a conflict arose between his closest religious advisors, Konchiin Sūden 金地院崇伝 (1569–1633), abbot of the Zen temple Nanzenji 南禅寺 in Kyoto, and Nankōbō Tenkai 南光坊天海 (1536?–1643), abbot of the Tendai temple Kan'eiji 寛永寺 in Edo. What was at stake was the ritual system by which Ieyasu was to be elevated to the status of a *kami*. This elevation was inspired by the apotheosis of Toyotomi Hideyoshi, which had been performed by Yoshida priests according to their specific ritual system. Hideyoshi had been deified as Toyokuni Daimyōjin 豊国大明神, literally the "Great Bright Divinity of the Abundant Country." Based on this precedent, Sūden argued that Ieyasu should equally receive the posthumous title of "bright deity" (*myōjin* 明神).[27] Tenkai, however, came up with his own teaching, which he called *Sannō ichijitsu shintō* 山王一実神道 (lit. "Shinto of the All-Encompassing Truth of Sannō"), and proposed from this angle the divine title of "avatar" (*gongen* 権現). Like *myōjin*, this was a common title for shrine deities at that time, but the term had a more explicit Buddhist connotation in that it refers to a manifestation (*gen* 現) of a buddha in the temporal guise (*gon* 権) of a *kami*.

An initial clash between Tenkai and Sūden had already taken place at Ieyasu's residence in Sunpu 駿府 castle shortly after his death on 1616/4/17.[28] The precise nature of this clash is not entirely known,[29] but it is clear that Ieyasu's heir, the second Tokugawa shogun Hidetada 徳川秀忠 (1579–1632), first accepted Sūden's claim for the *myōjin* title, but then had second thoughts after his return to Edo, where he consulted with Tenkai, finally deciding in line with the latter that Ieyasu's last wish demanded the *gongen* title.[30] The actual content of Ieyasu's testament was probably a matter of secondary importance in this debate, however. Sūden's diary, *Honkō kokushi nikki* 本光国師日記 (1610–33), for instance, states that "something like *Sannō shintō* will not help build up Japan" (1616/5/21).[31] This reveals not only Sūden's indignation about the change from *myōjin* to *gongen*, but also hints at his conviction that the confirmation of

Figure 2.1 Tokugawa Ieyasu as Tōshōgū Divinity (*Tōshōgū goshin'ei*).[32] Image: Hickman 1996, 77.

the *gongen* title implied a change from Yoshida Shinto to *sannō ichijitsu shintō* as the religious core of the Tokugawa regime. This was, in his eyes, detrimental to a sustainable religious system. In other words, the question of Ieyasu's divine title entailed consequences of utmost relevance for the entire religious system of Japan.

What, then, was the real difference between Yoshida Shinto's notion of *myōjin* and the notion of *gongen* as advocated by Tenkai? The greatest contrast is certainly to be found in their respective relationship to Buddhism. For Yoshida Shinto, Buddhism was an inferior teaching,[33] while for Tenkai, Buddhism and Shinto were identical. In this sense, a *myōjin* title along the lines of Yoshida Shinto would have excluded any Buddhist flair from Ieyasu's cult. In the end, however, Tenkai's *gongen* title, which implied the amalgamation of Shinto and Buddhism, prevailed. Ieyasu's deified form became known as Tōshō Dai*gongen* 東照大権現 ("Great *Avatar* Illuminating the East") and was worshipped in Nikkō 日光, a temple-shrine complex under Tenkai's supervision (Figure 2.1). Until now, scholars have regarded this outcome of the divine title debate as an isolated, accidental power contest within a world of religious specialists. According to my interpretation, however, it was a struggle about whether the official religion of the early modern Japanese state should include Buddhism or not.

Together with Ieyasu's Tōshōgū Shrine in Nikkō, two temples in Edo—Kan'eiji, which served for everyday rituals (*kitōji* 祈祷寺) of the Tokugawa family, and Zōjōji 増上寺, the Tokugawa ancestor temple (*bodaiji* 菩提寺)—formed the pinnacle of this state-sponsored, Buddhism-focused religious system. The leaning of this system to regard the state of Japan not only as a land of the *kami* but also as a "buddha land" became plainly visible in Ieyasu's divine title.[34]

Shinkoku in Tōshōgū Ritualism

In the concluding part of this chapter, I would like to focus on the early modern *shinkoku* discourse as it appeared in the ritual context of ancestor veneration by the shogun and the daimyo. There are two ritual text genres that concern us here, namely, *ganmon* 願文 ("prayers" or "wishes"), by which the direct descendants of a deceased person express their thoughts, and *hyōhyaku* 表白 ("dedications"), in which religious specialists explain the purpose of a ritual in place of the respective sponsor.[35] I will hereafter refer to these texts as "eulogies." Such texts had to follow the demands of classical modes of writing and of the specific ritual context. Therefore, they were usually written by scholar monks or other intellectual specialists in the service of a daimyo or shogun. These formalisms have created ample doubts as to whether such texts ever expressed a person's real intentions at all. This may be one reason why eulogies have rarely been used as historical documents before now. Considering the mentality of early modern historical agents, however, I find it hard to believe that they would offer a text in front of their ancestors that went against their own convictions. Therefore, we should indeed treat eulogies as public expressions of feelings towards ancestors that go beyond the confinements of rhetorical ornamentation. Starting from this assumption, it seems possible to verify the general importance of *shinkoku* by analyzing shogunal eulogies, and in particular their depiction of Tokugawa Ieyasu (referred to here as Tōshō Gongen 東照権現), starting from the eulogies by Ieyasu's grandson, the third shogun Tokugawa Iemitsu 徳川家光 (1604–51).[36]

At the twenty-first commemoration of Ieyasu's death in 1636, a eulogy (Figure 2.2) praised the deceased in the following way:

> His divine authority extends beyond the borders of Japan and his virtues illuminate our country like the sun. On the battlefield, no other hero excelled his martial skills, and when he took the seat of honor at a Buddhist gathering, even the greatest monks regarded him their master.[37]

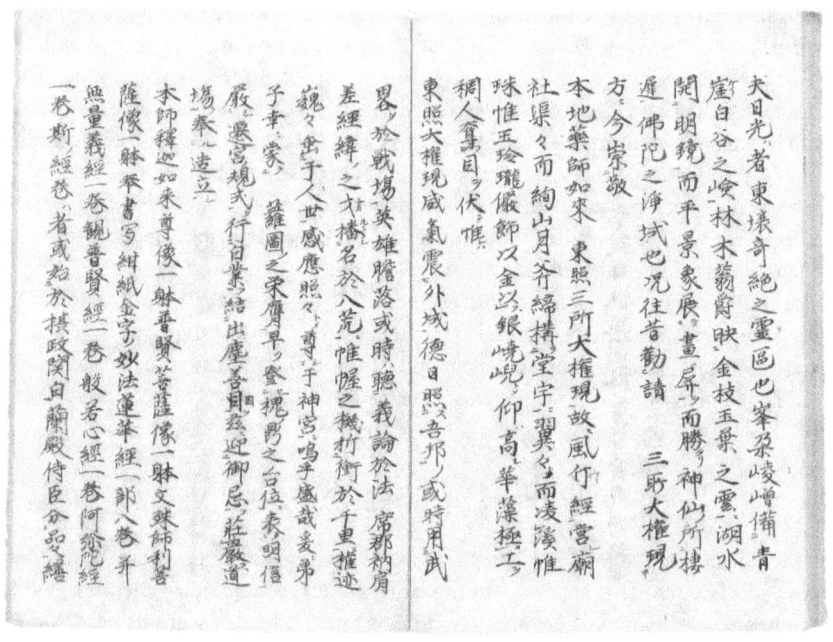

Figure 2.2 Eulogy by Tokugawa Iemitsu, twenty-first commemoration of the death of Ieyasu, 1636.[38] Image: NationalArchives of Japan, Digital Archive.

These phrases are presented as the humble words of Iemitsu, who identifies himself with his public titles as "descendant of Tōshō Gongen, shogun, chancellor to the left, following first rank, Minamoto no Ason." Moreover, the eulogy mentions that Tōshō Gongen is worshipped in a *jingū* 神宮, a "divine palace." This term or its shortened form -*gū* 宮 ("palace") was traditionally reserved for shrines of imperial ancestor deities such as Amaterasu or Hachiman. Ieyasu's shrine was officially designated such a "palace" only in 1645, and is since known as Tōshō*gū*. In 1636, however, the official designation was Tōshō*sha* 東照社.[39] This reveals that Iemitsu tried, in his eulogy, to exalt the status of his deified grandfather even higher than it already was.

At the thirty-third commemoration in 1648, we see a certain development in Iemitsu's ideas, with his eulogy (*ganmon*) praising Tōshō Gongen in the following way:

He achieved great merits by governing the eastern regions, protecting Kyoto in the west, obeying the tenno's rule of the entire country, and thus made the ideal government of old become reality.

In contrast to the twenty-first commemoration, this text makes explicit mention of the tenno. This seems to reflect the expansion of direct Tokugawa control from eastern to western Japan, which took place under Iemitsu's reign.

Some scholars believe that Iemitsu regarded the tenno and the court to have superior status than himself. I, however, assume that his submission to the imperial ranking system reflects his endeavor to create one source of authority by uniting the warrior and court nobility. In reality, the Tokugawa solidified their political control of the country around this time due to two major factors: 1) the intermarriage between the Tokugawa and the court (Iemitsu's niece became Meishō Tennō 明正天皇 [1623-96, r. 1629-43]);[40] and 2) the crushing of various uprisings such as the Shimabara rebellion 島原の乱 (1637-8).

Tokugawa support of Buddhism materialized among other things with the first printed edition of the Buddhist canon (*Tripiṭaka*, Jp. *Daizōkyō* 大蔵経) in Japan, which was initially entrusted to the above mentioned Tenkai. This so called *Tenkai Tripiṭaka* (*Tenkaiban daizōkyō* 天海版大蔵経) was completed in 1648, five years after Tenkai's death. At the thirty-third commemoration of Ieyasu in the same year, Tenkai's successor Kōkai 公海 (1608-95), who acted as the Buddhist supervisor (*dōshi* 導師) of the ceremony, alluded to the completion of the *Tripiṭaka* in the following way:

> Tōshō Gongen was able to grasp the real meaning of all Buddhist schools by following the true teaching of Tenkai. [...] When Tenkai proposed the edition of the *Tripiṭaka*, Iemitsu praised this as a deed without comparison in Japan, and completed it as a national project.

In this way, Kōkai stressed the continuity of Ieyasu's and Iemitsu's religious projects, presenting the Tokugawa dynasty as the embodiment of Japanese Buddhist culture.

At the fiftieth commemoration of Ieyasu's death in 1665, Shogun Ietsuna 徳川家綱 (1641-80, r. 1651-80) praised Ieyasu's divine virtue by which he had unified and protected the country. There is also a eulogy in the name of Shogun Ietsugu 徳川家継 (1709-16, r. 1713-16) from the centenary of Ieyasu's death in 1715,[41] which praises Tōshō Gongen in Confucian terms for uniting the imperial court and the warrior nobility. It seems safe to say that praising the Tokugawa ancestor as a protecting deity of Japan in Buddhist, Confucian, and Shinto terms became a part of the early modern *shinkoku* discourse.

This discourse existed also in the world of the daimyo. At the inauguration of a Tōshōgū branch shrine in Kagoshima 鹿児島 in 1710, for instance, the fourth daimyo of Satsuma-han 薩摩藩, Shimazu Yoshitaka 島津吉貴 (1675-1747), offered a eulogy that stressed Ieyasu's military virtues: "By the Mandate of Heaven, Tōshō Gongen accomplished the fate to bring uprisings to an end and let culture flourish, saving the people from bitter destitution." Daimyo Ikeda Yoshiyasu 池田吉泰 (1687-1739) of Tottori-han 鳥取藩 (present-day Tottori prefecture), on the other hand, offered a eulogy to the local Tōshōgū upon Ieyasu's centenary in 1715 that did not limit itself to Ieyasu's military accomplishments, but also praised him as "a model of a Confucian sage or a virtuous Buddhist monk." This imagery of Ieyasu, which sees him as a sage rather than a warlord or politician, casts doubts on the theory that the authority of Tōshō Gongen was dependent on the tenno or the imperial court.[42] Rather, sacredness was an intrinsic element of Tōshō Gongen, or perhaps even of the entire Tokugawa system.

Let me turn once more to the conception of Ieyasu (or Tōshō Gongen) within the Buddhist establishment: at a ceremonial reading of the *Lotus Sūtra* in 1714/7, which was done in preparation of the upcoming centenary, the eulogy referred above all to Ieyasu's religious charisma. Ieyasu appears as a sacred being from the beginning: born in the divine country of Japan, excelling in both military and civil accomplishments, and bringing peace to the world. He was not only of imperial pedigree,[43] he also received religious training by Tenkai and mastered the ultimate secrets of Tendai Buddhism, thereby amassing divine powers. For this reason, the sponsor of this ceremony (*ganshu* 願主) will gain luck in battle and a long life. The author of this text, a certain Ryōkai 亮海, was the abbot of Ten'yōji 天曜寺, which was both the ancestor temple (*bodaiji*) of the Tokugawa in Wakayama domain 和歌山 (Kishū) and the supervisory temple (*bettōji* 別当寺) of the Tōshōgū branch shrine in Wakayama. Thus, the merits promised to the sponsor of the ceremony seem to be limited to the head of the Kishū Tokugawa 紀州徳川 branch family.

One hundred years later, at the second centenary of Ieyasu's death in 1815, a eulogy (probably drafted by a monk from Enryakuji) also focuses on Ieyasu as a Buddhist divinity. According to this text, Ieyasu was originally Yakushi Nyorai 薬師如来 (Tathāgata Bhaiṣajyaguru) living in the world of the buddhas. He then manifested himself in Japan and performed all kinds of miracles, which resulted in two hundred years of peace in Japan. Moreover, Ieyasu is compared to the sage kings of China (King Tang 湯王 of Shang 殷, and King Wu 武王 of Zhou 周). Thus, the world of Buddhist clerics depicted Ieyasu rather as a Buddhist savior or a Confucian sage, not as a successful warlord.

Epilogue

In 1621, the head (*opperhoofd*) of the Dutch trading post in Hirado 平戸 (Kyushu) reported to the headquarters of the Dutch East Indian Company in Batavia (present-day Jakarta) that the shogun had prohibited any naval attacks on "enemies" (Portuguese traders, for example) by the Dutch or English along the coasts of Japan. The *opperhoofd* strongly suggested that the Dutch obey this order. He added the warning that the shogun was not like the Indonesian King of Makassar (whose kingdom was on Sulawesi [formerly Celebes] Island) and would not tolerate any violations of this order: "Makassar did not wish for this either, but lacked the strength [to prevent it from happening]. Japan does not lack that strength."[44] At the time, the Dutch East Indian Company had been given diplomatic autonomy, including the right of warfare, and therefore was basically able to act like an independent state. As this letter demonstrates, they were not inclined to obey the orders of a regional kingdom like Makassar, which lacked a firm fundament as a state. From the Dutch perspective, however, Japan under the Tokugawa shogunate was not a country of that kind.

If we want to explain why Japan posed a stronger resistance to Western supremacy than other countries in Asia (including all the positive and negative legacies of this development), the early modern *shinkoku* discourse, which found its physical equivalent in the Tōshōgū Shrine in Nikkō, may provide a viable starting point. Comparing this ritual and discursive system with the state ceremonies supporting the ruling dynasties in China and other East Asian countries, we notice a lack of the worship of Heaven, or rather, the idea that the dynastic rule was the result of a "Mandate of Heaven" (Ch. *tianming* 天命, Jp. *tenmei*). Japan had in fact a long tradition of circumventing this concept of Heaven and the corresponding Chinese state ceremonies. In their stead, political power was supported by anthropomorphic figures from the Shinto-Buddhist pantheon said to protect their descendants and religious followers. When early modern Japanese leaders were confronted with the incomprehensible teachings of Christianity, *shinkoku* conceptions, which supported the traditional syncretism, came back to their minds. Their concept of *shinkoku* differed from the modern *shinkoku* ideology, however, in that it included Buddhism.

The various eulogies for Ieyasu cited above demonstrate that the cult of Tōshō Gongen made use of Buddhism, Shinto, and *shinkoku* in order to create a sacred dynasty. This sacralization was one of the central activities of the government in early modern Japan. There is certainly a need to conduct further studies on how this endeavor was integrated into and reflected in the society at large.[45] There is no doubt, however, that the social elites shared the perception of living in a "divine country," the basis of this sacralization, and that it was this perception that kept the early modern state moving. Faced with the task of creating a unified state, the Tokugawa regime decided to integrate Buddhism into its administrative system. The debate regarding Ieyasu's divine title was probably the decisive event that triggered this decision. If so, the *gongen* title of Ieyasu can be seen as Tokugawa religious politics expressed in a single word.

Part Two

Unwanted Religious Groups

3

Anti-Christian Measures in Nagasaki During the Early Edo Period (1614–44)

Carla Tronu

Tokugawa policies of religious control are epitomized by the anti-Christian measures that started officially with the prohibition of Christianity in 1614. Buddhism was instrumental in de-Christianizing the population from early on, especially in Kyushu, where the new faith had spread most widely. In Nagasaki and the domains formerly governed by Christian daimyo such as the Ōmura 大村 or the Arima 有馬, however, there were practically no temples left. Buddhist and Shinto institutions had been dismantled during the 1570s, when these daimyo enforced mass conversions and allowed Christian missionaries to transform local religious sites into churches. After Christianity was banned, substantial resources were therefore invested in the building of temples in Nagasaki and the surrounding areas.[1] This rebuilding of Buddhism in Kyushu even superseded efforts of the shogunate to organize and control Buddhist sects (starting in 1615), which included a ban of temple construction without shogunal permission in 1631.[2]

This chapter examines the anti-Christian measures taken in Nagasaki after the prohibition of Christianity in 1614, focusing on the dismantlement of churches and the building of Buddhist temples during the Genna and Kan'ei eras (1615–44). These institutions were not only local religious centers, but also formed the bases for proselytization outside the city as well. In this sense, Nagasaki played an important role in both the Christianization and the de-Christianization of the entire larger region.

The Destruction of Christian Institutions

By the early seventeenth century, Nagasaki was the most important commercial port in Japan and the center of Japanese Christianity. The Jesuits (active in Japan from 1549 under Portuguese patronage) had established their headquarters there in 1584, while the Mendicant Orders (comprising Franciscans, Dominicans, and Augustinians under Spanish patronage, active from the 1590s) did the same at the beginning of the seventeenth century. After Toyotomi Hideyoshi's 豊臣秀吉 (1537–98) first attempt to expel the Christian missionaries (1587), he put the city under his control in 1592. Wards developed thereafter were called outer wards (*soto-machi* 外町), as opposed to the oldest or inner wards (*naka-machi* 中町), which were privileged by exemption from land tax. Nagasaki became all the more important for Japanese Christianity in this period: although most churches were dismantled, Jesuits managed to save Nagasaki churches from the same fate, allegedly to cater to the Portuguese merchant residents.

Tokugawa Ieyasu 徳川家康 (1543–1616) initially welcomed Christian missionaries for the sake of trade with Portugal and Spain. Both Jesuits and Mendicant Orders were allowed in cities under shogunal control, namely Kyoto, Osaka, Nagasaki, and Edo. Nagasaki became the seat of the Bishop of Japan immediately after Hideyoshi's death in 1598, and from 1601 there was a rapid increase in the number of churches in the city. By 1612, eleven parish churches existed in Nagasaki and the majority of its citizens took part actively in the Catholic liturgical calendar.[3]

However, once the Dutch offered purely commercial relations without any interference from religious dignitaries, Christians—now regarded as a potential threat for the on-going attempts to unify the country—lost the shogun's favor. In 1612, Ieyasu banned Christianity in the territories under his direct control and extended the ban to the whole country in January 1614 (Keichō 18/12).[4] Unlike Hideyoshi, the Tokugawa government enforced this ban with utmost determination. Instructions from February 1614 (Keichō 19/1) stipulated that all missionaries be captured and sent to Nagasaki, where trading ships should carry them abroad as soon as possible. This was swiftly done and in March (Keichō 19/2) missionaries from Kyushu and central Japan arrived in Nagasaki. However, the ships bound for Macao and Manila only left in the autumn and the missionaries were forced to remain in Nagasaki until then.[5] The concentration of foreign missionaries and the prospect of their exile led to the organization of pious displays such as penitential processions.[6]

In September 1614, sixty-three missionaries and several Japanese Christians (including daimyo Takayama Ukon 高山右近 [1552–1615] and his family) boarded ships for Manila. In early November, a pair of ships took around seventy missionaries and their Japanese assistants to Macao.[7] In total, around ninety-three foreign missionaries were expelled, although some managed to return secretly. A few days after the departure of the ships, all Nagasaki churches were closed. Their dismantling followed in two stages.

The first stage was the destruction of the eight churches within the city in 1614. This operation was handled by the Nagasaki magistrate (*Nagasaki bugyō* 長崎奉行) Hasegawa Fujihiro 長谷川藤広 (1567–1617), who had been in office since 1605, in collaboration with a shogunal envoy, Yamaguchi Naotomo 山口直友 (1544–1622), and three Buddhist monks. The magistrate asked the local *otona* 乙名 (ward heads elected by the citizens) to engage the citizens in the task of demolition, but they refused to take part in the operation, arguing that the residents were exhausted and unfit for such an endeavor.[8] This was a way to keep their integrity as Christians without defying the central authorities, but it hardly concealed the citizens' initial will to resist. To ensure that the people of Nagasaki did not interfere with the operation, Ieyasu ordered several daimyo from neighboring domains to assist the magistrate.[9]

According to the Spanish merchant Bernardino de Ávila Girón (?–*c.* 1619), who remained in Nagasaki, the first church to be demolished was the Cathedral, adjacent to the Jesuit headquarters, and dedicated to St. Mary of the Assumption. On October 27,

1614, the Jesuits said their last mass there and removed the altar to avoid its desecration. On the following day, they left the precincts and on October 29 demolition work started. In the first two weeks of November, another eight churches were torn down (see Map 3.2).[10]

All churches in the inner wards were dismantled except for St. Isabel (Santa Isabel), which was part of the Misericordia brotherhood's headquarters. It was used to store tatami and timber taken from the other churches.[11] Three churches in the suburbs were closed but not destroyed: All Saints (Todos os Santos); St. Michael (San Miguel) in one of the two cemeteries on Mt. Tateyama 立山; and St. Laurence (San Lorenzo), the church of the Korean community near Shin Korai-machi 新高麗町.[12] Non-religious institutions, like the seven Nagasaki hospitals, were allowed to stay active (including one for common illnesses, one for contagious illnesses, one for lepers, and hospices for widows and orphans). Although founded by missionaries, these hospitals were managed by members of the Misericordia brotherhood and were therefore treated as communal, not missionary, property. After 1614, four relatively quiet years followed. The Nagasaki magistrate and his assistants turned their attention to the persecution of Christians in territories formerly ruled by the Arima 有馬 and Ōmura 大村, while the Tokugawa had their hands full with fighting the Toyotomi.

The trigger for the second strike on churches in Nagasaki was a conflict over the office of magistrate of the city's outer wards (*Nagasaki daikan* 代官). In 1618, a powerful merchant, Suetsugu Heizō 末次平蔵 (?-1630) aspired to replace the *daikan* Murayama Tōan 村山当安 (?-1619). In their fight over the office, each accused the other of hiding Christian priests and missionaries.[13] The matter ended in favor of Suetsugu, who took over as *daikan*, and the extinction of the Murayama family. But more importantly, the conflict revealed the existence of underground Christian missionaries, which prompted a shogunal order to put an end to their presence.

In June 1619, the Nagasaki magistrate Hasegawa Gonroku 長谷川権六 (?-1630) directed several searches for hidden foreign missionaries and ordered the municipal authorities (the inner wards' four *otona* and the *daikan*, all former Christians) to combat Christianity more rigorously. All house-owners had to sign written declarations that they were not harboring foreign missionaries or Japanese clerics in their residences.[14] As a result, a total of sixteen European missionaries and their hosts were executed on November 18 and 27, 1619.[15]

These executions were followed by the second strike on Christian sites. First, the remains in three Christian cemeteries in Nagasaki, one in the Misericordia compounds, and the two on Mt. Tateyama, were exhumed and transferred outside the city.[16] Then the remaining Christian sites were destroyed, starting with the Misericordia headquarters, including the church of St. Isabel, and the outskirt churches of St. Michael, St. Laurence, and All Saints. Finally, the hospitals and hospices were torn down as well, leaving around 400 people without shelter. The Misericordia brotherhood members who had run the hospitals took care of them in their own houses, but this represented a heavy setback for the city's welfare.[17] When the Nagasaki magistrate left for Edo at the end of 1619, no Christian sites were left. Still, citizens feared another wave of persecution upon his return the following spring, since the magistrate usually obtained new instructions on local policies during his visits to the *bakufu*.[18] This indicates that the anti-Christian actions in Nagasaki were largely dictated by the shogunate.

In contrast, other former highly Christianized territories in Kyushu under the control of daimyo implemented anti-Christian measures at their own pace, even before the shogunate extended the anti-Christian ban to the whole country. In Hinoe domain 日野江藩 (later Shimabara-han 島原藩), for example, Arima Naozumi 有馬直純 (1586–1641) forced the apostasy of samurai (not of commoners) as soon as he replaced his father as daimyo in 1612, and by the time he was transferred to another domain in 1615 he had executed sixty Christian samurai. Under the next daimyo, Matsukura Shigemasa 松倉重政 (1574–1630), the anti-Christian measures relaxed until 1625, when Buddhist proselytizing and temple-building began to be encouraged.[19] In Nagasaki, however, the execution of hidden missionaries and their hosts started later, in 1619, although encouragement of Buddhism as an anti-Christian measure had started earlier, in 1614. Even before the Tokugawa banned Christianity, Nagasaki attracted Buddhist proselytizers tempted by the challenge posed by such a deeply Christianized city. Two temples were already established in 1604 (Shōkakuji 正覚寺) and 1607 (Kōtaiji 皓台寺), with the systematic building of temples gaining momentum from 1614.

The Appropriation of Christian Space

After the churches had been destroyed, the Nagasaki magistrate allocated former Christian sites to Buddhist or administrative institutions. This may be explained by the limited availability of urban space, but also by the fact that the location of religious institutions was traditionally determined by secular authorities in Japan. However, the appropriation of Christian sites was undoubtedly prompted by orders from Edo to use the proselytism of Buddhism to displace Christianity and motivate the population to apostatize.[20] Thus, while the general trend in the rest of Japan was to restrict religious institutions (especially Buddhist temples), in the Nagasaki area, the central administration fostered the establishment of new temples and shrines as part of its anti-Christian policy.

The establishment of new religious institutions on sacred sites of a different religion or belief system is a very common phenomenon, not only in Japan but around the world. In Japan, many early Buddhist temples were constructed on former *kami* abodes as a way to grant the new temples the "sacredness" of traditional religious sites. Similarly, in Europe, early Christian churches were founded on the grounds of former pagan temples. In Japan, too, we find Christian churches replacing Buddhist temples, even if this was due rather to local daimyo than to missionary policy. In 1551, Ōuchi Yoshitaka 大内義隆 (1507–51) granted the first Jesuits in Japan an abandoned temple in Yamaguchi 山口.[21] Similarly, the local lord Nagasaki Sumikage 長崎純景 (1548?–1622) assigned Jesuits an abandoned temple near his residence in Nagasaki village 長崎村. The Jesuits soon dismantled the temple and transformed it into All Saints' Church.[22] It remains unclear how the new building differed from the former, but this episode suggests that it was not by their own choice that the missionaries appropriated former

Buddhist temples. The dedication of abandoned temples to the missionaries by local daimyo can be explained by the fact that Jesuits were initially taken to be Buddhist monks coming from India. Moreover, constant warfare since 1467 had led to an increase in abandoned temples (*haidera* 廃寺), which were available for reuse. In addition, Jesuits were also granted non-religious sites, as was the case in Funai 府内 (today's Ōita prefecture, then part of the Ōtomo territories).[23]

After Christianity was outlawed in Nagasaki, the administrative authorities appropriated former Christian sites. As early as 1614, the Nagasaki magistrate accommodated the meeting hall of the representatives of the silk trade guild (*itowappu shukurō kaijo* 糸割賦宿老会場) in the former Jesuit headquarters near the Cathedral in Edo-machi 江戸町,[24] and a temple of the Ikkō 一向 sect, the Kōeiji 光永寺, was built on the former Augustinian residence and church in Furukawa-machi 古河町 (see Map 3.2–3).[25] In 1619, the *Nagasaki bugyō* donated the site of the Misericordia headquarters and St. John's church to Buddhist monks and supported the building of temples there (the Nichiren temple Honrenji 本蓮寺 and the Ikkō temple Daionji 大音寺, respectively). In the same year, after the Murayama family's extinction, the municipal authorities were able to confiscate their property, which included most of the non-Jesuit churches run by Japanese diocesan clerics and Mendicant Orders.[26] Suetsugu Heizō took for himself the site of the Dominicans in Katsuyama-machi 勝山町, where he built his residence in 1619. According to Jesuit sources, the *otona* and the new *daikan* Suetsugu wanted to save former churches from being turned into Buddhist temples by the Nagasaki magistrate. Although most local authorities had recanted their Christian faith, Jesuit sources reveal that many of them regarded the ban of Christianity to be a temporary matter and appropriated Christian sites with the intention of restoring them as soon as the ban was lifted.[27] This, however, never happened, and gradually all the remaining church sites were permanently transformed into administrative buildings or temples. The former site of the church of St. Francis in Sakura-machi 桜町, for example, was turned into Nagasaki's prison, and remained as such for the entire Edo period.

From 1633 onward, two *Nagasaki bugyō* were appointed. The two officials took turns in staying a full year in Nagasaki and Edo, respectively. This ensured a permanent *bugyō* presence in Nagasaki and better control of the population and the *Nagasaki daikan*. New residences for the magistrates were built on the former Jesuit headquarters. Later, in 1673, after the great fire of 1663, the magistrates decided to separate their residences for safety reasons, and a second *bugyō* residence was built in Tateyama, at the former site of the church of St. Mary.

Buddhist Temples in the Anti-Christian Policy

In order to prevent apostate Christians from returning to Christianity, the shogunate prioritized the building of temples and the preaching of Buddhism. In particular, during the Shimabara rebellion (*Shimabara no ran* 島原の乱, 1637/38), most temples in Nagasaki were required to pray for the safety of the country, and monks based in Nagasaki were invited to preach and establish temples in nearby domains. Moreover, temples became crucial for long-term anti-Christian measures, such as the annual

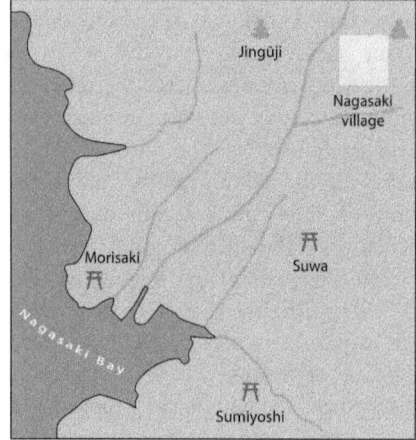
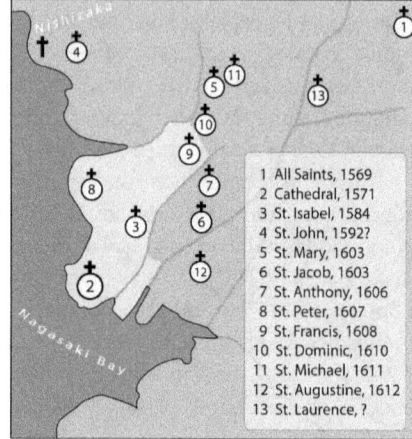

1 Nagasaki region before 1570

2 Christian Nagasaki, 1570–1614

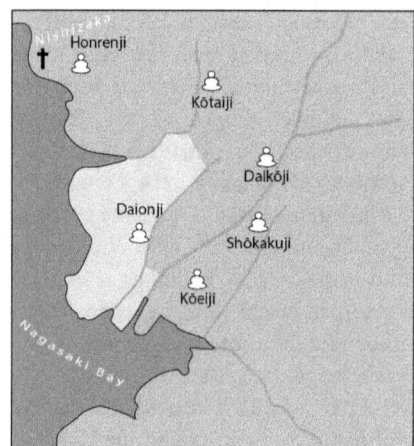
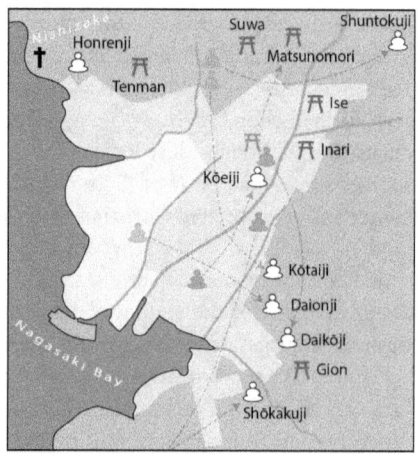

3 Inner wards and new temples, 1615–1624

4 New temples and shrines, 1624–1644

Maps 3.1–4 Major religious institutions in the Nagasaki region during the sixteenth and seventeenth centuries.

certification of religious affiliation (*shūmon aratame* 宗門改) and the compilation of registers of sectarian inspection (*shūmon aratamechō* 宗門改帳).

According to earlier scholarship, in the 1630s religious certification was made comprehensive and extended to the whole of the population (not just former Christians). However, reality shows considerable variations, depending on the particular socio-political circumstances of each domain. According to Ōhashi Yukihiro, there were four different patterns: 1) domains with a low number of Christians where systematic implementation was nevertheless undertaken early, such as the Obama domain 小浜藩 ; 2) domains with a low number of Christians where systematic implementation was undertaken late, as in Okayama domain 岡山藩 ; 3) domains with a high number of Christians where systematic implementation was early, such as Kumamoto-han 熊本藩 ; and 4) domains with a high number of Christians where systematic implementation was late, such as Ōmura-han 大村藩. Ōhashi argues that regardless of the number of former Christians, it seems that in domains were the ruling family remained the same after the ban on Christianity, the systematization of the temple certification system was slower, due to the strong bonds between the rulers and the former Christian population. In contrast, in domains where a new daimyo took over, the weaker bonds made systematic implementation easier and faster.[28]

In Nagasaki, a city that had been under the control of central authorities since 1592, the strong bonds between the citizens and local administrators were counterbalanced by the figure of the Nagasaki magistrate, who maintained constant contact with the shogunate and was detached from the local population. This was the key in the de-Christianization process of the city. The first systematic investigations of former Christians could have taken place as early as 1626, when *Nagasaki bugyō* Mizuno Morinobu 水野守信 (1577–1636) forced former Christians to trample on Christian images (*fumie* 踏み絵) to prove their recanting of the Christian faith.[29] Nevertheless, it is uncertain whether this was also the time when local authorities began to produce registers of sectarian inspection, since such documents dating to before the 1663 fire are extremely rare. The oldest extant register is from Hirado-machi 平戸町 and Yokoseura-machi 横瀬浦町 and dated 1634.[30] According to Nakamura Tadashi, this register shows that initially ward heads were in charge of carrying out the investigations and registering the outcome. In order to do so, they borrowed the *fumie* from the Nagasaki magistrate and conducted examinations house by house in their wards.[31] Thus, initially ward heads were in charge of civil certification (*zoku-uke* 俗請) and the recording of the sectarian inspection. The oldest extant registers of sectarian inspection through temple certification (*terauke* 寺請) date to 1641, which suggests that prior to that time the ward heads did not obtain confirmation of their registers from each temple involved. Thus, systematic temple certification was not implemented in Nagasaki until after the Shimabara rebellion (1637/38).

Another post-Shimabara anti-Christian measure was the shogunal Office of Sectarian Inspection (*shūmon aratame yaku* 宗門改役) established in 1640. Inoue Masashige 井上政重 (1585–1661) was the first to hold the office. He devised a restrained approach towards religious investigations based on fostering peer denunciation. He recommended using torture only moderately, sparing the life of Christians who had apostatized and persuading them to reveal "false apostates." Those who denounced other Christians were spared execution and placed under house arrest, as long as they had stepped on Christian images (*fumie*) to show their disassociation with Christianity. However, the continued exposing of Christians in practically all domains was taken as a sign that such methods were inefficient. After more than 600 Christian villagers were discovered in 1657 in Koori 郡村, Ōmura domain, the shogunate ordered a return to the use of execution. In the 1660s, the annual sectarian inspection through temple certification was forced on the whole population.[32] Through this system, Edo-period Buddhist temples played a significant role in religious control all over Japan.

The Establishment of Buddhist Temples

Resources used to reestablish Buddhist temples in Nagasaki included financial means and manpower for construction as well as stipends for Buddhist priests. They were provided by the *Nagasaki bugyō* and later also by the Ōmura daimyo house and the *Nagasaki daikan*. Between 1615 and 1624, twelve Buddhist temples had been constructed; by the end of the Kan'ei era (1644), thirty-four temples existed within the city limits and along the two mountain ranges surrounding the city (see Map 3.4).[33] This is a quite high number, given that there were approximately 3,000 households in the city at the time.[34] Assuming an average of five members per household, this meant one temple for approximately 440 parishioners. This surpassed the *per capita* ratio of temples in cities that did not have a strong Christian legacy, such as Edo, where around the year 1700 nearly 1,000 temples served about a million citizens, resulting in a 1:1000 ratio.[35]

The building of Buddhist temples on former Christian sites was ultimately a decision of the authorities, although most sources agree that the respective initiatives can be traced back to Buddhist practitioners. Apart from the above-mentioned two temples established by the Nagasaki magistrate on the grounds of former Christian churches in 1620, *daikan* Suetsugu Heizō established a Rinzai temple, the Shuntokuji 春徳寺 in 1630. Its first location was near Tateyama, but in 1640 it was moved to the former location of the Jesuit church of All Saints (see Map 3.2–4).[36] As mentioned above, this church had been established in an abandoned temple, so in a way, Buddhism gained the place back. In the following, I would like to examine the founding of Daionji 大音寺, which, in 1641, was the first temple in Nagasaki to obtain a vermillion seal from the shogunate (*shuindera* 朱印寺). This was the highest status recognized by the shogunate, and usually granted exemption from annual taxes and services.

Daionji

Daionji's founder was an Ikkō monk named Den'yo Kantetsu 伝誉関徹 (1588–1651) from Chikugo province. In 1614, he entered Zōtokuji 蔵徳寺 in Nobo village 野母村, Hizen province, where he took a vow to restore Buddhism in Nagasaki. He started to preach in the city in 1614, but found it difficult to establish himself, since initially no one would give him shelter.[37] After hearing about a man named Iseya Dennojō 伊勢屋傳之丞 (dates unknown) in Furu-machi 古町 who worshipped a statue of Amida 阿弥陀 Buddha, Den'yo visited him to pay obeisance to the Buddha as well. Dennojō let the monk stay with him and was able to gather people to hear him preach. Within three days, the audience attracted by his sermons increased from sixteen to more than forty people.

In August 1614, the Nagasaki magistrate Hasegawa Gonroku gave Den'yo official permission to settle in Nagasaki and asked him to preach Buddhism in accordance with the shogunal decrees.[38] Dennojō, as a resident lay believer, was allowed to build a "small hermitage" (*shōan* 小庵) on his own property in Furu-machi to enshrine the Amida statue, and Den'yo was officially appointed the hermitage's master (*anshu* 庵主).[39] In 1619 Den'yo received a permit to build a temple on the former site of St. Isabel, the church of the Misericordia brotherhood in Honhakata-machi 本博多町. After being received by Shogun Hidetada 徳川秀忠 (1579–1632, r. 1605–23) in Edo the following year, Den'yo went to Chion'in 知恩院 in Kyoto, the head temple of the Jōdo 浄土 sect, where he received the name Shōkaku-san Daionji 正覚山大音寺 for his new temple. In this way, Daionji was founded in 1620 as a branch temple of Chion'in.[40] Interestingly, the European-style bell of St. Isabel was kept and used in the new temple.[41]

Den'yo's efforts in Nagasaki were highly appreciated by the *Nagasaki bugyō* and other regional authorities, such as the daimyo of Hirado 平戸藩, who invited him to preach in villages of his domain that had been under strong Jesuit influence. Den'yo obeyed and helped establish a number of temples there. However, after three years of proselytizing in the Hirado domain, Nagasaki required his attention again.[42] During Den'yo's absence, citizens digging along the side wall of the easternmost side of Honhakata-machi unearthed human remains that had been buried in the former cemetery of the Misericordia brotherhood (established in 1583). Although in 1619 the *Nagasaki bugyō* had ordered the exhumation of the Christian cemeteries and the transfer of the remains to the outside of the city, some seem to have been missed. This episode suggests that former Christians had decided to recover the remains of their relatives on their own initiative. Den'yo perceived this as an attack on his institution, and in 1635 and again in 1637, requested that the *Nagasaki bugyō* prevent the residents of neighboring streets from digging and "causing landslides." The authorities ordered Den'yo to construct a stone fence to "prevent further landslides," but Den'yo regarded this as an unduly heavy burden. Instead, he submitted a claim for governmental help to the *bakufu* in Edo, but the Nagasaki municipal administrators (*machidoshiyori* 町年寄) prevented his petition from being processed.[43] Hampered by the local authorities, Den'yo took the opportunity to forward the Daionji question to senior councilor (*rōjū* 老中) Matsudaira Nobutsuna 松平信綱 (1596–1662) when the latter was in Kyushu in 1638 to put down the Shimabara rebellion. He argued that the Daionji compound was too cramped and that its location in the middle of a residential ward increased the risk of fire. In response, the *rōjū* urged the Nagasaki magistrate to grant Den'yo a larger plot of land in the southwest of the city, at the foot of Mt. Kazagashira 風頭山 near Kajiya-machi 鍛治屋町 (see Map 3.4). The *Nagasaki bugyō* granted Den'yo 100 silver pieces[44] to cover part of the costs of the relocation and ordered all wards of Nagasaki to support the construction of a large temple precinct (*daigaran* 大伽藍). Probably exhausted and frustrated by the hostility of former Christians, Den'yo decided to get rid of all Christian symbols and hid the bell of St. Isabel in the dry moat next to the new temple.[45] In this way, he disassociated himself and the Daionji from the memory of former Christian spaces.

The Establishment of Shinto Shrines

In addition to fostering Buddhist temples and rituals, from the Kan'ei era (1624–44) onward, the shogunate started supporting the construction of shrines and the worship of *kami*. The sources from religious institutions emphasize the initiatives of proselytizers, but the support of shrine worship also depended strongly on the policies of individual magistrates: Hasegawa Gonroku, who held the office from 1614 to 1626, established ten temples from 1614 to 1624, but only one shrine, in 1625 (Suwa Jinja 諏訪神社). In contrast, in the following four years, when his successor Mizuno Morinobu was in office (1626–9), five Buddhist temples and four shrines were established. Two of the shrines were independent institutions—Shin Daijin Shrine 新大神 (later renamed Matsunomori Jinja 松森神社), and Ise-no-miya 伊勢宮—and two were associated with temples—Tenmangū 天満宮 (1626) as a tutelary shrine of the Shingon 真言 temple Taishōji 体性寺, and Inari Shrine 稲荷社 of the Tendai 天台 temple Daigakuin 大学院 (later renamed Gyokusen'in 宝泉院) (see Map 3.4). The pace then slowed down, but by the end of the Kan'ei era (1644) there were eleven shrines in Nagasaki, eight of which associated with temples.[46] The following two examples reveal, how these shrines were connected to the anti-Christian policy of the *bakufu*.

Suwa

Suwa Shrine was established on Mt. Maruyama 丸山 in Nishiyama-mura 西山村, adjacent to Nagasaki, in 1625, enshrining an ensemble of three guardian deities (*ubusunagami* 産土神): Suwa Daimyōjin 諏訪大明神, Morisaki Gongen 森崎権現, and Sumiyoshi Myōjin 住吉明神, which before the region's Christianization had been worshipped in the area in three separate shrines. Little is known about the founding of these three pre-Christian shrines, but the gazetteer *Nagasaki zushi* 長崎図志 (1715) traces the origin of Nagasaki Suwa Shrine back to 1555, when Nagasaki Tamehide 長崎為英 (dates unknown)[47] obtained a "branch spirit" (*bunrei* 分霊) of the Kyoto Suwa Shrine and had it enshrined at the foot of Mt. Kazagashira 風頭山, near the current site of Chōshōji 長照寺. There was also a Morisaki Shrine 森崎神社 somewhere in the pine forest that covered the cape of Morisaki 森崎 (the site where the Jesuits built their church and residence in 1571) and a Sumiyoshi Shrine 住吉社 in Kojima-mura 小島村, the current site of Shōkakuji (see Map 3.1).[48]

The Jesuit missionary Gaspar Vilela (1525–72), who had settled in Nagasaki village in 1569, reported that he led the new Christian converts on an expedition to eliminate "some houses of local idols" in the area, which must have included these three shrines and the Jingūji 神宮寺 temple complex.[49] None of them was spared the Christian raid, but it is believed that a certain Kumon Kurōzaemon 公文黒郎左衛門 (dates unknown) secretly continued worshiping the three shrines' deities at a remote site in Hizen Province.[50]

In 1623, a *yamabushi* by the name of Aoki Kensei 青木賢清 (1582–1656) came to Nagasaki intending to re-establish *kami* worship. He was originally from Karatsu 唐津 in Hizen province, but related to the local Isahaya 諫早 and Matsura 松浦 families. According to the *History of Suwa Shrine* (*Suwa jinja engi* 諏訪神社縁起), his family had served the Matsura family in ritual functions.[51] When Kensei learned of Kurōzaemon's secret worship of the three deities, he met him and asked him to re-establish them in Nagasaki. However, since Kurōzaemon's family had fallen on hard times, he entrusted this task to Kensei. Thereupon, Kensei settled in Nishiyama-mura and formed a small community of local villagers who gathered to hear his teachings.

In 1625, Kensei sought the support of the *Nagasaki bugyō* and *daikan* to build a shrine in the city. Magistrate Hasegawa Gonroku accepted Kensei's request and obtained permission from Shogun Hidetada to establish what would become the Nagasaki Suwa Shrine. For this purpose, Kensei received land from Gonroku in the northwestern suburbs, in Nishiyama-mura (see Map 3.4), and was appointed head priest of the shrine, a position that was to remain in the Aoki family for generations.[52]

Although Christianity had been banned already ten years earlier, there was obviously still opposition by former Christian citizens against traditional forms of Japanese religion, since some residents tried to sabotage the shrines' construction and drive Kensei out of Nagasaki.[53] This began to change in 1634, when citizens were forced to become parishioners (*ujiko* 氏子) of Suwa Shrine as part of the increasing anti-Christian efforts. At that time, head priest Aoki Katakiyo 青木堅清 (Kensei's son, 1582–1656) organized a shrine festival (*matsuri* 祭) around the city for the first time, which gained the support and participation of the *Nagasaki bugyō* and all of the municipal authorities. This was the beginning of the Kunchi くんち festival.

The first-day procession, which took place on 1634/9/7, was meant to cross the city from north to south, ending at a resting place (*tabisho* 旅所) in Ōhato 大波止, Edo-machi 江戸町, near the disembarking site of the trade ships. Residents of Maruyama-machi and Yoriai-machi 寄合町 marched at the front of the procession, followed by residents from the rest of the participating wards. After these came the *mikoshi* and the shrine priests, followed by the municipal authorities.

According to the founding legends of Suwa Shrine, there were still Christians in the city who opposed this first Kunchi. As the procession was about to enter the inner wards at Bungo-machi 豊後町, they began to throw stones causing confusion and disarray among the participants. However, one of the ward heads, Yakushiji Kuzaemon 薬師寺久左衛門 (?–1658), faced the Christians resolutely and dispersed them, and the procession was able to reach the *tabisho* safely. In recognition of this, the role of procession leader (*sendatsu yaku* 先達役) was created for Yakushiji the following year, and he was allowed to have a seat among the authorities during the festival rites.[54]

On the second day of the Kunchi, official Shinto ceremonies (*shinji* 神事) took place, ending with a purificatory rite with boiling water (*yudate* 湯立). On the third and last day, after the official ceremonies, each ward offered popular dances and the *mikoshi* returned in procession to Suwa Shrine. Here, the authorities advanced to the main hall and provided offerings of silver. After another *yudate* blessing of the audience, a performance of horseback archery (*yabusame* 流鏑馬) concluded the festival.[55] With time, dancing and popular celebrations developed, and the whole population took part in the Kunchi.[56]

The connection of Suwa Shrine with the anti-Christian initiatives became obvious again in 1637, during the Shimabara rebellion, when the Suwa head priest offered prayers to protect the country from Christianity. As a reward, in 1641 the *bakufu* recognized Suwa Shrine as a *yochi* 余地, that is, a fief exempted from the land tax in silver (*jishigin* 地子銀). Moreover, in 1648 the shrine was allotted land. Its privileged connection to the shogunate can also be seen by the fact that it celebrated various important events, such as the accession of Shogun Ietsuna 徳川家綱 (1641–80, r. 1651–80) and his recovery from small pox in 1656, with a celebratory Noh performance (*shugi nō* 祝儀能) added to the Kunchi. In 1669, Suwa Shrine was recognized by the shogun as vermillion-seal land (*shuinchi* 朱印地), the shogunate's highest recognition for a religious institution, as mentioned above. It has remained the main shrine of Nagasaki up to the present day, and the Kunchi is considered one of the ten most popular festivals in Japan.

Ise-no-miya

The Nagasaki Ise Shrine (Ise-no-miya) was built in 1628 in Kōrai-machi 高麗町 (lit. "Korea town"). This ward was a poor area of the city, housing Korean artisans, most former enslaved prisoners of Hideyoshi's Korea Invasions (1592–98). Although in 1611, when Christianity was at its peak, they built their own church and founded their own brotherhood of St. Laurence, in 1626 they took the initiative to establish an Ise shrine. The Korean community claimed that a small shrine had existed for years in a bamboo grove near their ward. Because the church location is unknown, its connection to the shrine location remains unclear as well. But whether at the same site or not, this replacement of a church with a shrine may have been a move of the Korean residents to reassure the authorities of their disassociation with Christianity.

The community obtained permission from the *Nagasaki bugyō* to build a small shrine in 1628 and to have a Tendai mountain ascetic serve as its head priest. From 1629, some Nagasaki wards started sending one or two pilgrims a year to the Outer Shrine of Ise, through the Ise Confraternity (*Ise kō* 伊勢講) of Nagasaki. The number of pilgrims increased gradually during the Kan'ei era, peaking in the second half of the seventeenth century with an average of more than fifty pilgrims per year.[57] In 1639, the priest of Ise-no-miya obtained recognition from the Outer Shrine of Ise, whereupon the ward was renamed Ise-machi 伊勢町. In 1646 the Nagasaki magistrates provided a plot of land by the river in Ise-machi, and a shrine hall and other buildings were erected. Ise-no-miya would not become a *yochi* until the first year of the Meiji period (1868), but it was recognized as the third most important shrine in Nagasaki already during the Edo period.

Shrines in the Anti-Christian Policy

Most of the shrines built in the Kan'ei era were located in peripheral areas, either at the city limits at the foot of the two mountain ranges surrounding the port of Nagasaki, or in the outer wards near the confluence of the two tributary rivers of Hongawa River (see Map 3.4). This was not different for temples, especially after the dramatic fire of 1663 destroyed practically all of the wards in Nagasaki port city and most of the temples and shrines inside its residential areas. The magistrates relocated administrative and religious institutions to the suburban areas, for safety reasons as far as possible from the citizens' houses (*machiya* 町屋), forming two belts of "temple wards" (*teramachi* 寺町) surrounding the city. It must be noted here that in Japan, the status of religious institutions is expressed by the size (expanse) of their precincts, rather than the size (height) of their buildings (as in Europe). Thus, the higher status they gain, the further they move away from densely urbanized areas. For this reason, too, it is not surprising that the big shrines and temples of Nagasaki were relocated to suburban areas.

In sum, in Nagasaki the *bakufu* support for shrines came later and with lower financial investment than that for temples.⁵⁸ The number of new temples was approximately four times that of shrines, and in general, temples received larger grants of land. But Suwa Shrine was strongly involved in the *bakufu* enterprise of de-Christianizing Nagasaki and, accordingly, was rewarded with funds and privileges, such as exemption from land taxes.

With the exception of Suwa Shrine and Shin Daijin Shrine, which from 1658 also was recognized as a tax-exempted fief, shrines could not rely on shogunal funding and had to secure other sources of income. For example, in 1646, when Ise-no-miya's head priest received land from the Nagasaki magistrates to enlarge the shrine's precincts and built a proper shrine hall, he asked them for permission to raise funds among Nagasaki citizens. Since the magistrates obliged, further repairs and rebuilding were funded by donations from citizens.⁵⁹ However, much of the wealth of private donors, as well as that of the *Nagasaki bugyō* and *Nagasaki daikan*, depended on the success of trade with China.⁶⁰ For example, participation in annual pilgrimages to Ise fluctuated according to the current state of profits from Chinese trade.⁶¹ At the end of the Edo period, as Chinese trade declined and the *bakufu* weakened, stipends and donations to religious institutions diminished dramatically. While the major institutions managed to survive, many of the more minor shrines and temples were abandoned.⁶²

Conclusion

After the Tokugawa shogunate banned Christianity in all of Japan in 1614, several anti-Christian measures were implemented, but not in all domains, and not at the same time or speed. Substantial regional and temporal variations can be seen regarding when anti-Christian policies began, as well as regarding methods and developments. In this process, the building of temples and shrines was an important measure in areas where Christianization had involved the destruction of temples and shrines. This was the case in the territories of the Ōmura and Arima daimyo, and especially in the self-governed port city of Nagasaki.

Since Nagasaki had a much larger population than any village or castle town in the area, it also had the largest number of churches. When the shogunate ordered their destruction, they were appropriated by central or local authorities. In contrast to the *Nagasaki bugyō*, who were appointed on a temporary basis by the shogun, the local offices of *otona* and *daikan* remained in the hands of the same local families, all rich merchants. Since all of them had been Christians, they showed passive resistance to the building of temples on former church sites, even after having apostatized. For example, they appropriated several church sites with the intention of re-establishing them as soon as the prohibition was lifted. This, however, did not happen, and with time even the local authorities collaborated with the anti-Christian policy. Only one of the four ward heads avoided apostasy and, in the end, had to leave the city. Most former Christian sites were transformed into either civil administrative buildings or Buddhist temples; within three decades newly established temples and shrines outnumbered the former churches. The de-Christianization process also involved the loss of welfare and medical institutions that had been introduced by the Catholic missionaries, such as orphanages, hospices for widows, associations for collecting and distributing alms to the poor, hospitals, and lepers' hospices.

The establishment of Buddhist temples and Shinto shrines was vital for the de-Christianization process. For example, the Kunchi festival of Suwa Shrine gradually involved all citizens in a communal public ritual, and temples provided funerals and memorial rituals that strengthened family structures. Temples also played a crucial role in the long-term anti-Christian measures and religious control of the population, such as providing sectarian inspection through temple certification.

The anti-Christian policy of the Edo period was not a previously designed set of measures applied all at once and homogeneously. Rather it developed regionally in response to specific "problems," such as the discovery of missionaries hidden by Nagasaki citizens in 1619, the peasant revolt of Shimabara in 1637, or the discovery of Christian networks in Koori in 1657. Yet anti-Christian measures were gradually systematized and standardized, and by the mid-seventeenth century they were being applied at a national scale. Thus, by the end of the 1600s, what had started as local strategies targeting former Christians had become nationwide religious control of the entire population.

4

When the Lotus Went Underground

The Nichiren Buddhist Fujufuse Movement and Its Early Modern Persecution

Jacqueline I. Stone

During the Kanbun era (1661–73), a series of *bakufu* edicts suppressed the Fujufuse branch 不受不施派 of the Nichiren 日蓮 sect.[1] Fujufuse thus became the second religious group, after Christianity, to be proscribed in early modern Japan. Fujufuse priests refused, as a matter of principle, to accept offerings from a ruler who did not embrace the *Lotus Sūtra* and were persecuted in consequence. Considerable primary material remains concerning the suppression of Fujufuse adherents and their subsequent survival for some two hundred years as an underground community until achieving legal recognition in 1876. Nonetheless, outside sectarian circles, their story remains relatively unknown. This chapter explores what was at stake in the heated controversy over interpretation of the *fujufuse* principle within the Nichiren sect, as well as the significance of the *bakufu* crackdown on uncompromising Fujufuse proponents. The chapter has three parts: the first traces the background of the *fujufuse* controversy up through its first major eruption in 1595 and its immediate aftermath; the second examines mounting hostility between hardline Fujufuse advocates and their opponents within the Nichiren sect during the early decades of Tokugawa rule; and the third focuses on the persecution of the Kanbun era, when the *fujufuse* position was criminalized.

A Controversy Emerges

Fujufuse 不受不施 (literally, "neither receiving nor giving") means that priests of the Nichiren sect should not accept offerings from persons who do not embrace the *Lotus Sūtra*, and lay followers should not visit the temples and shrines of other sects, seek their religious services, or make donations to their priests. This stance derived from the sect's founder, Nichiren 日蓮 (1222–82). Nichiren had trained within the Tendai 天台 sect, which regards the *Lotus Sūtra* as complete and perfect, the Buddha's ultimate teaching, and all other teachings as his provisional "skillful means." But where Tendai stressed the suitability of different teachings for persons of differing capacities,

Nichiren's approach was exclusivist. Now in the degenerate Final Dharma age (*mappō* 末法), he asserted, only the *Lotus Sūtra* leads to liberation; other, incomplete teachings have lost their efficacy and must be set aside. Rejecting the *Lotus Sūtra* in favor of these provisional doctrines was for Nichiren equivalent to slandering or maligning the dharma (*hōbō* 謗法). To this gravest of all sins he attributed the calamities besetting Japan in his day: famine, epidemics, and the Mongol threat.[2] This conviction underlay Nichiren's confrontational mode of proselytizing (*shakubuku* 折伏) for which he is well known; his criticism of other Buddhist forms led to two sentences of exile and repeated attempts on his life. Nichiren condemned the giving of material support to priests who rejected the *Lotus Sūtra* as a form of the very dharma slander that had brought misery to the realm; thus, he clearly established the principle of "not giving." As for "not receiving," Nichiren is said to have refused an offer of patronage from the Kamakura *bakufu* if he would join with other sects in performing prayer rites to repel the Mongol invasion; only exclusive reliance on the *Lotus Sūtra*, he countered, could be effective. But because his following was small and marginal, the propriety of receiving offerings from nonbelievers did not become a major issue during Nichiren's lifetime.[3]

The issue grew pressing after his death, however, as the Nichiren sect spread from its home region, the Kanto provinces, to Kyoto and Sakai 堺 in the west, attracting patronage from influential warriors and aristocrats, and as some of its leading monasteries began to be designated as imperial or *bakufu* prayer temples (*chokuganji* 勅願寺, *kiganji* 祈願寺). Initially, exceptions to the principle of refusing offerings from "dharma slanderers" were often made for influential nobles and warrior officials. Some clerics within the sect even argued that accepting support from such persons could be an important means of leading them toward faith in the *Lotus Sūtra*. These more accommodating priests generally inclined toward *shōju* 摂受, a gentler mode of dharma teaching that leads others without rebuking their views, in contrast to the uncompromising *shakubuku* approach. From the fifteenth century, however, attitudes within the sect gradually hardened in the direction of growing exclusivism, strict *shakubuku* practice, and refusal to accept patronage from nonbelievers, including even the highest authorities. On several occasions, Nichiren clerics were able to obtain formal statements from the Ashikaga shoguns exempting them from participating in *bakufu*-sponsored ceremonies and temple fund-raising (*kanjin* 勧進).[4]

All this began to change, however, with the rise of Oda Nobunaga 織田信長 (1534–82), who was determined to break the power of medieval religious institutions. Nobunaga had humiliated the Nichiren sect in a rigged debate with the Pure Land (Jōdo 浄土) sect held at Azuchi 安土 castle in 1579 (*Azuchi shūron* 安土宗論). After declaring the Pure Land representatives victorious and executing the alleged instigators of the debate on the Nichiren side, he had forced the sect's leaders to submit a written apology, threatening that he would otherwise kill some two or three hundred Lotus devotees whom he had arrested and also destroy the Nichiren temples and believers in both Kyoto and his own domains.[5] Sensing early on the beginnings of an unprecedented consolidation of worldly power, sect elders in Kyoto began to retreat from hardline *shakubuku* and to adopt a more accommodating approach. In contrast, Nichiren clerics of the Kanto, Chūō, and Hokuriku regions criticized this attitude and redoubled their commitment to the exclusivist stance.

The Great Buddha Memorial Rites and Nichiō's Dissent

The *fujufuse* principle was generally shared by all Nichiren lineages (*monto* 門徒). While controversy over exceptions had occurred since the time of Nichiren's earliest disciples, it emerged as a decisive internal fracture line only in 1595, when Toyotomi Hideyoshi 豊臣秀吉 (1537-98) demanded that 100 priests from each of the ten sects take part in a series of monthly memorial services for his deceased relatives, to be held before the great Buddha image he had commissioned at Hōkōji 方広寺 in Higashiyama 東山. Cooperation would clearly violate the orthodox *fujufuse* principle, as it entailed participating in a religious rite not based on the *Lotus Sūtra* (an act of complicity in "dharma slander") and sponsored by a nonbeliever, Hideyoshi, along with accepting his offerings in the form of a ceremonial meal. Yet the Nichiren clerics felt themselves poorly positioned to refuse. Hideyoshi had warned them that, even though their traditional stance of non-participation might have been taught by their founder Nichiren, this time, it would not be tolerated.[6] Never before had the *fujufuse* principle been tested in connection with so powerful a ruler. A hastily gathered council of the Nichiren abbots in Kyoto agreed that refusing Hideyoshi would likely result in his suppression of the sect. Virtually all agreed to participate just once, in deference to his command, and then reassert their sect's policy.

Almost the sole dissenter was Busshō-in Nichiō 仏性院日奥 (1565-1630), chief abbot of Myōkakuji 妙覚寺 in Kyoto and a disciple of Jitsujōin Nichiden 実成院日典 (1528-92), who had studied in the Kanto and absorbed the strict ethos of *shakubuku* that prevailed there.[7] Nichiō argued that participating in the rites before the Great Buddha just once would not be possible and that taking part at all would be disastrous; once the sect's principle was broken, it could not easily be restored. The proper course, he said, would be to remonstrate with Hideyoshi, asserting the supremacy of the *Lotus Sūtra* in an act of "admonishing the state" (*kokka kangyō* 国家諫暁). Such admonitions had been carried out since Nichiren's time as an act of *shakubuku* directed specifically toward the ruler (*kokushu* 国主)—the emperor, the shogun, or their representatives—urging him to abandon support for clerics espousing provisional teachings and to endorse practice of the *Lotus Sūtra* alone, in order to ensure peace in the realm.[8] To meet persecution at Hideyoshi's hands, Nichiō said, would bear witness to the truth of the *Lotus*, which predicts that its devotees in an evil latter age will meet hostility from those in power. In his words:

> Refusing to accept offerings from those who slander the dharma is the first principle of our sect and its most important rule. Therefore, the saints of former times all defied the commands of the ruler in order to observe it, even at the cost of their lives. [...] If we fail to defy the ruler's stern command, how will we meet great persecution for the sake of our sect's dharma-principle? If we do not meet such persecution, the [*Lotus*] *Sūtra* passages about "not begrudging bodily life" will become all but false and meaningless. [...]
>
> If our temples are destroyed because we uphold our dharma-principle, that is [still in accord with] the original intent and meaning of this sect. What could there be to regret?[9]

As Nichiō had predicted, Nichiren prelates did not withdraw from the rites held before the Great Buddha after the first ceremony but continued to participate over the full twenty years that these memorial assemblies were conducted, in flagrant violation of their original agreement. Isolated by his refusal, Nichiō left Kyoto and eventually settled not far away at Koizumi 小泉 in Tanba province. From there he wrote and traveled to preach the *fujufuse* principle. He sent letters of admonition to Emperor Goyōzei 後陽成天皇 (1571–1617) and Hideyoshi and continued to denounce other members of his sect for their participation in the ongoing memorial rites. Eventually, abbots of the Kyoto Nichiren temples began petitioning the ruler—first Hideyoshi, and then Tokugawa Ieyasu 徳川家康 (1543–1616)—to punish Nichiō for his recalcitrance. A 1598 petition to Hideyoshi accuses Nichiō of luring away lay supporters and encouraging branch temples in both the capital and remote provinces to defy their head temples, suggesting that Nichiō's position was gaining considerable grassroots sympathy.[10] These early petitions also prefigure the major tactic that the sect's accommodationist faction would adopt in combatting their hardline Fujufuse opponents during the first decades of Tokugawa rule.

Hideyoshi died in 1598, and the following year, the Kyoto temples petitioned Ieyasu—who as inner minister (*naidaijin* 内大臣) had become the actual power-holder—against Nichiō.[11] Ieyasu saw their suit as an opportunity to suppress a potential source of conflict and summoned Nichiō to Osaka castle, to confront his opponents within the sect in debate. Like the Azuchi debate staged by Nobunaga some twenty years earlier, the outcome had been decided in advance. According to Nichiō's account, just prior to the debate, Ieyasu offered him every imaginable concession if he would participate in the memorial rites just once. He need not sit with the priests of other sects but could perform the sutra recitation in a separate room. If he did not wish to receive the offertory meal, he need only lift his chopsticks and bow toward the tray. Ieyasu even promised to provide Nichiō with a written statement that he had participated only under official duress. But he also threatened that, if Nichiō refused, punishment would fall not only on himself but on his disciples and relatives. Nichiō, however, declined to give Ieyasu even the semblance of complying. When Ieyasu tasked him with being a rebel who alone rejected the majority position of his sect, Nichiō replied that "the truth of Buddhism has nothing to do with the opinion of the majority. All that is important is whether a belief is in accord with the scriptures." Ieyasu retorted, "One who is this arrogant will surely be the cause of a crisis in the realm. He shall be exiled."[12] Ieyasu's assessment shows a keen awareness of the danger posed to his ambitions by even a single principled dissident. Nichiō was banished to the island of Tsushima 対馬, where he remained for over twelve years.

Nichiō's exile was a sanction imposed on a single individual seen as a potential threat to Ieyasu's vision of a new order, not—at this point—an outright ban on the *fujufuse* practice itself. After solidifying his authority and establishing his new *bakufu* in Edo (today's Tokyo), Ieyasu seems to have softened toward Nichiō, who was pardoned in 1612 and returned to Kyoto. There, several abbots of the Nichiren temples who had taken part in Hideyoshi's Great Buddha rites formally apologized to Nichiō and joined him in reaffirming the sect's *fujufuse* stance. The memorial rites had come to an end in 1615, when Ieyasu destroyed Hideyoshi's heirs, so participation was no longer an issue. In 1620, the Nichiren sect applied to the *bakufu* for official recognition of its *fujufuse* policy. Their request was granted on 1623/10/13 by Itakura Katsushige 板倉勝重 (1545–1624), who had served as Ieyasu's deputy and had also issued Nichiō's pardon.[13] However, this apparently successful resolution of the affair did not last long. Underlying tensions within the sect between hardliners and accommodationists, exposed by Hideyoshi's demands, still smoldered, and the *bakufu* would soon refuse to honor Katsushige's decree.

The Conflict Moves East

With Edo fast becoming the new center of commerce and politics, Buddhist schools and lineages, including the Kyoto-based *monto* of the Nichiren sect, also seized the opportunity to expand their influence in the eastern provinces. Around this time, the epicenter of the *fujufuse* controversy shifted from Kyoto to the Kanto. The Kanto provinces were a strict Fujufuse stronghold, and, in its eastward expansion, the conciliatory faction of the Nichiren sect met with hostility from their more rigorous counterparts. In this region, Chōon'in Nichiju 長遠院日樹 (1574–1631) now emerged as the leader of the hardline Fujufuse contingent. As chief abbot of Ikegami Honmonji 池上本門寺 in Musashi province, the leading Nichiren temple in the east with some 165 branch temples, he was well positioned to coordinate opposition to the accommodationists.

On the accommodationist side, a key role was played by the successive chief abbots of Minobu-san Kuonji 身延山久遠寺 in Kai province. Mount Minobu, where Nichiren had spent the last eight years of his life and which housed his grave, held special status within the Nichiren sect as a holy place and major pilgrimage site. Doctrinally, it became aligned with the accommodationist faction when Jakushōin Nichiken 寂照院日乾 (1560–1635), a bitter adversary of Nichiō, became its chief abbot (in 1602–03 and again in 1609–14); Minobu's next several chief abbots were all in Nichiken's lineage. Nichiken and his successors had close ties to the *bakufu*; Ieyasu's consort Yojūin 養珠院, or Oman no kata お万の方 (1577–1653), was among their influential patrons. They perceived the rise of the new shogunate as an opportunity to establish Minobu as the chief Nichiren head temple and to bring the entire sect under its governance. The *fujufuse* controversy now unfolded as a struggle between two factions, headed respectively by Ikegami and Minobu, for control of the Nichiren sect.

The mounting animosity between the two sides may be glimpsed from a suit filed in 1629 with the magistrate of temples and shrines (*jisha bugyō* 寺社奉行) by Chiken'in Nissen 智見院日暹 (1586–1648), then chief abbot of Minobu, against Ikegami and its chief abbot Nichiju.[14] Nissen's petition had three major points: First, he asserted, the Nichiren sect's leading scholar-priests had investigated and found participation in the rites sponsored by Hideyoshi to have been fully consistent with the sect's principles going back to Nichiren himself; Nichiō's denouncing of that participation as "slander of the dharma" was merely his own distorted view. Second, the position of Nichiju and his supporters was hypocritical and self-contradictory: While claiming that receiving donations from the ruler constitutes dharma slander, they themselves accepted official grants to temples of lands and land income. And third, Nichiju and his supporters were discouraging pilgrimage to Minobu and thus undercutting its economic base: they preached to lay believers that, because Nichiō's opponent Nichiken, a former Minobu chief abbot, had participated in Hideyoshi's rites, Minobu had become a place of dharma slander and that those who visited there would fall into the Avīci Hell, the lowest of Buddhist hells.[15]

Those Nichiren clerics participating in the rites sponsored by Hideyoshi had initially regarded their compliance as an expedient: regrettable, but necessary to protect their temples. As Nissen's petition indicates, however, in the intervening three decades, sectarian scholars had been laboring to find firm grounds that would justify exempting the ruler alone from the *fujufuse* restriction. By "scholars" Nissen specifically meant his own teacher, Shinshōin Nichion 心性院日遠 (1572–1642) and Nichion's teacher, the above-mentioned Nichiken, both Nissen's predecessors as Minobu chief abbots. In 1616, following Nichiō's return from exile, these two had engaged with him in a heated written exchange in which Nichiken leveled what would become a recurrent charge against strict Fujufuse proponents: while accusing others of dharma slander, they violated their own tenet by accepting official grants to temples of lands or land incomes.[16] Although Nichiken developed it at length, this was not altogether a new criticism. Ieyasu, before exiling Nichiō, had reportedly told him that if he were really determined to refuse the ruler's offerings, he should follow the example of the legendary Chinese sages Bo Yi 伯夷 and Shu Qi 叔齊, who, in protesting the misrule of the Zhou ruler, refused to eat the products of his realm and starved to death.[17]

In responding to Nissen's charges, Nichiju countered that official land grants to temples were merely an expression of the ruler's worldly benevolence (*ninnon* 任恩), not Buddhist offerings (*kuyō* 供養). The distinction dated back to the fourteenth century, when Nichiren temples in Kyoto first attracted elite patronage. Nichiō had addressed it in detail, offering doctrinal support, in his response to Nichiken. Only in worldly terms, Nichiō had said, did the land belong to the ruler. Like Nichiren before him, Nichiō asserted that, from an ultimate perspective, rulers of all countries hold their lands in fief from the eternal Śākyamuni Buddha of the *Lotus Sūtra*, lord of the threefold world. Thus there could be no objection to that Buddha's direct disciples—the priests of the *Lotus*—accepting the products of the land, as long as they upheld the *Sūtra*'s exclusive truth.[18] Nichiju now restated this position. Nissen's accusation, he added, committed the error of conflating worldly and transcendent registers.[19]

Probably in response to Nissen's petition of 1629, in the following year, on 1630/2/21, Nichiju of Ikegami, along with five elders of other leading Fujufuse temples and seminaries in the Kanto, were summoned to Edo castle along with their Minobu counterparts for what proved to be yet another rigged contest, known as the Minobu-Ikegami debate (*Shinchi tairon* 身池対論). Present on the Minobu side were Kuonji's chief abbot Nissen, the former chief abbots Nichiken and Nichion, and three others. Judges included the eminent shogunal advisor-monks Tenkai 天海 (1536–1643) and Sūden 崇伝 (1569–1633), among others. The two extant accounts of the proceedings, although each represent the opposing side, both indicate that the debate centered around two issues: whether refusing the ruler's donations was a criminal offense; and whether official land grants to temples constituted religious offerings. On the issue of legality, the Minobu faction invoked Ieyasu's precedent: "Gongen-sama" 権現様[20] had exiled Nichiō as a criminal. The Ikegami side retorted that Ieyasu's pardoning of Nichiō had indicated a change of heart; their opponents countered that the pardon had merely been part of a general amnesty, and so forth. Again, the outcome appears to have been decided in advance, and on 1630/4/2, the Minobu side was declared victorious. The above-mentioned official acknowledgement of the *fujufuse* position issued in 1623 was rescinded as illegitimate, and Nichiju and his five supporters were exiled. *In absentia*, Nichiō was also sentenced to a second exile on Tsushima—posthumously, as he had died the month before.[21]

In the aftermath of the debate, the two leading hardline Fujufuse temples, along with their hundreds of branch temples (*matsuji* 末寺), were placed under Minobu governance: Nichion was appointed chief abbot of Ikegami Honmonji, while Nichiken, Nichiō's arch-opponent, was given Nichiō's former temple Myōkakuji in Kyoto. Nichion is said to have arrived at Ikegami accompanied by an armed guard arranged for him by the shogun's widow, Yojūin.[22] Nissen, speaking as Minobu chief abbot and on behalf of the two former chief abbots, Nichiken and Nichion, issued a statement to all Minobu branch temples, including those newly acquired in the wake of the *bakufu* verdict, announcing that the Minobu-Ikegami debate had put an end to Nichiju's false interpretation. Offerings from the ruler alone were to be accepted as an undisputed principle, while in accord with time-honored usage, offerings from other nonbelievers would not.[23] Absent here was even the slightest suggestion that accepting the ruler's offerings had become a necessary expedient, let alone that it violated majority understanding of the *fujufuse* principle as upheld since the fifteenth century. Hardliners mocked Minobu and its supporters as the "not giving but receiving" (Jufuse 受不施) faction and claimed the name of Fujufuse for themselves.[24]

Accommodationist Attacks and Fujufuse Resistance

In theory, the accommodationists had won a great victory in the 1630 debate, but in fact the conflict intensified. The banishing of Nichiju and the other five clerics, like that of Nichiō thirty years before, was an action directed against specific individuals seen as troublemakers, not yet a ban on *fujufuse* practice itself. Moreover, hardline Fujufuse adherents still represented a majority within the Nichiren sect. In fact, their major strength lay in the Kanto region, at the very heart of the Tokugawa administration.[25]

Resistance began immediately in the temples turned over to Minobu following the ruling in the debate.[26] At Ikegami Honmonji, three clerics committed suicide to protest the change in leadership, while others left to join Fujufuse temples not under Minobu's oversight. Priests of Ikegami's branch temples refused to acknowledge their newly appointed chief abbot. One strategy of resistance was to abandon their branch temples, taking their lay followers with them, and build new, independent temples, which they termed "hermitages" (*anshitsu* 庵室). Defining these structures in this way enabled them to evade both Minobu's oversight and a 1631 *bakufu* prohibition on unauthorized temple-building.[27] Defiance on the part of branch temples persisted for decades. In Kyoto too, the abbot of Myōkakuji, determined not to practice under Minobu's governance, abandoned his temple and, along with more than thirty disciples, established an independent hermitage north of the city.

The Fujufuse side mounted a grassroots proselytizing effort to win over lay followers, thus undermining their opponents' support base. They established new seminaries (*danrin* 檀林) in Awa, Shimōsa, and Kazusa provinces, linking their temples in Edo to other strongholds in nearby provinces. Priests graduating from these seminaries were dispatched to preach the *fujufuse* doctrine among Nichiren Buddhist followers and to discourage pilgrimage to Minobu and other sites controlled by their opponents. Some carried out these preaching activities while living in the homes of lay supporters. The networks formed thereby with the laity would enable the Fujufuse faction to survive when it was eventually forced into hiding.[28] More immediately, the support of lay patrons enabled the building of new Fujufuse temples, again in defiance of repeated edicts prohibiting new temple construction. Tamamuro Fumio has estimated that, in the roughly thirty years between the Minobu-Ikegami debate and the Fujufuse suppression, no fewer than 242 Fujufuse temples were built in Edo alone.[29]

While the Fujufuse hardliners concentrated on spreading their message and winning lay support, the Minobu-led accommodationist faction, relying on their ties to the shogunate, mounted a relentless petition campaign. They repeatedly appealed to the magistrate of temples and shrines, demanding increased powers for the chief abbot, punishment for recalcitrant branch temples, and a ban on preaching *fujufuse* doctrine. Almost invariably, these petitions urged that lands and land incomes granted to temples be defined as dharma offerings, which would have rendered Fujufuse priests unable to accept them. These petitions escalated after the death of the third shogun, Iemitsu 徳川家光 (1604–51), when Fujufuse attacks on their opponents for participating in the funeral rites incited the latter to joint action. Tsūshin'in Nikkyō 通心院日境 (1601–59), who would succeed Nissen as Minobu's chief abbot, remained in Edo for eight years, from 1652 to 1659, to carry on this lobbying.[30] One Eitatsu Nittai 叡達日体 (1622–74) of Zuirinji 瑞輪寺, a leading Minobu branch temple in Edo, is said to have submitted anti-Fujufuse appeals three times each month over a ten-year period.[31] Representatives of nine leading temples and seminaries of the conciliatory faction submitted petitions in 1652 and twice again in 1656. Along with their prior demands, they now urged that "the disposition ordered by the three prior shoguns" (*gosandai no oshioki* 御三代之御仕置) be imposed on the entire Fujufuse contingent—in other words, that they should all be banished, as Nichiō and Nichiju had been. Such a move, of course, would have left their own side in undisputed control of the entire Nichiren sect.[32]

The Kanbun-Era Persecution

The dogged petitioning of the accommodationists began to bear fruit in the early years of the Kanbun era, when the *bakufu* strove to strengthen its control of religious activity by issuing a series of directives. Some targeted specific sects, such as edicts issued in 1663, in virtually identical language, to the Pure Land sect and to the Nichiren temples at Minobu, Ikegami, and Nakayama, that forbade religious disputes as well as "praising oneself and attacking others," suggesting efforts to silence ongoing disputes between

Pure Land and Nichiren Buddhism. Other edicts had broader scope: Temple ordinances (*jiin hatto* 寺院法度), previously issued only for specific sects or head temples, were now issued for Buddhist temples in general. One edict promulgated in 1665 stressed the need for branch temples to maintain allegiance to their head temples and forbade preaching innovative or heterodox teachings. Another, issued the same year, aimed at control of wandering ascetics and forbade Shugendō 修験道 practitioners, Buddhist priests, and other religious specialists from preaching, performing rites, or advertising their religious services in public places.

As part of the same regulatory effort, a survey of vermillion seal (*shuinchi* 朱印地) and other official land grants to temples was conducted by the magistrates for temples and shrines, Inoue Masatoshi 井上正利 (1606–75) and Kagatsume Naozumi 加々爪直澄 (1610–85), between the third and ninth months of 1665. The *bakufu* reconfirmed these grants but—in a clever move no doubt influenced by decades of petitioning from the Minobu faction—stipulated that these lands were "the ruler's dharma offerings." Fujufuse temples were required to submit written statements (*otegata* お手形) acknowledging receipt of these lands as dharma offerings, in exception to the *fujufuse* rule.[33]

Suddenly, priests adhering to the *fujufuse* principle were trapped in a dilemma, in which loyalty to principle and their socio-economic survival became mutually exclusive. To write statements acknowledging receipt of lands as the ruler's offerings was to betray their most cherished conviction. Appeals for permission to omit the word "offering" from these statements went unheeded.[34] While priests might leave their temples rather than subsist on impure offerings, they could not survive by itinerant preaching, as one of the 1665 edicts, mentioned above, forbade it. Some Fujufuse temples and seminaries did not have land grants, but they did not escape. On 1666/4/13, the *bakufu* issued the so-called "land and water offerings edict" (*dosui kuyō rei* 土水供養令). This edict proclaimed that the earth one treads and the water one drinks, the five grains, and the light of the sun, moon, and stars were all the ruler's offerings, and demanded written statements of their receipt.[35]

Ankokuin Nichikō 安国院日講 (1626–98), a leading scholar-priest active in the *fujufuse* cause, wrote an eloquent refusal. In it, he mocked the edict's claim by carrying it to its logical but absurd conclusion:

> If you insist that all things are [the ruler's dharma] offerings, then what about my own person, which Buddhists term the result of past karma, and Confucians, the workings of the five elements? Is my own person, formed by heaven and earth, also an offering from the ruler? If you insist that [all things] are the ruler's dharma offerings, then I refuse the specific offering of temple lands, but I accept the general offering of water to drink and roads to walk upon, and I will use them to spread the [*fujufuse*] teaching throughout the country.[36]

Disregarding such arguments, the *bakufu* now enacted a far more devastating ordinance in 1669, according to which temple certification (*terauke* 寺請) by Fujufuse temples would no longer be recognized. Temple certification of (non-Christian) religious affiliation and the subsequent "sectarian registration" (*shūmon aratame* 宗門改)

conducted by village or ward officials had become necessary in order to work, marry, travel, or change residence; unregistered persons had no legitimate social place.[37] The 1669 edict in effect banned hardline *fujufuse* practice, not only for priests, but also for their lay supporters.

Faced with the demand for *otegata* acknowledging the ruler's dharma offerings, Fujufuse priests had three choices: to accept the *bakufu*'s demand and go over to the accommodationists or convert to another sect; to attempt somehow to evade the demand; or to defy it outright. The majority chose the first course, a few converting to the Tendai sect but most joining their former opponents, the Jufuse contingent. Even priests who were staunch *fujufuse* advocates capitulated and submitted *otegata*. Behind their actions, perhaps, lay the judgment that, after all, it was better to compromise and preserve the temples than allow them to be destroyed in the name of the *fujufuse* principle.

Others sought ways of evading the dilemma. Abbots of six temples decided to comply with the letter of the *bakufu*'s requirement but defy its spirit by inserting the word "compassion" (*jihi* 慈悲) in their statements of receipt. This strategy rested on a distinction, found in Buddhist scriptures and long invoked by the Fujufuse side in debate with their opponents, that divided merit fields (*fukuden* 福田)—that is, recipients of offerings—into three kinds: fields of reverence (*kyōden* 敬田), that is, the Buddha, dharma, and *saṃgha*; fields of obligation (*onden* 恩田), parents, teachers, and others to whom a debt of gratitude is owed; and fields of compassion (*hiden* 悲田), namely, the sick, destitute, or others in need. These temples submitted *otegata* stating, for example, "We respectfully receive the grant of vermillion-seal lands; with gratitude for your compassion, we accept these lands and their income as offerings." In this way, they sought to reclassify the land grants, not as the ruler's dharma offerings, but as his worldly compassion, a stance known as *hiden fujufuse* 悲田不受不施. Initially the ploy seemed to have worked: the six temples concerned were confirmed in their vermillion-seal land grants. However, the Hiden faction was criticized by both Fujufuse hardliners, who dubbed them the "new" Jufuse movement, and the Jufuse accommodationists, who accused them of being unregenerate Fujufuse adherents hiding behind a conciliatory mask. When the matter came to light, the *bakufu* banned the Hiden Fujufuse in 1691, occasioning a massive roundup of adherents in which more than seventy priests and lay people were exiled to the Izu islands.[38]

Refusing to submit the *otegata* was deemed an act against the ruler, and priests who left their temples rather than do so were arrested, imprisoned, exiled, and in some cases put to death.[39] Some committed suicide in protest; others went underground. Some deliberately sought opportunities to admonish the authorities, knowing the result would be criminal sentence; some priests who went underground wore statements admonishing the ruler on their person, in case they should be captured. They must have been sustained by the *Lotus Sūtra*'s urging to be ready to give one's life, if need be, to propagate its message; by the examples of Nichiren and Nichiō; and by Nichiren's teaching that encountering persecution for the *Lotus Sūtra*'s sake guarantees one's future buddhahood. Lay Fujufuse devotees faced the same bitter choice—conversion to a non-Fujufuse temple; arrest, followed by imprisonment, banishment, or execution; or a furtive life in hiding as unregistered persons. One Taguchi Heiroku 田口平六 (Anjūin

Nichinen 安住院日念, 1656–1732), who would later join the above mentioned Ankokuin Nichikō in exile and become his disciple, recalled the moment:

> In the sixth year of the Kanbun era (1666), the fire-horse year, when the true dharma was utterly destroyed, I was still a child, but I remember faintly. Several believers gathered. "Shall we commit suicide? Drown ourselves? Or abandon our homes and flee, and simply die wherever we drop? Alas, how sad!" I watched them as they neglected their work to talk over possible courses. "We should not throw away our lives just yet; better to wait until there is no other choice," they concluded, and each sought out a [new] family temple. But among them were some persons of intense faith who hung themselves and died.[40]

It is difficult to know just how many people were arrested, exiled, or committed suicide rather than compromise the *fujufuse* principle. Striking examples occurred in Okayama-han, where the domain lord, Ikeda Mitsumasa 池田光政, destroyed 313 Fujufuse temples out of a total of 1,044 Buddhist temples in his domain and banished 585 Fujufuse priests, out of a total of 1,957 Buddhist clerics.[41] One Myōkakuin Nichikan 妙覚院日閑 (?–1668) of Honkuji 本久寺 in Saeki village 佐伯村, Iwanashi district, Bizen province, had secretly fled his temple and was hiding in a ruined *kofun* tomb in Yatabe 矢田部, supported by lay devotees. In 1668, as the persecution worsened, he was discovered and seized. Hearing of his arrest, his followers and relatives abandoned their fields to follow him. They too were arrested; twenty-eight were exiled, while six—including Nichikan—were beheaded. In 1669, Nichikan's teacher Kenjūin Nissei 堅住院日勢 (?–1669) similarly secluded himself in a *kofun* tomb in Fukuda 福田 in Mimasaka along with four nuns; there they fasted to death while chanting the title of the *Lotus Sūtra* (*daimoku* 題目), Namu Myōhō-renge-kyō. Nissei watched over the nuns until the end and then drowned himself in a nearby pond. Suicides by fasting, possibly in protest of the "land and water offerings" edict, are well attested. Throughout the archipelago, known Fujufuse hideouts were burned down; other suicides, arrests, executions, and deaths in prison, including those of small children, are also recorded.[42]

The persecutions following the edicts of the mid-1660s are referred to in the annals of the Nichiren sect as *Kanbun no sōmetsu* 寛文の惣滅, the "utter destruction" of the Fujufuse contingent in the Kanbun era. In fact, it was by no means completely eradicated but rather went underground. Only the barest sketch of its subsequent history can be given here.[43] Unlike the crypto Christians (*kakure kirishitan* 隠れキリシタン), the underground Fujufuse organization was able to maintain clerical leadership and communication networks throughout the archipelago. Fujufuse communities were linked by bonds of family and geography; many centered around Edo—in Kazusa and Shimōsa—as well as in the Osaka area and the nearby provinces—Bitchū, Bizen, Mimasaka, and Sanuki in Shikoku. Fujufuse priests lived disguised in the relative anonymity of urban areas or in huts concealed by thickets in out-of-the-way rural places; some were hidden in the homes of lay followers. Devotees met secretly in one another's houses, or in warehouses, chanting quietly, with a guard posted outside. Sometimes they attended such gatherings dressed in traveling garb, so that they could flee, if necessary, at moment's notice. The organization of Fujufuse quickly stratified into three divisions: 1) *hotchū* 法中, underground priests; 2) *hōryū* 法立, lay devotees who had themselves gone underground, following their clerics; and (3) *naishin* 内心, devotees who inwardly adhered to the *fujufuse* principle but had outwardly joined Jufuse Nichiren temples or converted to other sects. *Naishinji* 内心寺—temples whose entire membership, priests and laity alike, publicly dissembled while inwardly honoring the *fujufuse* doctrine—provided leadership for subsequent generations. Living off register, with no legal place in society, the first two groups, the *hotchū* and *hōryū*, depended upon the third for survival. However, the compromises made by the *naishin*, who had joined non-Fujufuse temples to maintain a social identity, unavoidably implicated them in dharma slander; thus their offerings could not be made directly to the *hotchū* but had to pass through the *hōryū*, being purified, it was thought, by their mediation. These intermediaries thus had to be persons whose purity of practice could be guaranteed. Under such circumstances, *fujufuse* understanding of Nichiren's teachings contracted around a core tenet of refusing alms from dharma slanderers. As with the crypto Christians, secrecy itself became the matrix of group identity, with a distinctive culture forming around it.

Conclusion

The *fujufuse* controversy changed character as its focus shifted eastward, following the establishment of the new *bakufu* headquarters in Edo. No longer was it merely an internal conflict over whether to compromise a sectarian principle as a temporary expedient, as it had been when Nichiō defied Hideyoshi's demands. Rather, it intertwined the conflicting interests and agendas of three sets of actors: the hardline Fujufuse faction, struggling to uphold their understanding of orthodoxy in the face of a politically changed world; their Jufuse opponents, bent on enlisting *bakufu* support to wrest control of the Nichiren sect from the numerically dominant Fujufuse adherents; and the Tokugawa *bakufu*, eager to bring religious groups under its control and to suppress dissident voices. In this struggle, the interests of the *bakufu* and the Jufuse accommodationists coincided, leading to Fujufuse defeat. Once that faction was outlawed, Jufuse clerics gained control of the sect's institutions. Their conciliatory reading of doctrine would dominate instruction in Nichiren Buddhist seminaries into the Meiji period.

The contest between the Fujufuse faction and their opponents was not purely an internecine power struggle. Figures on both sides wrestled with the question of how to preserve Nichiren's teachings under a new and powerful regime and differed sharply in their conclusions, the Jufuse side advocating rapprochement with the *bakufu* to preserve their sectarian institution, and the Fujufuse intent on upholding an absolute principle, even if it meant that institution's destruction. Jufuse proponents invoked Nichiren's admonition that the *Lotus Sūtra* must be taught in a manner according with time and circumstance, while Fujufuse adherents embraced his conviction that one should give one's life, if need be, to uphold the exclusive truth of the *Lotus Sūtra*. The standoff between the two factions represented an especially fierce and prolonged iteration of a recurrent conflict within the sect over this very issue.[44]

Why did the *bakufu* so ruthlessly suppress the Fujufuse? "The ruler is a follower of the Nenbutsu 念仏 [Pure Land] sect," Nichō had written of Ieyasu, "so he naturally dislikes our sect."[45] Personal animus against Nichiren Buddhists on the part of Tokugawa rulers may have played a partial role; so did officials' perception of confrontational *shakubuku* as a source of social discord.[46] However, broader ideological issues were at stake. Herman Ooms has discussed how the early *bakufu* drew on the absolutizing language of the very religious institutions it subjugated, in order to sacralize Tokugawa rule and the normative social regime that it sought to impose.[47] The given order was itself to be the sacred order, and, at the time of the Kanbun-era persecution, dissidents were rigorously suppressed.[48]

In deciding to accept the ruler's offerings, the conciliatory wing of the Nichiren sect relativized the *fujufuse* principle and thus neutralized the challenge it posed to the *bakufu*'s self-absolutizing stance. In contrast, uncompromising Fujufuse refusal to accept those offerings relativized *bakufu* authority, asserting a transcendent principle whose claims superseded those of worldly rule. Here Fujufuse invites comparison with Christianity. To be sure, Christianity drew hostility for reasons not found in Fujufuse: its foreign origins, its social practices deemed inimical to Japanese custom, and its associations with the imperialist ambitions of European powers. But in positing an absolute authority, transcending that of the Tokugawa regime, Kirishitan and Fujufuse devotees shared common ground.[49] Under the ideology of Tokugawa rule, radically competing notions of the absolute such as those embraced by these two groups could not be tolerated and were suppressed as heretical.

5

"Deviant Practices" and "Strange Acts"
Late Tokugawa Judicial Perspectives on Heteropraxy

Kate Wildman Nakai

"Heteropraxy" is a convenient catch-all term for summing up rites, beliefs, and activities that government authorities and established religious groups hold to be subversive or problematic. We should keep in mind, though, that it carries some potentially misleading connotations for the Tokugawa context. "Heteropraxy" implies the existence of its antithesis, "orthopraxy." And even if to a lesser degree than the cognate "orthodoxy," "orthopraxy" suggests a norm regarded as universally applicable. The evidence from a body of excerpts from late Tokugawa judicial precedents points, however, to a more complicated situation.

The excerpts were collected under the rubric "deviant practices, strange acts, and deviant theses" (*ihō, kikai, isetsu* 異法奇怪異説) in a series of compilations dating from the early to mid-nineteenth century that came to be known as *Criminal Judgment Precedents Organized by Category* (*Oshioki reiruishū* 御仕置例類集). The excerpts' content indicates that the officials who handled the underlying cases took little interest in questions of doctrine or belief. Their concern was above all activities that might undermine legitimate authority or social order. Nor did they presume a uniform orthopraxy. The shogunal government operated through multiple semiautonomous and segmented channels of control. In its approach to the regulation of religious life, it required near universal affiliation with a Buddhist temple, as several chapters in this volume document, and it expected people to adhere to the sectarian practices of their declared temple. But the government sanctioned multiple sectarian lineages, and it left it up to these lineages to determine the orthopraxis particular to each. Reflecting these orientations, shogunal officials tended toward a situational view of heteropraxy. For them, what determined whether a particular practice was "deviant" could depend as much on who did what in which context as on the practice's intrinsic character.

The lack of comparable materials for earlier periods makes it difficult to know if the approaches seen in these precedents prevailed in preceding eras as well, and the excerpted nature of the material means that one often has to read between the lines to try to reconstruct the underlying incident. The cases categorized as involving "deviant practices, strange acts, and deviant theses" nevertheless offer a reasonably reliable and systematic overview of perspectives within the late Tokugawa shogunal government on religious activities regarded as in some sense subversive. By exploring the features of these cases we should be able to gain a more nuanced understanding of what "heteropraxy" might have meant in the Tokugawa judicial context.

Rules and Precedents

The existence of *Criminal Judgment Precedents Organized by Category* bespeaks the great weight Tokugawa criminal jurisprudence put on precedent. The officials directly responsible for the administration of shogunal territory had substantial leeway in conducting investigations, but to varying degrees depending on the office, they were expected to consult their superiors regarding sentences. Cases involving complications or expected to result in a severe penalty of death or "exile to a remote island" (*ontō* 遠島) were routinely referred to the senior councilors (*rōjū* 老中) in Edo, the pinnacle of the shogunal government. The senior councilors in turn frequently handed such cases down to the deliberative council (*hyōjōsho* 評定所) for review.[1]

The deliberative council was not a court of appeal. It did not reconsider the facts of the case or seek new evidence. Rather, it evaluated the appropriateness of the proposed sentences on the basis of the evidence provided by the official who had conducted the investigation and in the light of judgments made in previous cases. It might affirm the investigating official's proposed sentence, or it might recommend its adjustment in one way or another.

From the middle of the Edo period, the deliberative council relied on two basic resources in conducting its review of the criminal cases referred to it. One was *Rules for Deciding Judicial Matters* (*Kujikata osadamegaki* 公事方御定書, hereafter referred to as *Rules*), compiled in the 1730s and 1740s at the direction of the eighth shogun, Yoshimune 徳川吉宗 (1684–1751; r. 1716–45). The *Rules* synthesized earlier edicts and decisions so as to set standards for meting out punishments for a wide range of crimes. It formulated these standards in general and abstract terms with the assumption that its stipulations would serve as parameters rather than be applied as is. The sentence in a specific case was to be decided in reference to the parameters but also by taking into account factors that made the crime in question more or less serious than the model described in the *Rules*.

A necessary adjunct to the *Rules* in the process of calibrating sentences and the second major resource relied upon by the deliberative council were the precedents offered by previous cases. These stood as examples of the kind of circumstances that might call for adjustment of the letter of the *Rules* and provided guidance as to the degree of adjustment. With the accumulation of precedents, the need developed for a mechanism to identify the most appropriate among them. This led to the compilation beginning in 1804 of collections of excerpts from exemplary cases, what we know today as *Criminal Judgment Precedents Organized by Category* (hereafter referred to as *Precedents*). By the early 1840s there were four such compilations, covering precedents dating from 1771 to 1839.[2]

The *Rules* included two articles concerning subversive or unsanctioned religious activities. Article 52 takes up the banned Nichiren 日蓮 offshoots Fujufuse 不受不施

and Sanchō-ha 三鳥派. As Jacqueline Stone shows in this volume, the shogunate saw Fujufuse as setting its doctrines (and thus those who propagated and followed those teachings) above shogunal authority, and in the 1660s the Edo government implemented a series of measures that effectively proscribed the sect.[3] Reflecting officials' general tendency in judicial matters to focus on matters of law rather than belief, article 52 does not say anything about the reasons for the proscription; its focus is rather how to deal with those who defy it. The article covers various hypothetical types of engagement with the proscribed teachings, specifying the punishments appropriate to each. Simultaneously it illustrates the situational approach to unsanctioned religious activities typical of Tokugawa jurisprudence. The article first addresses the most egregious level of engagement: those who propagated the teachings were to be exiled to a remote island, "even if they have declared that they will [recant and] convert to another sect." It then takes up those who had not actively propagated the teachings but were implicated by relationship to the propagators or had facilitated the propagation in some fashion. In contrast to the propagators, people in this category were generally to receive a reduced sentence if they apostatized. Those who had simply received the teachings were to be exiled to a remote island if they refused to renounce the practice, but should be let off without punishment if they swore an oath of apostasy and converted to another sect.[4]

The following article 53 shows the same formalistic and situational orientation. Designating punishments for those who engage in "novel shrine and Buddhist rites, strange acts, and deviant theses," it is basically directed at activities that contravene the regulations on temples, shrines, and other religious practitioners promulgated by the shogunate in the 1660s. Those regulations stipulated that temple and shrine priests should uphold the established practices specific to their own sect or shrine. Buddhist priests should not disrupt sectarian norms by introducing the rites of another sect. They should not "devise novel doctrines or expound strange rites." Activities proper to a temple should not be conducted in the houses of laypeople. Miscellaneous practitioners (*sho shukke* 諸出家) should not set up temple-like structures in their residences or preach among the urban populace.[5]

The addition of "deviant theses" (*isetsu*) to "novel shrine and Buddhist rites" expanded article 53's scope to activities of a secular nature. What exactly "deviant theses" meant is not indicated, but from the context, most likely the compilers of the *Rules* had in mind disseminating rumors about current events or otherwise stirring up popular curiosity. "Strange acts" (*kikai*) would seem to encompass everything from conjuring up fanciful stories to dubious invocations of the supernatural. Compared to article 52, the punishments stipulated in article 53 are relatively mild. Temple and shrine personnel who performed novel rites were to be banished from the locale (*tokorobarai* 所払) if the matter were grave and sentenced to strict seclusion (*hissoku* 逼塞) in less serious instances. Laypersons were to be sentenced to a fine.[6] Perhaps because the sentences specified in article 53 were quite light, the cases categorized in *Precedents* under the rubric "deviant practices, strange acts, and deviant theses" do not cite it that often compared to article 52, which appears repeatedly as a benchmark for measuring the relative gravity of unsanctioned religious activities. The premises to which article 53 pointed underpin virtually all the cases, nevertheless.

The four extant compilations of *Precedents* include eighteen cases under the rubric "deviant practices, strange acts, and deviant theses," ranging in date from 1774 to 1839. As some refer to precedents not listed separately in their own right, the overall total of precedents mentioned is somewhat larger.[7] For reasons of space and given the subject of the present volume, I will set aside three cases that revolve around secular "deviant theses" and focus on the fifteen that bear on religious issues. These fifteen fall broadly into three groups: cases involving the propagation of deviant practices; cases concerning charlatanry; and cases of clergy engaging in rituals and imprecations with a malevolent intent.

Notably none of the cases covered in *Precedents* under this rubric deal with Christianity. Nor do the *Rules* include any article regarding it. Despite Christianity's strict proscription, it constituted a black hole in eighteenth- and early nineteenth-century jurisprudence concerning subversive religious activities. This situation would change only in the 1830s, when an incident that occurred in Osaka and Kyoto in 1827 led to the creation of a new rubric in *Precedents* covering Christian devotees.

Propagation of Deviant Practices: Hiji Hōmon

Five of the cases in *Precedents* concern the propagation of deviant practices. Although Fujufuse stood as the benchmark for this issue in Tokugawa jurisprudence, none of the five deal with Fujufuse as such. Perhaps the provisions in article 52 of the *Rules* were seen as readily applicable to whatever instances of Fujufuse may have come up and no need was felt to amplify those provisions through the inclusion of an exemplary precedent. Instead, four cases address Hiji Hōmon 秘事法門, an underground Amida 阿弥陀-centered tradition that the established Pure Land sects condemned as heretical and which researchers often pair with Fujufuse as an example of persistent heteropraxy in the Tokugawa context. These cases offer a window into shogunal officials' perspective on this matter compared to that of the sects concerned.

Hiji Hōmon is associated foremost with Jōdo Shinshū 浄土真宗, which pursued investigations of Hiji Hōmon groups in Kyoto in 1755 and in Edo in 1767. On the first occasion Nishi Honganji 西本願寺, the head temple of the Ryūkoku 龍谷 branch of Jōdo Shinshū, acted on its own against temples and priests under its authority who were involved in the promotion of Hiji Hōmon activities; on the second it appealed to the shogunal authorities, who investigated and took punitive action against a substantial number of those who had participated in Hiji Hōmon groups.[8]

Hiji Hōmon was above all a movement centered on laypeople. The followers gathered in private residences to listen to sermons by members of the group and took part in rituals of figurative death and rebirth intended to ensure a safe transition to paradise (ōjō 往生). These rituals were typically conducted by a lay leader who was held to be endowed with special insight. Rather than chant the *nenbutsu* 念仏, which Hiji Hōmon practitioners held to be a form of "self-reliance" and an impediment to putting total trust in Amida, the supplicant seeking assurance of rebirth in paradise fervently chanted a plea to Amida for salvation ("Save me, I beseech you!"; *tasuke tamae*), continuing until the point of collapse. At that moment the lay leader would push the supplicant's head to the floor and pronounce that rebirth in Amida's paradise was certain; in fact, the soul had already been reborn, and only the physical body would eventually succumb to death.⁹

For the Jōdo Shinshū leadership these features that deviated from some of the sect's basic tenets marked Hiji Hōmon as heterodox. For shogunal officials the situation was more complex. Unlike Fujufuse teachings, Hiji Hōmon doctrines and practices did not incorporate a direct challenge to the supremacy of shogunal authority. Initially, at least, officials did not see the doctrines as necessarily deviant in and of themselves. What made Hiji Hōmon problematic was rather that its proponents did not keep to the framework of the particular sectarian lineage with which they were affiliated and the leading role taken by laypeople, a circumstance that officials always regarded with concern.

The first of the cases in *Precedents* related to Hiji Hōmon, dating to 1774, makes clear that from shogunal officials' perspective Hiji Hōmon doctrines as such were not the issue. A lay figure living on shogunal territory in Hida province (part of modern Gifu prefecture) had propagated teachings he had learned from a priest associated with a (presumably) local Jōdo Shinshū temple. He had continued to hold to these teachings himself even after Nishi Honganji had sent an inspector and it had been established that the doctrines were "improper." He had, however, ceased organizing meetings of followers, and once shogunal authorities began to investigate the matter, he declared that he had totally renounced the doctrines as well.

Article 52 of the *Rules* specifies that those who propagated Fujufuse teachings were to be sentenced to exile to a remote island even if they subsequently recanted. If that provision were to be applied in the Hida case, the lay figure should have received the same sentence. In its comments on the case, however, the deliberative council emphasized factors that distinguished it from Fujufuse cases. The incident "did not entail a challenge to shogunal authority, [the lay leader] did not propagate particularly deviant teachings such as that one should not hesitate to die [for one's faith], and no strange elements were involved. It is simply a matter of a wrongful interpretation of the doctrines of one particular sect [by someone affiliated with that sect]." The council proposed accordingly that the sentence be reduced to indefinite incarceration (*nagarō* 永牢); it also called for more lenient treatment of the lay leader's sons than was stipulated in article 52 for the offspring of someone who had propagated Fujufuse.¹⁰

The council made the same points and recommended the same sentence of indefinite incarceration for the lay leader in a second case dating from the following year, 1775. The lay leader had become familiar with Hiji Hōmon practices while in Kyoto to visit Higashi Honganji 東本願寺, including a "strange way of chanting." He went on to transmit these to followers who gathered in private residences or storehouses.¹¹ Hiji Hōmon groups often met in storehouses to avoid drawing attention to their activities, behavior that contravened the general shogunal prohibition of holding organized religious services at places other than sanctioned sites such as temples or shrines.

Although the deliberative council concluded that the practices figuring in these two cases were not so subversive as those associated with Fujufuse, it still recommended punishments for the key figures that were substantially more severe than what article

53 of the *Rules* stipulated for people who performed novel rites. Indefinite incarceration was not a routine punishment but was sometimes used as a substitute for exile to a remote island (which was considered tantamount to a death sentence) when exile was held to be inappropriate. What accounts for this severity? Most likely it was because the leaders had disregarded the basic principle that lay people should not arrogate functions reserved for licensed clergy and had behaved in a manner that was disruptive of the status categories and compartmentalized channels of control basic to the Tokugawa system of rule.

Two further Hiji Hōmon cases dating from the end of the eighteenth century reinforce this supposition. In these two cases, which were related, the key issue was not laypeople taking on roles proper to priests, but priests moving outside their own sectarian boundaries and transmitting Hiji Hōmon practices to lay people. The first, initially investigated by the Osaka magistrate and discussed by the deliberative council in 1788, revolved around Raigōji 来迎寺, the head temple of a small Amidist sect known as Yūzū Dainenbutsu 融通大念仏 and located in Kawachi province near Osaka. The second, which arose a decade later in 1797, involved a smaller temple of the same sect located near Kyoto. The two cases arose out of the activities of the previous Raigōji priest, one Jiun 慈雲 (dates unknown), who had taken up Hiji Hōmon practices and transmitted them to both laypersons and priests of other temples, including a temple affiliated with the Tendai 天台 sect and the Kyoto temple that was the focus of the 1797 case. By the time the Raigōji case came to light, Jiun evidently was no longer alive, and so the investigation centered on his successor, Jikū 慈空 (dates unknown), who had continued the Hiji Hōmon practices transmitted to him by Jiun.

In the writ against Jikū the magistrate detailed the practices the priest had "injudiciously" transmitted to laypersons: At his direction they had chanted "Save me, I beseech you!" until their breath gave out, at which moment he pronounced that they had secured a certain rebirth in paradise. He had further instructed them that since their soul (*shinkon* 心魂) had already been reborn, their body was no more than an empty shell for which they should conduct funerary rites. And he had sworn them to secrecy and threatened that they would meet with punishment should they traduce these practices. This, the magistrate concluded, was unquestionably "a deviant doctrinal form equivalent to Hiji Hōmon."

Jikū evidently attempted to defend himself by claiming that Jiun, from whom he had received the practices, had told him that this was the Yūzū Dainenbutsu way to obtain the secure faith in Amida essential for a safe transition to paradise (*ōjō anjin* 往生安心). The magistrate countered by invoking one of the fundamental articles of the shogunal regulations concerning the Buddhist sects: a priest who did not know the doctrines and rites of his own sect should not be put in charge of a temple. Whatever Jiun might have said, his successor, Jikū, "as the priest of the head temple of a particular sect," should have known what its true doctrines were as passed down by Jiun's predecessors. A second charge indicates how finely the distinctions between different doctrinal traditions might be drawn. Jikū, the magistrate pointed out, had received the doctrinal transmissions of the Chinzei-ha 鎮西派 lineage of the Jōdo sect. Rather than holding to these, however, he knowingly had utilized elements from the traditions of the Seizan-ha 西山派 lineage of the same sect (perhaps concerning the meaning of the *nenbutsu*). Worst of all, he had "injudiciously formulated ceremonies where he conveyed to laypersons the oral transmissions [intended for priests] of his sect."[12]

Despite this enumeration of serious charges, the Osaka magistrate proposed a relatively mild punishment more or less in line with the provision in article 53 of the *Rules* regarding priests who propounded novel doctrines: Jikū should submit an oath that he had recanted his wrongful views and be expelled from his temple. The deliberative council took a sterner stance. The council noted that although the doctrines Jikū had propounded were not those of Sanchō-ha or Fujufuse, they were "unquestionably of a pernicious and deviant character. For the priest of the head temple of a particular sect [...] to lead benighted ordinary laypersons astray in this fashion closely resembles Sanchō-ha and Fujufuse." It thus would be appropriate to sentence Jikū to exile to a remote island, the punishment for propagation of Sanchō-ha and Fujufuse beliefs.[13] The council applied the same standard in the 1797 Kyoto incident.[14]

The council's recommendations suggest that with the establishment of precedents of the shogunal government taking action against Hiji Hōmon, officials increasingly came to see the movement's practices as *ipso facto* problematic. Indeed a later citation in *Precedents* of another Hiji Hōmon case indicates that exile to a remote island came to be regarded as the standard punishment for propagating Hiji Hōmon as well as Fujufuse.[15] But the major factor behind the council's call for strict punishment of Jikū and the Kyoto priest seems to have been their status as clerics expected to know and propagate the doctrines of the particular sect with which they were affiliated. That status brought with it a higher level of accountability than what was to be expected of a layperson. Reflecting this distinction, the council recommended sentencing the laypeople involved to lesser penalties than those stipulated in article 52 of the *Rules* for followers who facilitated the propagation of Fujufuse. In the Raigōji case, the council noted, the situation of the laypeople was "different from that of the temple [priests] involved in the matter. They had simply once become believers out of benighted ignorance and were nothing like followers of Sanchō-ha and Fujufuse."[16]

Charlatanry and Clerical Imprecations

Slightly over half (eight out of fifteen) of the cases in *Precedents* dealing with problematic religious activities concern charlatanry. In most of these the accused were unlicensed practitioners or marginal members of society (including a number of *mushuku* 無宿, or unregistered persons), and the cases often involved using supernatural elements to play on the gullibility of others and extract payments for services. The issues these cases raised were not ones by and large of the propagation of a deviant doctrine but behavior contrary to the norms of social order. The cases might easily have been subsumed under other standard rubrics in *Precedents* such as "extortion" or "chicanery." What led to their inclusion instead under the rubric "deviant practices, strange acts, and deviant theses" was presumably the dubious "strange acts" (*kikai*) figuring in them. (Although, it should be noted, at least some of those acts likely would have been seen as acceptable if performed by licensed clergy.)

Officials sought severe punishments in these cases, typically exile to a remote island. This was probably owing in part to the irregular status of many of the protagonists, something that officials tended to regard suspiciously to begin with. The strict approach indicates that the officials held the types of charlatanry described in *Precedents* to be as egregious as propagating Fujufuse.

Several of the "strange acts" cases involved unlicensed practitioners performing healing rituals. In one, dating from 1827, an unregistered person pretended that he was a Nichiren priest with a proper temple who had received a formal transmission for how to perform healing rituals using a medium. He got the maid of an acquaintance to serve as the medium and had her put on a show of being possessed by the spirits that were troubling the sick person. Then he charged exorbitantly for rites to drive the spirits away. He also asserted that the medicine a doctor had prescribed for a sick woman was inappropriate and had her use instead a medicine of his own concoction, claiming that Nichiren had transmitted the formula for this prescription to him in a dream. The woman consequently died. For such "deceitful deluding of multiple people" the temples and shrines magistrate (*jisha bugyō* 寺社奉行) who initially investigated the case proposed a sentence of exile to a remote island.

As the precedent for this sentence the magistrate cited a comparable case from 1813. A Yin Yang diviner (*onmyōji* 陰陽師) had arranged for a woman to act as his assistant. When someone consulted him, he would say that the person was afflicted by the curse of a spirit or fox and have the woman hold a wand and babble incoherently as he intoned prayers to transfer the spirit or fox to her. To gather additional clients he hit on the idea of making paper effigies. He would give these to those who asked him to perform healing rituals, telling them to place the effigy under the sick person. For his "greedy extraction of fees for prayer rituals and deceitful deluding of multiple people," the Yin Yang diviner had been sentenced to exile to a remote island. The deliberative council agreed with the magistrate that the precedent was appropriate and that the fake Nichiren priest should receive the same sentence.[17]

Two instances where a yet more severe sentence of death was handed down confirm that exile to a remote island was considered the norm for cases of charlatanry. Only in aggravated circumstances involving additional serious crimes was this norm overridden. In one case, from 1838, the accused had engaged in forgery, for which the usual punishment stipulated in the *Rules* was decapitation with display of the head (*gokumon* 獄門).[18] Two unregistered persons plotted to print copies of an amulet from Daitake-san 大嶽山, a Shugendō 修験道 center in Kai province (present-day Yamanashi prefecture). Presenting themselves as representatives of the center, they went around distributing the amulets and performing imitations of rituals and incantations. Warning people that they were in danger of being possessed by *tengu* 天狗 if they did not solicit the rituals, the self-proclaimed Daitake-san representatives then extracted payments in return. The sentence recommended was simple decapitation (in other words, more severe than for the examples of charlatanry described above, but less than the norm for forgery). As the deliberative council explained, the forgery was of a relatively minor sort and the deceptions perpetrated were "typical of what swindlers do."[19] Here the religious elements were evidently secondary to the deliberations' main focus: calibrating the punishment for a case of swindling involving forgery.

The second case, from 1836, involved repeated use of fox witchery that resulted in several deaths. The council noted that precedents from earlier cases of fox witchery all pointed to exile to a remote island as the normal sentence, even when the witchery had inadvertently led to the death of the targeted party. What tipped the balance in this instance was that the perpetrator had engaged in the fatal witchery because of an unwarranted grudge. This fit the *Rules*' specification of the death penalty for killing or wounding someone out of anger for having one's own wrongdoing brought to light.[20]

One additional case dating from 1835 that straddled the boundary between charlatanry and propagation of a deviant doctrine offers further evidence that using dubious invocations of the supernatural to extract money added gravity to the offense in officials' eyes. The case concerned a small, private cult promoted by a family of some local prominence based near Kyoto. The cult centered on a figure named Kyūi 及意 (1563–1619), who had founded a short-lived offshoot of the Tendai sect and from whom the family claimed descent.[21] The accused in the case was a woman, the grandmother of the current family head. According to the writ, she conducted meetings at night in people's houses where, swearing the attendees to secrecy, she had them worship a portrait of Kyūi. "Deluding ignorant and benighted farmers," she promised that they were sure to achieve buddhahood if they received the breeze wafted from a fan he had owned. She then took money and cloth from them as "offerings in return for divine grace." The deliberative council concluded that misleading people with "such absurd claims [...] unquestionably is something totally deviant and improper." Comparable in gravity to propagation of Sanchō-ha and Fujufuse, it merited a sentence of exile to a remote island.[22]

The final type of irregular religious activities covered in *Precedents* under the rubric "deviant practices, strange acts, and deviant theses" are instances of clergy performing rituals or imprecations out of a malevolent purpose. *Precedents* includes two such cases and the first cites a third. All suggest that in these instances, too, situational factors colored officials' perspective: their primary concern was not so much the ritual's intrinsic nature as its target and the status of the person who performed it. The first case, dating to 1810, is difficult to parse. The accused was the priest of a Shingon Ritsu 真言律 sect temple in Izumi province, south of Osaka. It appears that his temple, or a temple with which he had connections, was involved in a legal dispute that did not go as desired and that a temple administrator asked him to conduct prayer rituals directed against the official in charge of hearing the dispute.[23] The priest's actions were investigated by the Kyoto magistrate, who confirmed with the head temple that the ritual in question was intended to "drive away the evil intentions of sworn enemies," not to kill them. Nevertheless, the Kyoto magistrate pointed out, the ritual was something "dangerous," and in accepting the request to perform it, the priest had shown "a lack of awe for shogunal authority." For this the magistrate recommended a sentence of exile to a remote island, normally the most severe penalty for "deviant practices, strange acts, and deviant theses."

Emphasizing the underlying implications of the priest's act, the deliberative council took an even sterner view, however. To regard the official who had handled the original dispute as "a sworn enemy" and conduct rituals to overcome him, the council argued, was an "act against shogunal authority." It thus warranted a penalty heavier than the norm. As a precedent, the council referred to the disposition of a large-scale popular protest in 1774 against the shogunal intendant (*daikan* 代官) in Hida province. In that incident the priests (*kannushi* 神主) of an important local shrine had been held culpable of abetting the protest by performing "criminal prayer rituals" and of receiving payments in return, and for this they had been sentenced to crucifixion. The council acknowledged that there were mitigating factors in the case of the Shingon Ritsu priest that made his actions somewhat less heinous than those of the Hida shrine priests: he had conducted the rituals at the request of a temple administrator rather than of farmers engaged in protest against the local shogunal official, and he had "not done so out of greed." Instead of the extremely severe punishment of crucifixion, the council thus recommended the standard death penalty of decapitation.[24]

The second case involving clerical imprecations confirms that the target was a crucial factor in weighing the crime's gravity. Dating from 1838, it concerned a shrine priest who tried to use the threat of imprecations to intimidate his opponents in a lawsuit. Both the investigating magistrate and the deliberative council agreed that in this instance a sentence of exile to a remote island was appropriate. The council contrasted the 1838 case to that of the Shingon Ritsu priest, noting that as the former did not involve action "against shogunal authority and is altogether of a less grave nature, it is not a crime that warrants the death penalty."[25]

The Kirishitan Issue

As noted above, the *Rules* did not contain any provision concerning Christians (or Kirishitan 切支丹, as they were termed), perhaps because no known Kirishitan had been detected for half a century. The first three compilations of *Precedents* (covering cases up to 1826) likewise did not include any cases involving Kirishitan.

This does not mean that there were no incidents involving probable Kirishitan activity in the latter part of the eighteenth century and early nineteenth. Shogunal and domain authorities in Kyushu confronted what today are assumed to have been underground Kirishitan in Urakami village 浦上村 in 1790 and Amakusa 天草 in 1805. On both occasions, however, the authorities handled the matter gingerly. They as well as the villagers avoided making Christianity the issue. The two sides alike framed the matter as a question of adherence to an unspecified "deviant creed" (*ishū* 異宗), and it was resolved on those terms.[26] It is almost as though the officials tacitly agreed not to get entangled in the complications of identifying the villagers as likely Kirishitan and then investigating and dealing with them as such.

A sharp break with this approach occurred in Osaka in 1827. The Osaka magistrate Takai Sanenori 高井実徳 (1763–1834), and most particularly the senior staff official (*yoriki* 与力) in charge of investigating the case, Ōshio Heihachirō 大塩平八郎 (1793–1837), concluded that they had uncovered a group of Kirishitan based in Kyoto and Osaka.[27] In forwarding the case to higher levels, however, they noted an obstacle to proposing appropriate punishments: the lack of pertinent precedents. In Edo the senior councilors and the deliberative council, to which the senior councilors handed the case down for review, noted the same problem. Deliberations over this issue resulted ultimately in the creation of a new frame of reference specific to Kirishitan. The new framework shared several premises with the precedents covered under the rubric "deviant practices, strange acts, and deviant theses"—most notably the assumption that subversion of shogunal authority constituted the most heinous of crimes—but it also established that Kirishitan represented a level of subversion beyond "ordinary" deviant practices. The fourth compilation of *Precedents*, put together sometime after 1839, reinforced this point by including extensive excerpts from this case and the deliberative council's review under the new rubric "devotees of the Kirishitan sect" (*Kirishitan shūmon osame sōrō rui* 切支丹宗門修候類).[28]

All evidence indicates that the small Kyoto-Osaka group accused as Kirishitan had no connection to underground Kirishitan communities in Kyushu. Its members, who were linked only loosely and included both men and women, had obtained their knowledge of purported Kirishitan practices directly or indirectly from a shady figure named Mizuno Gunki 水野軍記 (?–1824). Gunki had once been employed as a scribe by Kyoto noble houses but was already dead by the time the group came to the attention of the Osaka magistrate. He appears to have combined elements drawn from Chinese texts on Christian doctrine by Matteo Ricci (1552–1610) and such with the popular image of Kirishitan as possessing powers of sorcery. To this mixture he and his followers added common ascetic practices such as dousing oneself with water and climbing deserted heights at night with the goal of securing "an unwavering mind."

Gunki's male followers largely kept their Kirishitan practices to themselves, but the women fused them with activities they were already performing as Inari mediums (*Inari myōjin sage* 稲荷明神下げ) and Yin Yang diviners. For them, the powers to be obtained from worshiping the Lord of Heaven (Tentei 天帝) and chanting his mantra *zensu maru paraizo* ("Jesus, Maria, paradise") enhanced their ability to perform divinations and healing rituals. They also used those powers to gain clients by promising to expand their wealth. It was this last activity that initially brought one of the women to the magistrate's attention. The ensuing investigation led to the arrest and questioning of a large number of people in Osaka and Kyoto. It also produced confessions by the principals that they were devotees of the "pernicious creed" (*jashūmon* 邪宗門) transmitted by Gunki.

Takai and his staff presumed that the principals deserved severe punishments for "showing not the slightest awe for the shogunal authorities" and contravening the proscription of Christianity. Stretching to find a frame of reference in the absence of direct precedents, they turned to the 1788 case of Jikū, the Yūzū Dainenbutsu priest who had propagated Hiji Hōmon practices, and the case of the Hida shrine priests cited as a precedent in the 1810 case of the Shingon Ritsu priest. Takai also applied the criterion of mercenary greed seen widely in the cases examined above, using it to distinguish between the degree of culpability of the female and male principals. The crimes of the three women principals were more reprehensible, he argued, because they not only were "devotees of the strictly proscribed pernicious creed," but also had "used [its] practices to appropriate money." Their crimes were thus far graver than that of Jikū, who had been sentenced to exile to a remote island; they were comparable to those of the Hida shrine priests, who had charged "money for performing heinous prayer rites" and who for this had been sentenced to crucifixion. Gunki's two primary male disciples were one grade less culpable because they "did not use the practices of the pernicious sect to appropriate money from others (pp. 169–70)." On these grounds, Takai proposed to sentence the women to crucifixion and the men to decapitation with subsequent display of their heads. All were to be paraded through Osaka beforehand.

The deliberative council took a different approach. When it received the dossier on the case from the senior councilors, its initial reaction was to question whether the accused were really Kirishitan. In a confidential inquiry to the senior councilors, the council first took note of the difficulty in obtaining reliable information about Kirishitan. Because there was nothing in the *Rules* nor any precedents specifying the punishments meted out previously to devotees of the Kirishitan creed, there also were no records detailing the nature of Kirishitan practices.

Given these circumstances, the council suggested, the Osaka magistrate's conclusion that the accused were Kirishitan was overly hasty. The dossier on the case indicates that the investigators had paid almost no heed to questions of belief or doctrine. Their main focus had been the practices of the purported Kirishitan, which the evidence suggests had much in common with the examples of charlatanry considered above. In its inquiry to the senior councilors, the deliberative council pointed this out: "If it is a matter of using strange arts (*ijutsu* 異術) to startle people with extraordinary things, devotees of the Kirishitan sect are not the only ones to do so (p. 176)." The council likely had in mind instances such as the 1827 case of a fake Nichiren priest and his use of a fake medium, which it had considered only recently. The council's preferred approach to the Osaka Kirishitan matter presumably would have been to refer to such cases as precedents and recommend the same sentence of exile to a remote island.

The dossier received from the Osaka magistrate was formulated, however, around the supposition that the accused were Kirishitan. For the council to take a different approach would require that the senior councilors first send the dossier back to the magistrate for reconsideration. This was almost never done. In this instance, too, the senior councilors demurred when they received the deliberative council's proposal that they order the Osaka magistrate to redo the investigation. Such an unusual step, they responded, might cause doubts "about this matter in the world at large, and this might well result in laxity in enforcement of the proscription of this sect." The senior councilors therefore directed the deliberative council to determine that the accused were "devotees of the Kirishitan sect, in accordance with the conclusions of the investigating officials," and to recommend appropriate punishments on the basis of that premise (pp. 177–8). Setting aside its initial reservations, the deliberative council proceeded to follow these directions and to develop a frame of reference for punishments befitting Kirishitan.

We may assume that once it had been decided to deal with the parties to the incident as Kirishitan, the deliberative council, like the Osaka magistrate, saw crucifixion as the appropriate penalty. But it took a different route to that conclusion. The Hida shrine priest case that the Osaka magistrate cited as a precedent for levying a sentence of crucifixion entailed a direct challenge to shogunal authority of a sort that did not figure in the Osaka incident. The Osaka investigators had presumed that as Kirishitan the accused had likely engaged in seditious activities, but they admitted that they had not been able to find evidence corroborating these suspicions. The council thus looked for an alternative basis, grounded in the *Rules*, for establishing the heinous nature of the crime of being a Kirishitan.

The council first pointed to regulations that had been promulgated in the late seventeenth century for ongoing surveillance of the relatives and descendants of apostate Kirishitan (*Kirishitan ruizoku* 切支丹類族).[29] The requirement to continue this surveillance for generations attested to the enormity of the threat Kirishitan posed, making it "difficult to apply to the case at hand [the less stringent] provisions in the *Rules* concerning those who proselytize [banned] teachings such as those of the Sanchō-ha and Fujufuse (p. 179)." The council then argued that a more appropriate point of reference than article 52 would be article 20 of the *Rules*, which specified crucifixion as the punishment for circumventing the barriers set up at checkpoints along the major highways.[30] The council did not explain its reasoning, but we might surmise that it saw an analogy in that the prohibition of circumventing the barriers and the proscription of Christianity were both fundamental shogunal laws, made known to all by being posted on signboards throughout the country. Since what the Osaka Kirishitan had done was yet worse than circumventing a barrier, the council recommended that "to set a warning example," they should receive the additional penalty of being paraded through Osaka prior to crucifixion (p. 180).

Whereas the Osaka magistrate had continued to take into account the sort of situational factors typically applied in instances of ordinary deviant practices, the deliberative council also argued that the gravity of being a Kirishitan overrode such considerations. Contrary to the distinction made by the Osaka magistrate between the nature of the activities engaged in by the female and male devotees, the council thus concluded that the men's actions were "no less egregious" than those of the women (p. 183). Even if the men had not deceived others or appropriated money from them, they had engaged in the practices of the Kirishitan sect. Therefore, the council recommended, they should be sentenced to the same punishment.

Conclusion

The deliberative council acted for essentially expedient reasons in setting aside its initial doubts and formulating a new frame of reference for dealing with Kirishitan. The framework itself nevertheless made clear that being a Kirishitan was a more absolute evil than ordinary "deviant" practices. The inclusion of materials concerning the Osaka case in the fourth compilation of *Precedents* under the new rubric "devotees of the Kirishitan sect" reinforced this perspective. The incident likewise seems to have spurred attentiveness to the possibility that deviant religious activity might entail a Kirishitan connection. In the case, for example, of the woman who promoted worship of Kyūi, which occurred a few years after the Osaka Kirishitan incident in the same general region, the investigators evidently considered that possibility before dismissing it.[31] One might thus argue that Kirishitan came to represent heteropraxy in the late Tokugawa judicial context in a sense that "deviant practices" did not.

Yet, questions remain. The dousing with water and other austerities performed by the Osaka Kirishitan to obtain an unwavering mind were part of the repertoire of ascetic practices shared by a wide range of Tokugawa religionists. As the deliberative council pointed out in its initial comments to the senior councilors, the purported Kirishitan were hardly the only ones to use "strange arts to startle people," and the arts employed by those directly investigated were not particularly notable either. The 1827 case served to strengthen an existing abstract image of Kirishitan as sorcerers who would not hesitate to subvert authority and social order. But how, speaking concretely, might the Kirishitan incident have fed into new notions of heteropraxy or established what set Kirishitan practice on a plane of its own, distinct from other irregular and not-so-irregular praxis? The evidence available from the extant fourth collection of *Precedents* does not allow us to address this issue, and the loss of a fifth collection, compiled sometime after 1852, means we cannot know if it continued the rubric concerning Kirishitan or if the 1827 Osaka case was subsequently cited as a precedent. Discussion of its wider impact on official attitudes towards heteropraxy must await exploration from a different angle.

Part Three

Intellectual Challenges

6

Shinto as a Quasi-Confucian Ideology

Inoue Tomokatsu
Translation by Brigitte Pickl-Kolaczia

Among the religious policies of early Tokugawa Japan, the reforms in Aizu, Mito and Okayama during the Kanbun years (1661–73) are comparatively well known. They were shaped by Confucian ideas and included the reduction of Buddhist institutions, the removal of "illicit shrines" (*inshi* 淫祠),[1] and the revival of ancient shrines. Hitherto, most studies have tended to emphasize the destructive aspects of these reforms, namely the demolition of temples and *inshi*, interpreted as attempts of the political leaders to control the population's religious beliefs. However, the constructive characteristics—namely, the reconstruction of ancient shrines—deserve more attention.

It is easy to understand that Buddhist temples and *inshi* contradicted Confucian ideas and were therefore rejected by a political ideology based on Confucianism. Why, however, did the revival of ancient shrines conform to Confucian ideas? To explain the logic behind these religio-political measures, we should regard their underlying ideology not simply as Confucian. Rather, these reforms were the inevitable consequence of a certain Shinto ideology.

This chapter aims to shed light on the religious policies by feudal lords in the second half of the seventeenth century and argues that they were based on the idea of reconstructing Shinto as a quasi-Confucian teaching. In addition to this argument, I would like to point out two things: First, the reconstruction and appreciation of ancient shrines did not happen in Aizu, Mito, and Okayama alone. Rather this was a mainstream policy shared by many feudal lords of that time. Second, the source of this ideological trend was the need of the Tokugawa regime to legitimate its own rule by rejecting the political legacy of the Toyotomi. Moreover, the religious reforms in question resulted not only from the great social and political shifts that occurred in Japan between the late medieval and early modern periods, but were also shaped by the changing relations between East Asian countries.

Religious Policies in the Second Half of the Seventeenth Century

Reforms in Domains

The Kanbun reforms of Aizu, Mito, and Okayama show significant similarities. All three lords, Hoshina Masayuki 保科正之 (1611–72) of Aizu 会津藩, Tokugawa

Mitsukuni 徳川光圀 (1628–1701) of Mito 水戸藩, and Ikeda Mitsumasa 池田光政 (1609–82) of Okayama 岡山藩, ordered investigations into their domains' ancient shrines—in particular the so-called *shikinaisha* 式内社[2]—and restored a number of them that had fallen into disrepair. On the other hand, small shrines of unknown provenance that were based on popular beliefs were abolished or merged into "collective shrines" (*yosemiya* 寄宮). Another measure they shared was the removal of Buddhist elements from shrines.[3]

Scholars have tended to regard the religious policies of these three domains as exceptional cases implemented by three daimyo who were particularly fond of Confucian learning.[4] However, other domains carried out similar measures as well. In the Kanbun era, Matsudaira Yorishige 松平頼重 (1622–95), Mitsukuni's elder brother, had regulations and registers for shrines drawn up in Takamatsu 高松藩, his domain in Sanuki province. Around 1668, he, too, implemented *yosemiya* measures, whereby small shrines with little land and few parishioners were merged with larger shrines in their vicinity. In 1669, he had Takamatsu shrine histories compiled in the *Shrine Histories of Our Domain* (*Goryōbunchū miya yurai* 御領分中宮由来). Similar to Aizu, Mito, and Okayama, Yorishige promoted ancient shrines and had Buddhist elements removed from them. One example is the ancient Shiratori Shrine 白鳥神社, which in 1665, Yorishige gifted with a fief of 200 *koku*, summoned a Shinto priest from Kyoto to be installed there, and expelled the shrine's Buddhist monks (*shasō* 社僧).[5]

Measures to revive ancient shrines and *shikinaisha* by restoring them can also be seen in a number of other domains in the second half of the seventeenth century.[6] An early example is Wakayama domain 和歌山藩 in Kii province, where ancient shrines that had fallen into oblivion were investigated. In 1650, memorial stones were erected at some of their former locations. In 1678, the domain administration rebuilt the *shikinaisha* Sasutahiko Jinja 刺田比古神社 and removed all Buddhist elements, including its supervising temple (*bettōji* 別当寺).[7] In 1657, Kōchi domain 高知藩 in Tosa province consulted with the Yoshida 吉田 family—the superintendents of the office of deities (*jingikan* 神祇官) in Kyoto—concerning the enshrined deities of their *shikinaisha* and started a "restoration of ancient shrines" six years later, in 1663. In 1676, the domain of Hirado 平戸藩 in Hizen province conducted research on *shikinaisha* locations and deities on Iki Island, which was part of their domain. In Iwaki-taira domain 磐城平藩 in Mutsu province, the *shikinaisha* shrines Samakumine 佐麻久嶺神社 and Futamata 二俣神社 were restored in 1680 and 1682, respectively. Another example of appreciation for ancient shrines is Matsuyama domain 松山藩 in Iyo province, which restored Yuzuki Hachimangū 湯月八幡宮 in 1667 and Misake Shrine 味酒神社 (together with an allotment of shrine fiefs) in 1668/69.[8] These examples show that Aizu, Mito and Okayama were not the only domains that implemented policies to reorganize the religious landscape.

Policies of the *bakufu*

The active promotion of ancient shrines as well as the exclusion of Buddhism from their precincts was not limited to regional politics. The *bakufu* implemented similar measures. The most significant was the removal of Buddhist elements from the Ise

Shrines in the Kanbun era[9] in the context of the ritual rebuilding (*shikinen sengū* 式年 遷宮) of the entire site. Since the antiquity, this rebuilding was supposed to take place every twenty years, but the pace had dropped since 1462. Among the driving forces to rebuild the shrines after some longer, irregular, intervals, were the so-called *kanjin bikuni* 勧進比丘尼, Buddhist nuns from Keikōin 慶光院 in Uji (the shrine town of Ise's Inner Shrine), who used to raise funds for the shrines. For this reason, they had received a fief from the Tokugawa and had been requested to perform religious duties on behalf of the shogun through a vermillion-seal order (*shuinjō* 朱印状). However, in 1666, three years before the scheduled rebuilding ceremony, they were informed that a vermillion-seal order related to the *shikinen sengū* had never been issued to Keikōin. This was explained by the "wish" of Shogun Ietsuna 徳川家綱 (1641–80) that the Ise Shrines return to the "old ways." Eventually, the Keikōin nuns were excluded altogether when the *shikinen sengū* was performed in 1669.[10] In other words, the expulsion of Buddhist elements was an important factor for returning Ise to the "old ways."

The measures of the *bakufu* to erase all Buddhist elements from Ise did not end with the exclusion of Keikōin. Ise was at that time administered by the *Yamada bugyō* 山田 奉行, a *bakufu* official overseeing the towns attached to the Ise Shrines, Yamada and Uji. Besides public safety, his responsibilities included guarding the Ise Shrines and managing the *shikinen sengū*. In 1671, the *Yamada bugyō* Kuwayama Sadamasa 桑山貞 政 (1613–1700) ordered the Inner Shrine's head priest, Fujinami Ujitomi 藤波氏富 (1606–87), to remove the "dual parts" (*ryōbu* 両部)—that is, all Buddhist elements[11]— from the shrines. This was in line with the intentions of the *bakufu*'s senior council (*rōjū* 老中), Sadamasa's immediate superiors. However, Ujitomi felt it would be difficult to expedite such demands and opted for a slower approach to the separation of Shinto and Buddhism in Ise. Thus, the driving force behind the purge of Buddhist elements was the *bakufu*, not the shrines. Moreover, the *Yamada bugyō* was critical of the presence of Buddhist temples in the shrine towns, which were part of Ise's "shrine estate" (*shinchi* 神地). When a great fire destroyed 189 Buddhist temples in Yamada in 1670, he denied permission for forty-seven of them to be rebuilt and thus by default had them abolished. Other temples, such as the powerful Segidera 世義寺, were relocated outside the town's center.

The separation of Shinto and Buddhism (*shinbutsu bunri* 神仏分離) in Ise was carried out in the name of Shogun Ietsuna and his senior council. However, it is generally assumed that it was Hoshina Masayuki who directed these policies. As Ietsuna's uncle and legal guardian, he was able to exert substantial influence on the government. Masayuki is also considered to have proposed the relocation of the aforementioned Keikōin in 1666 to an area beyond the Miyagawa, which marked the border of Ise's "shrine domain" (*shinryō* 神領).[12]

Furthermore, Masayuki is assumed to have suggested the removal of Buddhist elements in the case of Izumo's grand shrine Kizuki Taisha 杵築大社 (today's Izumo Taisha 出雲大社), which was reconstructed around the same time.[13] As detailed in Mark Teeuwen's chapter in this volume, Kizuki Taisha had been strongly exposed to Buddhist influence during the medieval period. In the Kanbun era, however, Buddhist elements were removed from the shrine by Matsudaira Naomasa 松平直政 (1601–66), as well as by his Confucian tutor (*hanju* 藩儒) and the *bakufu*.

Another example for the *bakufu*'s *shinbutsu bunri* policy during the Kanbun years is Shimotsuke Utsunomiya Shrine 下野宇都宮 (today's Futaarayama Shrine 二荒山神社 in Utsunomiya, Tochigi-ken), which, in 1669, was ordered by the *bakufu* to abolish the office of *shasō* in its Lower Shrine (Shimonomiya 下宮) and to exchange its Amida statue with a non-Buddhist object of worship (*shintai* 神体).[14] Cases like these clearly demonstrate that religious reforms such as the revival of ancient shrines or the removal of Buddhist elements from Shinto sites were not only conducted by individual daimyo, but also by the *bakufu*.

The Ideology behind the Shrine Regulations and the Resurrection of Ancient Shrines

The previous section described how anti-Buddhist policies, the closing down of *inshi* and the restoration of ancient shrines were not measures limited to Aizu, Mito, and Okayama, but were indeed widespread. The following part aims to shed light on the ideologies that were the basis of these policies.

Mito

Tokugawa Mitsukuni started his religious reforms in 1663 with an investigation on the history and current situation of temples and shrines. Thus, he identified a number of *shikinaisha* that had fallen into disrepair, including Shizu Jinja 静神社. In 1668, Mito's magistrate of temples and shrines (*jisha bugyō* 寺社奉行) informed the Shizu Shrine in a letter about Mitsukuni's intent to restore it:

> Shizu Shrine in the Kuji district of Hitachi province [...] is a Grand shrine listed in the *Engishiki*. [...] However, as times have gone by the shrine has fallen into decay [...] and corrupt and impure fellows (i.e. Buddhists) have [...] interfered and defiled the water of our Ancient Source (*sōgen* 宗源).[15] Our Lord of Mito [...], who reveres [Shizu Jinja's] divine virtues, planned to remove ruin and defilement from ancient shrines and to restore their purity by newly built structures. [... He reformed their ritual system by] removing shrine monks and having shrine attendants study the Way of the Gods (*jingidō* 神祇道), thus restoring the Only Ancient Source (*yūitsu sōgen* 唯一宗源). [...] If [Shizu Jinja] shines with divine virtue and might, ruler and ruled will rejoice together, [Mito] will be peaceful and the people will forever be safe from harm.[16]

We can infer from this citation that the restoration of ancient shrines was part of Mitsukuni's scheme to realize an ideal society in his domain: Shrines should facilitate good governance based on rightful relations between lord and subject and should bring peace and safety to the people.

Mitsukuni's measures did not stop at individual shrines, but permeated the entire field of religious policies in Mito. In 1667, Mitsukuni initiated the compilation of various materials about Shinto and shrines in the *Shintō shūsei* 神道集成 (*Compilation of Writings on Shinto*).¹⁷ The biggest contribution to this work came from his vassal Imai Tōken 今井桐軒 (1646–83, also known as Ujun 有順). In a report on the *Shintō shūsei*, Tōken explains the guiding principle behind this work's compilation:

> In ancient times, an ideal society based on the Way of the Gods (*shintō*) took shape. Since the middle ages (*chūyō* 中葉), however, heretic teachings and Buddhism have flourished and defiled Pure Shinto. Even if we want to know more about the government of the ancient society and its way of sacred divine mystery (*seishin ōmyō no michi* 聖神奥妙之道, i.e. Shinto), it is difficult to make them clear to us, because historical documents are missing. Sensible men have lamented this state of affairs. Tokugawa Mitsukuni read the classic transmissions of foreign countries (i.e., the Confucian classics) and became increasingly aware of the magnificence of Japan's divine law. At the same time, the decline of Shinto pained him in his heart. Mitsukuni ordered us to clarify the history of the Ancient Source (*sōgen*, i.e., Shinto), and to clean it from the confusion caused by deceitful and heretic teachings.¹⁸

This passage confirms that Mitsukuni's measures were based on the notion of an ideal past before the advent of Buddhism. They aimed at a return to this past by clearing "heretic teachings" (*isetsu*)¹⁹ and Buddhist elements from shrines. Of course, it is impossible to know whether such an ideal society really existed in ancient times. Early Tokugawa political leaders, however, took "Shinto" as a symbol of this idealized societal order.

Aizu

The religious reforms of Aizu's Hoshina Masayuki were shaped by the same ideas as those in Mito. In addition to his shrine reform, which started around 1667, Masayuki ordered the compilation of the *Aizu jinja-shi* 会津神社志, a list of 260 main ancient shrines of Aizu domain (completed in 1672), and the *General Shrine Register* (*Jinja sōroku* 神社総録), which contains the names of all shrines confirmed by the domain administration (completed after Masayuki's death). The *Aizu jinja-shi* contains a preface by Hayashi Gahō 林鵞峯 (1618–80) that exemplifies Masayuki's thinking as follows:

> *Kami* exist, therefore we have to build shrines to worship them. This is the reason why the Zhou court in China established an office of rites whose officials were concerned with [ritual ceremonies]. Additionally, kings, lords, and high bureaucrats, and all kinds of people below them worshipped [different deities according to their rank]. Conducting rites specific to one's role and rank has been common law from ancient times to the present. In Japan, we have revered Shinto since the beginning of time. [...] However, because of Śākyamuni (Shaku-shi 釈氏) we have lost our origins. Because of new shrines, ancient customs were lost. Many *shikinaisha* fell into oblivion and their faded nameplates are no longer recognizable. Illicit shrines deluded people and caused harm. Fragrant herbs and rotten grass were put into the same vessel. Sensible men lamented this state of affairs vigorously. The lord of Aizu,

Hoshina Masayuki, holds fast to the Way of the Gods and in these past years he has dispatched officials to inspect the origins and locations of shrines [... in Aizu] in order to preserve useful shrines and to remove shrines without use. [...] To erect shrines and worship the *kami* is an essential task of the country. To follow the past and revive what was lost is an indication of good governance. To revere the Ancient Source (*sōgen*) is the Japanese style of rites. To destroy illicit shrines (*inshi*) is the wise decision of good rulers.[20]

Similar to Imai Tōken, Gahō regards the revival of ancient shrines and the destruction of *inshi* as a symbol of good governance that should improve the present state of society. Masayuki's Shinto advisor Yoshikawa Koretaru 吉川惟足 (1616–94) expresses a similar sense of crisis in the afterword to the *Aizu jinja-shi*:

When [the ancient government] divided the country into provinces and districts, they certainly erected shrines for the *kami* worshipped there. Since the middle ages, however, the gods, great and small, have been mingled with illicit shrines and false gods. Many were relocated into temples or polluted in private houses. [Under such circumstances,] we must fear that in the future no one will know the places of the *kami*'s original appearance.[21]

Here, too, Buddhism and *inshi* are regarded as a source of pollution that had caused confusion to "Shinto," which was understood as Japan's faith since its foundation. Thoughts like these motivated Masayuki to implement measures similar to those of Tokugawa Mitsukuni, such as the revival of ancient shrines, the regulation of existing shrines, the destruction of *inshi* and the removal of Buddhist elements from Shinto sanctuaries.

In his afterword, Koretaru further describes the specific places and concrete measures of Masayuki's shrine reforms. In conclusion, he states:

When the true *kami* prosper, the false gods will lose their power. When the false gods lose their power, the land will know peace. I pray that [Masayuki's] good [governance] will spread in all directions.[22]

Thus, Masayuki and his advisors were convinced that the religious policies in Aizu during the Kanbun years were the right way to keep peace within the entire country. Koretaru's words are further reminiscent of Kumazawa Banzan's 熊沢蕃山 (1619–91) opinion that false gods would lose power and true *kami* would gain it by turning *inshi* into collective shrines (*yosemiya*).[23] We may infer, therefore, that religious policies in Okayama, which were influenced by Banzan's ideas, were based on the same ideals as the religious policies in Aizu.

Pioneering the Idea to Revere Ancient Shrines: *Jingi hōten*

The reforms of the Kanbun era were based on notions of returning to the assumed ideals of ancient times. This line of thought, however, appeared well before the 1660s.

In 1646, Tokugawa Yoshinao 徳川義直 (1601–50)—uncle of both Mitsukuni and Masayuki—discusses this in the preface to his work *Treasure Books of the Deities of Heaven and Earth* (*Jingi hōten* 神祇宝典):

> Japan is the place where the divine spirits came into being and dwell, therefore it is called a divine country (*shinkoku*). Its treasures are the divine regalia, and he who guards these great treasures is the divine ruler (*jinnō* 神皇). He who subdues the barbarians (*seii* 征伐) is the divine warrior (*shinpei* 神兵), and the practice [of Japan] is the divine Way (*shintō*).[24]

The text continues with a brief explanation of shrine worship from the times of Japan's purported first emperor, Jinmu Tennō 神武天皇, until Daigo Tennō 醍醐天皇 (885–930), when the list of 3,132 deities in the *Engishiki* was drafted. This ancient Japanese shrine system is compared to the system of rites during the Zhou dynasty, which represents the ideal Confucian state based on propriety:

> The sages worshipped the deities of heaven and earth (*jingi*), performed sacrifices for them and respected human work. As it was in China, so it should be in Japan.[25]

Because of the introduction of Buddhism, however, Japan's shrine system had deteriorated. The *honji suijaku* 本地垂迹説 theory[26] in particular, which regards the buddhas as the original deities and the *kami* as their manifest traces, caused much confusion. The wish to remedy this situation was the major reason for compiling the *Treasure Books of the Deities of Heaven and Earth*.[27]

Thus, the *Jingi hōten* is based on the same logic as the *Shintō shūsei* and the *Aizu jinja-shi*, including: (1) the notion of an ideal society guided by the "Way of the Gods" as it existed before the advent of Buddhism; and (2) the idea of reviving the ideal rites for the *kami* by removing all Buddhist elements. These ideas appeared in the first half of the seventeenth century and were shared by the *bakufu*.[28] During the 1660s and 1670s, they were finally put into political practice.

Reconsidering the Unity of Shinto and Confucianism: Shinto as Martial Confucianism

As becomes clear in the preface to the *Jingi hōten* or in the *Shintō shūsei*, the three daimyo mentioned above regarded "Shinto" as a "Way" to lead society back to the ideals of "ancient Japan." At the same time, they all referred to the ideal society of China. To them, the ideal "ancient society" of Japan had been permeated with the same morality as Confucianism. In the *Aizu jinja-shi*, Hayashi Hōkō 林鳳岡 (1644–1732), Gahō's son, specified what this Way encompassed:

> [As a divine country originating from the *kami*] Japan possesses "distinction" (別) between man and woman, "affinity" (親) between parent and child, "righteousness" (義) between ruler and subject, and "ritual propriety" (禮) between high and low.[29]

Here, Hōkō claims that the order of human relations in the divine country of Japan contained specific virtues. These were clearly the virtues of Confucianism.[30] Thus, for intellectuals such as Hōkō, "Shinto" corresponded to Confucian virtues, and consequently these thinkers often related "Shinto" to Confucianism and Japan to China. We can see this tendency in the prefaces to the *Jingi hōten* and *Aizu jinja-shi*, where the ideal society of "ancient Japan" is perceived as corresponding to the ideal Zhou dynasty, or in Imai Tōken's claim that Mitsukuni, while reading the Confucian classics, began to yearn for a Japanese equivalent in the form of Shinto. The declaration "as it was in China, so it should be in Japan" from the preface to the *Jingi hōten* shows the conviction that Japan should possess a civilization of the same quality as China, the center of Confucian civilization.

The idea that Shinto and Confucianism were in essence the same—the so-called unity of Shinto and Confucianism (*shinju itchi* 神儒一致)—can be seen from the beginning of the early modern period. A number of scholars—among them three generations of the Hayashi family, Razan, Gahō, and Hōkō—adopted this stance. This unity of Shinto and Confucianism is also reflected in the preface to the *Jingi hōten*. Even though this text was in fact written by Razan,[31] there is no doubt that it expresses Yoshinao's way of thinking. Passages from the preface and afterword to the *Aizu jinja-shi*, composed by Gahō and Hōkō, show that Hoshina Masayuki held similar views. The same is true for Ikeda Mitsumasa, who introduced Confucian style funerals, shrine regulations, and *shintō-uke* in Okayama.[32] He certainly shared the ideas of his Confucian tutor Kumazawa Banzan, another adherent of *shinju itchi*.[33] Thus, all of the daimyo who realized anti-Buddhist reforms from the middle to late seventeenth century believed in the unity of Confucianism and Shinto and implemented their policies on the basis of this belief.

Confucian scholars and domain lords were not the only representatives of Shinto-Confucian syncretism. Another example is Deguchi Nobuyoshi 出口延佳 (1615–90), a priest of Ise's Outer Shrine, who is famous for having revived Ise Shinto. He also believed that "Shinto and Confucianism share the same principle" and that "the Way of Confucius is the same as the Way of the Gods (*shintō*) in our country."[34] Moreover, Nobuyoshi thought that Buddhism destroyed the ideal form of Shinto: "With the appearance of a Shinto merged with the dual parts [of Esoteric Buddhism] (*ryōbu shūgō shintō* 両部習合神道), Shinto's origins were increasingly lost. The writings of Shinto (*shinsho* 神書) were turned into Buddhist writings and Shinto started to decay."[35] These parallels between Nobuyoshi and the aforementioned scholars and daimyo point to a common discourse in the middle and late seventeenth century, according to which Buddhism had to be removed from shrines in order to revive "Shinto," which was in essence identical with Confucianism. Of course, Shinto did not possess such virtues in earlier times. As explained below, they were borrowed from Confucianism.

However, it is not without pitfalls to designate such ideas as the "unity of Shinto and Confucianism," since Shinto and Confucianism were not congruent in all aspects. Above all, Japan was not China, but a "divine country."[36] When Hayashi Gahō writes in the preface to the *Aizu jinja-shi* that "in our country, we have been revering Shinto since the beginning of time," or when Deguchi Nobuyoshi emphasizes the "differences in institutions and language" of China and Japan,[37] it becomes clear that in their opinion, the Way of the divine country ought to be Shinto and not Confucianism. And yet they insisted that "Shinto" was compatible with Confucianism, since according to their view, the virtues of Confucianism were universal.

While Confucianism and Shinto were both "Ways" that had to be put into practice, some differences still existed. At the end of the preface of the *Jingi hōten*, Razan writes:

> The conscience of the *kami* and the heart (*kokoro*) of man are originally the same. If we compare them with objects, then they are sword, jewel and mirror. [...] The jewel and the mirror stand for the civil aspects (*bun* 文), the sword for martiality (*bu* 武). [...] They [correspond to] the Way of the Just Ruler (*ōdō* 王道), the Confucian Way, the Way of the Sage.[38]

The Three Sacred Treasures (sword, jewel and mirror), which symbolize "Shinto," are related here to the Confucian way. In this sense, Shinto and Confucianism are the same.[39] On the other hand, Razan says that the sword stands for martiality. Kumazawa Banzan's interpretation of the Three Sacred Treasures is very similar.[40] Thus, "Shinto," which, in their view, contained the same values as Confucianism, values "martiality," a virtue that is depreciated in traditional Confucian thought. Even if these scholars insisted that "Shinto" taught the same morals as Confucianism, their "Shinto" was a quasi-Confucianism that held the military in high esteem, a "martial Confucianism," so to speak. Conversely we may say that the esteem of martiality was the only non-Confucian element of "Confucian Shinto."

The Formative Process of Quasi-Confucianism

"Shinto" at the Beginning of the Early Modern Period

How did the discourse described above emerge and why was it not only shared by Confucian scholars, but spread also among daimyo and Shintoists? How was it related to the transition from the medieval to the early modern period, as well as the political concerns of the *bakufu* at the beginning of the seventeenth century? Let me turn to these questions in the present section.

With the unification of Japan by the military under Toyotomi's reign, Japan's medieval period ended. Oda Nobunaga 織田信長 (1534–82), Toyotomi Hideyoshi's 豊臣秀吉 (1537–98) predecessor as unifier of Japan, fought fiercely against Buddhism's influence and dealt it a serious blow. Erecting a consolidated government through the military would not have been possible without diminishing Buddhist influence, which dominated the medieval period to such a degree that contemporary discourse explained Buddhism and secular powers as "mutually dependent" and the foundation of good governance. Buddhism's religious influence was so dominant that it is safe to subsume medieval religion in Japan under the term Buddhism. Even the native deities were regarded in Buddhist terms as "manifest traces" of "original [Buddhas]" (*honji suijaku*).[41] There were certainly attempts in the later Muromachi period to disengage Buddhism from Japan's original religious tradition, which came to be called "Shinto," in particular Yoshida Shinto 吉田神道, which was expounded by Yoshida Kanetomo 吉田兼倶 (1435–1511) (and may have been inspired by Neo-Confucian teachings). However, "Shinto" never developed a systematic worldview that could rival the sophistication of Buddhism.

Nobunaga's blow against the power of Buddhism diminished its position within Japan's religious sphere massively. This was the literal one-time opportunity in a thousand years for "Shinto" to gain independence from Buddhism. However, separation from Buddhism also implied that "Shinto" had severed its ties to the Buddhist all-encompassing view of the world including its explanation of the *kami*. If "Shinto" no longer held a role subordinate to Buddhism, it had to create its own systematic worldview or to find a substitute paradigm to replace Buddhism. This proved to be difficult, however. At the beginning of the early modern period, Shinto still consisted of nothing more than what Kumazawa Banzan called the "laws of priestly families" (*shake no hō* 社家の法), which he explained as "rituals according to the manner of individual priests."[42] At this point, Confucianism was joined with Shinto to create a paradigm that could be a substitute for Buddhism. By making use of Confucian concepts and terminology, "Shinto," which up to this point had been confined to *kami* ritualism, was able to explain and justify its own existence. According to Banzan, "the Way does not become clear without Chinese writings,"[43] and Deguchi Nobuyoshi stated that "one must not refrain from borrowing Confucian terms" in order to explain Shinto.[44]

Before the early modern period, Confucianism was not on equal footing with Buddhism. Both had come to Japan around the sixth century, but in contrast to Buddhism, Confucianism took root only as a scholarly discipline, not as a religious doctrine.[45] Until the medieval period, only a small number of intellectuals, such as courtiers or Zen 禅 priests, concerned themselves with Confucianism, and consequently its influence remained limited. When Confucianism began to be promoted by the Tokugawa administration, however, Confucianism's influence on society increased enormously. By linking itself with this socially invigorated Confucianism, "Shinto" was able to gain independence from Buddhism at the beginning of the early modern period.

Promoting Confucianism to Reestablish International Relations

This still leaves open the question of why the early Tokugawa regime promoted Confucianism in the first place. The most general reason is certainly the fact that Confucianism was regarded an effective tool for creating and governing a feudal society based on social rank (*mibun* 身分). However, the *bakufu* faced additional political challenges, which I will discuss in this section.

One of the *bakufu*'s initial objectives was to reestablish diplomatic relations with the countries of East Asia. Japanese piracy in the Sengoku period had seriously disturbed these relations and Toyotomi Hideyoshi's invasion of Korea (1592–8) destroyed them completely, turning Japan into a "barbarian country." In order to get rid of this bad reputation, the Tokugawa regime had to convince the international community—first and foremost Ming China—of its legitimacy and its high level of civilization. In 1610, the *bakufu* sent a diplomatic message to the governor of Fujian province claiming that "our manners have changed" since the times of Hideyoshi and that the rule of Ieyasu followed the model of the Three Dynasties.⁴⁶ Neighboring countries now adored the virtues of Japan, and have "started to pay tribute."⁴⁷ Conversely, Japan would pay "increasing adoration to China."⁴⁸

Another official letter explained that Tokugawa Ieyasu cherished China's habits (*fū* 風).⁴⁹ A diplomatic message sent in 1625, again to the governor of Fujian, claimed that "Japan has followed the lead of Chinese habits for a long time."⁵⁰ These letters demonstrate that in its inceptive phase, the Tokugawa regime tried to emulate Chinese "habits" (civilization) with the aim of reestablishing its relations with East Asian countries. The author of these diplomatic letters, by the way, was once again Hayashi Razan.

The "habits" admired by China's "barbarian" neighbors were nothing other than Confucianism, or rather, the Neo-Confucianism of Zhu Xi 朱子 (1130–1200). This was the model of civilization in all East Asian countries—at that time China, Japan, Vietnam, and Korea.⁵¹ Accordingly, the early Tokugawa considered making Japan a Confucian country an effective way to gain recognition as being civilized.

However, early modern Japan could not attain the same level of Confucianization as the continental East Asian countries for several reasons. First of all, Japan had virtually no experience with Confucian rites, which were the foundation of a Confucian state. With the exception of *sekiten* 釈奠,⁵² ancient Japan had not adopted any Confucian rites. In fact, it had been Buddhism that gained a strong position in Japanese religion, especially its funerary rites.

The second obstacle to the diffusion of Confucianism was the important role of Buddhism in defending Japan against the perceived Christian threat. While the political power of Buddhism had waned since the beginning of the early modern period, it still proved useful to the Tokugawa regime within the system of religious certification through temples (*terauke*). This, however, created an inextricable link between Japanese funerary rites and Buddhism, which made it nigh on impossible for Confucianism to take roots in this most important field of religious ritualism. Although political figures such as Tokugawa Yoshinao showed a predilection for Confucian funerals, the Christian threat was a problem of higher priority than introducing new funeral practices.

The third reason for the difficult situation of Confucianism was the military legacy of the regime. In Confucianism, the "civil" (*bun*), which appeals to self-control through virtue, has a higher value than the "martial" (*bu*), which subdues people by force. Nevertheless, the Tokugawa regime was established by a warrior endorsed by the tenno, who had appointed him as "barbarian-subduing general-in-chief" (*seii taishōgun* 征夷大将軍, generally shortened to "shogun"). Since this military regime regarded "martiality" as a key virtue, basing its legitimization on a Confucian paradigm proved a difficult task.

For these reasons, Tokugawa Japan failed to be accepted as a genuine Confucian civilization by other East Asian countries. Nevertheless, the government tried to establish Japan as a state endowed with a civilization similar to Confucianism.⁵³ Under such conditions, "Shinto," which was in the process of disentangling itself from Buddhism, became a useful tool for the Tokugawa regime. As it consisted of nothing more than *kami* ritualism, it could easily be assimilated into a moral system of Confucian virtues. Therefore, "Shinto" came to possess similar universal values in order to be compatible with Confucianism. In this way, the notion took shape of a "divine country" possessing a civilization as superior as that of China, but based on the Way of the Gods.

Conclusion

The ideology discussed in this chapter can be described as quasi-Confucianism, or more precisely as a kind of "Shinto" reimagined as "martial Confucianism." Religious reforms from the middle to late seventeenth century, such as the reconstruction of ancient shrines, shrine regulations, or the removal of "illicit shrines," owed their existence to this ideology. It derived from two concurrent intellectual developments: Shinto's search for a new dogmatic foundation after its emancipation from Buddhism; and the quest of the Tokugawa regime for an ideological foundation that was based on Confucian-style virtues. The political leaders were convinced that these measures would enable them to restore the ideal "ancient society" and to present Tokugawa Japan as a civilized country within East Asia. This was, at the same time, the paradigm that validated the Tokugawa regime and its power to readjust social norms after the "confusion of the middle ages."

While Shinto shared and used Confucian virtues, the inclusion of "martiality" turned this image of civilization into something specifically Japanese. This quasi-Confucian "Shinto" was carried on into modernity, when Shinto in the early Meiji period became closer to Confucian ritualism than ever before.[54] In the following decades, "martiality" would bare its fangs: After its victory in the First Sino-Japanese war (1894–5), Japan's self-image rose to that of the leader in the East, with once again its feral cries of "martiality" resounding all over East Asia.[55]

Buddhist-Confucian Polemics and the Position of Shinto

W. J. Boot

The old historiographical scheme, in which the Edo period was equated with Confucianism, will find few supporters nowadays, but the consequences have yet to be drawn. The study of Buddhism and the study of Confucianism still tend to be two different worlds—to the extent that the Buddhism of the Edo period *is* studied, of course. If one wants to remedy this situation, one must be aware of three things. First, in early modern Japan, Buddhism was far from dead; for practical purposes, it was the state religion during the whole of the Edo period. Second, early modern Confucianism was the preserve of a small group of intellectuals, and most of its rank-and-file adherents were not much interested in Confucian thought and thinkers, but rather in producing Chinese verse. Third, in the Japan of the Edo period, intellectual and religious circles formed a continuum, which was based on texts in classical Chinese and on Chinese notions of propriety and social organization.

Many years ago, I decided that the best way to explore this intellectual continuum was the study of polemics, because polemics would give access to the self-perceived differences between the Three Ways of Buddhism, Shinto, and Confucianism, and would indicate which arguments were expected to appeal to the interested public. The present chapter explores in some depth one strand of such polemics, namely, the antagonistic exchanges between proponents of Neo-Confucianism and Buddhism in seventeenth-century Japan. However, by way of introduction something must be said about the broader context.

Grosso modo, there are three positions East Asian scholars took in regard to the relation between Buddhism and Confucianism. The first is the universalistic, holistic claim that they are fundamentally identical—different formulations of the same truth. Add Daoism, and you have *sankyō itchi* 三教一致, i.e. the claim that the Three Teachings (Buddhism, Confucianism, and Daoism or, in Japan, Shinto) are identical. The second position is that the two are complementary—Confucianism for running the state, Buddhism for personal salvation. The third takes the antagonistic position—the two are completely different, and only one of them can be true.

In Japan, until the end of the sixteenth century, the first position prevailed. Confucianism was studied by Zen 禅 monks, who regarded it as a propaedeutic for

Buddhist studies, or by court nobles, who were not about to stress the differences, either. This applies both to Ichijō Kanera 一条兼良 (1402–81) and to members of the Kiyohara 清原, one of the families at the imperial court that was traditionally in charge of Confucian education.¹

The antagonistic position arose when Confucianism began to present itself as a way of personal, moral self-cultivation. The program of self-cultivation followed the eight stages outlined in the Confucian classic *Great Learning* (*Daxue* 大學); it involved the training of the individual through study, contemplation, and practice, and culminated in socially useful political activity. It competed with Zen Buddhism, the other great seducer of serious young men, but it differed from Buddhism in two important respects: Confucians studied *things*, not "nothing," and after they had finished their studies, they did not disappear into nirvana, but did useful work for emperor and empire. In China, this new attitude arose during the Song; its most famous representative was Zhu Xi 朱熹 (1130–1200). In Japan, it happened around 1600.

The shift is ineluctably bound to the names of Fujiwara Seika 藤原惺窩 (1561–1619) and Hayashi Razan 林羅山 (1583–1657). The latter presented himself as the disciple of the first, and claimed that his teacher had been the first, in Japan, to realize and preach the essential truth of Confucianism. As Razan tells the story, Seika had been a Buddhist monk for many years, but he turned layman again and propagated his new convictions, e.g. by appearing in front of Tokugawa Ieyasu 徳川家康 (1542–1616) in a Confucian robe (the *shenyi* 深衣). From that moment on, the triumphal march of Confucianism began.

Now, this was mostly self-advertisement of the Hayashi, and especially of Razan and of his son Gahō 林鵞峰 (1618–80). It remains true, however, that Razan was the first Japanese on record who took a strongly anti-Buddhist position.² Apparently, Razan *believed* the anti-Buddhist elements in the Neo-Confucianism of the Song. The decisive episode occurred when he was fifteen years old: the monks of the Kenninji 建仁寺, where he was studying, tried to force him to take the vows, but the young Razan refused, giving as his reason that Buddhism was contrary to filial piety. There was no greater sin than not having produced any offspring.³

Razan was not the only one to present himself as a Confucian scholar, critical of Buddhism. There were Seika's other disciples,⁴ as well as a number of younger contemporaries of other affiliations such as Nakae Tōju 中江藤樹 (1608–48), Yamazaki Ansai 山崎闇斎 (1618–82), Kumazawa Banzan 熊沢蕃山 (1619–91), and Yamaga Sokō 山鹿素行 (1622–85). Their appearance indicates that at the time the conditions were right for young men with intellectual aspirations to establish themselves as "independent" intellectuals who earned their own income—not as monks or samurai, but as teachers of Confucianism (*jusha* 儒者) and/or as physicians (*jui* 儒医).

The Confucians earned their money through their knowledge of Chinese and of the classical Confucian medical and literary Chinese corpus. The other group of people who knew Chinese was the Buddhist clergy. To them, it was the language of the Buddhist canon. The Confucians, on the other hand, had been exposed from their youth to Buddhist influence, and most of them were buried according to Buddhist rites.⁵ *Jusha* and priests agreed on the importance of Chinese, and on the necessity of knowing at least the introductory Confucian corpus of the *Four Books*. In this way, Buddhist priests and Confucian scholars together constituted an "intellectual world" in which Chinese

Figure 7.1 Portrait of Hayashi Razan.[6] Photo reproduced courtesy of the Kyoto University Museum.

was the *lingua franca*. The situation is comparable to early modern Europe, where ecclesiastics, humanists, lawyers, and physicians used Latin to conduct their serious discussions, and everyone shared a common Christian *and* classical background.

There were differences, however, between the two groups. Buddhist priests belonged to an immeasurably larger organization than the Confucians. This Buddhist church was recognized by the *bakufu* and the imperial court, both of which also made use of it for their own purposes. We may assume that the large majority of the courtiers and the samurai were sincere believers, but there were common interests between the ruling elite and the Buddhist church, exemplified, for instance, by the worship of Tokugawa Ieyasu as Tōshō Daigongen 東照大権現,[7] by the system of religious certification of the population through Buddhist temples (*terauke* 寺請), or by the temples tied to individual families of the court aristocracy (*monzeki dera* 門跡寺).

Scholars propounding Confucianism found themselves in a completely different situation. Confucians had to fend for themselves; there was no nation-wide organization on which they could fall back. In Japan, a Confucian scholar was a teacher of Chinese. His knowledge of Chinese gave him access to the Chinese classical corpus, and made him the representative of the superior culture of China. This gave him a certain status, but not the status a real Confucian aspired to—that of advisor to the shogun or a daimyo in political matters, as a member of the executive branch. Only a few reached this position, such as Kumazawa Banzan and Arai Hakuseki 新井白石 (1657–1725), but those who did were all samurai. In Japan, you were born to rule.

To sum up, Buddhists and Confucians belonged to the same social layer of educated intellectuals, but the Buddhists were better off in terms of numbers, connections, and wealth. What the Confucians had going for them was the prestige of "China," and their greater interest in, and relevant skills for, governing the realm.

Polemics

In its early modern guise of Neo-Confucianism, Confucianism must be understood as a young and upcoming movement that needed to attract attention and to spell out its differences with Buddhism. In this situation, the Confucians had something to gain from engaging in adversarial polemics.

The Buddhists, on the other hand, stood to gain little from acknowledging an adversary as insignificant as Confucianism. Moreover, polemics that created too much of an uproar ran the risk of drawing the ire of the authorities. From an administrator's point of view, the practical usefulness of Buddhism was clear, but the *bakufu* was averse to getting involved in sectarian quarrels. In religious matters, it stuck to the ancient East Asian rule that the state was supreme, and that religious organizations had to obey the authorities and behave harmoniously amongst themselves.

The clearest case *against* engaging in polemics was put forward by the Jōdo 浄土 monk Ninchō 忍澂 (1645–1711):

> In ancient and in modern times, you see a great many people who make it their business to condemn Buddhism. However, they are dogmatic and superficial. The people of the world have not heeded them, and our Way has only thriven more and more. From the beginning, they have never been able to damage the Great Law even one little bit. [It is like] taking a knife and cutting the wind: what harm will there be to the wind? Why, then, should I let my heart be bound by these various disputatious attacks on Buddhism? Moreover, when I am exposed to the full fury of those Japanese books about Shinto,[8] I can understand what their message is, and this I regard as a special favor. Therefore, I remain silent and do not argue with them. The confusion comes from them; what is it to me?[9]

These were wise words, but few heeded them. As the ten volumes of *Polemics in Japanese Thought-Sources* (*Nihon shisō tōsō shiryō* 日本思想闘諍史料, NSTS) bear witness, polemics throve.

In practice, we see that in both the Buddhist and the Confucian camp, a distinction can be made between polemics that took the adversarial position, and those that took a conciliatory stance. The latter we find exemplified in such texts as *On the Feet of the Tripod* (*Teisoku-ron* 鼎足論) by Taiga 大我 (1709–82)[10] on the Buddhist side, and *On Protecting the Law and Assisting Government* (*Gohō shiji ron* 護法資治論) by Mori Genjuku 森儼塾 (1653–21) on the Confucian.[11] In the first of his prefatory notes, Genjuku says the following:

Now and formerly, Confucian-Buddhist discussions have been rife. Each held fast to his own sect and did not [attempt to] understand the other's intention. They merely attacked the skin, and did not hit the meat-and-bones. Each formed [his own] biased faction, and, in the end, they lost all objectivity. The Confucians desired to destroy the Buddhists, and the Buddhists, in their turn, fought with their brothers. I deplored this, and composed this discussion. Prejudices are rooted in ignorance. Therefore, it is necessary to spread knowledge. This is the main objective [of this book].[12]

The adversarial strand of Confucian-Buddhist polemics was initiated by Hayashi Razan in *Dialogue between a Confucian and a Buddhist* (*Ju-butsu mondō* 儒仏問答), which he composed together with his older friend, the poet Matsunaga Teitoku 松永貞徳 (1571–1653); Razan upheld the Confucian cause and Teitoku defended Buddhism. The book must have been printed in the 1630s or 1640s.[13] Judging by the number of surviving copies, and by the paucity of references to this text, it cannot have been a bestseller. It does contain, though, all the topics that are discussed in later polemics, so in that sense, if not very influential, it was at least archetypical.

Razan uttered further criticisms of Buddhism in his *Examination of the Shrines of our Realm* (*Honchō jinja kō* 本朝神社考) and in the "essays" (*ron* 論), "disquisitions" (*ben* 弁), and "reading notes" (*zuihitsu* 随筆) published in Razan's *Collected Works* (*Bunshū* 文集). Once these texts had become available to Buddhist priests,[14] they prompted similarly polemical responses. Two representative texts are *Explaining my Doubts about* Jinja-kō (*Jinja-kō bengi* 神社考辨疑) and *On the Protecting Buddhas and Gods of our Land* (*Fusō gobusshin ron* 扶桑護仏神論), both of which I will discuss here in more detail.[15]

Jinja-kō bengi (hereafter *Bengi*) was written by the Shingon 真言 monk Jakuhon 寂本 (1631–1701). It was first printed in 1686 as *On* Jinja-kō *being a Heterodox Criticism of Buddhism* (*Jinja-kō jahai bukkyō ron* 神社考邪排仏教論), and reprinted in 1716 as *Jinja-kō bengi*. *Fusō gobusshin ron* was written by a monk of the Ōbaku 黄檗 Zen sect, Chōon Dōkai 潮音道海 (1628–95), and contains a preface dated 1687.[16] The text was never printed, and the database of Kokubunken (National Institute of Japanese Literature) lists only three manuscripts, so it cannot have been widely known.[17]

In their prefaces, both Jakuhon and Chōon give as their reason for writing the texts that they could not let Razan get away with his attacks on Buddhism. In Jakuhon's words: "[…] maligning [Buddhism] to his heart's content, and going to the depth of his poisonous envy. He did nothing but revile the splendid achievements of the sages and thus led astray the foolish feelings of ordinary people." Jakuhon even claims that he was not merely encouraged, but *forced* by his fellow monks to write his text.[18] Chōon describes how he realized, as he was reading Razan's writings, that Razan made a pretense of supporting Shinto, but was in fact aiming to suppress it, and also, that Razan was openly criticizing Buddhism. He, Chōon could not possibly keep silent.[19]

The format of *Bengi* and *Gobusshin-ron* is the same: each section begins with a quotation from Razan, followed by a rebuttal by Jakuhon or, respectively, by Chōon. As the title *Jinja-kō bengi* makes clear, Jakuhon directed his criticism specifically at *Honchō jinja kō*. Chōon targeted the same work but criticized also the essays etc. in Razan's *Bunshū*.

In rebutting Razan, Jakuhon tends to rely on personal invective, common sense, and logical arguments, but Chōon, apart from the inevitable personal invective, tends to counter with long quotations from a text entitled *The Classic of Great Accomplishment [Containing] the Annals of Bygone Matters from Previous Generations* (*Sendai kuji hongi taisei kyō* 先代旧事本紀大成経; hereafter *Taisei kyō*).[20] This text had been identified as a forgery and was therefore proscribed by the *bakufu* in 1681. Chōon, when writing *Gobusshin-ron*, must have been aware of this fact. Nevertheless, he argues throughout as if *Taisei kyō* had canonical status. In his view, it was the oldest of the national histories (older than *Kujiki* 旧事記, *Kojiki* 古事記, *Nihon shoki* 日本書紀, and *Kogo shūi* 古語拾遺), *and* it was written by no lesser person than Shōtoku Taishi 聖徳太子 (574–622).

Chōon felt free to quote from *Taisei kyō* in this context, because he was convinced that Razan had read the text, and hence, that Razan was acting in bad faith when he ignored it. Chōon's proof was the otherwise uncorroborated story that Tokugawa Iemitsu 徳川家光 (1604–51) had given Razan a copy to appraise, whereupon Razan had judged it to be a forgery.[21]

Choosing *Taisei kyō* implied choosing in favor of Shōtoku Taishi. Both Jakuhon, who had also read *Taisei kyō*,[22] and Chōon were in effect adherents of Shōtoku, whom they regarded as a superior being, a "true and perfect one" (*shinjin shijin* 真人至人), several cuts above the Confucian Holy Ones (*seijin* 聖人). Razan, on the other hand, was completely dismissive of the Crown Prince. Shōtoku, Razan maintained, was unfilial. Moreover, he was responsible for the murder of Emperor Sushun 崇峻天皇 (521?–92, r. 587–92), and he was a Buddhist, responsible for the spread of Buddhism. All miraculous stories about him were later inventions. The evidence Razan uses to prove that Shōtoku was unfilial is the orders he gave to trim down his tumulus while it was under construction, "because he would have no children to succeed him."

In rebuttal, Jakuhon praises the Buddhist succession—not from bodily heir to bodily heir, but from virtue to virtue—as preferable to the biological lineage. Even great sages like Yao 堯, Shun 舜, Tang 湯, and Wu 武 did not have worthy biological heirs.[23] Chōon supplies a lengthy quotation from *Taisei kyō*,[24] which tells "the whole story," including the explanation Shōtoku himself gave of his reasons to have his grave reduced in size: "Thinking back to the karma of his former lives, [he realized that] his descendants would not succeed him. Therefore, while his tumulus was being built, he told the workmen to slash it here and to cut it there. His words did not mean that it is all right that one's line be cut."[25] In other words, Chōon exculpates Shōtoku from the charge that he had himself refused to have descendants and was, therefore, unfilial. It was a matter of karma.

Another argument of Razan against Shōtoku that angered Jakuhon and Chōon was that Shōtoku had "killed" Emperor Sushun. Of course, Razan knew that Soga no Umako 蘇我馬子 (?–626) was responsible for this famous case of regicide and that the actual killing had been done by again a different person, but Umako and Shōtoku were allies. Together, in 587, they had defended Buddhism against Mononobe no Moriya 物部守屋 (?–587) and since then, under Suiko 推古天皇, they had become the major powers at court. In *Jinja-kō*, Razan maintains that Shōtoku should have executed Umako for killing Sushun, and in the second of the two essays he devoted to the matter, which is quoted by Chōon, Razan goes even further, saying that "according to the method of the *Spring and Autumn Annals* (*Chunqiu* 春秋)" one could maintain that it was Shōtoku who killed the emperor, even though the deed was done by somebody else.[26]

In rebuttal, Jakuhon writes: (1) Moriya disliked not only Buddhism, but also Confucianism for being a foreign creed; (2) in his *Sendai kuji hongi* 先代旧事本紀,[27] Umako goes out of his way to praise the gods, while there is no proof of Moriya ever having done so; (3) Razan is partial to Moriya because he, too, hates Buddhism; (4) Umako fought Moriya because Moriya wanted to kill all imperial princes in order to put his favorite, Prince Anahobe 穴穂部, on the throne; (5) it was Sushun who wanted to kill Umako, so what happened afterwards was his own fault; (6) Shōtoku wisely did not insist on punishing Umako, because then the disturbances would never have ended; (7) afterwards, Umako composed *Sendai kuji hongi*, which is how he redeemed himself.[28]

Chōon, in turn, says that Razan hated Buddhism; hence, he hated both Shōtoku and Umako. In order to defend them, Chōon declares that Sushun was a very wicked ruler, far worse than the Chinese archetypical tyrants Jie 桀 and Zhou 紂. This comparison implies, of course, that Sushun no longer was a sovereign, but that he was, in Mencius' words, "just a man" (Ch. *yifu* 一夫),[29] and that killing him was not regicide. Shōtoku, on the other hand, was "a true and perfect one," whose judgment could not be queried.

This brings us to Shōtoku's most famous remark, which is central to this whole strand of polemics: "Shinto is the root and trunk, Confucianism is the branches and leaves, and Buddhism is the flowers and fruit."[30] Razan's comment, quoted both in *Bengi* and in *Gobusshin-ron*, is that these words cannot possibly have been spoken by the Crown Prince; they are out of character, and were foisted upon him by the Urabe 卜部 and Nakatomi 中臣. What Shōtoku "really believed," says Razan, "was that Buddhism was the root and trunk, and that Shinto and Confucianism were the branches and the flowers."[31]

Neither Jakuhon nor Chōon agrees with this; both vouch for the historical truth of the attribution, adducing as proof a passage in *Taisei kyō*, which tells how Emperor Bidatsu 敏達天皇 (538?–85, r. 572–85) summoned the seven-year-old Shōtoku and "asked him about the words of Confucius and the Buddha."[32] In answer, the young boy produced the metaphor. Jakuhon's reacts with personal invective: Razan's mentality, he says, is that of "a foolish child trying to keep the precepts," which is the "second mental stage" as described by Kūkai 空海 (774–835); "the meritorious achievements of the Crown Prince do not fall within Razan's mental purview."[33] Chōon, after quoting *Seikō hongi*, adds a second metaphor: "[...] our country is the sun; China is the stars; India is the moon. The stars and the moon increase their luster through the [rays of] the sun. How could [our country] not be the root?" He concludes that, "therefore, the two Ways of Confucianism and Buddhism are brought forth by the Way of the Gods."[34]

The Position of Shinto

The importance that is attached to Shōtoku's dictum indicates that Shinto occupied a pivotal position within the context of Buddhist-Confucian polemics. The reason is, I think, that both Confucianism and Buddhism came from outside Japan. Both had to prove, therefore, that fundamentally they were Japanese, or at least, *more* Japanese, in the sense of "*closer to* Shinto," than the other party. For the adherents of the conciliatory position, Shōtoku's remark implied a redefinition of *sankyō itchi*, from Confucianism, Daoism, and Buddhism to Shinto, Confucianism, and Buddhism. Razan, of course, disagreed. His aim was to equate Shinto with Confucianism. This explains why his *Honchō jinja kō* is not merely a straightforward, historical account of Shinto shrines, but turns, at times, into an anti-Buddhist pamphlet. This also explains why he developed his own *ritō shinchi shintō* 理当心地神道, which was heavily indebted to Neo-Confucian metaphysics.[35]

Two further issues, apart from Shōtoku, that were raised in relation with Shinto were, first, Razan's position that the introduction of Buddhism had caused the decline of Shinto and, second, the definition of "gods"—basically, whether the Japanese word *kami* 神 means the same as its Chinese character equivalent *shen* 神 (or the generic *guishen* 鬼神) in a Confucian or Chinese context.

In the preface of *Jinja-kō*, Razan writes that the Royal Way (*ōdō* 王道), established in Japan by Emperor Jinmu 神武天皇 (the mythical founder of the imperial dynasty), fell into decay due to the influence of Buddhism as it expanded in the course of the Heian period, and that the decay of the Royal Way in turn caused the decay of the Way of the Gods.[36] In rebuttal, Jakuhon points out that Buddhism was the *second* foreign way to be introduced into Japan: Confucianism had arrived under Emperor Ōjin 応神天皇 (trad. dates 200–310), Buddhism only under Emperor Kinmei 欽明天皇 (509?–71). Secondly, he argues that "a Way may have come from a strange clime, and yet its transformations are immediate," adding:

> If [Razan] dislikes the teachings from another region, then neither should he [want to] practice the teachings of benevolence and righteousness (*ningi* 仁義, i.e. Confucianism) in our country.[37]

As for Buddhism, it is not inimical to the Royal Way or to the Way of the Gods. History is proof:

> Since olden times, foreign lands have not been able to attack our country. Even though subjects occasionally battled for power, they still served their king and did no [such thing as] robbing him of his throne. The masses did not transfer [their loyalty] and they lived at ease in their dwellings. This was because they were subject to the supreme order of the Royal Way. Furthermore, as regards [Buddhism in its relation] to the Way of the Gods, naturally, among the large numbers of Shinto shrines that are listed in this volume (i.e. in *Jinja-kō*), there are few that do not support the Buddha. And [it goes without saying that] the Buddha [sides] with the Gods! [Buddhism] was elevated because it was considered to be the basis; it expanded because it was considered to be virtuous. By flourishing more and more, it has increasingly manifested itself. The Shinto shrines in the realm have become prosperous. How was that before, when this Buddhism had not yet come [to our

land]? Why is it that you say that because of Buddhism the Way of the Gods has gradually fallen into disuse?[38]

Chōon begins the second fascicle of *Gobusshin-ron* by quoting the preface of *Jinja-kō*, and follows up with a lengthy rebuttal, which contains a completely original theory about the nature of the gods.[39] Amongst other things, he takes exception to charges Razan makes in his preface that the Buddhists identified Japanese gods with buddhas and bodhisattvas, and that shrines and temples were combined into single complexes. According to Chōon, *honji suijaku* 本地垂迹 (the theory that regarded *kami* as local manifestations of Buddhist deities) was not of Buddhist origin, but was first formulated in an oracle of the God of Miwa, and the first *gongen* to appear in Japan was Emperor Ankan 安閑天皇 (trad. dates 466–536; r. 531–6), who after his death manifested himself as Yoshino Gongen 吉野権現, a manifestation of the bodhisattva Maitreya.

Combining shrines and temples, too, was the result of a divine oracle. Chōon offers no proof, but he argues that priests and monks could not possibly have been living together, were it not for an oracle of the gods. The fact that they do, is evidence in itself. Moreover, it is evident that the gods prefer Buddhism to Confucianism. That is why temples prosper and Confucian schools do not.

This brings Chōon to the well-known pronouncement of Yamato-hime 倭姫, the imperial princess who in legend is presented as the founder of the shrines in Ise. Chōon quotes it from *Taisei kyō* as follows: "You, Shinto priests, listen properly to my words. *Avoid even the breath of teachings from other countries and of other beliefs* that [claim that] souls will ever be exhausted." Note that the phrasing in *Taisei kyō* is different from the usual phrasing, based on the medieval *Account of Yamato-hime* (*Yamato-hime no mikoto seiki* 倭姫命世記),[40] which is "avoid the breath of Buddhism," supposedly a warning addressed to the Shinto priests of Ise.

Chōon points out that Yamato-hime spoke these words in the days of Emperor Yūryaku 雄略天皇 (trad. dates 418–79; r. 456–79), at a time when Buddhism had not yet arrived in Japan. So, logically speaking, the words *could* not have been directed against Buddhism. *Yamato-hime no mikoto seiki* is a late fabrication, hence, less reliable than *Taisei kyō*. Moreover, the words "beliefs that [claim that] souls will ever be exhausted" clearly refer to Confucianism.[41]

Razan's crudest response to the identification of the gods with buddhas and bodhisattvas may have been the so-called Taibo theory (*Taihaku setsu* 太伯説), discussed by Razan and also, later, by Kumazawa Banzan.[42] Briefly, this theory, which has its basis in several Chinese dynastic histories, claims that Taibo 太伯, the uncle of the Chinese sage King Wen 文王, gave up his claim to the succession in the House of Zhou and went to live among the aboriginals of the Yangzi delta. From there he went to Japan, where, it is then claimed, Taibo became the founder of the imperial house. Whether he is to be identified with Amaterasu 天照, with Ninigi 瓊々杵, or with Jinmu remains a moot point. But, in any case, if Japan were founded by a scion of the House of Zhou, clearly, Confucianism is native to Japan. Razan introduced this theory in an essay which his sons included in his *Bunshū*, but he did not mention it in *Honchō jinja kō*. He may have thought it too controversial.

It is interesting to see that the Buddhists and Confucians have parallel strategies of arguing their compatibility with Shinto:

1. Outright identity: all gods are *suijaku* of buddhas | the ancestor of the imperial clan is Taibo.
2. Spiritual agreement: the gods welcomed the buddhas | Confucianism and Shinto are basically one.

The other point at issue is the theory of the nature of the gods advanced by Jakuhon and Chōon in answer to Razan's Confucian interpretation of Shinto. Jakuhon makes a differentiation between "god" in the Confucian sense of the term and "god" in the traditional Japanese sense: "What the Confucians call 'gods' 神 are the traces of the creative transformations and the intrinsic potential of Yin and Yang. They are different from the gods of our country." He even implies that Razan's ulterior aim is to destroy Shinto in this way: "[…] borrowing the name of our gods, he will abolish Buddhism; then he will lead our gods into Confucianism, and eventually he will destroy our gods."[43]

In Chōon's *Gobusshin-ron*, too, the nature of the gods is very much under discussion. Halfway through the first fascicle, Chōon criticizes Razan's *Disquisition on the God Ho no Ikazuchi* (*Ho no Inazuchi no kami ben* 火雷神辯),[44] in which Razan states that "the thunder god has no form," and that he, Razan, "explains everything through Principle." Quoting from the annals of Emperor Yūryaku in *Taisei kyō* under Yūryaku 12/4/27, which relates the physical encounter of the emperor with a thunder god, Chōon argues emphatically that the thunder god figuring there *did* have a form, and not only he:

> The gods of our country are mostly living gods (*ikigami* 生神), and therefore they have a form. In the foreign country (i.e. China) they worship the souls of dead men and consider those to be gods. It is for that reason that Confucians think they have no form. *Do not treat the gods of our country and those of the foreign country as identical.* In our country, even the souls of dead men massively [manifest] divine transformations and mysterious wonders. Usa and Yoshino[45] in the past and Kitano Tenjin more recently are proof of this.[46]

This quotation is followed seamlessly by a discussion of a god's three bodies.[47] Quoting *Taisei kyō*, Chōon distinguishes between the transcendent principle body (*rikyū* 理躬), the pneuma body (*kikyū* 気躬), and the seed body (*seikyū* 精躬).[48] Although a concept of the three buddha bodies exists in Buddhism, the present terminology seems to be unique to *Taisei kyō*. (At least, I have not encountered it elsewhere.) Chōon formulates a whole theology in these terms: Originally, the gods were in the eternal world and were identical with their transcendent principle body. After heaven came into existence, they used the pure *qi* 気 of heaven to make their material force bodies, while their transcendent principle body became their divine souls. In the next stage:

> With their transcendent principle bodies, or again with their material force bodies [the gods] entered into the material force of their fathers and mothers, and from

that material force they made their [own] bodies. The gods who have been born from [this] pure essence are called [the gods of the] seed bodies. They will, therefore, come to an end before heaven [ends]. Such is the case with our living gods. In case of the material body or the seed body—when [a god's] body ends, he will [again] become his transcendent principle body. If [the god has committed] any offences, he will not [again] become [his transcendent principle form], but will go to the nether world (*yomotsukuni* 黄泉国); if he has not [committed] any offences, he will [again] become [his transcendent principle body], and thus return to the eternal world (*tokoyo no kuni* 常世国).[49]

There is more to it than this (the discussion continues until 1:18a), but we will let that be for the moment. The point is that this innovative theology was prompted by the need to give an account of the Shinto gods as distinct from the Chinese (Confucian) ones. The writers of *Taisei kyō* wanted their gods to be individual, personal, everlasting deities. Therefore, they had no use for the standard Neo-Confucian metaphysics, which Razan followed in his *ritō shinchi shintō*.[50] They did not, however, devise a completely new system, but improvised on the Neo-Confucian scheme—original, but recognizable.

Jakuhon also attacks Razan's *ritō shinchi shintō*. He quotes Razan as saying: "The Shinto [which believes] that principle is present in the heart has been transmitted from god to god, from emperor to emperor. The Way of the Emperors and the Way of the Gods are one and indivisible."[51] Next, he counters as follows:

> [Razan] has plagiarized his talk about "the heart" from the Buddhist sutras. The Ways that gods transmitted to gods are the Sōgen 宗源 and the Saigen 齋源 schools of Ame no Koyane no mikoto 天兒屋根命 and Ame no Futodama no mikoto 天太玉命. These are quite different from the Confucian theories that [equate the gods with] the innate capacities of the two *qi*, or [with] the traces of creative transformation. If [Razan] thought that he himself was [the spokesman of] our national Shinto, then he lost himself. If he made [Shinto] fit his own [ideas], then he lost this (i.e. Shinto). What he seems to be calling Shinto must be regarded with suspicion.

Both Jakuhon and Chōon also criticize Razan for being inconsistent. On the one hand, they say, Razan claims that when a man dies, his *qi* dissolves and his soul disappears. On the other hand, Razan seems to believe in ancestral sacrifice, as is witnessed by his paraphrase of the *locus classicus* in the *Doctrine of the Mean* (*Zhongyong* 中庸 16): "When someone who is sacrificing to his ancestors maintains perfect sincerity, then [the ancestral spirits] 'will be all over'; it will be as if one sees them, 'as if they are present'". Quite correctly, Jakuhon comments: "When he treats something that is not present as *seeming* to be visible and *seeming* to be present, he is not being sincere, he is distorting [the truth]."[52]

A second instance of Razan's inconsistency, mentioned in *Gobusshin-ron* but not in *Bengi*, is that he denies rebirth, but accepts that *tengu* 天狗 (a class of demonic beings) are former (dead and therefore reincarnated) emperors and monks. In *Bengi*, Jakuhon merely remarks, after quoting the long section in *Jinja-kō* about *tengu*, that Razan relies on "slanderous words" and "popular rumors," and more specifically on *Taiheiki* 太平記 (*Record of Great Peace*).[53]

Jinja-kō bengi and *Fusō gobusshin ron* address many more topics and issues than the few I have treated above; curious readers will have to read the texts for themselves. However, the figure of Shōtoku Taishi, the relative positions of Shinto, Buddhism and Confucianism, and the definition of "gods" are the central issues in the adversarial strand of Buddhist-Confucian polemics these texts represent.

Conclusions

The discussions introduced above clearly show that there was an intellectual continuum between Confucians and Buddhist monks. They may have disagreed, but they certainly read each other's books and communicated with each other. This having been said, many problems remain that should be the object of further research. I will mention three.

First, how did these adversarial, antagonistic polemics relate to the other two positions outlined in the introduction? For the Buddhist clergy and Confucian scholars involved, the importance of these polemics ("the battle for Shinto") must have been self-evident, but one wonders how much appeal these polemics actually had outside the intellectual circles that produced them. *Ju-butsu mondō* and *Denchū mondō* (never printed) were written in a fairly simple kind of classical Japanese, which indicates that a wider audience was intended, but few copies survive (sixteen and thirty-nine, respectively). On the other hand, judging by the number of surviving copies (easily more than one hundred), *Honchō jinja kō* was a bestseller, but this was due, probably, to its value as a handbook on shrines, rather than to its polemical content. The two editions of *Jinja-kō bengi* together only come to sixteen surviving copies,[54] and *Gobusshin-ron* was never printed. On the whole, it therefore seems, outside interest was meagre. Question: how was the situation for the other types of polemics?

Second, if we assume the intended audience to have been the *bushi* 武士, daimyo, and *bakufu*, can any relation be established between the contents of these polemics and the competition for influence, patronage, and money that was going on between the Buddhist priests and the Confucian intellectuals? As we saw, Ninchō advised against engaging in polemics. Why did the Buddhists not heed his advice and ignore the Confucians? And, *if* they wanted to engage in polemics, why did they not address those aspects of Confucianism that in principle undermined the position of the ruling class, such as its insistence on meritocracy and on applying correct rules for adoption, burial, etc.? These were the areas in which Chinese norms and Japanese realities clashed most fiercely, but they remain unmentioned.

Politically speaking, the Buddhists' strongest card was Crown Prince Shōtoku. He was the ideal symbol of the conciliatory approach that *ex hypothesi* would please the authorities. He was of imperial descent, and in the course of the middle ages he had become a cult figure in his own right. With his simile of the tree, he was able to weld together the Three Ways and to symbolize their basic unity. It is understandable, therefore, that Shōtoku's importance is stressed by Jakuhon and Chōon; Razan clearly took a risk when he attacked him.

Third, can these polemics be regarded as symptoms of a process of gradual secularization, related to a growing influence of Confucianism? It cannot be denied that the Confucians made some inroads on the Buddhist position. Though individual officials were hardly likely to be swayed in their opinions by books written in Sino-Japanese (*kanbun* 漢文), a few did take a personal interest in Confucianism. Some daimyo even tried to put it into practice, the best known examples being Tokugawa Mitsukuni 德川光圀 (1628–1700), daimyo of Mito 水戸藩, and Ikeda Mitsumasa 池田光政 (1609–82), daimyo of Okayama 岡山藩.

There were other indications of increasing influence: In the course of the seventeenth century, Confucian scholars replaced Buddhist monks as tutors and clerks of the daimyo and *bakufu*; all samurai who attended the domain schools (*hankō* 藩校) received a Confucian education; and the number of Confucian private academies increased. At the end, the Meiji Restoration was in many respects a Confucian revolution; minds must have been prepared for that. The question remains, however, whether these trends were also perceived by the contemporaries and, if they were, whether the Buddhist camp considered them a threat. And, finally, one must ask whether there is a link between those possible perceptions and the contents of the Buddhist-Confucian polemics.

8

Ikeda Mitsumasa and Confucian Ritual

James McMullen

During the early Tokugawa period, several Japanese feudal rulers attempted to realize Confucian ideals of governance and to implement Confucian style rites of passage and administrative control in their domains. Four daimyo, in particular, have been recognized for this role: Tokugawa Mitsukuni 徳川光圀 (1628–1700) of Mito 水戸藩; Ikeda Mitsumasa 池田光政 (1609–82) of Okayama 岡山藩; Hoshina Masayuki 保科正之 (1611–72) of Aizu 会津藩; and Maeda Tsunanori 前田綱紀 (1643–1724) of Kaga domain 加賀藩.[1] These men have been grouped together as the illustrious lords (*meikun* 名君) of the early Tokugawa period. According to Azuma Jūji, they "demonstrated a strong concern not only with Confucian 'thought,' but also with its 'rituals' (*girei* 儀礼)."[2] Mitsumasa's reputation in particular spread beyond Japan; he is mentioned for instance in Engelbert Kaempfer's (1651–1716) account of the country.[3] For J. W. Hall (1916–97), he was a "great daimyo," whose rulership embodied "benevolent authoritarianism based on Confucian principles of government."[4] This chapter pursues Mitsumasa's interest in Confucian ritual. It argues that among the Confucian-minded illustrious lords, he initiated the most radical program of Confucianization. Notably, he extended the project to the ritual veneration of Confucius himself.

Mitsumasa publicly dedicated his life to Confucianism. Symbolically, on his journeys to and from Edo he took with him in mulberry wooden chests the canonical *Notes and Commentaries on Thirteen Classics* (*Shihsan jing jusu* 十三経注疏). His commitment is illustrated by his new year's *essai de plume* (*Gantan shihitsu* 元旦試筆) of 1676:

> I vow to illumine true righteousness
> Broadly, to foster a flock of outstanding men
> Above, to honor the chief virtues,
> Below, to foster the common people,
> O that, morning and night,
> I may not dishonor those who gave me birth,
> That the Confucian Way may rise and prosper
> And the realm may be at peace.[5]

Mitsumasa's Confucian mission statement, written at the age of sixty-eight, is deeply felt, retrospective, and, given his life story, carries a nuance of defiance. If the term

Figure 8.1 Ikeda Mitsumasa.[6] Image: Wikimedia Commons.

"existential" is defined as what an individual "makes himself by the self-development of his essence," then Mitsumasa's attempt to live his life by Confucian precepts, and to realize Confucian ideals both as person and as ruler, suggests this quality.[7]

The narrative that follows will confirm the religious character of Mitsumasa's Confucian thinking. Over his long experience of the tradition, however, his approach to rulership and his thinking changed. Five main phases, with some overlap, may be distinguished:

1. The Shingaku years, when Mitsumasa first looked to Confucianism as a gospel of social harmony and personal moral empowerment (later 1640s to 1654, but surviving thereafter as a private faith);
2. The evocation of Confucian humanism to justify an open-handed approach to relief from natural disaster, accompanied by tightened administrative control over the Okayama domain (early to mid-1650s);
3. A display of personal Confucian ancestor worship, accompanied by a shift of Confucian sectarian allegiance (from mid-1650s to later 1660s)
4. An overt program of Confucianization by building rural literacy schools and by promoting Confucian funerals and ancestor worship, culminating in a rite to venerate Confucius (later 1660s up til 1671);
5. The dismantling of his Confucianization programme by his son after Mitsumasa's retirement (1672 to 1682).

The chapter concludes with a discussion of the general features and problems of Mitsumasa's approach to Confucianism.

Phase 1: Mitsumasa's Early Engagement with Shingaku

Mitsumasa's was a *tozama* daimyo of a substantial domain, but linked to the ruling Tokugawa house by marriage, a relationship that protected him and at the same time allowed him a certain confident independence. His serious introduction to Confucianism took place in his thirties with a "soft" version of Neo-Confucianism that stressed individual moral empowerment. He owed this to Kumazawa Banzan 熊沢蕃山 (1619–91), a forceful Confucian scholar ten years his junior. Banzan had served Mitsumasa as a teenage page. During an interlude away from Okayama he became acquainted both with rural life and poverty, as well as with the distinctive Neo-Confucian practice known as Shingaku 心学 (Learning of the mind) advocated by Nakae Tōju 中江藤樹 (1608–48) in Ōtsu. Tōju was a follower of the Ming Chinese philosopher Wang Yangming 王陽明 (1472–1528). His "soft" Neo-Confucianism stressed followers' motivational "mind" over conformity to objective rules or institutions. Domestic rituals should be "clear and simple"; ritual practice was identified subjectively as "follow[ing] the moral knowledge in our hearts."[8]

Returning to Okayama around 1645, Banzan communicated Tōju's Shingaku to Mitsumasa, who greeted the practice as "like the promise of rain in a great drought."[9] He formed a lifelong respect for Tōju that can only be described as religious:

> On his journeys to and from Edo he visited Ōtsu and granted him audience or, inviting him to his inn, provided a repast and held quiet conversation. After his death, he placed his spirit tablet in the western enceinte of his castle.[10]

From the late 1640s, Mitsumasa's Confucian "aspirations" took shape within the military organization of his vassal household. He created a loosely formed unit of samurai called the Flower Meadow (Hanabatake 花畠) group or New Brigade (Shingumi 新組), led by Banzan.[11] This community pursued Confucian moral self-realization and the extension of "good knowledge," a faculty akin to conscience. Its members sought to "grow together in teaching and study, and together bear the fruits of sagehood."[12] There is, however, no evidence of any ritual veneration of Confucius. Nor does Mitsumasa seem to have embraced Confucian ritual at this time; in fact, the Ikeda ancestral rites appear to have continued on Buddhist premises during this period.[13]

Nonetheless, the creation of the Hanabatake group may be claimed as Mitsumasa's first step in applying Confucian tenets to governance. The group was distinctive; it recruited students not only from Okayama samurai, but from outside the Okayama feudal community, "easterners in large numbers" and "many *rōnin*."[14] The staff was also chiefly recruited from outside the domain, many from the family and disciples of Tōju himself.[15] As the Okayama scholar Ōsawa Sadao 大沢貞夫 (1698–1771) put it, Mitsumasa "devoted his energy to good government, and so made obtaining [men of] cleverness and talent his task. Therefore outstanding and excellent men gathered at the domain capital."[16] Confucian universalism taught that men who mastered the teaching be meritocratically rewarded with administrative office. Applied to the "easterners" and "*rōnin*" of the New Brigade, this policy constituted a Confucian challenge to the hierarchical hereditary privileges of feudal domain society.

Phase 2: Mitsumasa's Evolving Approach to Governance

The death of the third Tokugawa shogun Iemitsu in 1651 and the accession of Ietsuna, who was still a minor, precipitated a crisis for the regime. Abroad, the Manchu conquest of China in 1644 suggested the possibility of an invasion of Japan; domestically, the samurai revolts of Yui Shōsetsu 由井正雪 (1651) and Betsuki Shōsaemon 別木庄左衛門 (1652) shook the regime and led to calls for a tightening of *bakufu* ideological control.[17] Followers of Banzan were identified as participants. His subjectivist Confucianism was condemned by the senior councilor (*rōjū*) Matsudaira Nobutsuna 松平信綱 (1596–1662) on the grounds of making men "insubordinate."[18] Mitsumasa was urged by the *bakufu* to suppress the public role of Shingaku in Okayama and had little alternative, however reluctantly, to comply. On 1654/8/19, he forbad his vassals to study Confucianism as a group activity, because "the household becomes carried away, as though in the thrall of a decoy."[19]

A second major crisis, however, paradoxically intensified Mitsumasa's commitment to Confucianism. In 1653 a flood damaged the Okayama castle town and the surrounding area, resulting in loss of life, starvation, and deaths. Mitsumasa introspectively linked the suffering to his own confessed failures as a Confucian benevolent ruler. Compassionately conducted disaster relief measures brought Banzan's "soft" Confucianism to the fore and represented a peak in his influence over Mitsumasa. The next few years saw heightened Confucian rhetoric and a paternalism that would treat the people in the canonical phrase "like a child."[20] Mitsumasa attacked the "misapprehension" among his vassals that peasants should eat "rice bran, and the beard of wheat for their food." He invoked a Confucian belief in a universal humanity: "since peasants also are all men, they ought to eat rice."[21]

The same period saw another, more institutional form of Confucian influence that was also based on Confucian humanism attributed to Banzan: temporary adoption of a Confucian redistribution of wealth, involving a 10 percent fiscal rate and a flat rate of taxation to save the burden of annual assessments.[22] Such policies inflamed resentment among Mitsumasa's vassals. Banzan's position became insecure; in 1657 he resigned.

The Beginnings of a Change in Thinking

From around the mid-1650s, probably in response partly to the *bakufu*'s intervention and partly to enhance his own power within the domain, Mitsumasa showed signs of rethinking the nature of Confucian authority. Implicitly repudiating any sense of potentially subversive autonomy that his subjects might derive from Shingaku, he interposed himself between Shingaku and the authority delegated to him from the shogun, and stressed personal loyalty to himself.[23] "This province is my province," he told his vassals: "notwithstanding, to tell people that the Mitsumasa style is forbidden [...] is surely simply to put one's lord to one side."[24] Reconstruction following the flood offered Mitsumasa an opportunity to consolidate autocratic, authoritarian power over his vassals and the various strata of rural society, and at the same time to pursue the vision of his domain as a Confucianized community.[25] This gathering of power in the ruler's hands was consistent with Confucian models of paternalistic autocracy delegated to officials chosen for their ability. Mitsumasa's New Brigade, it seems, had begun to bear fruit. A new structure of rural administration through centrally appointed local deputies (*daikan* 代官) drew on the men from the New Brigade to strengthen Mitsumasa's control. It has been suggested that these measures, dated to the early 1660s, were based on Banzan's proposals.[26]

Rituals of Filial Piety

Mitsumasa, however, proceeded cautiously over the promotion of overtly Confucian measures. He began from politically innocuous but symbolic gestures in his own ancestor worship, an early indication of his intensified commitment to "visible Confucianism"[27] not long after the flood. In 1655/2/15, he led a group of senior housemen and others in a ceremony within Okayama castle in the presence of newly-made ancestral Confucian spirit tablets of his ancestors.[28] This constituted a dramatic break with the Buddhist ritual culture of the past, as Mitsumasa himself noted in his invocation:

> Before now, my sacrifices to ancestors have wholly been entrusted to Buddhists, and have not on my part exhausted sincerity and respect. Now I believe in the Way of the Sage and desire to erect a new lineage shrine and myself offer sacrifice and worship. However, because of crop failure and famine, I have not been able to effect this reform. And so roughly following the old [Confucian] system I have provisionally made tablets and for the first time use the mid-spring month respectfully to make offerings.[29]

This Confucian ceremony was only a beginning. In 1658 a disciple of Tōju was appointed "magistrate for the daimyo's ancestral shrine" (*gōbyō bugyō* 御廟奉行), and a ruler's ancestral shrine was built in the second enceinte of Okayama castle shrine. It consisted of a hall with three feretories. Two were built for Mitsumasa's ancestors, his grandfather Terumasa 池田輝政 (1564–1613) and his father Toshitaka 池田利隆 (1584–1616), together with their wives. One was reserved for Mitsumasa himself. This shrine became the main site of Mitsumasa's Confucian filial religiosity, with regular visits on new year's day. A climax came in 1667 with the exhumation of the previous two generations of Ikeda ancestors at Myōshinji 妙心寺 in Kyoto and their Confucian-style reinterment at Waidani 和意谷 in the west of Okayama domain (see Figure 8.2).[30]

Figure 8.2 Ikeda tombs at Waidani.³¹ Image: Wikimedia Commons.

Phase 3: Public Shift of Confucian Sectarian Allegiance

Mitsumasa's new interest in political realism was consolidated from the mid-1650s in a shift from Shingaku towards the less subjective Neo-Confucian school of Zhu Xi 朱熹 (1130–1200). According to an eighteenth-century source, Mitsumasa had concluded that "though Wang [Yangming learning] was easily intelligible, it did not have much [to offer to] government, and he embraced the learning of Zhu [Xi]."³² Mitsumasa's choice of personal guidance was a group of Neo-Confucian scholars associated with the influential Kyoto commoner and orthodox Zhu Xi Neo-Confucian teacher, Nakamura Tekisai 中村惕斎 (1629–1702). This school attached importance to the outward objectification of "visible Confucianism," chiefly in the form of ritual, which it believed to have transformative power. It was also vigorously anti-Buddhist and critical of the *bakufu*'s use of Buddhist temples as official sites of certification (*terauke* 寺請) for the population. From 1656, Zhu Xi scholars were summoned to Okayama. Among them, Ichiura Kisai 市浦毅斎 (1642–1712) was the "central person" who instructed Mitsumasa on Zhu Xi learning. Subsequently he became his main Confucian advisor and replaced Banzan in Mitsumasa's counsels.³³

Consistently with this change of allegiance Mitsumasa adopted a harder-edged, top-down dependence on administrative and political authority. This rigor contrasted with the "soft" Shingaku subjectivism that Mitsumasa attributed to Banzan and later angrily condemned as the product of a "darkened mind."³⁴

Phase 4: Converting the Okayama Domain—Religious Reform, Confucian Education, Ritual, and the Peasantry

Mitsumasa's new reading of Confucian tradition, however, was not expressed in administrative policy until the mid-1660s, over a decade after his embrace of Zhu Xi Neo-Confucianism. Perhaps he remained wary of the *bakufu*'s earlier intervention to suppress the moral empowerment offered by his Shingaku Neo-Confucianism. However, the deaths of Matsudaira Nobutsuna and Sakai Tadakatsu 酒井忠勝 (1587–1662) in 1662 may have mitigated these constraints. Ichiura Kisai seems to have been absent temporarily in the interim period, and lack of Confucian advice might conceivably have delayed Mitsumasa's Confucianization program.[35] A more adventitious, but not mutually exclusive, cause is advanced in Stefan Köck's contribution to this volume: the *bakufu*'s legislation concerning Buddhism and Shinto and interdiction of the Fujufuse branch 不受不施派 of Nichiren 日蓮 Buddhism in 1665. These measures may have given Mitsumasa the sanction to initiate a wider reform of Buddhism and Shinto in Okayama and to promote Confucianism. It also seems circumstantially possible that the reform of Buddhism implemented in his Mito domain by Tokugawa Mitsukuni slightly earlier than Mitsumasa's own might have prompted Mitsumasa's action at this time.[36] Whatever the case, from 1665 Mitsumasa embarked on a bold mission to convert his domain to Confucianism.

There were two aspects to this policy, both congruent with the beliefs of Nakamura Tekisai. The first, negative, consisted of a concerted campaign to reduce the power of Buddhism, the strong religious and ideological rival to Confucianism within the domain. This was associated with the shift of religious certification from Buddhist temples to Shinto shrines (*shintō-uke* 神道請). This important measure, the theme of Köck's chapter, needs only brief mention here, beyond the reminder that from late 1666 and continuing until 1667/3, Buddhist monks were encouraged to resign their status and 583 of an original 1,044 temples were closed. Simultaneously, Mitsumasa ordered the drastic reform of Shinto shrines, closing and amalgamating 10,528 "illicit" shrines to reduce the total of shrines to 683. Mitsumasa's motivation for these religious reforms is usually attributed to the influence of Banzan. Their views of Buddhism as unfilial and immoral were similar, though Banzan, now no longer in Mitsumasa's service, protested the coercive implementation of the reforms.[37] With regard to "illicit" Shinto shrines, Mitsumasa's case for reform is recorded in domain sources as moral, based on condemnation of their venal sale of cures to the peasantry.[38] But he seems likely to have shared Banzan's view that pristine Japanese Shinto was identical to the transcendent teaching of Chinese Sages.[39] Mitsumasa's active patronage of reformed and amalgamated shrines in Okayama is confirmed by the invitation of Kyoto court musicians in 1669 to teach music to Shinto priests "from throughout the province" to enhance Shinto "worship."[40]

Tenaraisho

The second aspect of Mitsumasa's Confucianizing policy complemented his reforms. It was an attempt to promote Confucian beliefs and practices among the populace chiefly by education and ritual. Informing both, historians have seen not only religious motivation, but also Mitsumasa's desire to create a submissive and harmonious society under his autocratic rule. In the sphere of education, rural literacy schools (*tenaraisho* 手習所) had been founded in 123 places by 1668, staffed mainly from the village-head (*shōya* 庄屋) stratum, and by Shinto priests, doctors, occasionally *rōnin*, and others. These schools served a practical end: to secure the literacy essential for efficient rural administration threatened by Mitsumasa's assault on Buddhist temples and their associated schools. But this measure was certainly also driven by Mitsumasa's Confucian idealistic moral mission. Teaching of filial piety in the *tenaraisho* suggests an attempt to wrest this value from Buddhism and to provide the underpinnings of submissive rural society. His Confucian hopes for these schools were articulated in "a verbal memorandum for the persuasion of village heads and peasants" dated 1673/2/29 by his right-hand man Tsuda Nagatada 津田永忠 (1640–1707), according to which Mitsumasa stipulated that it would be "to the benefit of the moral climate of the rural districts," if talented peasant children would acquire literacy and numeracy, understand the Confucian *Four Books* and *Lesser Learning*, perform filial piety to their parents, and respect their superiors and the laws.[41]

Confucian Rituals

The *tenaraisho* did not directly impose Confucian practices on the populace of the Okayama domain. Confucian familial rituals associated with death, burial, and ancestor worship, however, offered a direct means to this end. This policy implemented an utterance of Confucius himself favored by Nakamura Tekisai: "Let there be a careful attention to perform the funeral rites to parents, and let them be followed when long gone with the ceremonies of sacrifice—then the virtue of the people will resume its proper excellence."[42] In 1666/7, Mitsumasa conferred rewards for adopting Confucian conduct.[43] In the next month, the domain issued an official notice entitled *Ceremonials for Obsequies and Worship* (*Sōsai no gi* 葬祭の儀).[44] This document prescribes procedures for burial after a family death and for "mid-autumn veneration" to ancestors. Instructions for the former concern treatment of the dying person, laying out and dressing of the corpse, preparation of the spirit tablet, encoffining, burial, wording of the accompanying prayer, return home of the bereaved and installation of the spirit tablet, construction of the tomb and burial stele, and subsequent ritual care of the spirit with incense and food offerings on the anniversary of the death. A special section prescribed a grave-side ceremony in the third month. For each stage, *Zhu Xi's Family Rituals* (*Zhuzi jiali* 朱子家礼) is held up as guidance for the bereaved "according to their circumstances." This text—the "chief *vademecum* of the people for their domestic rites and ceremonies"[45] in China—sacralized a rigidly patrilineal kinship organization throughout society. It also polemically condemned Buddhist cremation as a "desecration of the corpse."[46]

The final section of the directive prescribes a collective Confucian-style village ancestor worship ceremony for "the lowly people" (*kamin* 下民).[47] Patrilineally related groups should assemble their spirit tablets and "one of the group leader's lineage" (*sōryō suji* 総領筋) should "light incense and pour sake onto a tray of sand and reeds"; this libation should also be performed thrice in front of the other tablets. "Wives and children, as their hearts incline them, should attend the place of sacrifice and help in the sacrifice in whatever respect is appropriate. The offerings should be consumed back at home."[48]

Light on the thinking behind these ritual measures is shed by a second memorandum by Tsuda dated to 1673/2/29.[49] Tsuda judged that both mid-autumn sacrifices and funerals served the end of anti-Christian inquisition, for "without these two practices, there is no evidence of religious belief." Village deaths offered the village head an opportunity to observe behavior; Christians behaved distinctively around deaths. Village heads' personal attendance at minor peasants' obsequies also fostered communal closeness and obedience. The mid-autumn sacrifice, like the Buddhist *bon* 盆, should promote solidarity among kindred. Since it involved peasants who work relentlessly all year round, "it is fine for them to desist from agricultural occupations for this one day and divert themselves as they wish."[50]

Other propaganda wooed the populace to Confucian practices. In 1667, a polemical tract, *Sōsai benron* 葬祭辨論,[51] published in Kyoto argued that deputing funeral obsequies to Buddhists for payment was grossly unfilial and again pressed *Zhu Xi's Family Rituals* as a model. However, despite these efforts it is worth remarking that Mitsumasa's promotion of Confucian beliefs and practices in Okayama rural society compared, say, to neighboring Korea, was relatively superficial. No ritual veneration of Confucius himself was required of the Okayama rural population.[52]

Samurai Education and the Ritual Veneration of Confucius: Mitsumasa's Climactic *yomizome*

Confucian doctrine held that moral suasion and the exemplary conduct of those in authority constituted the appropriate way to improve society. On 1666/10/7 Mitsumasa ordered the establishment of a temporary school (*kari gakkan* 仮学館) in the western enceinte of Okayama castle for the samurai of his domain. It was staffed mainly by his newly appointed scholars of the Zhu Xi school; the curriculum was Confucian. However, there is still no evidence of any ceremony to venerate Confucius at this institution.[53]

This *kari gakkan* had 106 students and was soon found to be too cramped. On 1668/12/24 Mitsumasa ordered construction of larger premises on a more spacious site.[54] The curriculum again centered on Zhu Xi Neo-Confucianism,[55] but the school contained no separate Sage's Hall for venerating Confucius. However, on 1669/7/25, a formal opening of the still incomplete school in the form of ritual veneration and offering to Confucius took place.[56] Mitsumasa was in Edo, but invited Banzan, still in his personal favor, to Okayama to lead the ceremony. A scroll in the hand of Nakae Tōju, "Perfect Sage King of Culture Universal" (*Shisei bunsen'ō* 至聖文宣王), symbolized Mitsumasa's tenacious continuity with the past of Confucianism in the domain. The ceremony itself consisted of Banzan lighting incense and bowing twice, all present making obeisance to the scroll, recitation of a passage of the *Classic of Filial Piety,* and distribution of offerings. Though this was liturgically perfunctory,[57] it was attended by a total of 164 senior domain personnel and students. For the first documented time, the spirit of Confucius was admitted into the domain pantheon. Similar gestures followed. A few months after the inaugural rite, on the school's completion on 1669/9/20, Mitsumasa's son Tsunamasa 池田綱政 (1638–1714) offered incense and bowed to the Sage's altar. In the following days, he visited the school and audited lectures.[58] Banzan remained in Okayama into the next year, and on 1670/1/5 presided at a school ceremony to venerate Confucius similar to the one he had led the previous year, referred to in the domain records as a "first reading [of the Confucian classic in the new year]" (*yomizome* 読初) and "new year ceremony for start of work" (*nenshu kaigyō shiki* 年首開業式). In 1670, Mitsumasa himself, returned from Edo, on 5/14, audited a lecture and inspected the school buildings.[59]

But neither Mitsumasa nor his heir had hitherto personally performed any significant public sacrificial act to venerate Confucius. The following new year, however, saw a dramatic change. On 1671/1/2 Mitsumasa personally endorsed the sacrifice to Confucius in his domain school in the presence of the domain samurai hierarchy. He did so, however, not in the conventional Confucian way—a formal *sekiten* 釈奠 or *sekisai* 釈菜 ceremony—but in a form referred to in the domain records as *yomizome*, like Banzan's of the previous year.[60]

> The Lord [Mitsumasa] attended at the school, washed his hands and gargled. He proceeded before the Sage, offered incense and prostrated himself making two bows. He performed the first reading of the opening chapter of the *Classic of Filial Piety*; when done he took his seat on the lower floor of the middle room. [Following further reading and exposition of the *Classic*, . . .] [Hiki] Samon 日置左門 (1648–1718) removed the offerings and placed them in the center of the middle room, and the Lord washed his hands and gargled and received the offerings with his own hands.[61]

Next, most saliently, Mitsumasa himself, acting symbolically as steward of a beneficent Confucian natural order and as Confucian benevolent lord, distributed offerings to "all from the Senior Council on down [. . .] to captains of guards and personal attendants." Further offerings were distributed by his most trusted lieutenants, Tsuda Nagatada (school magistrate at this time) and Nakae Yasaburō 中江弥三郎 (1648–1709; Nakae Tōju's third son), to students and by other officials, musicians, school officers and even "children" (*sc.* "common country people attending the school").[62]

The new year of 1671 was Mitsumasa's last as daimyo in Okayama. A few months later he left for residence in Edo. There, on 1672/6/11, he submitted his resignation to the shogun, ceding power to Tsunamasa. The new year's *yomizome* ritual of 1671, therefore, was a climactic event and the only instance of Mitsumasa's participation in public sacrifice to Confucius.[63] The immediate liturgical precedent for this ceremony seems to have been Banzan's 1670 new year *yomizome* ceremony. But this was Banzan's ceremony writ large and carried a far more potent symbolic significance. The new year was when the ruler orientated himself to the cosmic powers, to his ancestors, and as lord over his domain. The daimyo's performance of the leading liturgical role in a service of homage and sacrifice to Confucius on this day in the presence of his domain hierarchy signaled the central place that he had identified for Confucianism to sanctify the life of Okayama domain. Yet, he performed it only on this one occasion, and that shortly before relinquishing office. It should be seen as the crowning measure of his Confucianization of Okayama and at same time a defiant valedictory gesture.

Confucianization: Success or Failure?

Contemporary testimony on Mitsumasa's attempt to Confucianize his domain is partisan and contradictory. In 1667/3, Mitsumasa himself wrote to the *bakufu* claiming widespread disaffection with Buddhism in his domain:

> Though of course there are local variations, in recent years the people of the province have despaired of the monks through their private greed fooling others, and persons preferring Confucianism preponderate everywhere.[64]

But he also admitted some excess in administering the policy.[65] Another contemporary witness, however, claimed success: the Confucian Matsubara Issei 松原一清 (dates unknown), on a stay in Ushimado village 牛窓村 of Okayama domain in 1669, reported in his *Effusions* (*Shusshi kō* 出思稿):

> Funerals and worship throughout the province follow *Zhu Xi's Family Rituals* and those who use Buddhist methods do not amount to one or two in every hundred. [...] The ruler of this province has rejected heterodoxy and has promoted Confucian learning. The people of the province joyfully and readily follow him.[66]

An alternative (but not exclusive) explanation discussed by Ikeda Mitsumasa's biographer Taniguchi Sumio 谷口澄夫 (1913–2001) attributes enthusiasm for Confucianism in this area to lateral influence on funerals across the Inland Sea from Tosa and the Confucian Nonaka Kenzan 野中兼山 (1615–63) who promoted Confucian burial there.[67]

Some Buddhists, unsurprisingly, responded to Mitsumasa's Confucian policies unfavorably. They confidentially told *bakufu* inspectors:

> Our ancestral religion has been quite wiped out. We have been asked to follow Confucianism, of which we knew nothing previously. [...] Many suicides have resulted among monks and laity.[68]

Criticism came also from Kumazawa Banzan, bitterly alienated from Mitsumasa from the time of the latter's retirement. He is said to have unsuccessfully protested that "although the authorities have not taken the trouble to transform [the Buddhists] by virtue, they have inflicted suffering on them."[69] He judged that Mitsumasa was guilty of failing in respect of the "deep love like holding an infant" required of a ruler, and of not knowing the "true Way" and the "human feelings that are the basis of government."[70] In short, to Banzan Mitsumasa represented an unacceptable "hard" Confucianism and moral failure.

Phase 5: Tsunamasa's Change of Style

The most telling verdict concerning Mitsumasa's attempted Confucianization policies, however, comes after his retirement from his heir Tsunamasa and his associates. Mitsumasa had devoted great effort on Tsunamasa's education. Confucian strictures, moreover, required that a son not depart from the "way" of his father for three years after his death.[71] Indeed, Tsunamasa was reported by Kaempfer still to be "following his father's path."[72] And not long before his death Mitsumasa had observed to his "great pleasure" that his son's "aspirations have for the most part become like mine."[73]

Mitsumasa's euphoria was misplaced. Tsunamasa did not share his father's passionate Confucian convictions, but was a Buddhist, an aesthete rather than a moralist, and despotic rather than philanthropic.[74] Under his rule, his father's one-off domain-wide new year *yomizome* settled back into a regular intramural rite for students held significantly later, on the fifth day of the new year.[75] After consultation with the great councilor Sakai Tadakiyo 酒井忠清 (1627–81), Tsunamasa drastically reduced funding and student numbers at the domain school. By 1675, the rural elementary schools had been abandoned. Professedly, the motivation was in part financial, but Taniguchi asserts that Tsunamasa's aversion to Confucianism was a major reason.[76] Mitsumasa, feeling hurtfully betrayed, responded with a moving but ineffectual letter of reproach to his son.

A few weeks before Mitsumasa's death, however, on 1682/2/16, Tsunamasa inaugurated the first formal *sekisai* in Okayama at the domain school.[77] The ceremony, designed by Ichiura Kisai, may have been intended as solace to Tsunamasa's dying father.[78] But this was a very different ceremony from Mitsumasa's encompassing *yomizome* of 1671.[79] Liturgically, Tsunamasa finally repudiated his father's links with Shingaku. The scroll extolling Confucius in Tōju's hand was replaced with one in the hand of Tsunamasa, who thus symbolically took possession of the rite, but whose own participation was minimal. He led the ceremony, but returned to the castle "when the rite was finished" and did not stay for the ensuing lecture, the "receipt of the oblations," or the feast for "the officials of the department concerned."[80]

These features point to a diminished commitment to Confucianism. Tsunamasa's *sekisai* seems to have been influenced by the climate of Hayashi *sekisai* ceremonies at the Shinobugaoka 忍ヶ丘 Shrine in Edo, the place of Tsunamasa's socialization. There is little around Tsunamasa's Okayama *sekisai* to suggest his father's intense Confucian mission. It belongs, rather, to the category of a ritual of "cultural display," a fashionable aesthetic and cultural exercise, a cultural affectation. It had rather little purchase on the values and functioning of the wider society under Tsunamasa's reputedly harsh administration.

Conclusion

Mitsumasa pioneered the application of Confucian ideals and practices to governance in the early Tokugawa period. Circumstances made this project complex and even at times risky. As Kate Nakai has argued, Confucianism ultimately remained a "nontranscendental sociopolitical philosophy firmly rooted in the fabric of Chinese society and history." Its practice in Japan required "total faith."[81] The gap between the Chinese ideal Confucian society and the reality of the Japanese late feudal order caused especially great problems for such a temperamentally idealistic and tenacious man as Mitsumasa. The Confucian ideal privileged meritocratic, universalistic, and achievement-based bureaucratic civil values rather than their martial equivalents. The values of Japanese late feudal society were hereditary, particularistic, and ascriptive. Culturally and politically, Tokugawa Japan was martial, oligarchic, its order backed by the threat of violence, highly authoritarian, and instrumental. In mid-seventeenth century Japan, especially in the military estate, attitudes to the tradition were generally unsympathetic and inhospitable. Influential leaders of the Tokugawa *bakufu*—men such as Matsudaira Nobutsuna, Sakai Tadakatsu or Doi Toshikatsu 土井利勝 (1573–1644)—were "actually almost entirely uncomprehending concerning [Confucian] learning."[82] In times of tension, open advocacy of Confucianism risked reprimand from such powerful figures, as Mitsumasa experienced. Nor were lower-ranking warriors necessarily more favorably disposed. Mitsumasa himself had to contend with a senior vassal's objection that Confucian learning was "useless."[83]

Further circumstances complicated the Confucian project in the early Tokugawa period. Japan was a land of religious pluralism with an established religious culture, some elements of which were informed by values at variance with Confucianism while others could be interpreted as congruent. There were rival cults and rituals in Mitsumasa's world: the cult of Tokugawa Ieyasu as Tōshō Daigongen 東照大権現 (Avatar Illuminating the East) in Mitsumasa's own Okayama castle commanded attendance at dawn on the second day of the year.[84] On the day itself, his own ancestral shrine had priority. Shinto, the widespread indigenous tradition among the populace, was often superstitious but, atomized and doctrinally vague, offered potential ground for a syncretic alliance with Confucianism. As Stefan Köck shows, Mitsumasa saw this potential as an opportunity to wrest Shinto from its syncretic association with Buddhism. The elephant in the room, however, was deeply entrenched Buddhism itself. Until the attempted reforms of Mitsumasa and others, Buddhism remained a little challenged pillar of the Tokugawa polity. Yet, although Mitsumasa regarded Buddhism as unfilial, immoral and deluded and tried to reduce its influence in Okayama, he remained culturally imbricated with it. He piously copied Buddhists sutras for the favorable reincarnation of deceased family members and others and ritually visited Buddhist temples at the new year.[85]

The Chinese Neo-Confucianism to which Mitsumasa was dedicated encompassed holistic metaphysical assumptions about the world and the nature of man, as well as personal and family morality. Its norms and rhetoric ideally informed administration, access to political office and the exercise of administrative authority, land distribution, and the distribution of wealth. But it had become fragmented. After the long period of medieval upheaval, Japanese awareness of continental and peninsula developments was initially patchy. A provincial ruler such as Mitsumasa might adventitiously encounter different forms of Confucian doctrine ranging from subjectivist Wang Yangming Shingaku, Mitsumasa's first encounter, to the sterner objectivist school of Zhu Xi.

Against this complex background, Mitsumasa's commitment to Confucianism confronted him with unavoidable choices. He was an idealist to be sure, but neither a Confucian fundamentalist nor unrealistically utopian. He wrestled pragmatically with such problems as the choice of Neo-Confucians sectarian allegiance; the reconciliation of the imperative to "benevolent government" with the need to discipline a restive community, and the appropriate treatment of beliefs and practices that he believed morally confounded. His engagement with Confucianism suggests an evolving understanding but a consistent ambition to disseminate its principal values, especially filial piety. As he grew older, his Confucianism became less hortatory and more authoritarian. He rejected the subjectivist counsels of Banzan in favor of more direct intervention in the lives of his subjects.

But Mitsumasa's approach to such problems was conditioned by further compelling considerations deriving from his own inherited elite status within late feudal society. Mitsumasa not only genuinely aspired to be a Confucian ruler, but also inherited the prestigious role of warrior commander of a provincial army. He was obliged by the *bakufu* to maintain and lead an army ready for the field. He was perhaps aware of possible dissonance between his military and Confucian roles. In 1661, as he embarked on a program of Confucian inspired reform, he wrote in his diary: "there are two great matters of state: one is the military (*gunjin* 軍陣); the other is [ancestral] sacrifice (*sai* 祭)."[86] The introspective, self-demanding, sometimes irritable, aspiring benevolent and compassionate Confucian ruler was also an absolutist and military-style disciplinarian, a warrior ruler determined to protect his patrimony.

In the background was a constant meta-narrative in tension with, or separable from, Confucian ideals: the political survival of the Ikeda lineage in Okayama in the face of a changing socio-political order. This was the story of a ruler faced with multiple practical challenges to his rulership ranging widely from an expanding population and economy, a sometimes resentful feudal household, rising expectations among sectors of the governed, and natural disaster. Mitsumasa needed to secure his authority, legitimacy and honor, both domestically as ruler of his domain and among his elite feudal colleagues. In his perception, Confucianism was the true path, but was also instrumental to this end. He justified his endorsement of Confucian "learning" to unsympathetic senior vassals on the grounds that he had "become aware that it brought benefit to the state."[87] Mitsumasa chose between different styles of Confucianism similarly on the basis of the utility of each to promote harmony, moral rectitude, and loyal submission among his subjects.

What was Mitsumasa's legacy? After his retirement, his attempt to Confucianize his domain was largely dismantled by his son, but not wholly consigned to oblivion. His *tenaraisho* were amalgamated with financial support from his retirement benefice at Shizutani 閑谷. Here, his dream of a Confucianized domain survived, attenuated to a single rural school (*gōgaku* 郷学) which offered Confucian education inclusively to commoners. There, a small but purpose-built Sage's Hall, the first in Okayama domain, was constructed.[88] Mitsumasa, who hunted in the region, visited it several times. After his death, his latter-day Confucian mentor Nakamura Tekisai himself came and subsequently wrote a recension of Zhu Xi's retreat liturgy to venerate Confucius intended for performance at the Hall. Later, a bronze image of Confucius was commissioned for the Sage's Hall and an adjacent Shinto-style shrine to Mitsumasa and a reliquary mound were constructed (see Figure 8.1). His spirit received offerings in a ritual sequence immediately following those devoted to Confucius.[89] This was an early example, albeit local and small scale, of the resolution of the tension between a particularistic warrior daimyo ancestor and universal Confucian cults. Today, Mitsumasa is venerated as a resolute, idealistic, and compassionate ruler, an exemplar to posterity.

Calendars and Graves

Shibukawa Harumi's Criticism of Hoshina Masayuki and Yamazaki Ansai

Hayashi Makoto
Translation by Stefan Köck

Introduction: The Calendar Reform of Shibukawa Harumi

Open a book on the history of science in early modern Japan, and you will find without fail that the Jōkyō calendar (*Jōkyō reki* 貞享暦) was implemented by Shibukawa Harumi 渋川春海 (1639–1715) in 1685 (Jōkyō 2). This was the first calendar reform since the Chinese calendar *Xuanming li* 宣明暦 had been introduced in the mid-Heian period (823 years earlier). It was thus an epoch-making achievement. Accordingly, Harumi has been studied until now primarily as the genius who developed the first Japanese method of calendrical calculation.[1] However, in my own recent biography of Shibukawa Harumi,[2] which focuses on his life and intellectual background, I argue that more attention should be paid to the human networks that unfolded around him during his lifetime. Harumi did not carry out this calendar reform in isolation. He started his calculations only after Hoshina Masayuki 保科正之 (1611–73), the daimyo of Aizu 会津藩 and one of the central political figures in the *bakufu*, urged him to do so.[3] According to my opinion, it was Masayuki who realized the importance of a calendar reform and thus searched for someone capable of carrying it out. Eventually, his choice fell on Harumi. Most earlier studies claim that it "all started with Harumi's genius." In their overemphasis of Harumi's skills, they tend to overlook not only the political intentions of Hoshina Masayuki, but also the general circumstances of the period.

The new calendar was one part of Masayuki's program of political reforms. While not realized in Masayuki's lifetime, the idea of a calendar reform was taken up again by Shogun Tokugawa Tsunayoshi 徳川綱吉 (1646–1709), who continued Masayuki's political path and ordered Harumi to carry it out.

In the course of my research on this topic, I encountered a surprising detail: According to Harumi's principal student Tani Jinzan 谷秦山 (1663–1718), Harumi was severely critical of the funerals and graves of his mentor, Hoshina Masayuki, and his teacher, Yamazaki Ansai 山崎闇斎 (1618–82). This led to my examining their posthumous cults; I present the results in the later part of this chapter. This will include information gathered from the graveyard of Masayuki in Inawashiro 猪苗代 City, Fukushima prefecture, as well as the gravesites of Ansai in Kyoto, and of Harumi in the Shinagawa district of Tokyo.

The general aim of this chapter is to portray the personal network of people around Harumi, which I shall call the "*salon* of Hoshina Masayuki." Its members supported and assisted Harumi wholeheartedly. After Masayuki's death, however, the salon gradually broke apart. These circumstances led to Harumi's eventual criticism of the funeral cults of Masayuki, Ansai, and their Shinto advisor Yoshikawa Koretaru 吉川惟足 (1616–94). In addition, I analyze the epistemological paradigms shared by the intellectual members of this salon. As we will see, these paradigms influenced not only Harumi's reform of the calendar, but also his critique of his mentors' funerals.

The Salon of Hoshina Masayuki

To say that Hoshina Masayuki was the key political figure in the second half of the seventeenth century is certainly no exaggeration. His status as the domain lord of Aizu should not distract from the fact that he continued to support the government as advisor of his nephew, the fourth shogun Tokugawa Ietsuna 徳川家綱 (1641–80). While famed as the benevolent lord of his own domain, Masayuki also abolished surviving customs from the Sengoku period and devised a new framework of shogunal politics, based on his devotion to Zhu Xi Confucianism. He mitigated the prohibition of death-bed adoption in daimyo families, reduced the practice of confiscating and reassigning domains (*kaieki* 改易), investigated and subsequently reduced the causes for uprisings among *rōnin*, abolished the system of keeping hostages in the daimyo residences in Edo (*daimyō shōnin seido* 大名証人制度), and prohibited the practice of retainers committing suicide after the death of their lord (*junshi* 殉死).[4] His reforms also concerned the relations between shogun and daimyo, as well as the daimyo and their retainers, which were to be based on Confucian ideals of lord and subject, rather than on personal loyalties. The warrior nobility was to cease their sole focus on martial accomplishments in favor of becoming politicians familiar with the Confucian classics and endowed with benevolence and virtue. Masayuki is also regarded as the architect of reforms such as fire prevention measures after the great fire of Meireki (1657) or the confirmation of domain property in the Kanbun era (*Kanbun inchi* 寛文印知). On the judicial level, the *Shrine Clauses* (*Jinja jōmoku* 神社条目, also known as *Shosha negi kannushi hatto* 諸社禰宜神主法度) of 1665 might not have been promulgated without Masayuki.[5] Indeed, the extent of Masayuki's influence on the political and intellectual climate of his time was particularly wide-ranging and substantial.

Masayuki's intellectual charisma derived from his wide interest in reading and engaging in lively intellectual discussions. As he suffered from an eye disease, he had retainers read him books, and if any doubts occurred to him, he instantly started a discussion. He invited gifted intellectuals to give lectures at his residence in Edo and engaged in debates with them as well. These lectures attracted a growing number of his retainers and acquaintances, and thus a salon took shape around Masayuki, with its members engaging in intellectual and social exchange. Most of them were erudite retainers familiar with Confucianism and Shinto, including Tomomatsu Ujioki 友松氏

興 (1622–87), Hattori Ankyū 服部安休 (1619–81), Yokota Shun'eki 横田俊益 (1620–1702) and Andō Yūeki 安藤有益 (1624–1708).⁶ In the world of intellectuals, Masayuki conversed not only with Yoshikawa Koretaru and Yamazaki Ansai, but also with *bakufu* Confucianists such as Hayashi Gahō 林鵞峰 (1618–80), his son Hayashi Hōkō 林鳳岡 (1644–1732), and Toki Nagamoto 土岐長元 (1599–1683), who was a *bakufu* physician. He was moreover in close contact with members of the warrior nobility, including Inoue Masatoshi 井上正利 (1606–75), lord of Kasama 笠間藩; Tokugawa Mitsukuni 徳川光圀 (1628–1701), lord of Mito 水戸藩; Maeda Tsunanori 前田綱紀 (1643–1724), lord of Kaga 加賀藩; and Inaba Masanori 稲葉正則 (1623–96), lord of Odawara 小田原藩. We will reencounter these figures in the context of Masayuki's funeral. Shibukawa Harumi frequented Masayuki's salon as well.

Masayuki's devotion to Confucianism, in particular to the works of Zhu Xi 朱子 (1130–1200), was constant throughout his life. In addition, he took an interest in Shinto due to the influence of Yoshikawa Koretaru. Their encounter originated in Masayuki's intention to study the *Nihon shoki*.⁷ At first, he had his retainer Hattori Ankyū—an educated man who had studied Confucianism under Hayashi Razan—read the fascicle on the Age of the Gods (*jindai* 神代) to him, but he soon roared with laughter because of its overall nonsense, rejecting the text as being absurd. However, Toki Nagamoto, who was considered Masayuki's "brain," pointed out that there were various ways to read the *Nihon shoki* and mentioned the name of Koretaru as a specialist giving lectures on the topic. Masayuki immediately dispatched Ankyū to attend some of Koretaru's lectures. Ankyū was struck by Koretaru's erudition and advised Masayuki to hear his words directly. This prompted Masayuki to invite Koretaru to visit him. Let me render this episode in the words of Tani Jinzan's report, *Jinzanshū* 秦山集, based on what he had heard from Shibukawa Harumi:

> Thereupon Masayuki invited Koretaru to lecture on the fascicle on the Age of the Gods of the *Nihon shoki*. The audience included Inoue Masatoshi, Toki Nagamoto,⁸ Nakane Heijūrō, as well as my venerable master (Harumi). Teaching the first session, Koretaru quoted the phrase *ame no michi hitori nasu* 乾道独化 (lit. "heaven-way-single-develop").⁹ According to Koretaru's explanation, this meant that mysterious principles (*genmyō na dōri* 玄妙な道理) emerged piece by piece. Masayuki and Inoue were extremely impressed. Although they belonged to the most educated men of these days, they accepted Koretaru's explanation on the spot. This single point illustrates the superior nature of Koretaru's scholarship. He gave approximately thirty lectures.¹⁰

In this way, Koretaru came to be known as the Shinto advisor of a seventeenth-century "illustrious lord" (*meikun* 名君).¹¹ Without Masayuki, however, Yoshikawa Koretaru would probably not have risen to the post of the first Shinto official (*shintōgata* 神道方) of the *bakufu*. Incidentally, the teaching of Suika Shinto 垂加神道 by Yamazaki Ansai can also be traced to a visit Ansai made to Masayuki's Edo residence. Here, the renown Kyoto intellectual engaged in a debate on Shinto with Hattori Ankyū. Ansai's loss in this debate is said to be the beginning of his interest in Shinto. He too became Koretaru's student right after he met him the first time.

Since Harumi attended the lectures of Koretaru regularly,[12] we must regard him as a member of Masayuki's salon. But at the time of the calendar reform, Harumi was not the only person approached by Masayuki. It seems that Masayuki planned to have Andō Yūeki and Shimada Kakuemon 島田覚右衛門 (dates unknown) do the calculations, and to have Harumi and Yamazaki Ansai supervise them. Thus, the project of the calendar reform started as a work of cooperation and was not the work of Harumi alone.

History of the Chinese Calendar

The Chinese calendar was a symbol of the emperor-centered civilization of China. In a long historical process, the calendar was also transmitted to the tributary kingdoms on the periphery of the empire, which accepted it as a token of cultural sophistication. Kings who adopted the calendar thereby acknowledged Chinese hegemony, even if only in a nominal sense. Usually, they would adjust the calendar at the beginning of each new Chinese dynasty, a custom called "to follow the legitimate rule" (*seisaku o hōjiru* 正朔を奉じる). As long as the ancient Japanese state held formal diplomatic relations with China and the Korean peninsula, it followed this custom and in 862 took over the *Xuanming li*, the calendar Tang China used between 822 and 892. However, after the breakdown of the Tang (907), direct diplomatic and cultural exchange ceased. Thus, Japan continued to use the Tang calendar for 823 years without interruption or change.

The reform of the calendar, which finally materialized as the Jōkyō calendar of 1685, was therefore long overdue. This time, the Japanese did not receive a new calendar from the Chinese emperor. Instead, Harumi developed new calculations from astronomical observations, based on his research of the *Shoushi li* 授時暦, the calendar of the Yuan period (1271–1368), as well as of Western astronomy, which had been introduced to China by Jesuit missionaries such as Matteo Ricci (1552–1610). The impact of these Chinese language versions of Western astronomical knowledge could be felt everywhere in seventeenth-century East Asia. In China and Korea they led to the implementation of the calendar *Shixian li* 時憲暦 in 1646, while in Japan, the Jōkyō calendar was realized a few decades later.

As a member of Masayuki's salon, Harumi naturally worked for Masayuki and respected Koretaru and Ansai as his teachers. They were all passionate readers of the *Nihon shoki* and shared a longing to restore its ancient world. This Japan-centric "restorationism" (*fukkoshugi* 復古主義) must be seen against the backdrop of the Chinese dynastic change from Ming to Qing in 1644, caused by an invasion of the Jurchen (a confederation of Tungusic nomads) in northern China. In Japan, this was perceived as "China's transformation from civilization to barbary" (*ka'i hentai* 華夷変態) and led to an increasing Japan-centric worldview. Harumi, for instance, regarded keeping a Chinese calendar a sign of submission to China. Calculating a new calendar was a tool for reconstructing the world of the *Nihon shoki* for him. In the wake of this restorationist mood of the later seventeenth century, various kinds of Shinto interpretations took shape as well. The teachings of Yoshikawa Koretaru and Yamazaki

Ansai—Yoshikawa Shinto and Suika Shinto, respectively—were merely the most representative examples of this movement. In this sense, we must regard Masayuki's salon as a breeding ground of Shinto ideologies.

Masayuki died in 1672 (Kanbun 12), but he left a will requesting Harumi to undertake a calendar reform. In the following year, Harumi began his preparations for the calendar revision by presenting a petition to Shogun Ietsuna. Unfortunately, however, Harumi's prediction of a solar eclipse proved incorrect, which prompted the great councilor (*tairō* 大老) Sakai Tadakiyo 酒井忠清 (1624–81) to halt the calendar reform. Harumi, however, continued his empirical studies together with Tsuchimikado Yasutomi 土御門泰福 (1655–1717), the hereditary head of the Yin Yang bureau (*onmyō no kami* 陰陽頭) at the imperial court and like Harumi, a student of Ansai.

In 1683 (Tenna 3), Tokugawa Mitsukuni presented an astronomical map prepared by Harumi to Shogun Tsunayoshi. This seems to have caused a revival of the plans to conduct a calendar reform. In the twelfth month of the same year, Tsunayoshi finally gave his consent to the reforms outlined in Harumi's proposals. Since the calendar was ultimately an imperial matter, this information was passed on to the court, where Tsuchimikado Yasutomi offered a detailed plan to Emperor Reigen 霊元天皇 (1654–1732). There was some irritation when, in the third month of 1684 (Jōkyō 1), Reigen Tennō reacted to this with an imperial order to adopt the *Datong li* 大統暦, the calendar of the Ming dynasty, while Harumi's calculations were based on the *Shoushi li* of the Yuan dynasty, as mentioned above. Harumi's subsequent appeal for the adoption of the Yuan-style calendar was finally granted and in the tenth month of 1684 a new imperial order paved the way for the calendar reform of 1685.[13]

The *Nihon chōreki*

Among the works written by Harumi is the *Nihon chōreki* 日本長暦 (*Comprehensive Calendar of Japan*), a chronological table starting with the accession of Jinmu Tennō 神武天皇 and proceeding until Harumi's own times. It contains calculations of long and short months, the cyclical calendar signs for the first day of each month, and the days of the winter solstice. The *Nihon shoki* also provides the cyclical signs of the first day of each month, starting from the reign of Jinmu. Based on this, Harumi concluded that Jinmu Tennō must have created a calendar of his own. Thus Harumi spared no effort to reconstruct what he called the ancient method of calendar-making (*korekihō* 古暦法). According to his theory, this ancient calendar was lost after the Chinese calendar was introduced. Thus, the *Nihon chōreki* was the result of Harumi's firm belief in the existence of a native Japanese method of calendar calculation, and it demonstrated the practical applicability of this method for his own time.

Let us look at some concrete examples to explain the methodology of the *Nihon chōreki*. As mentioned, the *Nihon shoki* gives the corresponding cyclical signs to each historical event; in turn, the *Nihon chōreki* reveals the day of the month to which these signs correctly correspond. According to a chronicle of the Inner Shrine of Ise (*Naikū chinza koki* 内宮鎮座古記), for instance, the enshrinement of its main deity, Amaterasu Ōmikami 天照大御神, occurred on a wood-rat day (*kinoe-ne* 甲子, the first day of the sexagenarian cycle) of the tenth month in the twenty-sixth year of Suinin Tennō 垂仁天皇.[14] According to the *Nihon chōreki*, however, there was no wood-rat day in the tenth month of that year. Therefore, as Harumi explains, the tenth month must have been a mistake and the wood-rat day actually corresponds to the seventeenth day of the ninth month. In Harumi's time, this was the day of the *kannamesai* 神嘗祭 at the Inner Shrine, when the new rice was offered. In other words, Harumi made it clear that Ise's *kannamesai* had its origins in the enshrinement of Amaterasu Ōmikami on the seventeenth day of the ninth month. Using the same method, he was able to date the enshrinement of Toyouke Ōmikami 豊受大御神, the main deity of the Outer Shrine of Ise, to the sixteenth day of the ninth month. That day, too, corresponded to the *kannamesai* of the Outer Shrine. While it was common knowledge that the *kannamesai* was a harvest festival for offering the new grains to the deities of heaven and earth, the *Nihon chōreki* revealed a much more profound meaning of this event by relating it to the enshrinement of the shrine's principal deity.[15]

The *Nihon chōreki* was therefore a practical tool, enabling shrine priests to determine the original meaning, or the original day of each festival. Based on his belief in an ancient native calendar that had been lost, Harumi's approach must be regarded as a kind of restorationism. In the words of Yamazaki Ansai, the *Nihon chōreki* was nothing less than "the second founding of our country."[16] In the same way, the calendar reform of the Jōkyō era did not follow the ideal of emulating the Chinese calendar, but strived to restore the presumed method of Jinmu Tennō's calendar.

Funerals and Cemeteries

After Masayuki's death, the cooperation and comradeship within his salon started to wane; the friendship between Masayuki's erstwhile intellectual advisors Koretaru and Ansai foundered as well. Harumi then began to criticize both of them. In order to explain this turn of events, I will now present the circumstances of the funerals and graves of Masayuki, Ansai, and Koretaru on the basis of various materials, including photographs, that I took at the respective sites.

The Funeral of Hoshina Masayuki

Masayuki returned to Aizu one year before his death, together with Yoshikawa Koretaru and some of his retainers, in order to search for a suitable place for his own burial. He found it at Mineyama 見禰山 in the vicinity of Iwahashi Jinja 磐椅神社 at the foot of Mt. Bandai 磐梯, a place that offered a picturesque view of Lake Inawashiro 猪苗代湖.

Masayuki passed away on the eighteenth day of the twelfth month 1672 (Kanbun 12) in his Edo residence.[17] According to his last will, his retainers Tomomatsu Ujioki and Toeda Hikogorō 戸枝彦五郎 (dates unknown) were to be responsible for his funeral, which was to be conducted according to Shinto rituals (*shinsōsai* 神葬祭). This raised the problem of how to deal with the sutra recitations by Buddhist monks, which would have been normally performed at the funeral procession of a high ranking member of the warrior nobility such as Masayuki. Tomomatsu conceded to the custom during a conversation and passed on this information to the senior councilor (*rōjū*) Inaba Masanori via his son Inaba Masayuki 稲葉正往 (1640–1716), who was also Hoshina Masayuki's son-in-law. When Yoshikawa Koretaru came to Masayuki's residence to perform the Shinto funeral rites, however, he rejected a sutra reading harshly. He argued that mixing a Shinto ceremony with Buddhist rites would depreciate all efforts of Masayuki to re-establish the ancient customs of Japan. Tomomatsu immediately changed his mind declaring: "I have made a dreadful mistake. I will correct it by all means, even if this means to be judged a criminal."

Thereupon Koretaru went to Inaba Masanori's home and asked him to cancel the sutra recitation. Masanori however answered: "The *rōjū* council has already decided. Sutra recitations should not pose a problem, since they will not be conducted in the residence but at a temple." Koretaru stubbornly disagreed, arguing that any sutra recitation for Masayuki, whether performed at a temple or his residence, was not compatible with "One and Only Shinto" (*yuiitsu shintō* 唯一神道). Masanori became angry and insisted that refusing the sutra recitations was unheard of. He went on to explain that a sutra recitation had even been performed at the funeral of Tokugawa Yoshinao 徳川義直 (1600–50) of Owari 尾張藩, despite his request for Confucian death rites. Koretaru nearly decided to conduct a *yuiitsu shintō* funeral ceremony in his private compound, but then, however, he decided to leave everything to fate, making his opinion public in a fervent speech:

> You said that it is the policy of the *bakufu* to utilize every religion whatsoever and to cast away none, but Buddhism is overwhelmingly prosperous, and Shinto is only like a drop in the ocean. Should they not be equally balanced? Although the people of our country are all descendants of the *kami*, Shinto is in decline. By virtue of his superior capacities, our lord [Masayuki] restored Shinto. Since he has passed away, the opportunity to restore the divine way of our country is lost as well.[18]

In addition, Koretaru presented a certificate to the *rōjū* that demonstrated that Masayuki had received the "secret initiation of the fourfold transmission" (*shijū sōden no hiden* 四重相伝の秘伝) of Yoshida Shinto. This left a deep impression on the *rōjū* and convinced him to cancel the sutra recitation. However, he advised Koretaru to perform his rites in a quiet way, because this was a matter without precedent.

On the last day of the twelfth month, Masayuki's remains arrived in Aizu and were placed in the third fortification (*sannomaru* 三の丸) of Aizu-Wakamatsu 会津若松 castle. The preparations for his funeral, however, were severely threatened by various rumors and conspiracies.[19] First, the rumor was spread that the supervisors of Masayuki's funeral, Toeda and Tomomatsu, were on bad terms. Matters were further complicated by the fact that both Inaba Masanori, the *rōjū*, as well as Masayuki's son, the new domain lord Hoshina Masatsune 保科正経 (1647–81), were not in favor of a large-scale funeral, which would impose a heavy load of corvée labor on Aizu domain. Masatsune's confidants Naruse Kazue 成瀬主計 (dates unknown) and Nagura Hanzaemon 名倉半左衛門 (dates unknown) tried to discredit Tomomatsu by secretly telling the young lord and the *rōjū* that Tomomatsu planned an ostentatious funeral. Thereupon Masatsune invited Tomomatsu to come to Edo, but Tomomatsu was too busy. In response, when Tomomatsu later requested a personal meeting, Masatsune declined. Tomomatsu, convinced he had lost the confidence of his lord, was about to resign from his post as one of the funeral's supervisors, when he received a sudden order to come to Edo. There he was able to clear up all the misunderstandings and was reconfirmed as the supervisor of Masayuki's funeral. On 1673/3/4, Naruse and Nagura were finally punished for causing this disturbance in the domain administration.

For the construction of the burial mound, a large number of domain officials and artisans, including carpenters, sawyers, blacksmiths, goldsmiths, plasterers and tilers, were mobilized. Many workers were also needed for supplying stones for the sarcophagus (*sekkan* 石棺) and its outer shell (*gaikaku* 外槨). The whole domain was involved in the construction of the temporary shelter (*kariya* 仮屋) and a procession road to the site (*sandō* 参道). In the third month the burial site was completed and on 1673/3/14 the coffin was brought from Aizu-Wakamatsu castle and placed in the temporary shelter at Mineyama.

On the twenty-seventh day of the third month, the funeral took place in the presence of the new lord, Hoshina Masatsune.[20] The coffin was taken from its temporary shelter to the burial ground and placed in the sarcophagus, which was made of a single stone with a carved-out trough. Hattori Ankyū took a *katashiro* 形代[21] and placed it in front of the coffin. Tomomatsu and Toeda presented offerings. Facing north, Koretaru took a seat south of the coffin. Torches were extinguished and lit again. Flowers, sake, and fruits were offered on three tablets. Koretaru approached the coffin, rang a bell, performed a purification rite, and recited an address to the *kami*. The domain lord burned incense and left. In the evening of the same day, the "first sacrifice of repose" (*shogu* 初虞) was offered. This was a Confucian food-offering rite performed at the home for several days after a burial.[22] Masayuki's death rites also included other Confucian ceremonies, such "laying out" the body (*shōren* 小斂 and *dairen* 大斂)[23] and the "cessation of wailing" (*sokkoku* 卒哭).[24] The funeral-related rites ended on 1673/4/28, when the *katashiro* was moved to the "place for worshiping from afar" (*yōhaisho* 遥拝所) to the south of Aizu-Wakamatsu castle. There, a ceremony for the soul of the deceased (*mitama matsuri* 御魂祭) was held in the morning and the evening respectively.

In the fifth month (1673/5/18), the provisional hall (*karidono* 仮殿) of Hanitsu Shrine 土津神社 was completed, where Masayuki's spirit was then worshipped. In the seventh month (1673/7/17), a messenger from Kyoto brought calligraphies for the shrine tablet (*kaku* 額) and the Shinto mortuary tablet (*reiji* 霊璽), which had been drawn by Yoshida Kanetsura 吉田兼連 (1653–1732). In the tenth month (1673/10/11), an octagonal pacifying stone (*shizume ishi* 鎮石) was placed on top of the burial mound (Figure 9.1). It bears the inscription "Pacifying stone of the sacred grave of Hanitsu" (*Hanitsushinfun shizume ishi* 土津神墳鎮石), Hanitsu being the divine spirit of Masayuki. It is 3.9m high and just under 3m wide. Its octagonal shape may be related to vessels for coffins called *ohoto* 於保止 or *hitsuki* 比都器 used in other Shinto funeral ceremonies (see Figure 9.2).

In 1674, construction was started on a shrine where Masayuki was to be worshipped as the Hanitsu Divine Spirit (Hanitsu Reishin 土津霊神).[25] A stele of 5.5 meters with an engraved epitaph honoring Masayuki's achievements was completed in the fourth

Calendars and Graves 141

Figure 9.1 Pacifying stone on the grave of Hoshina Masayuki.[26] Photograph by the author, 2018.

Figure 9.2 Shinto-style vessel (*ohoto*) for a coffin.[27]

Figure 9.3 Turtle stone commemorating the life of Hoshina Masayuki.[28] Photograph by pasonisan.com, 2019

month. The text was composed by Ansai. The stele rests on a so-called turtle stone (*kifu* 亀砆), which gives the impression that a turtle is carrying the stone on its back (Figure 9.3). In China, turtle stones were popular in the Sui (581–618) and Tang (618–907) periods. The first Japanese examples, however, appear only in the early modern period.[29] The site of Hanitsu Jinja comprises a main hall (started in 1674/3), two *waka no miya* shrines, three branch shrines and one shrine for the protection of the stone stele. The roofing ceremony of the main hall took place on 1674/8/19 and on the twenty-third day, the *kami* was ritually enshrined (*sengū* 遷宮).

Summing up, Masayuki's death and deification rites actually consisted of a mixture of Yoshida and Confucian ritualism. It was Masayuki himself who had conceived this syncretic mix, while Tomomatsu, Toeda and Koretaru put it into practice.

The Funeral of Yamazaki Ansai

Yamazaki Ansai made even more unconventional arrangements regarding his funeral. In 1663, he had the graves of his grandfather and his grandmother moved from the Jōdo 浄土 temple Chion'in 知恩院 in Kyoto to the cemetery of Kurodani 黒谷. When his mother died in 1671, Ansai decided to conduct the funeral according to Confucian rites, against protests from Buddhist clerics. In the same year (1671/8/18), well in

Figure 9.4 Votive tablet of Yamazaki Ansai (Suikasha).[30] Photograph by the author, 2018.

advance of his death, he received the posthumous spiritual title Suika Reisha 垂加霊社 from Yoshikawa Koretaru, which he inscribed on a Shinto-style spirit tablet (*reiji*) and thereafter revered at his home. Later, he even attempted to place this tablet in the Shimo Goryō Shrine 下御霊社 in Kyoto (1673/2/22). When the authorities became aware of this in 1681, however, he was ordered to return it to his residence.[31]

In the third month of 1683, Ansai fell ill and had little hope of recovery.[32] Although his Shinto students took care of him, his Confucian students did not even pay him a visit. In the ninth month, his condition turned critical and Izumoji Nobunao 出雲路信直 (1650–1703), Nashinoki Sukeyuki 梨木祐之 (1659–1723) and Ōyama Tameoki 大山為起 (1651–1713) took turns in conducting prayers for Ansai, until he individually bid them farewell on the fifteenth day.[33] To avoid death pollution, he had a *sanja takusen* 三社託宣 scroll (bearing the names of Amaterasu, Hachiman and Kasuga) removed from his room, but asked his mistress Kachi 加知 (dates unknown) to stay at his side. He was well aware of the Chinese etiquette that "a gentleman must not die in the arms of his spouse," but Ansai rejected this as non-Japanese. He finally passed away on the sixteenth day, surrounded by his family and students.

In the hour of the ox (1 to 3 a.m.) of the twentieth day, a small number of students met, took the coffin with the corpse from Ansai's home and carried it to the Kurodani Cemetery. Other students joined them and together they buried him next to the grave of the Yamazaki family, where the remains of two generations of his ancestors were buried. According to Ansai's last will, he was buried facing east. No Buddhist cleric was present. In a letter, his students Asai Rin'an 浅井琳庵 (1652–1711) and Kataoka Tomonori 片岡友謙 (dates unknown) described this as follows:

> We carried his coffin as it was to the cemetery and buried it. Please rest assured that no Buddhist monk took care of it. At the temple, monks performed a burial

ceremony with an empty coffin. Regarding the posthumous Buddhist name, the monks called him something like "Mimuro Takatoshi." We were all greatly amused at hearing this.[34]

Obviously Ansai had prearranged this fake Buddhist funeral, having his students conduct his real funeral according to Confucian rites instead.

Ansai's Suika Reisha tablet, and the certificate of his posthumous name, were handed over to Izumoji Nobunao by Yoshikawa Koretaru. Later, the tablet became an object of worship as an associate deity (*aidono* 相殿) of the Sarutahiko subshrine 猿田彦神社 of Shimo Goryōsha, where it remains to this day (Figure 9.4).

The Funeral of Yoshikawa Koretaru

Accounts of the funeral of Yoshikawa Koretaru seem to be limited to his biography, *Yoshikawa Aremi no ya sensei gyōjō* 吉川視吾堂先生行状. Koretaru died on 1694/11/17, aged seventy-nine, surrounded by his wailing students. According to the biography, his face exhibited no trace of distress and had the same color as when he was alive.

Koretaru's burial mound was built within his private compound in Oshiage 押上, in the Honjo 本所 district of Edo. Since he had become a Shinto official (*shintōgata*) of the *bakufu* in 1682, he was allowed to be buried according to Shinto rites. In line with Yoshida Shinto, a shrine was erected on top of the grave. Today, the Yoshikawa family compound no longer exists; in 1896 their graves were combined and moved to a corner of Aoyama Cemetery 青山墓地. In 1936, Koretaru received a memorial stone.

Harumi's Criticism

Let me finally discuss the severe criticism of Shibukawa Harumi, which targeted precisely the funerals and graves of his masters and mentors Masayuki, Ansai, and Koretaru. In his own words rendered by Tani Jinzan, this criticism reads as follows:

> According to the burial customs of our country, there are no shrines on top of graves and there are no memorial stones. The imperial tombs of the Kinai area offer ample evidence for this. One should have looked at these. Nevertheless, the graves of Masayuki and Ansai follow Confucian customs and use stone steles. This is in no way compatible with ancient customs. There are endless reasons to regret this.[35] [...]
>
> Ansai received the burial rites from Koretaru, but they were not followed properly. At Masayuki's funeral, Confucian practices were used. At Ansai's funeral, Confucianism and Buddhism were mixed together. This is very lamentable.[36]

Harumi's understanding of ancient Japanese burial customs was based on a survey of imperial gravesites in the Kinai area. From this standpoint, he criticized the mix of Confucian and Japanese customs, including the placement of stone steles. He further maintained that:

Burials according to Confucian customs started with Razan 羅山 (1583–1657) and the Nonaka 野中 family of Tosa province. In Kyoto, Confucian burials have only been seen in the last thirty years.[37]

Thus, according to Harumi, Confucian funerals in Kyoto were a recent fashion rather than an ancient custom. Therefore, the fact that Masayuki and Ansai had included Confucian customs in their funerals was incompatible with Harumi's appreciation of the ancient Way of Japan.

Concerning Koretaru, Harumi's criticism was of a different kind. As mentioned, Koretaru's grave was placed inside the Yoshikawa compound in Edo. Other persons related to Aizu domain had their graves there too. The childless Tomomatsu Ujioki, for instance, asked Koretaru to build a shrine for him in the Yoshikawa compound and accordingly was entombed there in due course. Harumi visited the place together with Tani Jinzan on their way back from the Kameido Tenjin 亀戸天神 Shrine, in order to pay respects to Koretaru's son Yorinaga 吉川従長 (1654–1730) and to the graves of Koretaru and Tomomatsu. Upon seeing the graves, Harumi and Jinzan felt discomfort.

> We went to Koretaru's shrine. On top of each grave was a shrine. There were seven or eight shrines (*reisha* 霊社) for the souls of our deceased companions and all bore a tablet with their respective *reisha* title. On the northern side, there was something like a grave with a stone pagoda called the "Inner Shrine of the Tomomatsu family." It was utterly disgusting.[38]

What was the reason for the visitors' "disgust" at the sight of these graves? Most likely that a shrine was standing on a grave, that is, on a place affected by death pollution (*kegare* 穢れ). This was in line with Harumi's general criticism of Yoshida Shinto funeral rites, which disregarded this kind of pollution. Many people of that time were convinced that the funerals of the Yoshida house reflected original Shinto rituals, but in Harumi's opinion, funeral ceremonies directed to the *kami* had not existed in ancient Japan.

> Today, some people have their graves built in the compound of the Yoshida house and place a shrine on top of the grave. This is the worst case of pollution. Those who transmitted Shinto in recent times are completely wrong [in this respect]. There are no shrines on the top of imperial tombs, which are witnesses to the Age of the Gods. Whoever visits the Kinai area should go to the imperial tombs and acknowledge this.[39]

What Harumi calls "Shinto [of] recent times" refers to Yoshida Shinto. After the *Shrine Clauses* had been promulgated in 1665, Yoshida influence in the world of Shinto had become overwhelming. This must have increased the importance of Yoshida funeral rites as well. Harumi, however, was not at all in favor of this development.

Final Considerations

After his inspection of the imperial tombs in the Kinai area, Shibukawa Harumi was convinced that he had uncovered the burial customs of ancient Japan. In a similar way,

Figure 9.5 The grave of Shibukawa Harumi.[40] Photograph by the author, 2018.

Harumi "discovered" Jinmu's ancient method of calendar making, which became the basis of his *Nihon chōreki*. We might say that he applied the same restorative thinking in both cases. The hypothetical development "ancient calendar making by Jinmu → reception of the Chinese calendar → restoration of the ancient calendar" is repeated in the development "Shinto-style ancient funerals → funerals influenced by Buddhism and Confucianism → revival of ancient funerals." According to Harumi's hypothesis, ancient funerals included neither a grave nor a memorial stele, not to mention a shrine on the grave as found in the Yoshida funeral style.

I should add, however, that although Harumi criticized the graves and funerals of Masayuki and others severely, he himself was not buried according to a presumed ancient Shintoist custom. Harumi's funeral took place on 1715/10/6 at Tōkai Zenji 東海禅寺 (today Tōkaiji) in Shinagawa. The graves of the Shibukawa family are still lined up there and Harumi's grave is one of them. Since his gravestone bears the Zen-style posthumous name Daikoin Tōun Shōtetsu Koji 大虚院透雲紹徹居士, his was doubtless a Buddhist funeral (Figure 9.5). We may conclude that in contrast to Masayuki and Ansai, Harumi did not want to eliminate Buddhist elements from his own funeral. But how was he able to criticize Masayuki and Ansai, if his own funeral did not confer to ancient customs? Is there indeed a contradiction between theory and practice in Harumi's case?

A Confucian funeral was unacceptable for Harumi. In this regard, he was definitely different from Masayuki and Ansai. They were Confucian scholars who had devoted themselves to the teachings of Zhu Xi, searched for a Japanese form of the way of the sages, and studied the fascicle of the age of the *kami* of the *Nihon shoki* from that point of view. For Harumi, in contrast, the world of the *Nihon shoki* represented an ideal in and of itself. Harumi's restorationism was at once a belief and a method. The *Nihon chōreki* constituted a chronological bridge between the time of Jinmu Tennō and that of Harumi, based on the assumption that Jinmu Tennō had established a calendar. If one accepts this restorative method, it is possible to apply it to all kinds of phenomena. In Harumi's *Nebokoro shūi* 瓊矛拾遺, for instance, the written characters, sounds, garments, and houses of the Age of the Gods are discovered and explained one after the other. In addition to the *Kojiki* and *Nihon shoki*, Harumi detected ancient customs in remote places in the provinces too. His explanations even seem to anticipate the ideas of the pioneer of Japanese folklore studies, Yanagita Kunio 柳田国男 (1875–1962). Thus, he declared that it was possible to understand ancient burial customs by looking at the imperial tombs of the Kinai area. This leads me to the conclusion that he would have opted for an ancient funeral, if he had been free to choose his own funeral style.

Wealthy people built giant graves where offerings and prayers could be performed, but according to Harumi these were all "foreign customs that came from the west" and did not adhere to the "manners of our divine country" (*shinkoku no fū* 神国の風). Taking these "manners of the divine country" as Harumi's standard, the funerals according to Yoshida Shinto as well as the Shinto-Confucian death rites of Masayuki and Ansai became objects of his criticism.

As regards Buddhism, Buddhist-style funerals were forced upon society due to the *terauke* system, within which each individual school decided on their own funeral procedures. In contrast, Shinto funerals were particular to Shinto priests and required special permission from the *bakufu*. While they gradually increased in number from the middle of the early modern period onward, they continued to be rare when compared to Buddhist funerals. We could say that Shinto death rites and funerals lacked a place for developing in Edo-period society.

The persons who gathered in Hoshina Masayuki's salon supported the calendar reform of Harumi, but their opinions differed greatly when it came to funerals and burials, matters concerning the hereafter. Masayuki and Ansai could stick to their beliefs and enforce funerals according to their own wishes because they had received posthumous spiritual titles from Yoshikawa Koretaru during their own lifetimes.[41] Moreover, both had loyal retainers and faithful students who carried out their wills after their deaths. These were certainly exceptional cases.

Harumi's eldest son Hisatada 渋川昔尹 (1683–1715) died six months before his father. Both were buried at Tōkai Zenji according to their traditional religious denomination, the Zen 禅 sect. This was a natural process in Harumi's eyes, since it was done for the preservation of the Shibukawa house. His opinion that one had to follow the traditional protocol of the divine country (*shinkoku*) pertained only to exceptional figures like Masayuki or Ansai, who had rejected Buddhism and selected funerals composed of their own beliefs combined with Confucian rites. But not even in his dreams would Harumi have agreed that ordinary Japanese should do the same. For those living within the confines of the *terauke* system, no alternatives to Buddhist funerals existed. Even individuals with strong Shintoist beliefs like Harumi succumbed to the norm of a Buddhist funeral according to the religious affiliations of their family. However, Harumi believed that if someone possessed the power to choose his own funeral, he should adhere to ancient Shinto rites. Harumi's severe criticism of Masayuki and Anzai was rooted in precisely this way of thinking.

Part Four

Institutional Challenges

10

Shinto in the 1660s and 1670s

The *Shrine Clauses* of 1665 as an Expression of Domain Shinto

Mark Teeuwen

On the eleventh day of the seventh month of Kanbun 5 (1665), the shogunate issued a law that is known as either the *Shrine Clauses* (*Jinja jōmoku* 神社条目) or the *Law for Shrine Priests* (*Shosha negi kannushi hatto* 諸社禰宜神主法度). It consisted of five articles:

1. Shrine priests must study the Way of the Gods (*jingidō* 神祇道), be knowledgeable about the deity bodies they worship, and perform customary rites and ceremonies. Henceforth, those who are negligent in their duties will be discharged of their priestly office.
2. With regard to ranks for shrine houses: those who have been receiving such ranks through the mediation of a particular noble house will continue to do so.
3. Shrine priests without ranks must wear white robes. Other robes require a certificate from the Yoshida house.
4. Shrine lands may not be sold, bought, or pawned.
5. Minor damages to shrines must be repaired in an appropriate manner.[1]

The main policy aim of these *Shrine Clauses* was to establish a national licensing system for shrine priests. This would supply the warrior authorities with a mechanism to dismiss or punish "negligent" priests, identify "illicit shrines" (*inshi* 淫祠), and handle conflicts between priestly houses over the control of legitimate shrines. The *Shrine Clauses* seek to achieve this by confirming already established procedures to obtain priestly court ranks (item 2) and by regulating the use of priestly robes (item 3). Applications for court rank were to be mediated through customary channels in the case of shrines with existing court connections. Unranked priests, moreover, were to wear white garb, or obtain licenses from the Yoshida house of court priests if they aspired to a higher status and the corresponding apparel. In 1668, the Yoshida appealed to the shogunate, asking it to specify that they held the absolute monopoly on mediating priests' applications for court ranks on behalf of all shrine houses without established court connections. This triggered a long legal battle that ended in defeat for the Yoshida in 1674, opening the way for other noble houses to enter this market (notably the Shirakawa, who also served as specialists of shrine ritual).[2]

The issuance of the *Shrine Clauses* was closely connected to the experiments with "Domain Shinto" (*hanryō shintō* 藩領神道) by Tokugawa-related daimyo in the mid-1660s (see the introduction to this volume). In Mito domain 水戸藩, the daimyo Tokugawa Mitsukuni 徳川光圀 (1628–1701) surveyed temples and shrines in 1663 with the intention of instigating radical reforms. As explained in detail by Brigitte Pickl-Kolaczia in this volume, Mitsukuni sought to enhance the status of shrines in his domain, but was hindered by the fact that some shrines were under the "supervision" (*shihai* 支配) of the Ise shrines, others of the Yoshida 吉田 house, and others again under the Shugendō 修験道 head temple of Daigoji Sanbōin 醍醐寺三宝院.[3] Mitsukuni used Yoshida advisors in designing his shrine reforms. These reforms involved the destruction of countless illicit shrines and the protection or even reconstruction of shrines with "correct" credentials, which were to be staffed by ranked priests with proper licenses. Mito domain was able to push through these reforms with much greater effect after the promulgation of the *Shrine Clauses* in 1665. In 1666, the daimyo of Aizu domain 会津藩, Hoshina Masayuki 保科正之 (1611–73), implemented similar reforms. Masayuki maintained close relations with Yoshikawa Koretaru 吉川惟足 (1616–95), a Shinto teacher in possession of the secret transmissions of Yoshida Shinto. As such, Masayuki lobbied actively for recognition of the authority of the Yoshida house over Shinto matters, and he is often credited as the main political force behind the *Shrine Clauses*.[4] These clauses, then, were arguably the most influential legacy of Domain Shinto on a national level, reaching far beyond the domains that experimented with Shinto policies in the 1660s and 1670s.[5]

The *Shrine Clauses* are mostly discussed as an administrative tool, designed to extend warrior control to the disorganized field of shrines and shrine priests. On a conceptual level, they are sometimes referred to as an initial step towards the institutional establishment of Shinto as an autonomous, non-Buddhist sect of its own. Inoue Tomokatsu writes: "The rise of Yoshida Shinto and the activities of the Yoshida house increased Shinto's autonomy from Buddhism, and the *Shrine Clauses* inspired shrine priests to seek emancipation from the temples that kept them in a subordinate position."[6] In this chapter, I will investigate three prominent sites where such battles for emancipation in the name of an autonomous Shinto were fought in the 1660s and 1670s. The different outcomes of these battles raise the question to what degree the realm of "Shinto" had indeed gained autonomy as a general principle of governance.

A point that is seldom made about the *Shrine Clauses* is that they were issued on the same day as the *Law for Temples of All Sects* (*Shoshū jiin hatto* 諸宗寺院法度). The *Shrine Clauses* extended legislation previously addressed to Buddhist temples to Shinto shrines, and thereby placed Shinto in the same category as the sects of Buddhism. As we shall see below, the *Law for Temples of All Sects* was issued as part of a policy to strengthen the system of temple certification (*terauke seido* 寺請制度), which aimed to suppress "pernicious creeds" by checking the faith of laypeople. What was the place of Shinto in this policy?

The *Shrine Clauses* and the Control of "Faith"

The *Shrine Clauses* of 1665 were clearly modeled on the first wave of Edo-period temple laws (*jiin hatto* 寺院法度), imposed on Buddhist sects between 1601 and 1615.

Like the *Shrine Clauses* half a century later, those laws had stressed priests' duty to pursue learning, established structures of administration and control, and banned the sale of lands. They had also laid down rules concerning more specific issues of the temples and sects to whom they were addressed. While "learning" (ritual and/or doctrinal) figured in many of the temple laws as the primary task of monks, this does not necessarily mean that these laws were intended to encourage such learning, let alone sanction sectarian theology. The shogunal officials who designed these laws sought to reduce temple autonomy and establish mechanisms that subjected the monastic community to the hegemony of the new regime. When lawmakers stressed the duty of monastics to exert themselves in "the way of learning" (*gakudō* 学道), this was not so much because they were concerned with doctrinal issues, but rather because this duty offered a rationale for punishing lax or unruly priests.[7]

But as all laws do, the temple laws had intended as well as unintended effects. The laws issued to temples in the Kanto region in particular ordered minor temples to affiliate themselves with a single sect and charged head temples with educating and certifying monks. This laid the foundation for the development and codification of sectarian learning and practice.[8] The authority of the Yoshida over shrines and shrine priests was not identical to that of head temples over branch temples, but the shared format of the *Shrine Clauses* and the early temple laws indicates that the shogunate saw the Yoshida house as comparable to a Buddhist head temple. Perhaps unwittingly, the *Clauses* gave official status to Shinto (*jingidō*) as a "Way" on a par with Buddhism. This opened a new door to those who wanted to argue that Shinto and Buddhism were incompatible, and that it was wrong to place shrine priests under the supervision of Buddhist temples.

After Ieyasu's countrywide ban of Christianity (1614), the temple networks institutionalized by the temple laws were put to a new use: certifying the faith of laypeople. This introduced a wholly new, and wildly ambitious, objective to shogunal policy regarding temples: to solve the contradictions of faith and loyalty. The shogunate now saw an urgent need to break up communities whose faith undermined the social order. To achieve this, the regime compelled people to commit to one of the faiths that *were* deemed acceptable. This concern led shogunal officials to impose on all sects a model that closely resembled that of the Ikkō 一向 sect (which it actually regarded with suspicion): communities of laypeople with a clear-cut sectarian identity, whose contributions supported temple networks with a tightly organized hierarchical structure, from head temples at the top to village halls at the bottom. The premises of the temple certification system were: first, that temples served dedicated lay adherents; and second, that laypeople committed themselves to a single sectarian faith under the guidance and supervision of their temple of choice. The assumption was that temple membership would stop laypeople of all classes from slipping into a "pernicious creed" (*jashūmon* 邪宗門)—notably Christianity. "Temple certificates" (*terauke shōmon* 寺請証文), introduced from the mid-1630s onwards, stated that the priest was prepared to guarantee the carrier's legitimate sectarian identity.

This brings us to the 1660s, a period of administrative consolidation. In this decade, national laws replaced particularized arrangements within the worlds of warriors, courtiers, and temples alike. In the realm of temples, the 1665 *Law for Temples of All*

Sects performed this function. This law drew on the earlier temple laws of the 1610s but added articles related to temples' relationship with their "patrons" (*danna* 檀那), whose faith they were now obliged to certify. The law's fourth item states that "patrons will select their temple of affiliation according to their own understanding (*kokoroe* 心得)," while in the same breath banning priests from "contesting others' patrons." These two phrases clearly contradicted each other. The first allowed laypeople to register as they saw fit, while the latter prevented them from doing so, because a temple that accepted a new patron was liable to be sued for *danna* theft. Thus, this clause encapsulates an uneasy compromise: it balances the need to ensure that people will not fall into the clutches of a pernicious creed (by allowing them to have their chosen faith strengthened and certified by a temple), against the need to prevent unmanageable conflicts between temples or even sects (by rendering any change of temple affiliation difficult, or even illegal). This created a situation where faith was fossilized, and temples certified people's faith on the presumption that faith is hereditary.

In contrast to temples, shrines were to play no part in the management of faith. Shrine priests, like *shugenja* 修験者 and many other religious figures, existed outside of the affiliation system. As a result, the dimension of controlling faith in *Law for Temples of All Sects* highlighted a new contradiction that inspired some to protest: shrine priests who rejected Buddhist faith were nonetheless obliged to affiliate with a temple, have their faith certified annually by that temple, and be buried there.[9] The admonition to study *jingidō* (item 1 of the *Shrine Clauses*) could be understood to imply that Shinto had a status equivalent to, and incompatible with, the Buddhist sects. As explored in other chapters in this volume, there were indeed some domains that briefly experimented with that logic by introducing a system of shrine affiliation. The fact that there was a historical moment in the 1660s and 1670s when this was deemed possible (or even desirable) is highly significant. In the end, however, shogunal support was withheld from these experiments.

This must mean that ultimately, shrines and their Shinto were regarded as somehow different in nature from the logic of faith that formed the rationale of the affiliation system. Shinto could not overrule Buddhist faith for individual patrons. Yet the view that Shinto and Buddhism are incompatible did gain strength, and shrine priests were able to draw on this view in institutional struggles with Buddhist overlords or competitors. From the 1660s onwards, there arose a number of cases where shrine priests challenged the control of temple monks over their shrines, or even the presence of monastics at their rituals. In the next section of this chapter, I will briefly explore three examples of conflicts where the autonomy of Shinto was invoked in order to expel Buddhists.

Izumo

The rebuilding of Izumo 出雲 (or Kizuki 杵築) Shrine in the 1660s is often cited as the first instance of a physical separation of Buddhism and Shinto (*shinbutsu bunri* 神仏分離), prying apart an integrated shrine-temple complex.[10] Izumo was redesigned with shogunal funds as a Shinto shrine devoid of any Buddhist presence. Even the Buddhist mendicants called *hongan* 本願 ("[mendicants dedicated to Amida's] original vow"), who had raised money for the maintenance of the shrine's precincts, were expelled in 1662, and their headquarters were turned into a shrine archive. In 1664 and 1665 all Buddhist buildings and objects were removed from the shrine grounds, including a three-story stupa, a Buddha hall, and a sutra hall. Subsequently monks from the nearby Tendai 天台 temple Gakuenji 鰐淵寺 were banned from participating in the shrine's annual rituals, cutting the late-medieval ties between shrine and temple.

In the words of both the Izumo priesthood and the shogunal magistrate of temples and shrines (*jisha bugyō* 寺社奉行), Izumo Shrine had now become a site of *yuiitsu shintō* 唯一神道. *Yuiitsu*, meaning "only one; monistic; non-dual," had been a central term of Yoshida theology ever since Yoshida Kanetomo's 吉田兼倶 *Yuiitsu shintō myōbō yōshū* 唯一神道妙法要集 (*Essence of the Wondrous Dharma of the One-and-Only Shinto*, c. 1485). As demonstrated by Bernhard Scheid (2003), however, the term spread in the broader meaning of "non-Buddhist Shinto" in the seventeenth century. In this usage, *yuiitsu shintō* was the opposite of *ryōbu* 両部 ("two-part") or *shūgō* 習合 ("combined") *shintō*, which referred to shrines that integrated *kami* and buddhas, priests and monks. As we shall see, in Izumo the term *yuiitsu shintō* was used not with reference to Yoshida theology but rather in this latter sense of "Shinto only," exclusive of Buddhism.[11]

Izumo's rebuilding as a *yuiitsu* shrine was unprecedented, and a result of unique circumstances. The success of the shrine priests in removing all Buddhist presence from Izumo is often credited to the daimyo of Matsue domain 松江藩, Matsudaira Naomasa 松平直政 (1601–66), one of Ieyasu's many grandsons who appears to have had a special interest in Shinto. Already in 1638—the year he arrived in Matsue—he issued shrine laws (*Kizuki shohatto* 杵築諸法度) that called for "regular rites to be restored to ancient Shinto protocol." In 1653 Naomasa invited Kurosawa Sekisai 黒澤石斎 (1622–78) to Matsue as the domain's Confucian adviser. Sekisai was a student of Hayashi Razan 林羅山 (1583–1657) and an outspoken proponent of Razan's Confucian Shinto. He was explicit about his disgust at the Buddhist "infiltration" of the ancient Shinto site of Izumo, and inspired its priests to think along the same lines.[12] By this time, Naomasa had already succeeded in gaining shogunal approval and support for a ritual rebuilding of Izumo Shrine in its "correct" dimensions. Izumo Shrine had earlier been rebuilt in 1609, on orders of Toyotomi Hideyoshi (1537–98). That rebuilding, however, resulted in a relatively small "basic hall" (*honden* 本殿) surrounded by many Buddhist structures. A new rebuilding in the form of a more prestigious "correct hall" (*seiden* 正殿) offered the shogunate a chance to display the superiority of Tokugawa rule over Hideyoshi's regime.[13]

Separating Shinto from Buddhism became part of this project only at a very late stage.[14] Initially, negotiations in Edo were conducted by the above-mentioned *hongan* mendicants, whose main task was to procure offerings from sponsors and devotees around the country. The *hongan* mediated between the shrine and the public, while the priesthood, led by the two hereditary houses of head priests (*kokusō* 国造) Senke 千家 and Kitajima 北島, dedicated itself to shrine ceremonial. In line with established protocol, it was the *hongan* leader Mon'yō 文養 (dates unknown) who led the effort in Edo to secure permission and funding for the rebuilding; a report that he sent to Matsue in early 1662 envisioned not only the construction of a new *seiden*, but also extensive repairs to the shrine's various Buddhist facilities.

Perhaps emboldened by the knowledge that they had Naomasa's and Sekisai's backing, the priesthood immediately sent its own representatives to Edo, two high-ranking priests named Sakusa Yorikiyo 佐草自清 (dates unknown) and Shima Ichinojō 島市之丞 (dates unknown). Through undocumented channels, they gained the ear of the magistrate for temples and shrines in Edo, Inoue Masatoshi 井上正利 (1606–75, in office 1658–67). Masatoshi was a student of Yamazaki Ansai 山崎闇斎 (1619–82) and a member of Hoshina Masayuki's "salon," a circle of neo-Confucian intellectuals and warrior leaders who developed an interest in Shinto in the early 1660s.[15] We have already encountered Masayuki as a central figure of Domain Shinto and a decisive lobbyist for the *Shrine Clauses*. Masatoshi introduced Ansai to Masayuki in 1665, and Ansai would spend the next seven years in Masayuki's service. In the early summer of 1662, Mon'yō protested against the meddling of priestly representatives, but this merely gave Masatoshi a suitable excuse to abolish the *hongan* altogether and expel them from the shrine. The decision to eradicate all Buddhist presence from Izumo Shrine and turn it into an exemplary site of *yuiitsu shintō* was taken immediately after this expulsion.

It appears that Masatoshi's ambitions went beyond Izumo; if he had not retired in the twelfth month of 1667, he might have done more for the cause of *yuiitsu shintō*. Earlier in 1667, Yorikiyo visited Masatoshi to report on the completion of the Izumo rebuilding. At this time, delegations from the Inner and the Outer Shrine of Ise were in Edo in connection with a conflict that I will return to below. Masatoshi summoned them to witness Izumo's moment of glory. He congratulated Yorikiyo on the fact that Izumo now had become "a site of Shinto," and he pointed out that Izumo had been "restored" to *yuiitsu shintō* even before Ise itself.[16] This performance was clearly designed to signal that the shogunal magistrate of temples and shrines frowned upon Buddhist involvement in shrines, and that he would support initiatives to further marginalize Buddhists in Ise as well.

When the *Shrine Clauses* were issued in 1665, in the midst of Izumo's rebuilding process, the Izumo priests had been among the first to protest against the prerogatives that these clauses granted to the Yoshida house. In 1666 they filed a petition arguing that the two *kokusō* houses of Izumo should not be forced to subject themselves to the supervision of the much inferior Yoshida, and should be allowed to continue their practice of supplying priests in the Izumo region with Yoshida-like licenses. They succeeded in pushing through both these demands thanks to Masatoshi's unwavering support. In 1667, the emperor granted the Izumo *kokusō* an *Edict of Eternal* [*Priestly Office*] (*Yō senji* 永宣旨), rendering them permanently independent of the Yoshida. This was taken to also imply recognition of the right of the *kokusō* to serve as the supervisors (*sō-kengyō* 総検校) of all priests in Izumo province.

The importance of Masatoshi's support became clear in the 1690s.[17] In 1693, Sada Shrine 佐太神社 (located some forty kilometers west of Izumo Shrine, near the castle town of Matsue) claimed that it held an ancient prerogative to license priests—that is, grant them permission to wear priestly robes—in three and a half of Izumo's ten districts. Sada allied itself with the Yoshida before attempting this coup. This alliance impressed the domain authorities, and Matsue officials tried to mediate between Sada and Izumo to hammer out a compromise. The Izumo priests, certain of their unassailable authority, refused and took the matter straight to Edo. However, they soon found that the new magistrate of shrines and temples had no sympathy for their cause. The magistrate reacted negatively to the disrespect Izumo had shown to Matsue's Tokugawa-related daimyo and granted complete victory to Sada, depriving Izumo of a considerable source of income. To underline the displeasure of both the magistrate and the domain, both *kokusō* were forced to retire and saw their divine heirlooms temporarily confiscated (1697). The Izumo priesthood suffered severe repercussions that were lifted only in 1705.

The Shintoization of Izumo, then, was directly connected to the Domain Shinto of the 1660s. Izumo's rebuilding as a *yuiitsu* shrine was made possible by the intervention of figures who were central both to Domain Shinto and to the issuance of the *Shrine Clauses* that so offended the Izumo priests. Powerful figures like Inoue Masatoshi and Hoshina Masayuki believed that Shinto offered an effective way to inculcate Confucian morals in the populace, while Buddhism undermined those morals. It was such views that informed their support for the removal of Buddhism from Izumo. Matsudaira Naomasa was also sympathetic to these ideas; one could even argue that Matsue domain, too, experimented with its own version of Domain Shinto, though on a less grand scale than Mito, Aizu, or Okayama 岡山藩. As a result, the notion that Buddhism and Shinto are incompatible was for the first time implemented on the ground, at one of Japan's most prominent shrines, through determined political action.

However, the case of Izumo also shows that when the Domain Shinto moment passed, the reforms that had been carried out in its name were insecure. The *hongan* mendicants were defeated once and for all, but the Yoshida, through their allies at Sada shrine, proved that the Izumo priesthood defied them at their peril.

Hie

Soon after the *Shrine Clauses* were issued, another Shinto-Buddhist conflict erupted at the Hie shrines 日吉神社 on the eastern foot of Mt. Hiei 比叡山.[18] In 1669, Hie's shrine priests filed a protest with the Kyoto magistrate (*Kyōto machi bugyō* 京都町奉行) against interference in shrine matters by the Hiei monks. The monks reacted by airing the suspicion that the shrine priests were challenging Hiei's authority over Hie by scheming to convert their shrines from *shūgō* (Buddhist) to *yuiitsu shintō*.

The matter was solved temporarily in a negotiated settlement, but eleven years later, in 1680, the conflict re-erupted. Again, the Hiei monks feared that the true intention of the priests was to adopt *yuiitsu shintō*—and indeed, the priests had already applied for permission to acquire Yoshida-type altars.[19] Matters came to a head in 1684, when the priests removed the Buddhist statues that served as the objects of worship at all of the seven Hie shrines. The statues were taken away in the dead of night; it later emerged that they had been burned. This was one step too far, and in 1685 the priests not only lost their cause but were also handed verdicts of exile and expulsion by the Kyoto magistrate. After this, the abbot of Rinnōji 輪王寺, an imperial prince who was the highest authority of the Tendai sect (including Mt. Hiei and the Hie Shrines), summed up the priests' "crimes" at the end of a document that spelt out new regulations for the priests' conduct:

Sannō ichijitsu shintō is the foundation of *ryōbu shūgō shintō*, founded by Saichō.[20] Evildoers among the Hie priesthood have been scheming to ban monks and nuns from the shrines and convert them to *yuiitsu shintō*, but they could not escape punishment for their crime of secretly stealing the deity bodies.[21]

In his study of these events, Satō Masato points out that they bear witness to the influence of the Yoshida, their non-Buddhist *yuiitsu shintō*, and their official status as overseers of shrine priests, recognized in the *Shrine Clauses*.[22] The outcome, however, was radically different from the case in Izumo. The regulations issued by the Rinnōji abbot to the Hie priests in 1685 specified that Tendai monastics had access to the inner precincts of the shrines when they worshipped there, and that future rebuilding of the shrines would be planned and attended by "senior monks of Mt. Hiei as well as senior Hie priests."[23] Priests' applications for court rank were to be approved and handled by Hiei's monastic hierarchy. These regulations had the explicit aim of isolating the Hie priests from the *yuiitsu shintō* of the Yoshida, and of solidifying their integration in Tendai's Buddhist-dominated *ryōbu shūgō shintō*.

The reason why the Hie priests failed where the Izumo priests succeeded is obvious: While Hie was a subsidiary of the mighty temple complex on Mt. Hiei, Izumo was never in a subordinate position in its longstanding relationship with the Shugendō temple of Gakuenji. In both cases, the strongest party got its way. It is all the more striking, under these circumstances, that even Hie priests found inspiration in *yuiitsu* ideas, absorbed them into their practice as early as the 1580s,[24] and found the courage to aspire to *yuiitsu* autonomy right after the *Shrine Clauses* were issued.

Ise

While Izumo and Hie are often brought up in the context of the *Shrine Clauses* and the ascendancy of the Yoshida in the 1660s, Ise is rarely mentioned. Yet it was in the 1660s and 1670s that Ise was transformed into a site of Shinto, both discursively and institutionally.[25] This is hardly a coincidence; at the very least, it says something about the general atmosphere in which Domain Shinto could thrive in these decades.

In the 1660s, Ise was a complicated place. Its two constituent shrine complexes, the Outer and the Inner Shrine, had been rebuilt in 1563 and 1585 through the combined efforts of the new warrior hegemons—Oda Nobunaga (1534–82) and Toyotomi Hideyoshi—and monastics specializing in *kanjin* 勧進 fundraising (not unlike the *hongan* of Izumo). When Hideyoshi donated funds for the 1585 rebuilding, he also took measures that decided the economic and political situation of the shrines and the towns in front of them for centuries to come. He exempted the area east of Ise's Miyagawa River from his cadastral surveys and turned it into the domain of the shrines, to be governed by the town councils of Yamada and Uji where the Outer and Inner Shrine were located. This arrangement was rendered permanent by Tokugawa Ieyasu in 1603. In the 1630s, the shogunate appointed a Yamada magistrate (*Yamada bugyō* 山田奉行) who was tasked with overseeing the Ise shrines and the councils of both towns.

Needless to say, the economy of Ise was dominated by the pilgrimage trade. This trade was based on contracts between Ise pilgrimage entrepreneurs (*oshi* 御師) and their "patrons" (*danna*), giving the *oshi* a monopoly on providing services both in their *danna*'s home provinces and in Ise. Leading *oshi* of the Outer and Inner Shrines dominated the Yamada and Uji town councils. These towns accommodated numerous temples where *kanjin* monks and nuns were based. Many *kanjin* temples also held portfolios of *danna* contracts and doubled as *oshi*. The largest among them, the Keikōin 慶光院 nunnery, both oversaw the rebuildings at Ise and served as the *oshi* of the Tokugawa.

In 1635, anti-Christian legislation came to Ise, and with it, the issue of certifying faith. The Yamada town council received instructions that all inhabitants—male, female, as well as servants—needed to "decide on their sectarian affiliation (*shūshi* 宗旨)" and procure a *danna* certificate from a temple. Ise's priests were not exempted, and in 1638 the head priest of the Outer Shrine petitioned the magistrate to "disregard" temple affiliation for shrine priests and their families and offered to guarantee for all priests personally. The head priest explained to the magistrate that "Buddhism offends the ancient law of Shinto;" therefore, forcing shrine priests to submit to the supervision of monastics would be an affront to the gods.[26] This exception was granted and remained in place until 1671.

Questions of faith also emerged in other ways. An *oshi* of the Outer Shrine, Deguchi Nobuyoshi 出口延佳 (1615–90), worked to recover Ise's ancient Shinto writings and reconstruct classical shrines and rituals. Nobuyoshi sought to redefine Shinto as a teaching and faith for laypeople, essential to all Japanese in their daily lives. Nobuyoshi argued that the deterioration of the Shinto creed (*shūshi*) was driving people into the arms of the Southern Barbarians (i.e., Christians).[27] His understanding of Shinto was fiercely anti-Buddhist, and from about 1650 onwards he wrote a number of works where he fulminates against Shinto's medieval corruption by *ryōbu shūgō* ideas and practices. Nobuyoshi singled out the Yoshida as the main source of such corruption. In 1666, a year after the *Shrine Clauses* were issued, he accused the Yoshida of inventing such practices as Shinto *goma* 護摩 and Shinto *kaji* 加持, both rituals strongly associated with Buddhism, and spreading them to priests around the country.[28]

The logic of faith also affected the *oshi* business. In 1634 and 1635, Outer Shrine *oshi* stopped all traffic to the Inner Shrine, claiming that they had exclusive rights to serve pilgrims with whom they had contracts.[29] Their argument was that since the gods worshipped at the Outer and the Inner Shrine are identical, pilgrims can only be under contract with one *oshi*; if pilgrims had contracts with two *oshi*, one at each of the two Ise shrines, the Inner Shrine contract was invalid. Inner Shrine *oshi*, on the other hand, claimed that both Ieyasu and his successor Hidetada had given them a vermillion-seal document stating that it was "up to the *danna*" (*danna shidai* 檀那次第) to perform the pilgrimage free from interference. They interpreted this phrase to mean that pilgrims were free to conclude contracts with *oshi* of both Ise shrines, because the gods of the two shrines are not identical but separate. This last point, at least, was recognized by the shogunal deliberative council (*hyōjōsho* 評定所) in Edo upon consulting the shogunal scholar Hayashi Razan; the fact that the shogun and many daimyo also had two *oshi* added weight to this view.

In the end, the discussion revolved around the question whether *danna* were to be free to worship where they wanted, as argued by the Inner Shrine *oshi*, or whether Outer Shrine *oshi* could stop their own *danna* from patronizing the Inner Shrine, as their Outer Shrine colleagues argued. To solve the matter, a new vermillion-seal document was issued with revised wording: It was confirmed that *danna* were "free to follow their own will (*kokoro* 心, *kokorozashi* 志)," while at the same time, *oshi* were warned not to "steal others' *danna* by cunning."[30] This formula foreshadows the almost identical structure of the fourth item of the 1665 *Law for Temples of All Sects*, discussed above. This 1635 document guaranteed the free "will" of pilgrims, and at the same time sought to prevent conflicts between *oshi*.

Although this verdict ended all attempts by the Outer Shrine to barricade the road to the Inner Shrine, the matter did not end here. In 1667/68 there was further wrangling about the *oshi* business. Local officials failed to cut through the Gordian knot created by the contradictions in the 1635 document, and the parties proceeded to Edo. There, the deliberative council concluded that it was up to the "faith of patrons" (*ganshu no shinjin* 願主の信心) whether they wanted to have one *oshi* or two—one for each of Ise's two shrines.[31]

The matter was complicated even further by the existence of *kanjin* temples that also held *danna* contracts. Already in 1654, three temples in Uji appealed to the Yamada magistrate, arguing that they should be free to distribute Ise amulets not only to the *danna* with whom they had contracts, but to all faithful, irrespective of any contracts that they might have with *oshi* of the Inner and/or the Outer Shrine. The reason for this, they stated, was that their temples were the official "shrine temples" (*jingūji* 神宮寺) of the Ise shrines; as such, they had since ancient times performed Buddhist rites for the protection of the realm. The magistrate gave these temples the cold shoulder but allowed them to take their case to Edo, where the magistrate of temples and shrines was equally negative. Yet at the very least, it was confirmed that these temples had the same right as the Inner and Outer Shrine *oshi* to serve the *danna* for whom they did hold contracts.[32]

After this, the matter of Ise's temple *oshi* remained pending for decades, until the 1670s, after the relationship between the Inner and Outer Shrine *oshi* had been clarified. The final outcome was dramatic: In 1675, the magistrate banned all "Buddhists" (*bukke* 仏家) from distributing Ise amulets and acting as Ise *oshi*. From this point onward, all *oshi* were to represent Shinto, and this excluded temples from the trade.

This was only one of a series of blows to the interests of temples in Yamada and Uji. Another setback befell the nuns of the Keikōin, who had been granted special privileges by Ieyasu in recognition of their key role in Ise's rebuildings. In 1666, a vermillion-seal document (*shuinjō* 朱印状) that Ieyasu had granted to the Keikōin was repealed and the nuns were denied their customary place of honor in the upcoming rebuilding of 1669. Further anti-Buddhist measures followed. In 1670 a fire consumed most of Yamada, including 189 temples there; the magistrate used this disaster to reduce the Buddhist presence in the vicinity of the shrines, forcing forty-seven Yamada temples out of existence.[33]

Shunning Buddhism as a source of pollution that might anger the gods was a traditional principle in Ise, and had its roots in classical times. Yet the inhabitants of the shrine domain, including even the Ise priests, were not exempt from the temple certification system, which could not function without the presence of numerous temples and monks. In addition, Ise was replete with prayer temples and Buddhist mendicants who catered to the religious needs of pilgrims. The livelihoods of Ise's *oshi*, merchants, and many others depended on the pilgrimage. While shunning Buddhism was a famous Ise trademark that enhanced its sacred appeal, strict bans on all things Buddhist would disrupt both the temple certification system and the pilgrimage trade. The solution was to maintain rules of shunning Buddhism, while taking care to create ways around them. Ise was, for example, a popular pilgrimage destination also for monastics, even though they were officially banned from entering the shrine precincts.[34] From the 1660s onwards, policies to enforce this ban were balanced with measures that sought to accommodate the wishes of monastic pilgrims. In 1665, a group of monks was allowed to worship in front of the main shrine halls as long as they refrained from chanting the *nenbutsu*. In 1672, a special worship site was created for monastic visitors further away from the shrines (*sōni yōhaisho* 僧尼遥拝所); in 1689, the worship site at the Inner Shrine was moved closer to avoid displeasuring visiting monks. There was, in fact, an even easier method to gain access: Throughout the Edo period, all who had taken the tonsure (or were naturally bald) had the option of dressing in lay garb and renting a wig.

Conclusion

Through the examples of Izumo, Hie, and Ise, I have reflected on the significance of the *Shrine Clauses* of 1665 and the official recognition that these clauses gave to the Way of the Gods (*shintō* or *jingidō*) as a teaching and creed of its own. The *Shrine Clauses* were issued at a time when the Tokugawa-related daimyo of Mito, Aizu, Okayama, and arguably Matsue were experimenting with "Domain Shinto," implementing policies that separated Shinto from Buddhism and shrines from temples. As noted above, these clauses would probably not have been issued without the effective lobbying by one of these daimyo, Hoshina Masayuki of Aizu; they are, therefore, a result of Domain Shinto spilling onto the national scene.

Yuiitsu ideas, claiming that Shinto and Buddhism are separate and incompatible, were already in play at shrine-temple complexes such as Hie and Izumo at the very beginning of the Edo period. In Ise, they dominated priestly learning by the 1650s. We have seen that "Shintoization" following a *yuiitsu* model succeeded in Izumo in 1662 and in Ise in 1675, while it failed in Hie in 1669 and again in 1685. The 1660s and 1670s were clearly *yuiitsu*'s "moment in the sun"—an historical juncture when Shinto ideas enjoyed active political support and were being implemented at some places, though only when the circumstances were favorable.

The *Shrine Clauses* formed a set with the *Law for Temples of All Sects*, which itself was a product of the ambition to strengthen the temple certification system so as to control laypeople's faith. As this volume illustrates, the 1660s saw the culmination of a concern with lay faith as a potential threat to the social order. Naturally, faith was defined by sect and teaching. The recognition of the Yoshida's Shinto as a non-Buddhist teaching raised questions about the status of the Shinto "creed" (*shūshi*) in the management of faith. If a non-Buddhist teaching was recognized as a legitimate creed, should this have implications for the temple certification system? Should, for example, Shinto priests have their faith certified by Buddhist temples?

These questions point at a defining dilemma in the Tokugawa system of controlling faith. Faith (referred to in the Ise conflicts by such terms as *shinjin* 信心 and *kokoro* 心, *kokorozashi* 志, or *kokoroe* 心得) was *in principle* regarded as an important matter of personal choice. In 1635, the *oshi* of Ise's Outer Shrine claimed that they had the right to buy and sell *danna* contracts at will without consulting the affected *danna*, as was indeed current practice. In Edo, this struck the warrior officials who adjudicated this matter in the deliberative council as unreasonable. One of the officials pointed out that he would call this *oshi shidai* 御師次第, "up to the *oshi*", rather than *danna shidai*—it was the will of the *oshi* that was being respected here, not that of the *danna*. Another compared the practice to horse-trading of the worst kind, and a third exclaimed: "None of us can be bought and sold like that!"[35] The Inner Shrine *oshi* were likewise guilty of selling *danna* contracts, but stressed repeatedly, though surely untruthfully, that they always respected the faith of the *danna* and asked their permission before proceeding with a sale. We see here the notion that a layperson's faith should have priority over the contracts he or she (or, more likely, someone in a previous generation) has concluded with religious professionals.

Such sentiments were prevalent in the 1630s, when the campaign against Christians was in full swing and the first steps towards establishing a system of temple certification were being taken. By the 1660s, however, complications had arisen. Laypeople's freedom to follow their faith had to be balanced against other considerations that were ultimately deemed more important: the institutional interests of the brokers of faith. Efforts to control laypeople's faith lapsed, while a less ambitious and more pragmatic concern took over: certifying the credentials and institutional structures of priests, and working out how to deal with their overlapping contracts with lay *danna*. A system that once sought to ascertain the orthodoxy of laypeople's faith gradually turned into a system of licensing priests and adjudicating their contractual rights. If proponents of Domain Shinto hoped that the *Shrine Clauses* would save the people in their domains from the clutches of Buddhism and give them the option to adopt Shinto as their faith, they failed. Instead, their initiative led to the development of an ever more intricate system of licenses for various kinds of ritualists who operated outside of the temple certification system, allowing them to legalize their trade. There is no doubt that this outcome would have offended the Confucian sentiments of the creators of Domain Shinto—the daimyo of Mito, Aizu, and Okayama and their advisers.

11

Domain Shinto and *shintō-uke* in Okayama-han

Stefan Köck

Introduction: A Reappraisal of Shinto Shrines in Early Tokugawa Japan

Toward the middle of the seventeenth century, a reappraisal of ancient shrines took place in several Japanese domains. Primary examples of domains in which this trend appeared in the 1650s are Wakayama-han 和歌山藩 in Kii province, Iwaki-taira-han 磐城平藩 in Mutsu province, and Kōchi-han 高知藩 in Tosa province.[1] Individual shrines considered of religious value for the domain lords were usually supported; while shrines dedicated to the religious needs of the general populace were seen as less important. Domain rulers even adopted a policy of destroying shrines they deemed illicit (*inshi* 淫祀).[2] From a wider perspective, these developments mark the beginning of a separation between Shinto and Buddhism, if only at a local level.

In the 1660s, *bakufu* legislation also supported endeavors to separate Shinto from Buddhism. The *Shrine Clauses* (*Jinja jōmoku*) of 1665, which aimed at the control of Shinto priests (*shinshoku* 神職) and shrines throughout the country,[3] were the first explicit laws concerning the "Way of the Gods" (*jingidō* 神祇道). They not only facilitated, but also expanded, the range and intensity of reforms that were subsequently undertaken in the domains of Mito 水戸藩, Aizu 会津藩[4], and Okayama in the late 1660s. For example, starting in 1666, Okayama domain (Okayama-han 岡山藩) was subjected to various radical reforms during the rule of Ikeda Mitsumasa 池田光正 (1609–82, r.1632–72). The underlying concept of these reforms has been described as to "persecute Buddhism and elevate Confucianism" (*haibutsu kōju* 廃仏興儒).[5] Succinct as this description is, however, it captures only a part of Mitsumasa's aims,[6] which also included Shinto, with shrine reforms a basic feature from the outset of the developments.

In these examples, domain rulers or, respectively, the *bakufu* decided to foster and actively push the development of Shinto forward in their dominions, leading to specific varieties in each domain. Yet, as is emphasized by Inoue Tomokatsu in this volume, they also shared common elements, such as the tearing down of illicit shrines, the separation of Shinto and Buddhist elements, and initiatives by the respective rulers to give Shinto a new shape in their dominions. I call the resulting domain-specific Shinto developments "Domain Shinto" (*hanryō shintō* 藩領神道).

In this chapter I will primarily discuss Ikeda Mitsumasa's religious reforms (also referred to as the reforms of the Kanbun era [1661–73]), with a focus on the measures linked to Shinto and their long term implications. In particular I will analyze the implementation of *shintō-uke* 神道請 (certification by Shinto shrines), which entailed the religious control of the domain's populace by means of Shinto shrines. This was different from the usual procedure of confirming the non-Christian status of inhabitants with certification from a Buddhist temple (*terauke* 寺請).[7] Although the *shintō-uke* and other measures introduced in the Kanbun era in Okayama prevailed for only a few decades, they mark the decline of the medieval Shinto-Buddhist syncretism (*shinbutsu shugō* 神仏習合) as well as the rise of *hanryō shintō* in Okayama-han.

Initial Reforms: Destruction of Shrines

Domain-wide religious reforms in Okayama-han started in the spring of 1666 through a extensive reduction in the number of shrines. In the fifth month of 1666, having just returned from Edo, Mitsumasa met with the three heads of his domain administration (*daikan gashira* 代官頭), eager to discuss his plans regarding Shinto shrines.

> (1666/5/18) I talked with the three *daikan gashira* [about the fact that] in the province there are [many] of those useless shrines. They will be concentrated in one place provided with land [the size] of 5,000 *koku*. We will approach the honorable Yoshida. Apart from that, the grand shrines and the *obusuna* shrines shall remain untouched. I have ordered them to proceed with the [next] step.
> Note on the small shrines in general: More than 11,100 will be torn down.[8]

Mitsumasa's journal entry is the first known reference to measures for the general restructuring of Shinto institutions in Okayama-han. The mentioned number of 11,100 small shrines is not a random figure and suggests that a thorough survey of shrines had already been conducted. Indeed, preparations must have been well under way between the spring of 1665 and the spring of 1666 while Mitsumasa was away in Edo.

Mitsumasa's number is confirmed by an only slightly different one in the *Ohiroma zakki* 御広間雑記, a historical account of the Yoshida 吉田 house that describes events from 1650 to 1869[9]:

> (1667/2/19) [The Okayama register] stated: "In total there are 11,128 shrines; among them are 601 *ujigami* shrines."[10]

These are probably the correct figures from the above-mentioned survey, and thus it seems Mitsumasa made a mistake in his journal: He confused the total number of shrines in his domain with the number that were to be destroyed. According to him, grand shrines (*taisha* 大社)[11] and tutelary shrines of villages (*ubusuna/obusuna* 産土, usually called *ujigami* 氏神 shrines) were to be left standing, but more than 11,000 small shrines were to be merged in one place and their original buildings torn down.

Domain Shinto in Okayama-han

The reference to "the honorable Yoshida" (*Yoshida dono* 吉田殿)[12] shows that he intended to enlist the help of the Yoshida Shinto 吉田神道 organization.

But Mitsumasa's plan of reducing the number of shrines was by no means exceptional in the 1660s, as indicated above. It was just the extent of these measures in Okayama-han that set it apart from other domains. The *Ikeda-ke rireki ryakki* 池田家履歴略記,[13] a historical account of the rule of the Ikeda family in Okayama, provides additional information on how Mitsumasa planned to put these measures into action:

> (1666/5/18) [Mitsumasa] talked to the *daikan gashira* Kawamura Heitaibei 川村平太兵衛, Nishimura Gengorō 西村源五郎 and Tsushi Gen'emon 都志源右衛門 and consulted with Matsuoka Ichinosuke 松岡市之助. [All shrines] except those of *ubusuna* deities were destroyed without pardon. The trees from the shrine grounds were taken and one shrine was built in each *daikan* residence. These were called *yosemiya* 寄宮 ("collective shrines") and [Mitsumasa] sought a seal of confirmation from the Yoshida.[14]

These lines sum up the developments in the months following 1666/5. They reveal that Mitsumasa consulted not only the heads of his government (*daikan gashira*), but also Matsuoka Ichinosuke (*fl.* 1664–1679), a Shinto priest whose responsibilities will be discussed in more detail below. The wording of the *Ikeda-ke rireki ryakki* ("without pardon" *nokorazu hakkyaku shi*) bears witness to the fact that the execution of these measures was absolutely systematic.

In his journal entry of 1666/5/18, Mitsumasa pointed out that any leftover devotional objects from the destroyed shrines were to be preserved in a collective shrine (*yosemiya*), a new category of shrine created specifically for this purpose. According to the *Ikeda-ke rireki ryakki*, however, initially one *yosemiya* was built in each district supervised by a local deputy (*daikan* 代官).[15] It has been calculated that a total of 10,528 shrines were destroyed, with only 612 tutelary and grand shrines remaining, along with seventy-one *yosemiya*.[16] In other words, 94.5 percent of the shrines in Okayama-han vanished. On average, less than one shrine per village remained (0.97). Thus, the reduction of shrines in Okayama was even greater than in Mito domain, where in 1696 shrines were also destroyed.[17]

Steps toward an Alternative Mode of Religious Certification

Religious certification was one step in the larger process of religious inspection. In its usual form, this process had two main agents: the domain administration; and the Buddhist clergy. In general, religious inspection was conducted as follows: A register of religious inspection (*shūmon aratame chō* 宗門改帳) was compiled once a year by the village headman (*shōya* 庄屋) or the village administration. It listed each individual member of every household in the village. This register was given to the Buddhist temples to which these villagers were affiliated. By attaching his seal to the name of each individual, the monk of a specific temple certified that they numbered among his temples' parishioners (*danna* 旦那/ *danka* 檀家). The register was then returned to the village administration. Usually the *shōya* then verified the religious affiliation of the individuals mentioned therein, stating explicitly that they were not Christians. Finally, the register was submitted to the domain's magistrate for religious inspection who produced the annual report for the *bakufu*.[18]

In Okayama-han, religious inspection (*shūmon aratame* 宗門改) was practiced even before the *bakufu* made it mandatory for the whole country in 1664. The domain's oldest extant register of religious inspection dates from 1655 and marks the beginning of monthly inspection of non-affiliation with Christianity in Okayama-han.[19] Extant registers from the following years show that the procedure was taken seriously.

Thus, in 1664 religious inspection was already established in Okayama-han; some administrative procedures were probably modified according to *bakufu* specifications. These demanded, for instance, that the domains employ a magistrate for religious inspection and that they submit an annual report. A system according to *bakufu* specifications was established in Okayama-han in the first month of 1665.[20]

As a consequence of the system of religious inspection, anyone who was not certified as a parishioner of a village temple was suspected of being a Christian and their case was investigated in detail. A special investigation was also required for individuals who moved from one village to another. They had to present a document stating that they had switched their temple affiliation—that is, left their former temple parish and joined the temple of their new residence. The relevant document was issued by the village administration and usually inserted in the register of religious inspection of the respective year.[21]

The changes introduced in the summer of 1666 by Mitsumasa directly addressed the administrative step of confirming an individual's religious affiliation. Journal entries from that time reveal his plans for treating Confucians in a separate way.

> (1666/8/4) I talked to the *daikan gashira* and to the district magistrates (*koori bugyō* 郡奉行) about the modalities for the certificates of [non-adherence to] Christianity for those who have expressed an inclination towards Confucianism.[22]

As when he decided to reduce the number of shrines, Mitsumasa first consulted his inner circle of advisors and the higher officials of the *han*. From the beginning, this also involved the domain's district officials.[23] As the above journal entry shows, Mitsumasa followed the *bakufu*'s campaign of religious inspection and anti-Christian certification. At the same time, however, he refers to the existence of individuals in Okayama-han who were inclined towards Confucianism. Clearly it had become an issue as to how such people should be certified after certification by Buddhist temples had become mandatory under *bakufu* law.

Mitsumasa may have had two groups in mind when he referred to people with "inclination towards Confucianism." While his long-time companion and Confucian advisor Kumazawa Banzan 熊沢蕃山 (1619–91) had left Mitsumasa's service in 1657, former Confucian pupils of Banzan constituted a significant group among the domain's leading administrators.[24] Also, according to a report of 1667 by itinerant inspectors of the *bakufu* (*junkenshi* 巡見使), Mitsumasa intended to make Confucianism known among the populace by visiting several places in Okayama domain in autumn 1666.

Following his visit some members of the populace actually turned towards Confucianism.²⁵ But assuming the report is correct in stating that Mitsumasa's tour took place in autumn this will place it some time after the discussion of an alternative certification procedure. And the fresh Confucian converts were not at all educated Confucians like the pupils of Banzan or Mitsumasa himself. It is best to consider them Confucians only in a nominal way. Whether Confucian values were at all relevant among the lower strata of the domain's populace at large, or even known, is doubtful.²⁶ Thus at this stage, these considerations regarding religious certification seem to pertain only to a rather limited group. In the long run, however, they proved to be the first step towards a reform that altered the religious affiliation of the entire Okayama population.

Mitsumasa's journal entry for the following day (1666/8/5) includes a template draft for an alternative "Certificate of (non-adherence to) Christianity," in two parts:

> Although my tradition for generations has been Shingon Buddhism, as parishioner of __ temple in __ village, __ district, I became interested in Confucianism and studied Shinto, and from this __ month, __ day onwards I reject Buddhism, and practice Confucian ceremonies (state reason for faith in the tutelary deity) (for outsiders not required). Accordingly, I request a certificate from the priest of __ shrine.²⁷

This is a hypothetical declaration by an individual member of the domain for announcing their decision to leave the Buddhist sect to which they adhere, denoted here as the Shingon 真言 sect. Instead of Buddhism, the individual plans to practice Confucian ceremonies and honor the tutelary deity of their village. In accordance with this intent, they request a certificate of confirmation by the priest of their village's Shinto shrine. As the second part of his draft, Mitsumasa provides a corresponding template for the "priest of __ shrine":

> Although the signee __ of __ district, __ village has until now been a parishioner of Shingon Buddhism at __ temple in __ village, __ district and requested certification accordingly, he has turned to Confucianism and studies Shinto and expresses faith in the tutelary deity of __ shrine (for outsiders not required). He is not a Christian. If there is anything suspicious, I will seek you out and explain. Accordingly, this is hereafter valid.²⁸

With this, the Shinto priest confirms that the applicant belonged to a certain parish of a certain Buddhist sect (again Shingon is used as an example), but had hence turned to Confucianism, was studying Shinto, and had started to worship the tutelary deity of his village. The priest also confirms that the applicant is not a Christian and offers to answer any questions regarding the applicant's intentions.

As mentioned above, changes of residence and parish affiliation had to be clarified on an individual basis, with an explanatory note inserted into the respective year's *shūmon aratame chō*. Mitsumasa's draft was meant to serve as a template for exactly this kind of document. Moreover, it documents a religious conversion: from a temple's *danka* parish to a shrine's *ujiko* 氏子 parish.

Mitsumasa's template marks the starting point of the practice of certification via Shinto shrines in Okayama-han. From his viewpoint, *shintō-uke* was merely a minor addition to the religious inspection procedure, the only change being that the *shinshoku* of the respective shrine henceforward certified in the register of religious inspection that certain individuals belonged to the *ujiko* parish of his shrine. The *shūmon aratame chō* would continue to be sent in the established way from the village administration to the village temple in order for membership in the temple *danka* to be certified. Additionally, the register would also be sent to the village's shrine to allow its *shinshoku* to certify membership in the shrine *ujiko* of his parish. Finally, the register would be returned to the administration for the concluding steps. Certification via shrines was thus just an additional administrative step in the religious inspection process.

Mitsumasa's template thus drafted a legal document that when submitted, that is, when an individual changed affiliation from a temple parish to a shrine parish, would serve several aims at once:

- documenting that the mentioned individual was not a Christian;
- identifying the individual as a former member of a specific temple parish;
- identifying the individual as a new follower of Confucianism and of Shinto;
- documenting the individual's departure from the aforementioned temple parish;
- documenting the individual's entry into the *ujiko* parish of the respective shrine;
- implying that henceforth in the annual religious inspection, the *shinshoku* of the respective shrine was responsible for certifying the membership of that individual in the *ujiko* parish.

One may deduce from the template that Mitsumasa regarded Confucianism, Shinto, and Buddhism as elements of a common category *shūmon* (religion)—at least for administrative purposes. It does not, however, support the view of the union or identity of Shinto and Confucianism.[29] The template clearly distinguishes between Confucianism (*judō* 儒道) and Shinto; no term for unifying the two traditions is found.[30] This suggests that Mitsumasa, a devotee of Confucianism, intended to employ the two traditions for different purposes.

And indeed, the template shows that Shinto was primarily used to have the *shinshoku* take over the administrative duties of religious control. It was a change that involved legal implications, since the respective individual no longer fell under the jurisdiction of Buddhism. Regarding this point, Mitsumasa distinguishes clearly between Buddhism on one side, and Shinto and Confucianism on the other, whereby he considers these two sides mutually exclusive.

Since Confucianism was—in Mitsumasa's view—no longer compatible with Buddhism, an alternative for certifying converts was necessary in order to meet the requirement of religious inspection as prescribed by the *bakufu*. No Confucian institutions existed, that could have provided an alternative to *terauke*. Shrines, however, existed in almost every village. And Shinto priests, unlike Buddhist monks, who often moved to village temples from afar, were usually deeply rooted in their village communities. Mitsumasa, it is assumed, had *shinshoku* do religious certification because their intimate knowledge of village affairs allowed for an even tighter control of the population.[31]

Shinshoku thus gained a function as quasi-officials of the domain administration that hitherto had been held exclusively by Buddhist clerics.

Mitsumasa's template foreshadows the religious restructuring of the subsequent period, which was to redefine the relationship between Buddhism, Confucianism, and Shinto. Having non-Christian certification conducted by shrines implied the potential weakening of Buddhism. And the template indeed seems to have coincided with considerations of Mitsumasa to cut back Buddhism as well.³² According to the *Ikeda-ke rireki ryakki*, only days later he delivered a lecture to the upper strata of domain officials in which he criticized the following aspects of Buddhism:

> (1666/8/23) Among those who have taken [Buddhist] vows, there are people who are old and sick, as well as uneducated and even illiterate. This state of affairs can no longer be tolerated. All in all, Buddhism is quickly impaired if clerics, despite the fact that they should be focusing their minds on administering graves and specializing in this, do not stop spreading subversive teachings; this encourages foolish monks.³³

Although Mitsumasa targets several points with this criticism, one statement stands out as a possible indication of what was to come: The clear warning that Buddhist monks should refrain from spreading subversive, heterodox teachings (*jahō* 邪法). Instead, they should occupy themselves with serving their parishes. In retrospect, this statement can be read as an indication that the reduction of Buddhist temples and monks, in particular the Fujufuse branch (Fujufuse-ha 不受不施派) of the Nichiren 日蓮 sect, was already being considered. At this point, however, the notion of the mutual exclusiveness between Buddhism and Confucianism does not seem to have led to any concrete measures. The drastic reduction of Buddhism started only a few months later.

Buddhist Persecution in Okayama

In Bizen province, the region encompassed by the Edo period's Okayama-han, the Buddhist sects Tendai 天台 and Shingon had originally been dominant. In the late fifteenth century, however, local rulers began to patronize the Nichiren sect which consequently started to flourish in this region. Many Nichiren temples in Bizen had ties to the temple Myōkakuji 妙覚寺 in Kyoto; in fact, they amounted to about one third of Myōkakuji's affiliated temples.³⁴

As is described in detail by Jacqueline Stone in this volume, the exclusivist concept of "neither giving nor receiving" (*fujufuse* 不受不施) was a basic stance of the Nichiren sect. Ultimately this meant the rejection of any relations with "non-believers" of Nichiren's doctrines, including the highest secular authorities. In the late sixteenth and early seventeenth century, this had led to conflicts with Toyotomi Hideyoshi 豊臣秀吉 (1537–98) and Tokugawa Ieyasu 徳川家康 (1542–1616). Nichiō 日応 (1565–1630), then abbot of Myōkakuji and thus also important for Okayama, was one of the most radical advocates of *fujufuse*. He refused to take part in all official ceremonies organized by the *bakufu*, and thus met with growing opposition, also within his own sect. The *fujufuse* principle thus led to Nichiren Buddhism splitting into an accommodating faction and a fundamentalist faction. The latter became known as the Fujufuse branch. Finally, the accommodating faction demanded the persecution of their Fujufuse opponents. Resultant measures were begun in the Edo region at the end of the fifth month of 1666.

Mitsumasa took this conflict as a precedent to proceed against Buddhism in his own domain. In the twelfth month of 1666, six Fujufuse monks were expelled from Okayama-han. By the third month of the next year, this number had risen to 585. Other Buddhist sects were affected as well, as the following tables show:

Table 11.1 Buddhist temples and clergy in Okayama-han.[35]

	1666	1667	net decrease	remaining %
Temples	1,044	481	563	46.1%
Monks	1,957	1,110	847	56.7%

Table 11.2 Persecution and religious affiliation.

	Fujufuse	Tendai / Shingon	net sum	Fujufuse %
Exiled monks	585	262	847	69.1%
Destroyed temples	313	250	563	55.6%

These figures show that the purges decimated the number of monks and temples. While Okayama-han had more than 600 villages, according to the *Otome-chō* 御留帳 of Kanbun 7, in early 1667 only 481 temples and 1,110 clerics remained. Thus, about 20 percent of the villages no longer had a temple, and close to 50 percent of the clergy had been either exiled or laicized.

However, the temples and their monks were important institutions in local communities. A major duty in their parishes, in addition to *terauke* certification, was performing funerals. They also held an educational role. Temple schools (*terakoya* 寺子屋), where the upper strata of the rural society acquired their education, were usually run by village clerics. Thus it is clear that the reduction measures caused serious problems in the areas of administration and education.

It is easy to imagine that the remaining temples were unable to perform their traditional duties smoothly. Moreover, the potential inoperability of the religious certification system also had implications at a supra-regional level, since certification was mandatory not only under domain law, but also under *bakufu* law. Thus, finding solutions for the administration and education of the entire Okayama-han became an urgent task.

The Implementation of *shintō-uke* Certification

Since Mitsumasa had already set a precedent by designating Shinto shrines as being responsible for the religious certification of Confucian converts, one obvious solution would have been to engage with Shinto on a larger scale after the purges of Buddhism. However, there was apparently a lack of educated shrine personnel, which complicated matters. In general, village shrines were not permanently equipped with professional *shinshoku*, but were rather attended by members of the laity, who acted as "part-time" or "lay" priests (*zoku kannushi* 俗神主).³⁶ The need to have a certain level of education narrowed the number of prospective *shinshoku* decisively. In addition to Buddhist monks, usually the only people with such skills were the members of the village administration—for the most part, hereditary offices held by a small number of families. Practical solutions for this dilemma can be inferred from the *Satsuyōroku* 撮要録, an Okayama-han administrative compendium. At first glance, the solutions offered here are quite surprising. To cite only one example, the Buddhist monk of Tōkaku-bō Temple 東覚坊 in Waita village 脇田村 was laicized. Subsequently, he became a Shinto priest at Sōja Myōjin Shrine 惣社明神 in the nearby village of Gion 祇園村.³⁷ His case is only one of many similar examples listed in this compendium. Obviously not all monks who were expelled from their temples had to leave the domain. On the contrary, a considerable number seem to have transitioned almost seamlessly into the office of *shinshoku*, often at the tutelary shrine of their place of residence.

No exact figures are available for the number of monks who became Shinto priests. For Tendai or Shingon clerics, whose sects had integrated *kami* already for centuries, becoming a Shinto priest probably posed few problems. At the village level, it had actually been more common for services at shrines to be conducted by Buddhist monks (usually called shrine monks [*shasō* 社僧]) than by fully fledged Shinto priests.³⁸ Educated monks without Fujufuse ties could therefore easily convert from *bōzu* 坊主 to *shinshoku* and continue to serve their community. For the *han* administration, this was a quite practical solution. Such former monks were also certainly already trained in anti-Christian certification, since most of them had been practicing *terauke* since 1655, when the procedure was introduced by Mitsumasa.

Thus, in terms of administration, the change from *terauke* to *shintō-uke* did not cause any formal changes of the certificates and registers as such.³⁹ In the case of *terauke* certification, a Buddhist cleric guaranteed that the registered individual belonged to his parish by attaching his seal. In the case of *shintō-uke*, the local Shinto priest guaranteed that the registered individual belonged to the shrine parish. Other than that, the processes were more or less identical.

It is hard to say, however, whether each individual now had to declare themselves a follower of Confucianism and Shinto in written form, as had been intended according to the plans for conversion on a smaller scale in 1666/8. It seems that no documents with information on this point are extant, which may be due in part to the administrative practice at that time of discarding *shūmon aratamechō* after a couple of years. From figures in *han* administration documents, we only know that in 1669 the religious certification of 97.9 percent of the population was done through Shinto shrines.⁴⁰ Thus, in terms of administration, the measures of 1666/67 proved quite successful. But this was only one aspect of the reform measures. When professional *shinshoku* began to conduct tasks such as *shintō-uke* in Okayama-han, the provisions of the *bakufu*'s 1665 Shrine Clauses had to be considered as well. Demands regarding the certification, training, and education of newly appointed shrine priests had to be met.

Matsuoka Ichinosuke's Role in Establishing *hanryō shintō* in Okayama

Tasks such as educating new shrine priests became one of the duties of the above-mentioned Matsuoka Ichinosuke, who in 1666 or 1667 was appointed general inspector of Shinto priests (*kannushi sōtō* 神主惣頭) in Okayama-han, and held that office until 1679 or 1680.[41] Ichinosuke was originally a *shinshoku* from the prestigious Atsuta Shrine 熱田神宮 in Owari province; he had entered Mitsumasa's services in the early 1660s. According to the *Ohiroma zakki*, he had established contacts with the Yoshida family already in 1664 and subsequently had become a licensed priest of Yoshida Shinto.[42] This qualification set him apart from other *shinshoku* in Okayama-han. Ichinosuke was an advisor to Mitsumasa regarding the shrine reduction measures of 1666. As *the* specialist on Yoshida Shinto in Okayama-han, he was the intermediary when Mitsumasa and his officials wanted to enlist the authority that had been transferred to the Yoshidas in the *Shrine Clauses* for their purposes in the process of their own Shinto reforms.

One of his first tasks involved legitimizing the newly established *yosemiya*. Being a shrine, a *yosemiya* needed to house a devotional object (*shintai* 神体). Okayama-han achieved this legitimization by having Matsuoka Ichinosuke approach the Yoshida family. The *Ohiroma zakki* contains the following record:

> (1667/2/19) The *shintai* of Bizen province were handed over to Matsuoka Ichidayū this morning, and they amount to seventy-two shrines. The *kami* names have been cataloged in detail in a separate register.[43]

What this record is referring to is clear: The seventy-two *shintai* were to serve as objects of worship in the *yosemiya*.[44] This number differed from Mitsumasa's plan as recorded in his journal on 1666/5/18. Originally, for the entire domain he had intended to build a single shrine with land attached yielding 5,000 *koku* per year. By early 1667, this plan had changed to constructing one shrine for each administrative district, over which a local deputy (*daikan*) presided.[45]

The *Shrine Clauses* also required *shinshoku* to be educated in Shinto lore, a provision also taken up in Okayama-han. Several documents mention priests being instructed by Ichinosuke. For example, the annual administrative volume *Ontome-chō hyōjōsho* 御留帳評定所 of 1669 notes:

> Item. Inakawa Jurōemon 稲川十郎右衛門 and Nishimura Gengorō 西村源五郎 went to Matsuoka Ichinosuke's residence for lessons.[46]

The *Otome-chō*[47] of 1670 contains a similar entry.[48] In addition to teaching Shinto priests, Ichinosuke had to attend to various ceremonial duties. These are also recorded over several years in the *Otome-chō*. For example, in the ninth month of 1669, Ichinosuke and other *shinshoku* performed a *kitō* 祈祷 prayer ceremony at Okayama castle, which replaced the established Shingon-Buddhist *kitō* rite.[49] Other records mention him as the officiant in shrine relocation ceremonies.[50]

Regarding his administrative duties, he was in charge of *shintō-uke* certification.[51] On occasion, he also confirmed the laicization of former Buddhist monks.[52] And last but not least, one further task of his office involved traveling through the domain to supervise local Shinto priests.[53]

Ichinosuke's many duties reflect the extent of the changes and innovations that were introduced by Mitsumasa's Shinto reforms. In fact, Ichinosuke's responsibilities provide an overview of the developmental phase of *hanryō shintō* in Okayama, of which he was a central figure for more than twenty years.

In 1680, the domain government appointed Ōmori Chikugo 大森筑後 (dates unknown), head priest of Kibitsu no miya 吉備津宮, the most prestigious shrine of Bizen province,[54] to be the new general inspector of Shinto priests and successor of Ichinosuke. The decision was confirmed by the Yoshida house in the same year. Administering the *shintō-uke* system became one of Chikugo's main jobs. His family held the office of *kannushi sōtō* throughout the Edo period, although at times members of two other shrine families, the Oka 岡 and the Migaki 見垣, also held this post.[55]

In general, however, after Mitsumasa retired as ruler of Okayama-han in 1672, *shintō-uke* certification and most of the Confucian educational reforms were gradually abandoned. In 1674, his son and successor Tsunamasa, yielding to demands of the *bakufu*, readmitted *terauke* certification, whereupon and the populace in many areas quickly reverted to certification via Buddhist temples.[56] The final blow to *shintō-uke* came in 1687, when the *bakufu* demanded that Okayama-han declare *terauke* certification mandatory and thus to conform to the prevalent type of religious certification in Japan.[57]

While domain-wide *shintō-uke* certification thus reached its end after twenty years, other reforms lasted longer. *Shintō-uke* actually continued on a small scale, since Shinto priests and their families were allowed to continue this form of certification for themselves.[58] Moreover, the administrative structures and Shinto institutions created under Mitsumasa's rule remained active as central elements in the special "Domain Shinto" of Okayama-han.[59]

Concluding Remarks

By the seventeenth century, a shift gradually took place from the all-encompassing *shinbutsu shūgō* paradigm of the medieval period to the interpretation of *kami* worship as a distinct religious tradition. While Yoshida Shinto had already prepared the ground in the Muromachi period, early modern scholars distinguished between Buddhism, Confucianism, and Shinto on an intellectual level.[60] Practical consequences of this shift became visible around the mid-seventeenth century, starting with the first steps taken to separate Buddhism and Shinto in various provinces, such as Kii, Tosa, and Mutsu. This was the first glimpse of domain specific forms of Shinto (*hanryō shintō*). The promulgation of the *Shrine Clauses* in 1665, through which *bakufu* law acknowledged Shinto as independent from Buddhism, was a decisive step in establishing what I call "Domain Shinto." From this point in time, various domains, including Mito, Okayama, and Aizu, initiated religious reforms, with Okayama taking the most radical course.

Traditional scholarship has depicted the religious reforms in Okayama domain as a carefully thought-out systematic policy. After reconsidering the relevant sources in this essay, I propose a different view: Mitsumasa originally intended to cut back the number of shrines drastically, to reduce the number of Buddhist monks, and wanted to establish an alternative way of religious certification for a rather small number of people devoted to Confucianism. However, following the major purges of Buddhism in the winter of 1666/67, urgent measures were needed to ensure the continuity of large segments of the administrative and educational system. It seems that the domain government of Okayama-han had not been aware that these consequences would arise when it initially conceived and executed its policies. A "master plan" did not exist. Decisions were taken when necessity arose, with Shinto and Confucianism utilized to solve the predicament resulting from the Buddhist persecution.

Shintō-uke certification as part of the *shūmon aratame* system of religious inspection was originally designed in 1666 as an alternative for those members of the Okayama-han populace who had converted from Buddhism to Confucianism. It was only applied as the sole and mandatory type of certification when in 1667 the breakdown of the former practice of *terauke* was imminent due to the purges of Buddhist institutions. But even then the changes were largely nominal, since in many cases defrocked monks became Shinto priests and continued to serve their communities. Nonetheless, although *shintō-uke* certification was made mandatory for the entire domain only out of necessity, the implications of this for establishing Shinto as a separate religion were profound.

Following the severe reduction in the number of shrines, in most villages only one tutelary shrine remained. Professional Shinto priests were installed at these shrines by the domain government to serve the shrine and its *ujiko* parish, which consisted of the populace of the respective village. These priests provided cultic as well as administrative services. Thus, village shrines, which had earlier been looked after merely by members of the laity or Buddhist shrine monks, were now staffed with permanent *shinshoku*.

This new class of *shinshoku* was supervised and educated by the *kannushi sōtō*. This newly introduced post was first held by Matsuoka Ichinosuke, an advisor to Mitsumasa and an intermediary between Okayama-han and the Yoshida house, which had been called upon to give legitimacy to Shinto-related reforms. Matsuoka Ichinosuke may be regarded as a major influence in shaping the characteristics of Domain Shinto in Okayama-han.

The countrywide authority of the Yoshida house had been boosted by the *Shrine Clauses* of 1665. Starting in the Kanbun era, it enjoyed influence in Okayama-han throughout the Edo period. Over time, however, a degree of control was taken back by the *han* administration as well as by local *shinshoku*.[61] Thus in Okayama-han, independent decisions were often taken on a case-by-case basis without recourse to an external source of authority.

This was very much in line with the main outcome of the Shinto reforms undertaken during Mitsumasa's reign. For the first time, Shinto was separated from Buddhism and established as an individual religion in an area extending over a whole province. *Hanryō shintō* in Okayama was created by strong impulses originating from the *han* government. It featured shrine parishes, as well as a defined organizational structure that consisted of trained religious specialists, separate sanctuaries, and distinct rites and ceremonies. In addition, Shinto priests served as quasi-officials of the domain administration by conducting the *shintō-uke* certification of the populace.

The institutions of Okayama's *hanryō shintō* as created under Ikeda Mitsumasa continued through the early modern period, even after the return to *terauke* certification in 1687. Many open questions and details still need to be considered. Its internal workings, its relevance in the wider development of Japanese religions, as well as its significance in the study of the formation of religions in general will therefore continue to be the subject of further research.

12

"*Kami* is *kami*, Buddha is Buddha"

Religious Policies in Mito Domain in the Later Seventeenth Century

Brigitte Pickl-Kolaczia[1]

> *The way of the* kami *is the way of the* kami, *the way of the Buddha is the way of the Buddha,* shugen *is* shugen. *[Mitsukuni] teaches us that each way must be considered separately and not to confuse things that are different.*[2]

In 1666, Tokugawa Mitsukuni 徳川光圀 (1628–1701), the daimyo of Mito domain (Mito-han 水戸藩), started a purge of religious institutions within his *han* that would result in the destruction of approximately 60 percent of Mito's Buddhist temples and the abolition of nearly all Hachiman 八幡 shrines. Parallel to these measures, Mitsukuni enacted policies that fostered a certain degree of Shintoization in Mito. Taken together, all these measures are part of a concept for which we propose the term *hanryō shintō* 藩領神道 (Domain Shinto), the attempt to reshape Mito's religious landscape according to a daimyo's own ideas of Shinto. The following chapter will give an overview over the *hanryō shintō* policies enacted in Mito.

In 1665, the *bakufu* had decreed two laws to regulate religious affairs within the whole country. The *Law for Temples of all Buddhist Sects* (*Shoshū jiin hatto* 諸宗寺院法度) regulated, among other issues, the conduct of monks and the relation between temples and parishioners. Together with this law, on the same day, the government had passed the *Shrine Clauses* (*Jinja jōmoku* 神社条目), also known as the *Law for Shrine Priests* (*Shosha negi kannushi hatto* 諸社禰宜神主法度), which gave the priestly family of Yoshida 吉田 official authority in almost all Shinto affairs, especially the licensing of shrine priests.[3] Although the Yoshida had issued licenses before that date—for Mito we see Yoshida certificates as early as 1651—this new law awarded those private documents official character.[4]

Controlling the population's religious affiliation was central to Tokugawa religious policy from the very beginning. The repression of Christianity grew more severe after the Shimabara rebellion (*Shimabara no ran* 島原の乱) of 1637/38[5] and the certification of religious affiliation (*shūmon aratame* 宗門改) became mandatory. In Mito, district officials (*gundai* 郡代) were charged with overseeing the process. From the 1620s, every village in Mito submitted registers of sectarian inspection (*shūmon tegata* 宗門手形), which confirmed that no Christians lived there. From 1639, information on the religious affiliation of every household was compiled in census registers of sectarian inspection (*shūmon ninbetsu aratamechō* 宗門人別改帳). Attached to the *tegata* and *aratamechō* were confirmations that neither Christians nor illegal *rōnin* 浪人 lived in the village and that the registers were complete. The registers were then signed by village and temple officials.[6]

In 1664, the *bakufu* ordered the domains to install local magistrates of temples and shrines (*jisha bugyō* 寺社奉行), who took over the task of overseeing the certification process from the district magistrates.[7] Family temples (*danna dera* 檀那寺) confirmed people's affiliation with them and their registers were forwarded to the *han* administration.[8] This task gave Buddhist temples *de facto* control over the population's religious activities and with that control, they gained considerable power. At least three daimyo sought to resist this development and took measures to weaken Buddhism's superior position within their *han*. These three were Hoshina Masayuki 保科正之 (1611–73) of Aizu 会津藩, Ikeda Mitsumasa 池田光政 (1609–82) of Okayama 岡山藩, and Tokugawa Mitsukuni of Mito.

Tokugawa Mitsukuni was the second daimyo of Mito and a grandson of Tokugawa Ieyasu 徳川家康 (1543–1616). The Tokugawa in Mito belonged to the Three Houses (*gosanke* 御三家), Kii 紀伊, Owari 尾張, and Mito, branches of the ruling Tokugawa dynasty. While Kii and Owari enjoyed higher social status and court rank, Mito's daimyo were exempt from the obligation of fluctuating their residence between Edo and their home domain (*sankin kōtai* 参勤交代); they were allowed to stay in Edo for long periods of time. Between 1661 and 1666, Mitsukuni visited Mito only twice, 1663/7–11 and 1665/8–12, spending the majority of his time in Edo.[9] This physical proximity to the center of political power enabled the Mito Tokugawa to exert greater influence on the government than the other houses.[10] Mitsukuni's position seems to have granted him some measure of freedom to adjust the *bakufu*'s orders to his own ideas and wishes.

Historians and biographers of the eighteenth, nineteenth, and even twentieth century depict Mitsukuni as a heroic figure who, although close to the shogun, so revered the emperor that his teachings are considered the foundation of the imperial restoration in Meiji Japan.[11] Natalie Kouamé has questioned this view, pointing out that the political circumstances of the early and the late Edo periods were completely different.[12] While the following analysis will provide no definite answer to this matter, it nonetheless aims to provide a concrete depiction of the nature and immediate implications of the Mito reforms in the late seventeenth century.[13]

These reforms, which took place over a period of approximately thirty years from 1666, resulted in a drastic rearranging of Mito's religious landscape. They involved the rejection of Buddhism, a severe curtailing of the Hachiman faith, and the strengthening of shrines and shrine priests by supporting Shinto funerals and allowing anti-Christian certification by shrines, albeit to a limited degree. After Mitsukuni stepped down as lord of Mito in 1690, his nephew and successor Tsunaeda 徳川綱條 (1656–1718) adopted his uncle's views and continued "Shintoizing" the domain.

Measures against Buddhist Temples

[...] in the small temples, there are only ignorant and vile simple-minded priests. They perform tasks that are outside their purview. It is not clear whether they are priests or laymen. They mislead the people, cost the country dearly, and corrupt the morals. We should investigate all the useless small temples and order their destruction.[14]

The changes in Mito's landscape are depicted in two main sources from that time: the *Foundation Register* (*Kaikichō* 開基帳) of 1663 and the *Register of Destructions* (*Hakyakuchō* 破却帳) of 1666. The central and perhaps the most prominent element of Mitsukuni's policies was the aforementioned destruction of a large number of temples. The commissioning in 1663 of the *Kaikichō*, a register of all temples and village tutelary shrines (*chinju* 鎮守) in Mito, seems to have been a first step in preparing the reforms, even before the *Law for Temples* and the *Shrine Clauses* were decreed in 1665. First, every village had to deliver a register containing details about its temples and shrines (*jisha o-aratamechō* 寺社御改帳). These were then gathered and consolidated to form the domain-wide *Kaikichō*, which today serves as the most important source on the state of religious institutions in Mito before Mitsukuni's reforms.

Two years later, in late 1665, Mito established the office of *jisha bugyō*, following the already mentioned *bakufu* order of the previous year. Until 1682,[15] the office was held by two individuals, later by only one. They received a stipend of 150 to 200 *koku* and were assisted by subordinate clerks, the *jisha yaku* 寺社役 and *jishakata tedai* 寺社方手代. The *jisha bugyō*'s duties included an inspection of temples and shrines (*jisha junken* 寺社巡見) every other year to check their economic and moral state,[16] and their administration. However, some sources indicate friction with local district magistrates (*koori bugyō* 郡奉行) regarding the jurisdiction over persons affiliated with abolished temples.[17] While installing the *jisha bugyō* was probably not Mitsukuni's own decision and instead ordered by the *bakufu*, it seems to have served well in the reforms' preparations and implementation.

As briefly described above, the status quo of Mito's Buddhist and Shinto institutions is thoroughly illustrated in the *Kaikichō*.[18] The register consists of fifteen volumes: five volumes for the Shingon 真言 sect; two volumes for tutelary shrines; and one volume each for the Buddhist sects Tendai 天台, Nichiren 日蓮, Rinzai 臨済 and Sōtō 曹洞, Jōdo 浄土, Ikkō 一向, Ji 時, as well as *yamabushi* 山伏, and *gyōnin* 行人. It contains information about each institution's name, location, affiliation, income, head temple (*honji* 本寺), additional titles and designations (*sangō* 山号 and *ingō* 院号), priest rank, certificate of tax exemption, foundation, founder, and, for the years before 1663, number of adherents (*monto* 門徒), attached temples, and number and social status of patron households (*danka* 檀家).

According to the *Kaikichō*, in 1663 Mito had 2,377 temples. Mito's population at that time was c. 290,000.[19] This means that the average parish size was approximately 122 persons, which is quite small compared to other regions in Japan. The majority of temples in Mito in 1663—namely close to 2,000—were affiliated with Esoteric Buddhism (Tendai, Shingon, *gyōnin*, and *yamabushi*). The second largest group, of 190 temples, had ties to Pure Land sects (Jōdo, Ikkō, and Ji). There were 174 temples belonging to Zen Buddhism (Rinzai and Sōtō), and thirty-five were Nichiren temples.[20]

A large number of temples had been founded between 1460 and 1660. There are several reasons for the increase during these years. One was the number of successful preachers of the various Buddhist schools, who were in need of buildings where they could speak to the people. Another is that itinerant monks increasingly wished to settle down and head their own temples.[21] The main reason, however, seems to be the Buddhist endeavor to take care of funerary rites for the population during this period.[22]

Beginning in 1666, of the 2,377 temples in Mito, 1,433 were destroyed within the next thirty to forty years (see Table 12.1). The Shingon sect, being the largest sect in Mito, suffered the most extensive damage: 769 Shingon temples were destroyed. The *yamabushi* came second, followed by the Tendai sect and the *gyōnin*. In terms of relative damage, the *gyōnin* were hit the hardest, losing 100 percent of their members. The *yamabushi* and the *gyōnin* were similar groups of ascetics, but the *gyōnin* had looser institutional ties. They were thus freer in their actions, which seems to have made them a primary target for Mitsukuni's radical measures.[23] Next came the *yamabushi* with around 80 percent of their members. On third place was the Tendai sect, with 71 percent. If the founding date of the temples is considered, we see that younger temples were at greater risk of becoming a target. The majority of destroyed institutions were built after 1500.

The orders for the destruction of various temples and shrines were issued between 1666/4/25 and 1666/8/26 and are compiled in the *Hakyakuchō*, our most important source for the first stage of the reforms in Mito.[24] The orders contain both general provisions and special instructions for individual cases. They also include information on the motives behind destroying the targeted Buddhist institution. Accordingly, the destroyed temples can be divided into six main categories.

1. Temples having no parish or priests, or those whose priests held more than one office.[25]
2. Temples with unscholarly priests (lit. "ignorant and vile simple-minded priests," *muchi muge no gusō* 無智無下之愚僧)[26], a clear reference to the *Law for Temples* that ordered priests to be well versed in their doctrine.
3. "Useless temples" (*mueki no tera* 無益之寺), considered as such because they did not conduct funerals and did not issue certificates of religious affiliation.[27] Those that did issue certificates but did not hold funerals were deemed unreliable, because if they did not see to their parishioners' funerals, the authorities doubted whether they could truly know that these parishioners were not following a heterodox religion.[28]
4. Temples bearing the same name as a temple in the castle town of Mito, these being regarded as redundant.[29]
5. "Temples built after 1615," referring to the first religious decrees issued by Ieyasu regarding Buddhist temples. Temples that had been built since the Genna era (1615–24) and thus after that first wave of regulations were not listed in the 1663 *Kaikichō*. In the *Hakyakuchō* there are two passages concerning this category: one quite general,[30] the second explicitly mentioning Nichiren temples.[31]
6. Temples in residential areas, referring to temples to be destroyed in order to make room for living space for *bushi* 武士 and merchants.[32]

Table 12.1 Temples and temple reductions by founding period and sect.[33]

	Shingon		yamabushi		Tendai		gyōnin		Sōtō		Jōdo		Ikkō		Rinzai		Nichiren		Ji		Total	
8th c.	2	1	8		1																11	1
9th c.	9				3																12	
10th c.	2				1																3	
11th c.	2	1			1																3	1
12th c.	8	3			2																10	3
13th c.	10	8			3	2			4	2	4	2	14	2			2	1	2		39	17
14th c.	42	16	6		14	6			12	2	5	1	4		14	1	3	2	4		100	28
15th c.	204	97	13		22	15	1	1	27	6	7	1	15		7	2			2	1	280	121
16th c.	580	371	54		33	18	27	27	53	17	42	24	15	6	7	4	6	3	3	1	820	469
17th c.	156	87	110		21	13	75	75	19	9	33	22	17	12	7		18	7	1		457	229
unknown	336	185	98	231	105	92	29	29	21	5	18	11	18	9	10	2	6		1		642	564
Total	1351	769	289	231	206	146	132	132	136	41	109	61	68	29	38	9	35	13	13	2	2377	1433

The first column for each sect shows the number of temples that existed in 1663 (according to the *Kaikichō*), the second, grey column shows the number of temples ordered to be destroyed.

These general provisions are mostly given in the first part of the *Hakyakuchō*. What follows is a large number of individual cases, which could be and were used as precedents. The following examples illustrate the nature of these cases and the measures that were taken against the culprits.

In the village of Sanzai-mura 三才村, the monk Hōrinbō 宝林坊 (dates unknown), on top of having relations with women and ignoring the orders of the village officials, enticed one of his disciples to usurp territory owned by Keijūin 慶寿院 (dates unknown). Both Hōrinbō and Keijūin belonged to the Tendai sect. The case was investigated and Hōrinbō found guilty on both counts. He received a prison sentence and his disciple was banished. In turn, Keijūin received Hōrinbō's temple lands.[34]

Here, only the offending monk and his collaborator were punished. In other cases, like that of the Tōkōji 東光寺 belonging to the Shingon sect in Ashiarai-mura 足洗村, not only the perpetrator himself was affected, but also other people connected to his misdeed. The case itself was similar to the one described above. Tōkōji's monk had openly lived with a woman for several years. In addition, he had usurped tax-exempt lands belonging to Shōtokuin 照徳院 and Kisshōin 吉祥院 in Ta-mura 田村. The monk was banished. His superior, the head priest of Tōkōji, was forced to resign, and orders were given for the temple to be destroyed.[35] However, those orders were not implemented until much later, in the Genroku era (1688–1704).[36] This example makes it evident that orders to abolish temples were not always executed immediately.

Another incident that led to the downfall of several people is that of a monk of Shōfukuin 正福院 in Tozaki-mura 戸崎村, who had lived with a woman for several years and even adopted a daughter. Village officials had warned him repeatedly about laws forbidding such things, but the monk did not heed them. As a result, he was banished and the two women incarcerated. The temple was to be destroyed and its possessions confiscated.[37] The husband of a woman having an illicit affair with a monk could also be affected in such cases as he could also be found at fault (and often was) for having an unfaithful wife and ordered to pay the cost of her incarceration.[38]

These cases show that the focus of penal action were mainly monks whose behavior was deemed unworthy of their station or who in some way disrupted communal life. Associates of the culprits were often prosecuted too, possibly as a means to involve the communities in preventing further transgressions.

The massive interference in the affairs of religious institutions described above naturally had an impact on individuals affiliated with these temples. The *Hakyakuchō* offers insight into how Mito dealt with this issue as well. The majority of priests whose temples were destroyed due to the six reasons listed above were defrocked, but they were then allowed to join the ranks of farmers, artisans, or merchants. Priests who had owned arable land before the destruction of their temple were allowed to keep it, provided they agreed to cultivate it as farmers. A large number of *yamabushi* became Shinto priests. It is clear that the officials of the domain administration actually had the continued livelihood of laicized monks in mind and wanted to prevent their impoverishment—although probably not out of the goodness of their hearts, but instead to avoid public unrest.[39]

Although temples were demolished and monks often forced to leave the premises, sacred objects and moveable possessions were confiscated by the authorities rather than destroyed. They were then either sold off through auction,[40] redistributed to other temples,[41] or even given to the former priests as funds to use for their relocation to a place of their own choosing.[42] According to Tamamuro Fumio, a leading authority on Japanese early modern social history, there were even a few cases in which priests, after their laicization, were allowed to stay in their temples until they died, whereupon the temple was eventually destroyed.[43] Priests who were found guilty of misconduct, however, were banished from their temple or, when the crime called for harsher punishment, incarcerated.

Parishioners who found themselves without a temple had to affiliate themselves with another institution. Burial grounds were relocated. In the castle town of Mito, the town magistrate (*machi bugyō* 町奉行) had to send information about changed affiliations to his superiors and issue the respective certificates immediately.[44] If a village lost its only temple due to circumstances such as those described above, the priest of another village performed funerals for the now abandoned flock and his temple received the destroyed temple's lands.[45]

Branch temples that lost their head temple (*honji*) were simply reassigned directly to the temple at the next higher hierarchical level, referred to as "superior head temple" (*daihonji* 大本寺). If possible, the *daihonji* had to be located within Mito domain. If it was situated outside the domain, a temple of the same sect within the domain that had lost many branch temples and had large estates was chosen.[46]

The solutions to problems arising from the measures against temples were quite pragmatic and designed to disrupt social and organizational order as little as possible.

As mentioned above, the reforms were not implemented overnight and thus it was necessary to keep an eye on their progress. In 1667, the year after Mitsukuni had decreed the destruction of numerous temples, village headmen and their assistants (*kumigashira* 組頭) were ordered to submit data on the results of the new measures. In 1675, domain officials conducted an inspection of Mito's temples, focusing on those whose destruction had been ordered nine years earlier. On the occasion of this inspection, it was discovered that seventeen Sōtō and seven Rinzai temples earmarked for demolition were still existing.[47] This shows that despite the apparent fervor behind the conception of these reforms, their implementation lagged somewhat behind.

Shintoization of Shrines

Before Mitsukuni's reforms, Shinto institutions in Mito, as in the rest of Japan, were characterized by syncretic Shinto and Buddhist practices, *shinbutsu shūgō* 神仏習合. Mitsukuni, however, understood Buddhism and Shinto as separate traditions. Under the slogan of "shrine reforms" (*jinja aratame* 神社改), he ordered several measures aiming at the dissolution of the usual syncretism. He started with Shizu Shrine 静神社 and Yoshida Shrine 吉田神社, traditionally ranked as the second (*ninomiya* 二之宮) and third (*sannomiya* 三之宮) shrines of Hitachi (the province in which Mito domain was located). In 1667, he had the office of Buddhist shrine monk (*shasō* 社僧) abolished at these two shrines and the respective monks transferred to temples. To further emphasize the shrines' emancipation from Buddhism, he appointed eight shrine maidens and five male *kagura* 神楽 dancers. At the same time, he dispatched the priests (*kannushi* 神主) of these two shrines to Kyoto to have them instructed in Yoshida Shintō 吉田神道.[48]

Two years later, Mitsukuni had noticeboards erected at the same two shrines[49] that reinforced the rejection of any Buddhist presence: monks and nuns were forthwith ordered to take off their Buddhist garb outside the *torii* gate if they wanted to enter the shrine precincts. Furthermore, people who had no serious business at the shrines, but had gone there only for the "obscene" reason of sightseeing, were forbidden to go beyond the fence around the inner shrine precincts (*aragaki* 荒垣). "Of course" (*mochiron* 勿論), unruly behavior was forbidden within the shrine buildings (*shaden* 社殿) and the *kagura* hall. Two further provisions prohibited graffiti on the walls of the *shaden*, the fences and the *torii*, as well as the presence of unclean persons—either due to mourning or other reasons—in front of the shrine.[50] While it is more than likely that disruptive behavior and ritually unclean persons had not been welcome at the shrines already before this time, the emphasis these orders put on the protection of Shintō institutions and the spatial exclusion of Buddhism was certainly new.

In 1674, the emancipation of Shinto priests from Buddhism went one step further, when Mitsukuni tackled the comprehensive obligatory certification of religious affiliation (*shūmon aratame*) at Buddhist temples (*terauke* 寺請). For shrine priests, such certificates were now to be issued by the aforementioned Yoshida and Shizu Shrines, which introduced a practice similar to Okayama's *shintō-uke* 神道請.[51] This was a complicated matter, since the certification of religious affiliation was closely related to the performance of funerals. Indeed, Shintō priests petitioned repeatedly for permission to have their funerals performed by their own priests.[52] In contrast to non-Buddhist funerals, which became the standard for the elite in Mito, certification at shrines was extremely short-lived as Mitsukuni's permission was superseded by a *bakufu* decree of 1687 that ordered *shūmon aratame* the exclusive purview of Buddhist temples.

A measure that can be deemed a success was the establishment of the "one village, one shrine" system (*isson issha seido* 一村一社制度). In 1663, the *Kaikichō*'s volumes on tutelary shrines list 186 shrines[53] with 211 shrine personnel (18 *kannushi*, 169 *negi* 禰宜, 18 *shanin* 社人, and 6 *ichiko* 市子). While the head priests (*kannushi*) seem to have been licensed by the Yoshida, this was probably not the case for other shrine staff, who were often laypersons.[54] In 1666, the same year Mitsukuni ordered the massive actions against Buddhist temples, he had also decreed that each village should have its own tutelary shrine. According to the register *Mito-ryōbun murawari* 水戸領分村割 (*The distribution of villages in Mito*), in 1781 there were 578 villages in Mito.[55] A register of all tutelary shrines in Mito from the early eighteenth century, the *Chinjuchō* 鎮守帳 (*Register of Tutelary Shrines*),[56] lists 551 shrines[57] at the time of its compilation. This means that the number of tutelary shrines had almost tripled (from 186 to 551) between 1663 and the end of the seventeenth century. Although there were a few villages without a tutelary shrine, it is safe to say that Mitsukuni and Tsunaeda more or less accomplished the establishment of *isson issha seido* within Mito. However, this does not mean that Shintō shrines were supported indiscriminately. It is important here to distinguish between tutelary shrines and small wayside shrines. The *Hakyakuchō* specifically mentions small shrines without pedigree (*yuisho naki ko-ho[ko]ra*),[58] which had to be destroyed.

Shintoization not only meant an increase in shrines but also a change in administration. Up until Mitsukuni's measures, many shrines had been supervised by Buddhist monks, *bettōsō* 別当僧 or *shasō*, and it was not uncommon for shrines to have images of Buddha statues as objects of worship (*shintai* 神体).[59] As part of the Shintoization process, of seventy-one shrines with Buddhist *shintai*, only twelve remained unchanged. In forty-four shrines, Buddhist statues were replaced by ritual wands (*gohei* 御幣), in fourteen by mirrors (*kagami* 鏡), and in one by a stone.[60]

The replacement of shrine monks was more difficult. While Mitsukuni and Tsunaeda might have aimed at substituting all of them with *shinshoku* 神職 (Shinto priests), by the 1690s only about 56 percent of Mito's village shrines were administered by Shinto priests, while 189 shrines (*c*. 34 percent) still had a Buddhist monk taking care of them.[61] Add to this the fact that Shintō priests often took on the role of *shasō* and conducted Buddhist funerals and memorial services (*hōji* 法事). These tasks constituted a considerable part of their income and giving them up would have robbed many of their livelihood.[62] A complete separation of Buddhism and Shintō was simply not feasible.

Hachiman aratame: Measures Against Hachiman Shrines

A notable peculiarity within Mito's religious reforms are the so-called "Hachiman reforms" (*Hachiman aratame* 八幡改). Hachiman (usually referred to as "Great Bodhisattva") is a deity with particularly strong Buddhist connotations, and also considered an imperial ancestor deity by identification with the prehistorical emperor Ōjin 応神天皇. Moreover, due to his special relationship to Seiwa Tennō 清和天皇 (850–81), Hachiman was held in high esteem by warrior clans (including the Tokugawa), who traced their ancestry back to this emperor.

In 1695, Tokugawa Tsunaeda issued an order to eradicate Hachiman shrines within his domain. The above-mentioned *Chinjuchō*, which documents the results of this order, lists 105 Hachiman shrines and the measures undertaken or planned for each of them. The reforms left just three shrines untouched: Arakawa Wakamiya Hachimangū 安良川若宮八幡宮, Baba Hachimangū 馬場八幡宮, and Ōta Hachimangū 太田八幡宮.[63] These were all influential shrines and presumably escaped the fate of their smaller counterparts only because of their pedigree. A special example is Tokiwa Hachimangū 常葉八幡宮, which used to be the principal Hachiman shrine in the town of Mito with an income of 300 *koku*. It was founded in 1592 by Satake Yoshinobu 佐竹義信 (1570–1633) and affiliated with a supervisory temple (*bettōji* 別当寺) of the Shingon sect. In 1694, the shrine was transferred to Nakasai-mura 那珂西村. However, it was brought back to the town of Mito a mere thirteen years later in 1707, where it still exists today.

The reforms of the Hachiman shrines can be categorized into four types: (1) rededication to a new deity; (2) downgrading from tutelary shrine and attachment to a different shrine as a branch shrine; (3) joint enshrinement with another deity (*gōshi* 合祀);

Table 12.2 Measures against Hachiman shrines as of 1696.[64]

measure	no. of affected shrines
rededication	86
downgrade	7
joint enshrinement (gōshi)	3
abolishment	6
no change	3

(4) complete abolition.[65] The majority of Hachiman shrines were rededicated, six shrines were abolished and, as mentioned above, only three shrines underwent no changes.

In his contribution to *History of the Town of Mito* (*Mitoshi-shi* 水戸市史), Tamamuro Fumio names four possible reasons or goals for the measures listed above: (1) the denial of the *honji suijaku* 本地垂迹 paradigm (the theory of *kami* as Buddhist manifestations); (2) Mitsukuni's possible doubts about the theory of Hachiman and Ōjin Tennō being identical; (3) his belief that the direct veneration of an imperial ancestor by the (common) people was not sensible; and (4) the rejection of the faith of the Satake, former lords of Mito.[66]

There has been some debate about the motives behind the Hachiman reforms. While these measures might indeed reflect a rejection of the *honji suijaku* theory, some doubts about this being the main reason have come to the fore. According to the historian Etō Yoshinobu, this is only one aspect, and it seems to have been a side effect rather than the main motivation. He also considers Tamamuro's second suggestion implausible. While Mitsukuni has long been considered to have been skeptical about the hypothesis that Hachiman and Ōjin Tennō are the same, to Etō this seems a misconception.[67] Point three has been named the most likely reason by historians such as Tsutsumi Teiko. Etō cites her work on the Satake's Hachiman faith, where Tsutsumi states that rejecting the faith of the domain's former lords was a natural aspect of the Tokugawa reign in Mito.[68] The treatment of the Mito Hachimangū in Tokiwa by Mitsukuni's father Tokugawa Yorifusa 徳川頼房 (1603–61), who installed a new *kannushi* with strong connections to the Yoshida, and then by Mitsukuni himself suggests that she is right. However, Etō argues that Mitsukuni's motivation lies elsewhere. On the one hand, Mitsukuni criticized worship of Hachiman as a war deity since Ōjin Tennō never showed military prowess. Furthermore, he believed that Hachiman's identification as the tutelary deity (*ujigami* 氏神) of the Genji[69] was unjustified. What seemed to rankle him most, though, was that an imperial ancestor was worshipped by warrior families (*buke* 武家) as their deity. He saw this as an act against the natural separation between sovereign and subject.[70] In the years before his death, his veneration for Hachiman as an imperial ancestor may even have led him to regret the destruction of a large number of small Hachiman shrines.[71] However, we must not overlook that the actual reforms of the Hachiman shrines were implemented after Mitsukuni was succeeded by Tsunaeda. It stands to reason that Tsunaeda's policies were probably heavily influenced by Mitsukuni, but Tsunaeda may have taken matters further than his uncle had intended.

Even if the exact motives behind the Hachiman reforms are not entirely clear, the measures indicate local variations within the framework of *hanryō shintō*. It seems that

Mitsukuni's and later Tsunaeda's ideas differed significantly from the general contemporary perception of Hachiman cults. The ensuing radical reduction of Hachiman shrines in Mito demonstrates a considerable degree of independence and intellectual autonomy of Mito's domain leaders and their conception of Shinto.

The Development of Non-Buddhist Funerals in Mito

The renunciation of Buddhist funerals, at least for the elite, seems to have been particularly important to Mitsukuni. Until the 1660s, virtually everyone in Mito received Buddhist death and memorial rites. Mitsukuni strived to change that. He began with the funerary rites of his own family. The first to receive a non-Buddhist funeral was Taihime 泰姫 (1638–59), Mitsukuni's spouse. Taihime was terminally ill and contemplated her impending demise. From her deathbed, she gave unambiguous instructions: "After my death, the Buddhist monks shall be donated no money. Together with ceremonies of our land (*honchō no rei* 本朝の礼), there shall be Confucian rites." She based her instructions on her belief that Confucian rites were similar to "the old funerary rites of our land" (*honchō no jōko no sōrei* 本朝の上古の葬礼).[72]

After Taihime's death in early 1659, Mitsukuni described the rites for her funeral in a letter to her parents. This letter mentions a number of Confucian terms that attest to a break with Buddhist tradition. Mitsukuni also recounts the search for a suitable location for her grave. In the end, he felt forced to have her tomb situated within the precincts of a Buddhist temple (Yoshida Temple 吉田寺, affiliated with the Yakuōin 薬王院, Tendai sect):

> Even though I detest the proximity of the tomb to a Buddhist temple, it is not as if I intended to search for a place that is definitely bad. [In accordance with] the customs of our land, seven or eight people in ten respect the monks who worship the Buddha. Therefore, [. . .] [. . .] the tomb is next to the Yoshida temple.[73]

Mitsukuni's compromise with native customs (and possibly with putative negative reactions by the shogunal government), was only temporary, however. In 1677, Taihime's tomb was transferred to the newly founded Zuiryūsan 瑞龍山 cemetery, which would become the Confucian family cemetery of the Mito Tokugawa.

In 1661, Mitsukuni's father Yorifusa, like his daughter-in-law, was buried with rites based on Confucian principles. In this aspect, both services followed the example of Hayashi Razan's 林羅山 (1583–1657) funeral and that of Razan's wife. Mitsukuni also had a Confucian shrine built for his father inside the town of Mito, the Ikōbyō 威公廟.[74]

When Mitsukuni himself died, he had not left any instructions for his funeral. It seems that he did not expect to be buried with Shinto rites, and so his successor Tsunaeda had him buried with Confucian rites as well,[75] however both Confucian and Buddhist spirit tablets were used.[76]

Attempts to exclude Buddhism from funerary rites were not limited to Mitsukuni's own family. For samurai, he had Confucian style cemeteries built in and around the Mito castle town.[77] The specifics are recorded in the *Hakyakuchō*.[78] Each cemetery was to be assigned two guards selected from the public. These guards received a stipend of five *koku* each. Additionally, they were allotted small pieces of land on the cemetery grounds next to the main gate where they could build their own houses. If the need arose, more land could be dedicated for burials, provided it was not farmland. Forested areas could be cleared and the wood used for building the guards' dwellings. The guards were allowed to dig a well in front of their houses, but were forbidden to have vegetable gardens on the premises.

The order to build cemeteries also contained detailed instructions on their layout including the erection of an open hall to protect mourners from the weather and exact plans on where to place the incense burner. The plots themselves were not to measure more than one *ken* in length for single graves, and one *ken* by nine *shaku* (c. 1.8 x 3m) for couples. Mitsukuni himself specified the design of the graves and wrote them down in a manual titled *Sōsai giryaku* (喪祭儀略; *Outline of Funerary Rites*), which he based on *Zhu Xi's Family Rituals* (*Zhu Xi jiali* 朱子家礼), a treatise on court etiquette that also includes instructions for mourning rites.[79] Thus, a permanent alternative to Buddhist funerals was established in Mito on the basis of Confucian rites. The cemeteries in Sakado and Tokiwa (see note 77) exist to this day.

Shinto priests were another group that rejected Buddhist funerals. From 1695, Shinto funerals were allowed not only for priests and their closest family members, but also for all shrine members (*shachū mon'yō* 社中門葉). However, this practice was extremely short-lived; the general population had already reverted to Buddhist funerals by the time Mitsukuni died in 1701. The issue of Shintō funerals, however, was not laid to rest entirely. From 1765, a law allowed only priests and their heirs to have Shinto funerals. In 1766, however, the Yoshida in Kyoto wrote a letter to Mito's Shinto priests encouraging them to petition for Shinto funerals for all members of all families of Mito's shrines, "in accordance with Lord Mitsukuni's order."[80] Over the years, and especially in the second half of the Edo period, funeral rites repeatedly became a point of contention between Buddhists and Shinto priests. With the dissemination of National Learning (Kokugaku 国学),[81] these discussions also spread geographically and Mito was often referred to as precedent.

As we have seen in this section, Mitsukuni put quite some effort into the establishment of non-Buddhist funeral rites. However, the time for Shintō funerals had not yet come. On the one hand, there were no guidelines available; on the other, it seemed near impossible to gain the *bakufu*'s permission for a Shintō funeral. Even Hoshina Masayuki had difficulties in this regard.[82] This does not change the fact, however, that Mitsukuni had a lasting impact on funerary customs. Shinto funerals continued to be a recurring topic in political and ideological discussions, with Mito often serving as a precedent. In the mid-nineteenth century, Tokugawa Nariaki 徳川斉昭 (1800–60) argued for using Shinto rites in ancestral worship within the imperial family. Among other things, his efforts eventually led, in the 1860s, to the restoration of the imperial tombs and the introduction of a system of Shinto-based memorial rites for imperial ancestors.[83]

Conclusion

Regarding the measures taken in Mito, one can hardly avoid the question of whether they were anti-Buddhist or pro-Shinto. A contemporary rumor suggested that

Mitsukuni's Confucian advisor, Zhu Shunsui 朱舜水 (1600–82), whom he had invited to become his teacher in 1665, prompted the destruction of Buddhist temples. Shunsui never denied these allegations; however, he also never openly attacked Buddhism.[84] It is indeed unlikely that Shunsui was the source of Mitsukuni's anti-Buddhist policies. However, it is not implausible that he encouraged Mitsukuni's actions, since Confucians tended to regard Buddhism, and in particular Buddhist prayers for secular ends (*kitō* 祈祷), as useless and wasteful.[85] Nevertheless, it somehow defies reason to claim that Mitsukuni acted against Buddhism itself. He targeted mainly institutions that did not fit the concept of Buddhism as devised by the Tokugawa, according to which temples should be led by erudite monks of irreproachable character and fulfil the administrative task of religious control assigned to them by the Tokugawa government.

On the other hand, Shinto shrines were not promoted indiscriminately. Shrines, too, were supposed to conform to a dictate from above, that is, from Mitsukuni. Proper Shinto shrines in Mito were tutelary shrines emancipated from Buddhist influence and administrated by a professional Shinto priest. In contrast, small wayside shrines without pedigree rooted in local folk beliefs were doomed to destruction.

The overall aim of these measures seems to have been neither an oppression of Buddhism nor an arbitrary promotion of Shinto, but to put Mitsukuni's mark on Mito's religious landscape. The version of Shinto promoted in Mito—and the other regions in Japan dealt with in this volume—we call *hanryō shintō*, a system of shrine worship based on the ideas of domain lords (in this case Mitsukuni), that was implemented, at least to some degree. It may even have had a long-term impact. However, we must keep in mind that political circumstances changed throughout the two centuries from Mito's reforms until the *shinbutsu bunri* measures in the early Meiji period. At least in the sphere of funerals, Mitsukuni induced a paradigmatic change that had a long lasting effect, even if he himself could not yet be buried with Shintō rites.

Although the separation of Shinto and Buddhism (*shinbutsu bunri* 神仏分) was one of Mitsukuni's chief goals, even his fervor knew limits. And so he never dared to enforce *shinbutsu bunri* at the Mito Tōshōgū 水戸東照宮, where Tokugawa Ieyasu was worshipped.[86]

13

Shinto Priests and the Yoshida in Izumi Province

Yannick Bardy

In the Edo period, every Japanese village maintained at least one structure that we now call a "Shinto shrine"—even though most of these structures showed traces of Buddhist beliefs or, more importantly, at that time displayed Buddhist icons. In Izumi province, south of Osaka, each village had ties to several Shinto shrines. Some of them were quite small (*hokora* 祠), while others were the family shrines of locally important clans. There were tutelary shrines for hamlets,[1] and, of course, the village tutelary shrines. In Izumi province, we also often find communal shrines (*gōsha* 郷社) that served several villages. Two of these *gōsha* are the subject of this chapter.

It is important to note here that community patterns had changed since medieval times. Having suffered several losses against autonomous rural communities in central Japan, the hegemon Toyotomi Hideyoshi 豊臣秀吉 (1537–98) and the subsequent Tokugawa shogunate tried their best to reduce the power of these communities. One of their methods was called "cutting villages" (*murakiri* 村切). In the course of cadastral surveys, by which each peasant's land ownership and fiscal obligations were determined, *murakiri* established new, smaller administrative and fiscal entities—the Edo period villages (*mura* 村). These new villages were still largely autonomous entities, but were subject to the authority of the shogun and the feudal lords as soon as conflicts arose. It has been suggested that *gōsha* shrine communities still accorded to pre-*murakiri* patterns.[2]

In the Izumi province, parishioner communities (*ujiko* 氏子) were often led by shrine assemblies conventionally called *miyaza* 宮座. *Miyaza*, however, is actually a term constructed later, during the Meiji period. It is used mainly in studies on Japanese folklore and religious history as a general description for various types of assemblies that originally led both religious activities and village affairs. Some of them were hereditary (reaching back to the privileged medieval class of field owners),[3] while others were open to all villagers. The hierarchy within these organizations was based on the age of its members, with a number of seats often reserved for the leading families for whom the shrine assembly was a means to maintain their influence on the community. Yet some of the *gōsha*'s *ujiko* were not led by a *miyaza* but by a loose organization, sometimes referred to as the committee of villages (*muramura tachiai* 村々立会), composed of representatives of each village's officials (*mura yakunin* 村役人).

These officials were also part of the village elite and represented both village and shrine interests toward the authorities when organizing rites and festivals.

Another important question concerns the ritualists in these shrines. In most cases, Buddhist shrine monks (*shasō* 社僧) were available. Some of them performed all the rites in a shrine, while others were only called in for the most important, or exceptional ones such as *sengū* 遷宮, the translocation of the main objects of worship, or *amagoi* 雨乞, the call for rain. Sometimes, these *shasō* had more responsibility and acted as formal Buddhist shrine supervisors (*bettō* 別当). However, not all shrines were supervised by a *bettō*. Only a few had professional Shintō priests called *kannushi* 神主, *shinshoku* 神職, or *shake* 社家. Surveys of these priests show a large diversity of status, power, and rights. The existence of a professional priest did not correspond to a shrine's physical size or rank, the number of its parishioners, or the village organization.

In Izumi province, most shrine priests were chosen from among the elders (*toshiyori-shū* 年寄衆) of the shrine assembly. In this case, the priesthood alternated between these elders, changing every two, three, or more years. In other cases, the priesthood was exclusive to one family, which tended to become partially or completely specialized in religious affairs. These families could be locally important ones, in which case the priesthood was an important asset in these families' strategies to maintain their status and to assure their continuity.[4] In other cases, these priests were subordinate to the villagers or the shrine monk.[5]

In Kanbun 5 (1665), the shogunate issued a regulation for priests of Shinto shrines, the *Shrine Clauses* (*Jinja jōmoku* 神社条目).[6] The third of its five articles decreed that priests without rank had to wear a simple white court dress (*hakuchō* 白張). For other apparel, priests had to obtain permission from the Yoshida 吉田.[7] This license, the *shintōsai kyojō* 神道裁許状, was a document consisting of four or five lines. Usually it provided the priest with an honorific ancient governor title and a family name linked to the court. A license from 1718/6/19, for instance, reads:

> Letter of authorization of the accomplishment of Shinto rituals in [formal court garb composed] of the *kazeori* hat and the *kariginu* dress, given to Yokota Iwami-no-kami Fujiwara Yoshikatsu, priest of the first rank divinity Kasuga of Mibayashi village, Izumi district, Izumi province.[8]

This license allowed its recipient to wear a colored costume quite different from the *hakuchō*: the black headdress (*kazeori eboshi* 風折烏帽子) and the "hunting dress" (*kariginu* 狩衣) originally sported by court nobles. It is through the issuing of these licenses that the Yoshida built their priest network throughout Japan.

As Maeda Hiromi[9] and others have pointed out, a similar practice boomed from the end of the seventeenth to the beginning of the eighteenth century. In this period, the Yoshida sold rank certificates called *sōgen senji* 宗源宣旨, which routinely credited "first court rank" to the respective shrines and their *kami*, until complaints by the court forced the Yoshida to stop doing so in 1738. Eleven *sōgen senji* were delivered to Izumi's shrines.[10] Since *sōgen senji* were sometimes issued together with *shintōsai kyojō*, it is not quite clear whether the priests actively applied for the *shintōsai* license or whether they were persuaded to buy one while originally requesting a *sōgen senji*.

Below, I will present the cases of priests of two rural shrines in Izumi province and their association with the Yoshida network. Both shrines had a parishioner community composed of several villages. For the first case, the Ōiseki Shrine, I draw from two types of documents. The first is a material collection of more than 200 pages published by the Izumisano City Historiographic Association in 2005,[11] consisting of a detailed chronicle and letters, complaints, extracts of family registers, etc. The text was written by a local shrine monk (*shasō*) from 1791 to 1808 in order to document an ongoing conflict with the local priest. The second type are mostly unpublished documents from an archive of the Furuya 古谷 (*Furuya-ke monjo* 古谷家文書), an important local family whose involvement in both village and shrine affairs will be mentioned below.

For the second case, the Kasuga Shrine of Ikeda valley, I make use of unpublished documents passed down in a former priestly family, the Yokota 横田 of Murodō (*Yokota Shigeru-shi shozō monjo* 横田滋氏所蔵文書). Composed of some 1,000 documents from the end of the eighteenth century (including some older ones), the archive focuses on agricultural matters and the shrine activities of this family.

Based on these documents, I will discuss how and why priests of such large community shrines joined the Yoshida network. By analyzing these processes, I hope to clarify in an exemplary way the relationship between rural priests and the Yoshida in early modern society.

The Case of Ōiseki Shrine

In 1666, less than a year after the *Jinja jōmoku* had been issued, a priest from the southern part of Izumi province associated himself with the Yoshida by obtaining a *shintōsai kyojō* license.[12] He was the priest of Ōiseki Jinja 大井関神社 (also known as Hine Jinja 日根神社) in Hineno 日根野 village (see Map 13.1), an old shrine included in the *Engishiki* 延喜式 (927). It belonged, moreover, to the network of six official shrines of Izumi, which dates back to the foundation of Izumi province in 740.[13] Ōiseki Shrine was initially run by priests of the Hine 日根 lineage, who maintained relations to the court all through the medieval period. In the early modern period, Ōiseki was the tutelary shrine of four villages: Hineno, Nagataki 長滝, Kaminogō 上之郷, and Usaida 兎田, this last village being in a different domain than the others during the Edo period. At first, the parishioners were organized in a complex *miyaza*, divided into sub-assemblies, one or more for each village, of which some were further subdivided, and its membership was hereditary based on blood relation. But during the last century of the Edo period, these families gradually lost their right to participate in the *miyaza* due to the lack of male heirs, until it was decided that village officials of Hineno should take over important decisions about the shrine.[14] In addition to the Hine priests, there were also some shrine monks (*shasō*) who resided within the shrine precinct in a temple called Jigen'in 慈眼院, which was in itself an important Shingon 真言 temple. In the early nineteenth century, one of these Jigen'in monks compiled some documents about the shrine's history,[15] on which the following account is based.

In 1585, Toyotomi Hideyoshi's forces came to the region to fight against an alliance led by the temple Negoroji 根来寺 (located ten kilometers to the south of Ōiseki Shrine, on the opposite side of Izumi's Katsuragi 葛城 mountains, which belonged to Kii province). Hineno village suffered heavy losses when Negoroji was defeated. The village head, who had sided with Negoroji, had to flee and the buildings of Ōiseki Shrine were destroyed. According to the Jigen'in documents, however, the priest of Ōiseki Shrine, a certain Hine Wakasanokami 日根若狭守, joined Hideyoshi's camp and later became a daimyo, due to his merits in Hideyoshi's Kyushu Campaign (1586–7). While there remain some doubts as to the truth of this story,[16] it can be regarded as an origin story (*yuisho* 由緒) to explain why there was no Shinto priest in the sanctuary from 1585 until 1658. The shrine regained most of its destroyed buildings, which were probably rebuilt on an order by Hideyoshi or his son Hideyori 豊臣秀頼 (1593–1615). By contrast, Hideyoshi confiscated the fiefs, which had been bestowed on the traditional shrine network by Oda Nobunaga 織田信長 (1534–82) through a vermillion-seal decree. The Tokugawa ignored this privilege as well and denied a return of these fiefs to the shrines in the middle of the seventeenth century.

Since Ōiseki Shrine lacked Shinto priests during the first half of the seventeenth century, exceptional rites, such as rain prayers and the central ceremonies of the main yearly festival were conducted by Jigen'in shrine monks. Other rites were performed by common villagers or parish elders.[17] This situation changed in 1658, after a flood had damaged the shrine buildings and repairs became necessary. In order to obtain authorization from the domain administration (at that time Kishiwada-han 岸和田藩), villagers and *shasō* decided to send a petition to the lord. However, a petition like this without the name of a Shinto priest, either as the author or at least as the signing party, was seen as a problem.[18] Thus, the villagers together with Jigen'in decided to appoint one.

A few years earlier, during the Meireki era (1655–7), the community had employed a certain Ukon 右近 (dates unknown) and his family as shrine servants. Ukon had lived under very poor conditions in a nearby hamlet, suffered from poor health and was not able to support his family. Therefore, the parish community decided to give him the job of lighting the lanterns and cleaning the shrine in exchange for a modest stipend and lodging on the shrine grounds. When forced to appoint a shrine priest, they chose Ukon as the *kannushi* of Ōiseki Shrine. Together with the shrine's *shaso* and the village officials, Ukon signed the application for shrine restoration, which was sent to the domain administration. When Ukon died a few months later, his son succeeded him as priest.

When the *Jinja jōmoku* were issued, the community soon tried to raise the status of their priest and began negotiations with the Yoshida for a license. In 1666, the head of Hineno village, together with a priest of the nearby Aritōshi Shrine 蟻通神社[19] and others, stated in letters[20] to the Yoshida that the priesthood of Ōiseki Shrine was hereditary, that the current priest (Ukon's son) was from a sacerdotal lineage, and that he would be the one to perform the rites from now on. They also formally acknowledged the Yoshida's authority and their right to investigate in case of any doubts about the priesthood.

The aim of the village community was probably to provide the village with some autonomy in all matters related to their shrine by obtaining protection from the Yoshida. However, they did not take into account the possibility that the Yoshida might support the priest *against* the community or the *shasō* in order to gain independence and take an active role in the main rites.

In reality, Ōiseki's shrine priest remained in a position subordinate to the *shasō* and the *miyaza*. Religious matters were left to the Buddhists and worldly issues such as the priest's income were decided by the parish. The priest was not even allowed to enter the shrine and had to stand still in the outer corridor (*engawa* 縁側) of the shrine while Jigen'in monks performed the rites inside. On one day in 1756, however, the rain was so heavy that the monks allowed the priest to enter the inner sanctum (*naijin* 内陣).[21]

In 1790, the priest, Ihara Shikibu 井原式部 (1743–1811) and his son Ōkura 井原大内蔵 (1769–1821) finally started long and complex negotiations to obtain better status and a real role in the rites. During these negotiations, the *shasō*, the community, and the domain administration gradually acknowledged that their shrine priest should have an active role, since he was after all associated with the Yoshida. First Shikibu was allowed to take a ritual wand (*gohei* 御幣) and pass it to a monk; later he even performed a full ceremony of Yoshida Shinto after the shrine monks finished their ceremonies. After a series of protests, negotiations with the villagers and the *shasō*, and ensuing investigations by the domain administration (who did not much more than give an order to find an agreement), the priest gained a substantial number of privileges, such as the right to use a family name and to wear two swords during formal occasions. And yet, he did not stop antagonizing the monks, the community, and even the domain administration. Finally, in 1804, that administration sent officials as witnesses of the fourth month rites, but the priest refused to perform the rites in protest at not having the most senior position in the shrine. The officials told him that such a refusal would result in his dismissal as priest and his banishment. In the face of such a threat, he ended his protest and performed the rites, bringing the argument to a definitive end.[22] One of the reasons these negotiations dragged on for such a long time was probably two intercessions by the Yoshida in response to the priest's appeals.

The first intercession came in the form of a letter sent to the domain administration in 1798. In this letter, the Yoshida wrote that it was unusual for one of their priests to be prevented from performing the rites of his sanctuary, quoting the two letters sent by the community in 1666. After this first intervention, the priest was given a more significant role in the rites. A second letter was sent in 1802, at a time when the priest was still not permitted to participate in the rites in the inner sanctum. The Yoshida had been called to resolve a similar situation in the nearby Aritōshi Shrine, and accordingly they sent two of their representatives into the region to seek a solution to both problems. These officials conducted a survey of the Ōiseki Shrine and discovered an old panel (*munefuda* 棟札) attached to a beam, according to which Jigen'in was the supervising temple (*bettōji* 別当寺) of Ōiseki. This upset the Yoshida's envoys: How could a Jigen'in monk be a *bettō* of that shrine, whose priest was one of the Yoshida's priest network, without seeking prior permission? After that, they asked both the monk and the priest about the enshrined deities' names and identities, and discovered a concerning lack of knowledge on the part of the priest. Having severely reprimanded both the priest and the *shasō*, they decided to return to Kyoto without presenting a resolution.[23]

When the Yoshida representatives were already on their way back, the domain officials in charge of religious matters (*jishakata* 寺社方) arranged a meeting between them and the leaders of the parish. It was decided that the monk of Jigen'in would purchase a *bettō* certification and the priest would purchase a *shintōsai kyojō*, renewing his affiliation to their organization. Incidentally, one of these leaders, a village official (*toshiyori* 年寄) named Furuya Rokuemon 古谷六右衛門 (dates unknown), was a descendant of an old family closely associated with Ōiseki Shrine. In all relevant documents of the period, the Furuya are frequently referred to as *shajin* 社人, *ji'nin* 神人 or *sewanin* 世話人. The first two terms usually designated low-ranking shrine servants, while *sewanin* was often used for other parishioners who were responsible for special tasks such as shrine repairs. The Furuya, however, was one of the oldest leading families in this region and had played a decisive role in the affairs of the shrine for a long time. In this case, therefore, these terms seem to be used as titles signifying a special relationship between this family and the shrine or the shrine assembly, akin to a patron.[24] In any event, the shrine assembly decided to send Rokuemon to Kyoto to acquire licenses from the Yoshida. He came back not only with one license for the *bettō* and one for the priest, but also with one for himself as *ji'nin*. Whether this was a move decided by the community to try to keep the priest in check, or a personal decision by Rokuemon to strengthen his own influence over the shrine or within the community, is unclear.

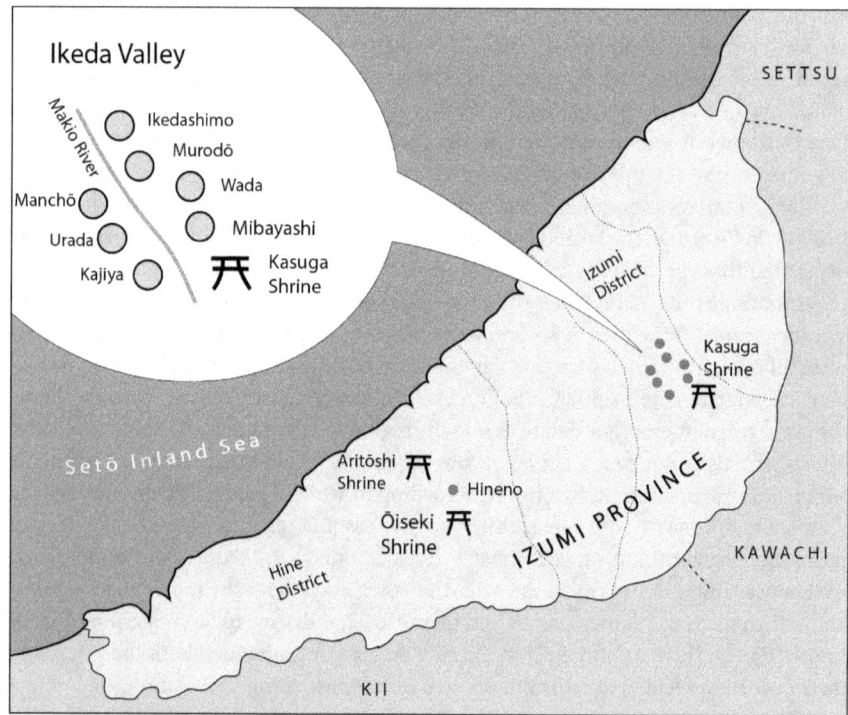

Map 13.1 Ōiseki Shrine and Kasuga Shrine in Izumi province.[25]

In the case of Ōiseki Shrine, it is clear that association with the Yoshida was instigated by the community, or the leading village officials, as soon as the *Jinja jōmoku* decree was published. Until the beginning of the nineteenth century, the priest occupied only an inferior role. The attempt to obtain Yoshida affiliation, therefore, cannot be understood as a means to raise the priest's prestige and status, but rather as a means to legitimate the shrine being staffed by a priest, perhaps in opposition to another unknown party, or in anticipation of such opposition. However, as time passed, Ōiseki priests—probably backed by the emergence of National Learning (Kokugaku 国学)[26]— began to fight for real recognition in their shrine's rites, which would allow them to perform Yoshida Shinto rituals. The Yoshida, on the other hand, also profited from this argument. By sending two agents to Aritōshi and Ōiseki Shrine they were able to strengthen their own authority in the region, gaining new members and confirming that their rituals would be used at the shrine, along with the syncretic (*ryōbu* 両部) rituals of the Buddhist shrine supervisors.

The Case of Ikeda Kasuga Shrine

The second case presented in this study concerns the Kasuga Shrine 春日神社 in Mibayashi village 三林村 of the Ikeda 池田 valley in Izumi district. This shrine was the tutelary shrine of seven villages in the valley (see Map 13.1), split between three domains (partly owned by the *bakufu*).[27] The parish community was composed of all families of the seven villages, and shrine affairs were handled by the "seven villages' committee" (*nanakason tachiai* 七ヶ村立会), as explained above. A professional priest shared administrative shrine duties with the leading officials of the villages, the village heads (*shōya* 庄屋) or *toshiyori*, forming some sort of council. The exact foundation date of the shrine is unknown. However, from the history of other Kasuga Shrines in the area, we can infer that it was built during the Kamakura era by a local lord. Perhaps to gain its protection, he dedicated it to the divinities of the famous Kasuga Shrine in Nara at a time when the site belonged to the land holdings of this same Nara Kasuga Shrine.[28]

The shrine rituals were performed by a priest from the Yokota 横田 family who belonged to Murodō 室堂, one of the six other villages of the valley. Until the beginning of the eighteenth century, priesthood was transmitted among three collateral branches of this extended family, the Shōbei 庄兵衛, Sajiemon 左二右衛門 and Jinsaemon 仁左衛門. When a priest died, the head of one of the other two branches would take over.[29] All branches were peasant families. The Shōbei were the second most important farmers of the village, owning fields worth around thirty *koku* 石 of rice, while at the beginning of the 1700s, the Sajiemon branch staffed the village head, until this office was abolished during this century. Little is known of the third branch, except that its head was the priest of the Ikeda Kasuga Shrine for forty-seven years, until his death in 1716, when Shōbei followed in the succession. At that time, Ikeda Kasuga Shrine did not have any relationship with the court or any other important center of Shinto.

In 1718, after a successful rain supplication ritual in a time of drought,[30] the parishioner community of the seven villages applied to the Yoshida for a court rank for their Kasuga Shrine. As noted above, a court rank for a community shrine was a popular means to gain fame and prestige at that time. Thus, with the permission of all respective domain authorities, the priest Shōbei and a village representative traveled to Kyoto to obtain a first-rank certificate for their *kami* in form of a *sōgen senji*. Upon their return, they announced to the lords that they had not only received a court rank for the shrine, but also a *shintōsai kyojō* license for the priest.[31] This was the document cited above, which granted Shōbei the family name of Fujiwara and the title of Iwami-no-kami, as well as the right to wear colored court dress.

Little is known about the process leading to the issuance of this *shintōsai kyojō*. However, the context makes it seem likely that it was not the initial intention of the community and the priest to obtain this license, but rather that it was suggested by the Yoshida themselves. In fact, we know that before issuing a *sōgen senji*, the Yoshida required the villagers to clarify who was in charge of the rites of the shrine.[32] Situations like these were also good occasions for them to gain new followers. In other words, we can infer that this priest's association with the Yoshida and their network was not planned by himself or the villagers before he went to Kyoto. Rather it was a sort of by-product, a corollary effect of the application to bestow a first court rank on Ikeda Kasuga Shrine.

When Yokota Iwami-no-kami died in 1732, the sacerdotal office was supposed to switch to the Jinsaemon branch, but one male representative was old and sick, while the other had just been born. Thus, the three Yokota branches decided that Iwami-no-kami's son, Shōbei, would become the new priest. When this Shōbei died in 1768, the Jinsaemon were ready to take over the priesthood. At this time, however, the next Shōbei kept the office in his branch, backed by the heads of all seven villages. When the Jinsaemon protested, village officials promised to return to the traditional pattern of succession at the next turn. However, when the next Shōbei (Iwami-no-kami's grandson) died in 1804, the village heads proclaimed his son, Jūemon 横田重右衛門, as the new priest, despite the protest of Jinsaemon descendant Uemon 横田宇右衛門 to the local lord.[33]

In this fashion, priestly succession evolved from a semi-hereditary pattern, alternating between three branches of one extended family, to a hereditary one. Even if this went against the traditional rights of the other branches of the Yokota family, this pattern was also fostered by the parish. It seems likely that the acknowledgment of Shōbei/Iwami-no-kami by the Yoshida provided this branch with more prestige, while accidental succession issues helped to sustain the new system of succession. Ultimately, acknowledgment by the Yoshida and support by the community contributed to a new priestly identity of the Shōbei lineage.[34]

However, Jūemon's position was soon contested. In 1805, Noguchi Tosa 野口土佐 (dates unknown), a priest of the Tenjin 天神 Shrine (today Sugawara Jinja) in the nearby town of Sakai 堺 and head of the Yoshida in Izumi province, started a tour of the province's shrines.[35] When he visited the Kasuga Shrine in 1809, he discovered that Iwami-no-kami's *shintōsai kyojō* had disappeared. According to local tradition, it was enshrined in the First Shrine of the Kasuga ensemble, but in fact it was not. In addition, Noguchi was upset by the fact that several generations of priests had not renewed their association with the Yoshida's network. He threatened to make the Kasuga shrine's priest his subordinate. Thereupon, the community decided to apply to the Yoshida for a copy of the old *shintōsai kyojō* and a new one for Jūemon.[36]

This episode reveals a couple of interesting facts. First, the inspection tour must be seen against the backdrop of the increasing competition in the field of Shinto between the Yoshida and other court families like the Shirakawa 白川.[37] The tour was clearly a means to assert the Yoshidas' authority over rural shrines. Moreover, it may be no mere coincidence that the Yoshida decided to visit Izumi's shrines in 1805, only a few months after the final solution of the Ōiseki Shrine incident had led to three new association licenses. This event might indeed have demonstrated the necessity to visit local shrines if the Yoshida wanted to keep and expand their influence. In this sense, Noguchi's tour was not only an investigation of existing relations, but also an opportunity to gain new priests for the network, by the use of threat if necessary.

The second fact of interest is the lack of knowledge by the priest and the villagers regarding the license, its significance, or the Yoshida. Prior to Noguchi's visit, the *shintōsai kyojō*—or, as they put it, "the thing called *gokyojō*"[38]—was just an additional item given to them at the same time as the wood panel with the "first court rank" title for the shrine. It was enshrined and treated the same way as a *gohei*.[39] Rather than a lawful certificate given to their priest to acknowledge his position within the shrine, it was viewed as part of a package given to the divinity together with the court rank.

Benefits and Costs of Yoshida Affiliation

Yoshida Protection of Priestly Status

When Jūemon renewed his affiliation with the Yoshida by buying the respective licenses, the affair of the lost *shintōsai kyojō* seemed to be settled. However, problems arose when the original reappeared at a certain temple on Mt. Kōya 高野山, the Renmyōin 蓮明院, in 1815. This temple used the fact that the original license was in its possession to claim that the monk of its branch temple in Murodō, the Seonji 施音寺, was actually the supervisor (*bettō*) or *shasō* of Kasuga Shrine and in charge of its most important shrine rites. Thus, it contested Jūemon's qualification as the leading priest and, in particular, his right to perform a *sengū* rite (i.e., the relocation of the main object of worship), which he had performed three years earlier. The issue was brought up with the Sekiyado domain, implying the danger that it might be advanced to the shogunal administration.[40]

Was this a case of Buddhist monks trying to wrangle away a shrine from a newly established Yoshida priest? To answer this question we have to identify the decisive agents of this story. According to the Seonji claim, this local temple had in the past performed rites at Kasuga Shrine, before Jūemon was formally recognized as a priest by the Yoshida.[41] It seems, however, that Seonji had no permanent staff at that time, and therefore other people from Murodō must have acted as Seonji's representative. We do not have definitive proof, but it is clear that Seonji was connected with someone from the Yokota family. We already know that some members of this family were upset by the usurpation of Kasuga Shrine by the Shōbei branch. Thus, the people behind the empty Seonji were probably family members of Jūemon who felt deprived of their right to priesthood.

Since this was a far-reaching religious affair, Jūemon and the village heads appealed to the Yoshida to investigate and decide the case. The Yoshida sent two officials and their investigation revealed that even Renmyōin on Mt. Kōya was without a resident monk: it was a cleric of another monastery who had written the plea in its name. Another point was that there had been a recent fire at the temple's archive, and thus Renmyōin was unable to provide any solid proof to its claims except for the lost and found again *shintōsai kyojō*. In the end, the Yoshida confirmed the priest's authority and ruled out most of Seonji's claims on the shrine, letting the village leaders write an arrangement with all parties, giving only a secondary role to the Seonji as a *shasō*.[42]

In this case, the community (except the few villagers behind Seonji) and the priests considered the Yoshida to be the relevant authority, and the priest Jūemon used his new relationship with them to ask for protection. The stance of local priests toward the Yoshida had changed from indifference or ignorance to close association with their network. The same had happened a few years earlier, when the priest of Ōiseki Shrine appealed to the Yoshida with the hope of gaining their support in his bid for a better position in the shrine/Shinto hierarchy. In the case of Ōiseki, we know from the letters of 1666 that the Yoshida were already considered a potential backup to which the priest and the parishioner community could turn in case of contestation or argument about the priesthood. What was considered a mere possibility in the mid-seventeenth century became a real means of support in the beginning of the nineteenth century.

The Costs of Entering the Yoshida Network

Yet entering the Yoshida network and renewing this association in each generation also meant a massive financial burden. In the case of Kasuga's Jūemon, he not only had to pay for a new Yoshida license itself, but also to finance the trip to Kyoto. Additionally, he had to offer presents and money to an intermediary and to Yoshida representatives, amounting to at least one *ryō*, two *bu* in gold and 113.5 *monme* of silver. Furthermore, he was obligated to buy some Yoshida Shinto paraphernalia—six golden *gohei*, a prayer, seven little golden fans, priestly garb, and a copy of the *sōgen senji*—for a total of three *ryō*, two *bu* of gold and thirty-two *monme* of silver.[43] In short, without counting the cost of the license itself, the total cost was already almost six and a half *ryō*, a significant amount for the priest, even if we take into account the probable support of the community. We know that in 1821, the renewal of the Ōiseki licenses forced the priest to ask the parishioners for 100 *monme* of silver, a bit less than two *ryō*, which also points to the significant cost for him.[44]

Another costly transaction occurred when Furuya Rokuemon's successor at Ōiseki had to renew his *ji'nin* license in 1858. Having lost much of his wealth, he asked for leniency and a lower price, which was fixed at around three *bu* of gold. This corresponds to 0.75 *ryō* for a license of a mere *ji'nin*. In addition, he had to pay a considerable amount as a handling fee in order to see a Yoshida representative,[45] and a further total sum of one *bu*, two *shu* as gratuity to a number of intermediaries. This does not yet include travel costs to Kyoto. The *ji'nin* license itself cost less than the priest patent twenty-five years earlier, but the collateral expenses were extremely high.

In addition, the Yoshida would sometimes call upon their network to help them cover extraordinary expenses, as was the case in 1821, when the head of the Yoshida household had to travel to Edo. To finance the trip, the household initiated a premodern form of crowdfunding, asking affiliated priests for "100 *hiki*" (about 0.4 *ryō*) each.[46] Considering that costs like these were due in each generation, it seems justified that the priests expected support in exchange for their money.

Conclusion

It is generally assumed that the *Shrine Clauses* from 1665 established the Yoshida as the leading authority of Shinto. As other chapters in this volume show in detail, however, the Yoshida were soon challenged by other important Shinto centers such as the Ise and Izumo shrines, or the Shirakawa house. They did not hold a monopoly on priestly networks in the Edo period. In addition, membership in such networks was not compulsory for ordinary shrine priests. The majority of them neither applied for nor conformed to the networks' rules of renewing membership in each generation, at least until the early nineteenth century, when the Yoshida began to be more proactive. It is not even certain that before the 1800s, priests were required to renew their license in each generation. The fact that renewing membership involved a heavy financial burden means that priests probably had high expectations of the Yoshida's help in case of arguments about their rights or status. For these priests, the burden of the cost of membership was worth it only when it helped them to gain influence.

However, the very meaning of membership in the Yoshida network should be investigated with regard to the period under consideration. As outlined in the following chapter by Anne Walthall, the first half of the nineteenth century was a time when the Yoshida recruited heavily and diffused their rites and doctrines among the rural priests affiliated to them. However, in the early Edo period, neither priests nor parishioners seemed to be aware that they were part of a network until it came knocking on their door. To them, the decision who should become a priest was a local matter, in the hand of the community that acknowledged a system of succession, changing it when necessary.

In the case of the Ōiseki priest, the legitimacy emanating from the possession of a *shintōsai kyojō* was sought after but soon forgotten. The priest of the Kasuga Shrine did not even actively apply for it, and chose to enshrine it like the other sacred items given to the shrine by the Yoshida. Even when the license disappeared, neither the community nor the priest was particularly concerned, at least until the Yoshida inspection. Eventually, however, the license turned into an effective asset of power and legitimacy: when a coalition of temples and villagers tried to oust the newly established priestly lineage, the Yoshida intervened and helped the priest to gain the upper hand in the argument; similarly, the Ōiseki shrine priest used his license to call upon the Yoshida for help and thus solidified his claims on the shrine rites.

Thus, to better understand the priestly networks of the Edo period, and in particular the Yoshida organization and their membership, it is not enough to analyze the situation top down. We also have to investigate the concrete situation of local shrines, their parishioners, and their ritualists, both Shinto and Buddhist.

14

Competing Claims for the Faith and Affiliation of Shrine Priests

The Shirakawa, Yoshida, and Hirata Atsutane

Anne Walthall

For much of the early modern period, the Yoshida 吉田 house dominated the world of shrine priests. Yet beginning in the late eighteenth century, it faced increasing competition from the Shirakawa 白川 house. Scholars of religion have compared the two institutions in terms of their strategies for gaining affiliates and their impact on local customs. The question of doctrinal differences has been put aside, the assumption being that these mattered less than financial considerations or ritual practices. I propose to investigate this issue through the lens of the nativist (Kokugaku 国学) scholar Hirata Atsutane 平田篤胤 (1776–1843), who advocated a "pure Shinto," unadulterated by Buddhist doctrine and practice. I will first introduce his writings on the two houses and then analyze a conflict in which shrine priests in Mikawa province, who likewise sought a return to the past, tried to switch affiliation from the Yoshida to the Shirakawa.

Starting with Yoshida Kanetomo 吉田兼倶 (1435–1511), who was a scion of hereditary diviners at the imperial court, the Yoshida titled themselves superintendent of Shinto (*shintō chōjō* 神道長上), claimed descent from Ame no Koyane 天児屋根, a deity who accompanied the sun goddess's grandson on his descent to earth, erected a new shrine to the eight imperial tutelary deities (Hasshinden 八神殿) that had previously been located inside the court's administrative offices, and promoted their vision and practice as the One-and-Only Shinto (*yuiitsu shintō* 唯一神道). In 1665 the shogunate issued the *Shrine Clauses* (*Jinja jōmoku* 神社条目, also known as *Law for Shrine Priests*, *Shosha negi kannushi hatto* 諸社禰宜神主法度) that largely but not entirely ceded authority over hereditary shrine personnel to the Yoshida family. In particular, they stipulated that priests without court rank and unaffiliated with other court families had to receive Yoshida permission to wear colored robes.[1] The clauses did not grant the Yoshida the exclusive right to petition the emperor to bestow court ranks (*shisso* 執奏), nor did they cover other kinds of affiliation; moreover, the most important shrines remained outside Yoshida jurisdiction. As noted below, the Yoshida tried to bring all shrine priests under their control and therefore urged the shogunate to revise these clauses, but to no avail.[2] In 1738, they were forced to stop selling ranks.

While they continued to use priestly licenses and established a network of thousands of adherents,[3] this was still a comparatively small portion of all shrine priests. As Hardacre has pointed out, many shrine personnel preferred autonomy in order to preserve local practices and customary rituals.[4] Some priestly families who had previously accepted Yoshida affiliation slipped away. The Yoshida pushed back, claiming that the *Shrine Clauses* of 1665 meant once a Yoshida affiliate, always a Yoshida affiliate. In 1782 they had the shogunate reiterate its support for Yoshida control over priests, and sent factotums to the countryside to demand submission from all who were performing rites without a Yoshida license.[5] The results were disappointing.

The Shirakawa house had unassailable jurisdiction over Shinto rituals inside the court owing to its hereditary position and title as kingly councilor of divinities (*jingi hakuō* 神祇伯王), which was based on its descent from the tenth-century emperor Kazan 花山天皇 (968–1008; r. 984–6). Nonetheless, it nearly became extinct in 1751 when the latest in a series of short-lived heads died. The five imperial regent houses of emperor Momozono 桃園天皇 (1741–62; r. 1747–62) saved it by having it adopt the maternal uncle of the tenth shogun Ieharu 徳川家治 (1737–86; r. 1760–86). They re-established the Hasshinden inside the court in addition to the one previously erected by the Yoshida, and revived the *chinkonsai* 鎮魂祭, an important imperial ritual performed at the Hasshinden by the Shirakawa to strengthen the emperor's spirit before he performed ceremonies leading to his enthronement.[6]

Following its revival, the Shirakawa house started encouraging local priests to seek its licenses, thus entering the Yoshidas' religious market outside the court. Priests and other shrine personnel wanted licenses for robes and initiation into the performance of specific rites because these gave them standing as religious practitioners. Similar to the Yoshida, the Shirakawa could approve the transfer of a deity to another shrine, i.e. the founding of branch shrines. Because they served as protector for the Fushimi Inari Shrine 伏見稲荷大社 and its network, 85 percent of the transfers they sanctioned were for Inari to be enshrined in village shrines, daimyo or wealthy commoner compounds, and even household god shelves.[7] The Shirakawa also took the lead in granting licenses to carpenters who built shrines and to other part-time shrine personnel such as groundkeepers, farmers, urban prayer specialists (*shintōsha* 神道者), pilgrimage entrepreneurs (*oshi* 御師), and female shamans (*miko* 巫女). At first, the Yoshida insisted that their licenses go only to priests, but in the 1830s, they started to follow the Shirakawa example.[8] The Shirakawa also sold exorcisms to commoners, court nobles, and daimyo to rid people of fox possession, curses, miscarriages, or other ills, while the Yoshida proffered charms to ward off potential curses by the gods or subdue crazy behavior, thus giving laypeople access to Shirakawa and Yoshida magic.[9] In other words, a contest over marketing Shinto paraphernalia arose between Yoshida and Shirakawa. In the early nineteenth century, both houses looked to Atsutane for help.

As an exponent of pure Shinto, Atsutane tried to spread his ideas not only through an expanding network of disciples, but also through the shrine priests affiliated with the Shirakawa and Yoshida. Yet before Endō Jun's recent work on the social context for Atsutane and his world view, historians, at least in the United States, paid scant attention to these connections.[10] H. D. Harootunian emphasizes Atsutane's message to farmers and makes no reference to either house;[11] Mark McNally mentions Hirata affiliations with both houses but provides no details.¹² In fact Atsutane had a great deal to say about each house, shrine priests constituted an important segment of his audience, and his writings shed light on early nineteenth-century religious beliefs.

What did shrine priests make of Atsutane's interventions into the rivalry between the Shirakawa and Yoshida? Both Yoshida and Shirakawa affiliates joined Atsutane's school, and even those who did not, visited him or read his texts. The Shirakawa record of disciples notes eighty-four instances in which men tried to escape Yoshida control, sometimes successfully and sometimes not.¹³ For a case study regarding an attempted transfer of allegiance, I will turn to the struggle by priests in Mikawa to free themselves from the Yoshida in order to affiliate with the Shirakawa. Men on the Shirakawa side of the conflict had close ties to Atsutane, while at the same time, Atsutane's chief disciple remained a Yoshida affiliate. For this reason, juxtaposing Atsutane's writings on the Yoshida and Shirakawa with actions taken by the Mikawa priests can help explicate both.

Hirata Atsutane and the Shirakawa House

Both the Yoshida and Shirakawa established branch offices in Edo, the Yoshida in 1791 and the Shirakawa in 1802. At that time the shogunate welcomed these moves in its efforts to delegate and strengthen supervision over religious personnel.¹⁴ The Yoshida also established a divinity school in 1798 for lectures and study on history and ancient customs based on canonical texts and to train priests in Yoshida protocols for transmitting the Way of the Gods.¹⁵ Atsutane came to know the staff in both these offices and later commented on their incompetence. Nevertheless, he performed services for both.

Service to the Shirakawa

According to Atsutane's biography by his adopted son, Hirata Kanetane 平田銕胤 (1799–1880), the Shirakawa were the first to appoint him to be a scholar-teacher (*gakushi* 学師). This may have been as early as 1808, when he was still struggling to establish himself as a scholar, or a few years later in 1811.¹⁶ As detailed below, he drafted a set of "principles" for the Shirakawa and a history of their house in this period. He resigned from the Shirakawa house in 1819, claiming that he was too busy to fulfill his duties.

Despite resigning his Shirakawa position, Atsutane continued to correspond with its adherents. Then the shogunate's Tenpō reforms (1837–43), which meant stricter control over all kinds of religious movements, inadvertently entangled the Shirakawa office and the Hirata family. In 1840, the Shirakawa established a school in Edo and appointed Atsutane to be one of the instructors. Before he had the chance to give a lecture, the shogunate proscribed his works and sent him into exile to his birthplace in Akita. As an Akita domain retainer, he acquired rank and a stipend from the domain, while his family in Edo, now headed by Hirata Kanetane, moved into the Akita domain's barracks near Asakusa.

The Shirakawa faced other setbacks during the Tenpō reforms. Several of their officials in Edo came under the scrutiny of senior councilor Mizuno Tadakuni 水野忠邦

(1794–1851), the chief architect of the reforms, who forbade religious leaders to live in central Edo. Just months before Atsutane's exile, the magistrate of temples and shrines (*jisha bugyō* 寺社奉行) forced the Shirakawa Kanto administrator into retirement for wrongdoing. Two subsequent administrators were exiled in 1843 and 1845, and two underlings died in prison. The reasons for these punishments ranged from fraud and embezzlement to accusations of heresy against Inoue Masakane 井上正鉄 (1790–1849), the founder of Misogi-kyō 禊教 who had become a Shirakawa affiliate in 1836.[17]

In accordance with the Tenpō reform's relocation decrees, the Shirakawa branch office settled in Torigoe Shrine 鳥越神社, just a few blocks away from the Hirata. During the complicated struggle to find an administrator for it, Kanetane's second son, Kaneya 平田鉄弥 (1830–?), held the office for four years but proved unequal to the task. Kanetane eventually sold the office to Furukawa Mitsura 古川躬行 (1810–?), who later suffered his own difficulties with the authorities. In 1860, Furukawa wrote a preface to and published a critique of the Yoshida house (to be discussed in the next section) that Atsutane had first penned in 1809.[18]

Thus, the relationship between the Hirata and the Shirakawa played out in various registers that enhanced the influence of both sides: from affiliation to doctrine to institutional support. In contrast to Atsutane's changing view of the Yoshida's claims to authority over shrine priests, he and his descendants never wavered in their understanding of the Shirakawa's preeminence in terms of historical pedigree and the purity of its teachings.

Atsutane's *Shirakawa House Principles*

In 1816, while he was still a Shirakawa *gakushi*, Atsutane became the ghostwriter for the *Principles of Study for the Shirakawa House* (*Hakke gakusoku* 伯家学則, hereafter referred to as *Principles*).[19] Even though he claimed no credit for it, an annotated copy remains in the Hirata family archives, and Kanetane later admitted that his father had written it. People who wished to study Shirakawa doctrine were to focus on the age of the gods, their deeds and lineages, the centrality of the emperor to the Japanese polity, indeed the world, and the Way of the Warrior (*budō* 武道).

The initial section of the *Principles* summarizes Atsutane's understanding of divine chronology starting with the primordial gods of the *Kojiki*, Ame no Minakanushi 天御中主尊, Takamimusubi 高皇産霊尊, and Kamumusubi 神皇産霊尊. In this section, Atsutane laid out lists of topics to be explored, from the origins of distance and weight to rites and ceremonies, the beginning of sacred dance, the secret formula for purification, the history of the age of the gods, the profound principle for pacifying the spirits of the dead, and much, much more. "Investigate everything from the original nature of the sun god and the moon god to the fundamental origin of the Warrior Way" (p. 3).

Studying Japan's ancient history did not preclude investigation into other countries, but the student must be careful. He must not carelessly confuse the Confucian canon or Buddhist exhortations with the true, pure ancient truths handed down from the age of the gods. There is ultimately no need to know the scholarship of other countries, which can lead a student astray, particularly the seductive theories found in Chinese learning. "Never deviate from the canonical precedent of respecting the domestic and despising the foreign" (p. 6).

The introduction of foreign ideas is blamed in the *Principles* for the ills that had befallen the imperial institution and the Way of the Gods (*shintō* 神道). When foreign teachings supplanted the Way of the Gods, private conflicts arose, and "there was no longer any reverence for imperial authority" (p. 10). The administrative hub moved to Kamakura, emperors were exiled when they tried to reassert their authority, and following the Ōnin civil war (*Ōnin no ran* 応仁の乱, 1467–77), "lords and retainers, fathers and sons, elder brothers and younger brothers raised private armies, challenged each other to battle, killed, and plundered" (p. 12). Fortunately, a revival of scholarship and a revival of the imperial house had come with the advent of Tokugawa rule. The emperor and court were now at the forefront of studying the Old Way, the Way of the Eternal Gods, the unique Imperial Way. Students in the Shirakawa house "should take this message to heart, pursue their research into the Old Way for the sake of court and military, and never stop praying for enlightenment from the gods with an ever more purified heart" (p. 17).

The *Principles* sets up a fundamental equation between the Way of the Gods, service to the emperor, and the Way of the Warrior. "Emperor Jinmu used the Way of Gods and Warriors (*jinmu no michi* 神武の道) to peacefully govern the realm" (p. 10). The characters for his name, 神 (deity) and 武 (warrior), recuperate this dual way. When Buddhism became Japan's dominant religion, "the Way of the Gods was despised and the Warrior Way was seen as vulgar while literary arts were respected. As a result, the simplicity of the Ancient Way gradually deteriorated" (p. 10).

Atsutane thus distinguished between the Way of the Warrior that supports imperial rule and individual warriors who selfishly disobeyed the court. His emphasis on martial practice perhaps owed something to his awareness that Japan needed to defend itself following the 1808 HMS *Phaeton* incident, in which a British ship sailed boldly into Nagasaki harbor and destroyed its shore batteries without meeting the slightest resistance. Refracted through current concerns, his message highlighted the importance of the military to Japan's history and religion. This martial legacy later resonated with priests, regardless of their affiliation with either the Shirakawa or the Yoshida.

Hirata Atsutane and the Yoshida House

Atsutane's relations with the Yoshida house were more complicated than those he had with the Shirakawa. On the one hand, he worked more closely—and for a longer time—with the Yoshida; on the other, despite a faint-hearted effort at being conciliatory, he remained more critical of their beliefs and practices. He never completely broke off contact, perhaps because the Yoshida had the largest shrine organization in the country and one of his chief disciples had Yoshida affiliations.

Atsutane's Yoshida Critique

Atsutane and the Yoshida got off to a rocky start. In 1809, when he was still an unknown thinker with only eighteen disciples, he produced *Outline of Vulgar Shinto* (*Zoku shintō taii* 俗神道大意), which contains his most severe critique of Yoshida or *yuiitsu shintō*. It was not published until 1860, but it circulated widely in manuscript.[20]

In this work, Atsutane first denigrated the Yoshida's inferior origins compared to the Shirakawa. Descended from the imperial line, the Shirakawa had served in the same position for 800 years and thirty generations. They took charge of everything related to sacred matters at court, they supervised the court bureaucracy, guarded the shrine located inside the palace, and conferred office on the regents. One of their original responsibilities was to perform services at the Hasshinden, at least until the Yoshida had it moved out of the palace to their own shrine.[21]

In contrast, the first known Yoshida ancestor was a diviner from Izu named Hiramaro 平麿, parentage and dates unknown, who was skilled at reading tortoise shells. He and his descendants, originally called Urabe 卜部, gradually rose from lowly attendants without rank or office to prominence. During the reign of Shogun Tsunayoshi 徳川綱吉 (1646–1709, r. 1680–1709), the twenty-ninth family head was promoted to the upper ranks of the nobility, even though he was still in charge of the tortoise shell diviners and from a base house (p. 140).[22] The only reason why the family, now calling itself Yoshida, got away with designating itself the superintendent of Shinto was because of its dirty tricks. It falsified documents, claimed more authority than it deserved, and fabricated a genealogy. "Claiming that it is so ordered by the military government, its officials deceive shrine personnel across the provinces and gull them into coming under Yoshida control. Since they do this out of greed, they are just like the monks" (p. 144).

Atsutane acknowledged that he was not the first to accuse the Yoshida of self-aggrandizement. In 1739 Yoshimi Yoshikazu 吉見幸和 (1673–1761), a Shinto priest from the Tōshōgū branch shrine in Nagoya, refuted claims that the Yoshida had descended from Ame no Koyane. Yoshimi's criticism of the Yoshidas' divine origin was widely known by the early nineteenth century, and Atsutane used it to great effect, putting all the blame on Yoshida Kanetomo: "The forgeries, false statements, and plots all come from his hand" (p. 146). Kanetomo had forged a genealogy that traced the Yoshida family back to Nakatomi no Kamatari 中臣鎌足 (614–69), the ancestor of the Fujiwara court nobles, and asserted that the Yoshida house possessed a secret transmission handed down by the divine Nakatomi ancestor Ame no Koyane. Descent from this deity mattered because he was the mythological originator of Shinto rituals and the divination that ascertained the will of the gods. Regarding himself as Koyane's direct descendant, Yoshida Kanetomo argued that his version of Shinto was superior to all others,[23] an example of how genealogy becomes important as a matter of faith.

Refuting such claims, Atsutane argued that there could be no secret transmissions apart from the prayers written down for all to see in texts from the age of the gods. Kanetomo's incantation originated in a prayer created by Kūkai 空海 (774–835) to further his teachings on *ryōbu shintō* (p. 147). Kanetomo also falsified imperial edicts and misinterpreted earlier texts to promote his house. He brought an eight-sided hall for the Bodhisattva Kannon 観音菩薩 into his shrine precincts, lied by claiming it had been a place of worship since the time of Emperor Jinmu, and called it the Hasshinden where the imperial gods were enshrined.[24] In 1489 he claimed that the god bodies (*shintai* 神体) stored at the two Ise shrines and other sacred treasures had emitted light and flown to his family shrine, thus providing the excuse for building a new shrine to Amaterasu. "He deserves the gods' punishment" (p. 149).

Atsutane further criticized Yoshida machinations to gain control over all shrines across Japan by calling for a revision of the *Shrine Clauses* immediately after they were issued in 1665. The Yoshida had faked imperial decrees to claim an appointment as councilor of divinities, the title held by the Shirakawa, and argued that traditionally they had been in charge of all shrines wanting imperial rank. While the imperial regent questioned the Yoshida's documentation, Asukai Masaaki 飛鳥井雅章 (1611–79), who served as liaison with the shogunate (*buke tensō* 武家伝奏), supported the Yoshida. The shogunate asked the regent to investigate the precedents further. When urged to present the original decrees instead of copies, the Yoshida pretended that they had been accidentally destroyed by fire on their way to Edo (p. 159). Unable to substantiate their claims, the Yoshida were forced to submit recommendations for rank to the emperor through the official on duty.[25] On the other hand, they retained the right to license priests without court rank to wear ceremonial robes above their station, which is, according to Atsutane, inappropriate in any case, since robes signify office at court. "This is outrageous and disrespectful" (p. 160).

Toward the end of *Vulgar Shinto*, Atsutane raises issues concerning practice. Here again he draws on earlier criticism. How can the Yoshida claim to believe in "One-and-Only Shinto" when almost all of their ceremonies come from Shingon 真言 Buddhism? Take the *goma* 護摩 rite of burning prayer sticks, performed in Esoteric Buddhism because burning wood represents people's suffering and calamities purified by fire. For shrine personnel to perform it is inappropriate. Later, by stealing the Yoshida's most prized secret traditions in the late seventeenth century, the former fishmonger Yoshikawa Koretaru 吉川惟足 (1616–95) changed the character of the Urabe house.[26] Neither Koretaru's descendants nor the Yoshida know what they are doing when they pretend to worship the gods, nor do they know the appropriate names for the gods (pp. 165–6).

From Critique to Cooperation

In 1822, shortly after quitting his service for the Shirakawa, Atsutane turned around and wrote something of an apology for his castigation of Yoshida Shinto—*Soliloquy* (*Hitorigoto* 独言). Here Atsutane acknowledges that while the Yoshida had accepted Shinto-Buddhist syncretism (*shinbutsu shūgō* 神仏習合) in medieval times, this was to prevent the true Old Way from disappearing. Yet in spite of this conciliatory acknowledgement, most of the text admonishes the Yoshida. Now that the Ancient Way was flourishing, it behooved the Yoshida to change their teachings to fit the times lest they alienate local priests who wanted to base their practice on ancient texts.

Atsutane urged the Yoshida to advance their scholarship by appointing scholars of the Ancient Way as teachers, opening a school for Shinto studies, and leading the priests in each region back to the past based on ancient studies that emphasized the great Way of the Emperor, not their personal, private ways. "By relying on ancient studies, the errors that have accumulated since the middle ages will be corrected, and we will return to the past in accordance with the emperor's beneficent mercy."[27] The Yoshida had to allow scholars to investigate the past, and when their interpretations conflicted with the doctrines and practices transmitted by the Yoshida, then both the Yoshida and the scholars would have to bring them into harmony. The Yoshida had to resist putting limits on scholarship, and the scholars must not embarrass them by making their differences public. This process of reconciliation thus had to be done in secret. If the Yoshida agreed, then "your household occupation of performing Shinto rituals handed down to you from Ame no Koyane will continue to be transmitted to both heaven and earth."[28] *Soliloquy* can thus be seen as mediating between the priests and the Yoshida while seeking a hearing for Atsutane's ideas in Japan's largest shrine organization.

Hattori Nakatsune 服部中庸 (1757–1824), Atsutane's devoted supporter in Kyoto, explained the extraordinary reversal found in *Soliloquy* in a letter to Motoori Ōhira 本居大平 (1756–1833):

> Since Hirata is trying to spread the Way of the Gods throughout the realm, he thinks that it will be easy for him to do this if he persuades the Yoshida house to reform its Shinto in line with the ancient studies handed down by Norinaga and if he uses that house to convey his teachings.[29]

Hattori also thought he understood why the Yoshida would accept this not-quite-an-apology:

> Lord Yoshida's beliefs typically have to do with his house's worldly affairs. In recent years Hirata has become famous in Edo, he preaches the Ancient Way, he has many pupils, and he has become powerful. I have heard that even the Yoshida Kanto administrator has become one of his disciples. He is reporting to the Yoshida house in Kyoto that if it doesn't co-opt Hirata, the situation will become impossible.[30]

But would this work? "The Yoshida style is just like that of Honganji 本願寺[31], and since they amass money whether asleep or awake, they are completely set in their ways" (p. 437). On the other hand, as he pointed out, since the Yoshida were losing ground to the Shirakawa, they needed Atsutane. Atsutane thought he could reach shrine priests through the Yoshida and they would provide cover for his publication projects. Each side hoped to use the other.

In any event, Atsutane's plans met with success. Soon after he wrote *Soliloquy*, he went to Kyoto, where he was introduced to members of the Yoshida house and met with them several times during his stay.[32] After he returned to Edo, he received an appointment from the Yoshida's Kanto administrator Miyagawa Danshō 宮川弾正 (dates unknown) to be its *gakushi*, a new position created possibly in response to his *Soliloquy*. The document confirming Atsutane's appointment states:

> Since you have been diligent in recent years in the study of the Way of the Gods, you are now appointed scholar-teacher. Henceforth you are instructed to educate the shrine priests attached to us and under our control. Moreover, whenever you travel around the villages, you are to admonish any priests guilty of misconduct and instruct them not to neglect their calling and their Shinto initiation.[33]

This appointment allowed Atsutane to keep doing what he was already doing—lecturing in Edo and trawling the countryside for recruits. Now, however, he was to advance the Yoshida agenda as well as his own.

Atsutane demonstrated further good will toward the Yoshida by revising their genealogy. For this he got help from four priests from Mikawa province who later became his disciples, in particular Hatano Takao 羽田野敬雄 (1798–1882), who appears again in this chapter. The revision was needed because the Yoshida claim that their ancestor, Urabe Hiramaro (mentioned above), was the son of a court priest named Nakatomi Chijimaro 中臣智治麿 (active around 800) lacked credibility. In order to link the Yoshida with the Nakatomi's divine ancestor, Ame no Koyane, Atsutane used ancient texts to construct a new lineage turning Hiramaro into a cousin, not a son of Chijimaro. Because Atsutane's work was based on evidence drawn from historical investigation, it superseded earlier attacks on the genealogy.³⁴

Despite this conciliatory gesture, clashes between the Yoshida and the Hirata school continued. The publication of a treatise on the Nakatomi purification ritual (*Nakatomi no harae hongi* 中臣祓本義) by the Yoshida official Miki Hirotaka 三木広隆 (dates unknown) in 1824 is a case in point. It was severely criticized by Atsutane's protégé Ikuta Yorozu 生田萬 (aka Michimaro 道満, 1801–37)³⁵ for its misunderstanding of Japanese and Chinese history. Later, in 1827, Ikuta wrote an appendix to his critique that castigated Kanetomo for nominating himself as the superintendent of the Office of Deities, thus challenging the Shirakawa-Yoshida hierarchy. Atsutane supported Ikuta's views. Atsutane even proposed him as an assistant scholar-teacher at the Yoshida school in Edo. Ikuta planned to get approval from the Yoshida to become an instructor and then go to Kyoto, an indication, perhaps, that he intended to force Yoshida adherents to repudiate Miki's ideas. These plans never materialized.³⁶

There were other differences besides intellectual ones. Starting in 1829, the Yoshida had to deal with problems in their Edo office when Miyagawa Danshō was caught up in a scandal that led to his banishment from Edo. Who was to serve as the next Kanto administrator? Atsutane's disciples in Kanto proposed that he be appointed to the position, but this suggestion horrified the conservative Yoshida officials. In 1831, a Yoshida house elder sent the following announcement to Atsutane:

> The shrine priests under our control have been complaining for years that the Edo office is poorly managed, and now they propose that since you have already been appointed teacher-scholar, you should become the administrator. Given how busy you are with your studies, we have decided to give the position to Matsuoka Sanai 松岡左内 (1791–1851, aka Motoatsu 帰厚). We have discussed this with the priests and warned them to submit. We instruct you to continue as scholar-teacher and redouble your efforts in matters of instruction.³⁷

At least the appointment had not gone to Miki, who, as Endō Jun points out, was trying to use Yoshida backing to force people in Kanto to buy his book and to get himself set up as another scholar-teacher with his own school to be funded by the Kanto priests. Not only did they not like Miki's work, he was costing them money.³⁸

Despite doctrinal differences and personnel problems, Atsutane never severed ties with the Yoshida, even when they tried to force the Shirakawa to relinquish their adherents in Mikawa, as we will see below. After all, he had students and disciples on both sides.

Conflicts over Priests Switching Affiliation in Mikawa

How did the emergence of the Hirata school intersect with Yoshida and Shirakawa priestly networks outside the urban centers? And how did provincial priests respond to Yoshida–Shirakawa competition? In order to explore these questions, we turn now to Mikawa province in central Japan, the cradle of Tokugawa Ieyasu's 徳川家康 (1542–1616) rise to power. Ieyasu had a particular attachment to Hachiman 八幡, worshipped by many warriors as their ancestor and a god of war, and invested a number of Hachiman shrines in Mikawa with vermillion-seal patents (*shuinjō* 朱印状) that provided them with an income guaranteed by the shogunate. In the nineteenth century, the hereditary priests at these shrines often worked together by organizing poetry meetings and setting up study groups to investigate Japan's history and theology. The Hirata school attracted many of these local intellectuals.

We have already encountered Atsutane's chief disciple in Mikawa, Hatano Takao, who assisted in creating a new Yoshida genealogy. He succeeded to a Yoshida-licensed house in 1818 when his father raised the money from parishioners to pay for his succession license, plus licenses for prayers, procedures, incantations, and costly paraphernalia.[39] Takao officiated at two important shrines (Hada Shinmeisha 羽田神明社 and Hachimangū 八幡宮) in Yoshida domain 吉田藩 (modern Toyohashi, Aichi prefecture; see Map 14.1). Living in the domain's castle town, he had close ties to its officials. In 1852 he convinced them to purge Buddhist elements from the castle shrine.[40] At the same time, he promoted Atsutane's teachings through financing the publication of Atsutane's works, introducing priests to the Hirata school, replacing Sanskrit letters with the ancient script of the gods (*jindai moji* 神代文字) on festival flags, and urging shrine priests to spread the dual Way of literary and martial arts in service to emperor and nation.[41] Takao remained a Yoshida adherent until the Meiji government abolished the system of court-issued licenses for priests in 1868. This is worth remembering when comparing his case with other shrine priests of his acquaintance who chose Shirakawa affiliation, some like him officiating at Hachiman shrines.

One dispute between the Yoshida and Shirakawa over who had the authority to issue licenses to local priests and who had the right to adjudicate conflicts, court or shogunate, also sheds light on reasons for opposing Yoshida affiliation. Two of Takao's fellow Hachiman priests in Western Mikawa took leading roles in this conflict: Watanabe Masaka 渡辺政香 (1776–1840), the shrine priest for Hachimangū in Terazu 寺津 village (in present day Nishio city in Aichi), then under the jurisdiction of Ōhama Fort (Ōhama Jinya 大浜陣屋),[42] and Takeo Masatomo 竹尾正靭 (1781–1861), the priest at Hachimangū in Maigi 舞木 village of Okazaki domain 岡崎藩 (present day Okazaki city in Aichi). Although the conflict erupted after Masaka joined the Shirakawa school in 1807, sponsored by Masatomo's father, its roots go back to 1797 when Masaka was

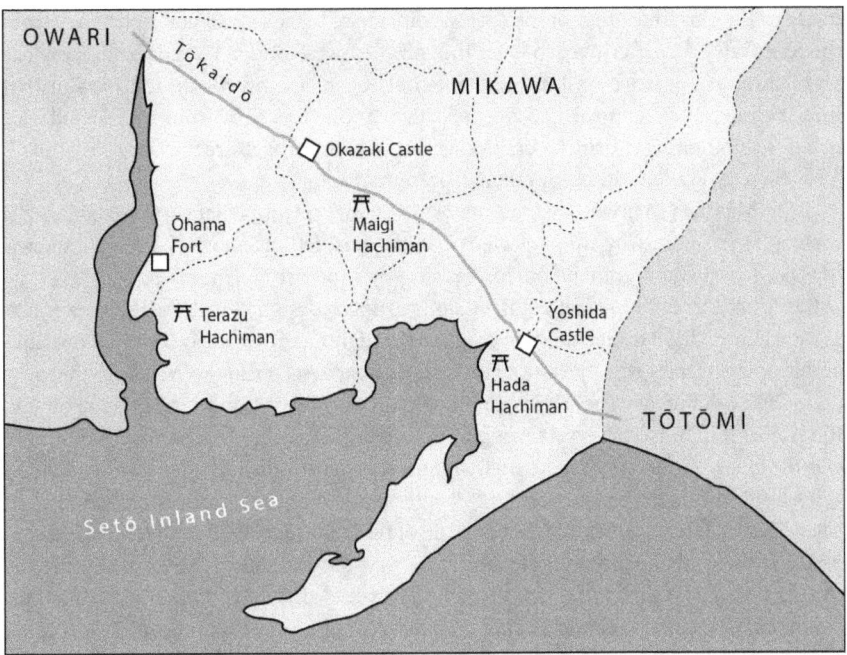

Map 14.1 Hirata-affiliated Hachiman shrines in Mikawa province.

forced to submit to the Yoshida. That year, a Yoshida factotum had summoned him to the residence of a nearby priest and bullied him into signing a document attesting to his acceptance of Yoshida jurisdiction. The factotum then informed him that within the next year, he was to request a license suitable to his status, submit to Yoshida instruction, and promise not to cause disorder. Masaka had to sign another document to this effect, an experience he found humiliating. His shrine had received a vermillion seal from the great Ieyasu. Why should he have to become a Yoshida subordinate? When Masaka asked to become a Shirakawa disciple, he wrote, "up to now I have not been affiliated with the Yoshida or any other house." Five other Mikawa priests also joined the Shirakawa, having suffered the same high-handed treatment at Yoshida hands.[43]

The Yoshida did not follow up their 1797 claims to jurisdiction over the Mikawa priests until 1814, when they sent a request to the Ōhama government office to inform shrines under its jurisdiction that Shinto initiation and licenses fell under Yoshida purview. The office refused because according to the shogunate's directive, government authorities were the ones to decide whether the Yoshida had control over local shrines, as the Ōhama priests pointed out.

Since they could not intimidate the local government, in 1815 the Yoshida appealed to the magistrate of temples and shrines in Edo. This time they invoked additional cases, complaining that Takeo Masatomo (the priest at the Maigi Hachimangū Shrine in Okazaki) plus four other Shinto priests outside of Mikawa had gotten licenses from the Shirakawa for priestly garb even though they were under Yoshida authority. The Shirakawa countered by asking the imperial regent to investigate their claim that priests under their control had no need to rely on directives from the Yoshida for licenses, thus hoping to use a favorable decision at court to pressure the Edo magistrate.[44] They then appointed Masatomo their representative for Mikawa.

Both Masaka (1816) and Masatomo (1817) wrote treatises that summoned nativist theology to explain why they rejected Yoshida jurisdiction in favor of the Shirakawa. Masaka based his argument on his reading of Motoori Norinaga 本居宣長 (1730–1801), who had called secret transmissions artifices designed to help their inventors make a living. Good things should be spread throughout the world as widely as possible, and keeping secrets was the sign of an impure heart. According to Masaka, "there are no hidden teachings in the Way of Buddhism or the Way of Confucianism; so how can the Way of the Gods, universal throughout the world, be limited to the Yoshida?" Shinto was the great Way of the Emperor, who reigns forever over heaven and earth in a direct line of descent from the sun goddess. People should obey him respectfully and live in accord with ancient traditions. The function of the traditional Office of Deities (*jingikan* 神祇官), rightfully headed by the Shirakawa, was to set an example for following the simple customs of the Way of the Gods honestly and sincerely.[45] Masatomo called his complaint *Treatise on Wrongs in Divine Affairs* (*Kamigoto no uretamigoto* 祭事冤論). It recapitulated the history of the age of the gods in accordance with Atsutane's teachings, criticized the confusion in rites and ranks wrought by the Yoshida, and justified Shirakawa Shinto as the one true tradition.[46]

Contrary to the expectations raised by the Shirakawa house and its adherents in Mikawa, the court decided in favor of the Yoshida. On 1816/i8/17, it accepted the Yoshida claims of authority over Shinto initiation and licenses to wear priestly garments for eleven priests from six provinces, including six from Mikawa (Masatomo was not one of them). Furthermore, the Shirakawa were forbidden to solicit applications for affiliation without getting permission from both the court and shogunate. At first, Shirakawa head Sukenobu 白川資延 (1770–1824) reluctantly accepted this decision. The Mikawa priests headed by Masatomo, however, urged him to stand up to the Yoshida. They argued that the court's decision was imprudent, all it worried about was its reputation vis-à-vis the shogunate, Sukenobu was weak, and they wanted their demands realized no matter what. Owing to this pressure, Sukenobu asked that the case be re-opened. In fact, he had an ace up his sleeve: Emperor Kōkaku 光格天皇 having abdicated, the new emperor was supposed to receive a Shinto initiation from him. Sukenobu, however, refused to appear at court until his demands (those of the Mikawa priests) had been met. This was a serious matter: Withholding the Shinto initiation would compromise the new emperor's authority as chief of worship. According to a letter from Masatomo to Watanabe Masaka, he had urged Sukenobu to stay home.[47] Thus, a remarkable feature of this conflict is the fact that it was the local priest Masatomo who pushed the Shirakawa to oppose the Yoshida.

Both court and shogunate launched investigations and issued findings, and Masatomo spent much of the following two and a half decades in Edo. He often visited the Hirata school, as did Masaka on his trips to the city. They corresponded with

Atsutane,[48] although neither became disciples. Other Mikawa priests and Masatomo's son joined the school along with Hatano Takao in 1827. In 1838, the shogunate asked questions about the Shirakawa's administrative duties as head of the *jingikan*, and Masatomo crafted the response.[49] Even though the shogunate ultimately ruled in the Yoshida's favor in 1840, granting them control over the six Mikawa shrine priests, the Yoshida never tried to make them accept Yoshida jurisdiction after this ruling. The shogunate never enforced its decision, and the court simply ignored it.[50]

Unlike the Mikawa conflict that lasted for decades, most attempts by shrine personnel to switch affiliation ended fairly quickly. When the Yoshida claimed that one of their own had tried to leave their control, the Shirakawa sometimes agreed and returned the would-be adherent. But when the applicant claimed a sincere faith in the Shirakawa house, especially if he had supporting documentation from his domain, the Shirakawa took him in.

Despite different religious affiliations and subordination to different political jurisdictions, Takao, Masaka, Masatomo, and their descendants worked together in multilayered and complex organizations. They shared an identity as priests who served the Hachiman shrines invested with vermillion seals and they had a common interest in nativist ideas. Watanabe Masaka's son and other Mikawa priests copied Masatomo's *Treatise on Wrongs in Divine Affairs*. In 1841 Masatomo's son sent a copy of it along with the statement on the *jingikan* made by Masatomo in 1838 to the Yoshida adherent/Hirata disciple Hatano Takao with a note saying, "Since we are of the same [Hirata] school, and we are on such friendly terms, please take a look at this."[51] In *Soliloquy*, Atsutane noted that the Hachiman priests in Mikawa were turning against the heretical teachings promoted by the Yoshida.[52] From his perspective, their affiliations with either the Yoshida or the Shirakawa mattered less than their adherence to his teaching on the Ancient Way of Pure Shinto.

Conclusion

Scholars such as Hatakama Kazuhiro argue that the Yoshida and Shirakawa cared more about expanding their control over local priests than they did about theology.[53] As far as they were concerned, what Atsutane wrote was less important than bringing in fee-paying bodies. For the priests, affiliation with one or the other of these houses was often a matter of habit. Hatano Takao accepted Yoshida control because his ancestors and his domain had long-standing ties to the Yoshida. Other priests preferred the Shirakawa house because affiliation with it came cheap, and the Shirakawa were not as doctrinaire as the Yoshida. Founders of new religions, Shugendō 修験道 practitioners, amulet sellers, and the like found a welcome with the Shirakawa regardless of their personal beliefs and practice. Yet Atsutane had a theological agenda. He wanted to train priests to return Japan not simply to the Age of the Gods, but to *his* particular view of the Age of the Gods based on his research into ancient texts. Only a small percentage followed him, but their presence speaks for the possibility that for some priests, at least, doctrine mattered.

Japanese historians have proposed various interpretations for the significance of the rivalry between the Yoshida and Shirakawa and Atsutane's role in it. In her article on the conflict in Mikawa, Mase Kumiko argued that the case demonstrates the shogunate's declining authority because Watanabe Masaka and his peers ignored the shogunate's decree that they affiliate with the Yoshida. Inoue Tomokatsu and Takano Toshihiko posit that the promise of court rank for shrine priests or even nothing more than a license to wear colorful priestly garb raised the emperor and court in local consciousness and proves that the emperor was not as irrelevant to the Tokugawa polity as was once thought.[54] Bob Wakabayashi also made this argument in examining the ways everyone from daimyo to commoners sought the markers of prestige offered by the court.[55] As for Atsutane, according to the literary scholar and historian Yamada Yoshio 山田孝雄 (1873–1958), once both the Shirakawa and the Yoshida turned to Hirata Shinto 平田神道, this was equivalent to uniting shrine officials across Japan in the Hirata school of Japan studies, before the Meiji government instituted a unified system for organizing shrine personnel.[56] Since not all shrine officials affiliated with the Shirakawa or Yoshida, let alone Atsutane, Yamada overstates the case for Atsutane's nationwide impact. Nonetheless, the initiatives taken by these various establishments gave radically new institutional contexts and meanings to Shinto in the nineteenth century, with nativist theology taking the lead.

Notes

Introduction

1. Hur 2007, 50–1.
2. For details, see the "Preface" to this volume.
3. On our conventions of dating, see the "Editorial Conventions" section in the prelims; on the specific problems to identify this edict, see Chapter 1, note 8.
4. As briefly mentioned by Sonehara (Chapter 2 in this volume, note 45), this text seems to have a faint relationship with Tenkai's Buddhist Shinto.
5. First orders in Mito are actually documented as having been undertaken on 1666/4/25 (see Chapter 12 in this volume, p. 180), while Ikeda Mitsumasa started his reforms on 1666/5/18 (see Chapter 11, p. 164).
6. Scheid 2004.
7. Conlan 2016.
8. Boot 2000.
9. Tendai scholar monks from the Tokugawa entourage such as Jōin 乗因 (1682–1739) compared Tōshō Daigongen to Tenshō Daijin 天照大神 (Amaterasu), the ancestor deity of the imperial lineage, maintaining that this kind of "Shinto" was in unison with the Buddhist *Sūtra of the Golden Light* (*Konkōmyō kyō* 金光明経) (Bodiford 2013, 279–82).
10. Inoue 2013, 50–1.
11. Scheid 2003.
12. The 1664 law also urged the establishment offices for religious investigation in each domain (Tamamuro 2001, 262).
13. According to Tamamuro Fumio, a nationwide prohibition of Fujufuse was officially enacted only in 1669 (Tamamuro 2001, 265). Nevertheless, the *Temple Laws* of 1665 seem to have had the persecution of Fujufuse already in mind, leading to comparable measures also outside Okayama (Kasahara 2001, 397–400).
14. On *shikinaisha*, see Chapter 6 in this volume, note 2.
15. *Gosanke* were the three distinguished cadet Tokugawa houses that could provide a successor to the shogun line in case of need, namely the daimyo of Owari, Kii, and Mito; *shinpan* refers to other daimyo related to the Tokugawa.
16. Taira 1983, 67–70; Scheid 2002, 311–12.
17. Taira 1983, 74–6.
18. Inoue 2007a, 2.
19. See Chapter 6 in this volume, p. 97.
20. Scheid 2002, 313–14.
21. Taira 1983, 84–6.
22. Inaba Masanori, referred in the text as Mino no kami 美濃守, was the daimyo of Odawara 小田原藩 and held the office of *rōjū* from 1657 to 1681. His son was married to one of Masayuki's daughters.

23 *Yoshikawa Aremi no ya sensei gyōjō* 吉川視吾堂先生行状 (*The Accomplishments of Master Yoshikawa Aremi [Koretaru]*), written shortly after Koretaru's death in 1694 by his adopted son and successor, Yoshikawa Yorinaga 吉川従長 (1654–1730). The account is certainly not free of hagiographic exaggeration, but its gist seems plausible. The passages on Masayuki's funeral follow a translation by Richard Bowring and I owe him deep gratitude for forwarding me this still unpublished material. For a parallel account contained in *Aizuhan kasei jikki* 会津藩家世実紀, see Chapter 9 in this volume or Roberts 2012, 145–7.
24 *Yoshikawa Aremi no ya sensei gyōjō*, 472.
25 *Yoshikawa Aremi no ya sensei gyōjō*, 472.
26 *Kotogoto shikaranu sama ni* 事々しからぬ様に (*Yoshikawa Aremi no ya sensei gyōjō*, 473).
27 This was cited as a precedent in the discussion about Masayuki's funeral (*Yoshikawa Aremi no ya sensei gyōjō*, 472). On Ikeda Mitsumasa's commitment to "erect a new lineage shrine," see Chapter 8 in this volume (p. 121). On Tokugawa Mitsukuni, see Chapter 12.
28 Roberts 2012, Chap. 5.
29 As analyzed in detail by Anton Schweizer, Ōsaki Hachiman Shrine emulated the architectonical and artistic design of Hideyoshi's Toyokuni Shrine in Kyoto. It is probable that Date Masamune, one of the most powerful figures of the day, envisaged himself as an avatar of Hachiman and had a self-deification similar to that of Hideyoshi in mind, when he erected this shrine in 1604 (Schweizer 2016, Chap. 4). On daimyo deification, see also Takano 2018.
30 Roberts 2012, 149.
31 See Chapter 8, p. 128.
32 Roberts 2012, 138–41; for Domain-Shinto-like phenomena in the nineteenth century, see also Haga 1998.

Chapter 1

1 Gonoi 1990, 2–4.
2 Gonoi 1990, 5–12. Ōhashi suggests that there were about 300,000 Christian followers in the early seventeenth century. See Ōhashi 2016, 125.
3 Shimizu 1981, 214–18.
4 For details, see Murai 1991, 85–6; and 2002, 36–43.
5 See, for instance, Chapter 2 in this volume.
6 *Kishōmon* 起請文, a blood oath that entailed divine punishment if broken (Hur 2007, 42).
7 Nakamura 1960, 662–6.
8 *Tsūkō ichiran* 5, 154–5. The document is actually known by various titles such as *Statement on the Expulsion of the Padres* (*Bateren tsuihō no bun* 伴天連追放之文) or *Statement against Christianity* (*Hai kirishitan no fumi* 排吉利支丹文). As described by Sonehara Satoshi in this volume (Chapter 2), it was drafted by the *bakufu*'s religious advisor Konchiin Sūden 金地院崇伝 (1569–1633) and contained the overarching principle to eradicate Christianity through the concerted forces of Shinto and Buddhism (see also Takagi 1992, 6–7; and Gonoi 1990, 202–07). At the same time, it had the covert purpose of warning the western daimyo who remained sympathetic to the Toyotomi legacy.

9   *Tokugawa jikki* 1, KT 38, 646; and *Tsūkō ichiran* 5, 35–9.
10 For a detailed discussion of the Kokura inspection, see Tamamuro (1998), 4–25; and Yokota 2014, 281.
11 Gonoi 1990, 11–12.
12 Shimizu 1981, 145; Endō 1992, 75–7.
13 *Tsūkō ichiran* 5, 214–18.
14 On anti-Christian measures in Nagasaki, see also Chapter 3 in this volume.
15 Among the documents identified, this one is considered the oldest register and the closest to the "register of sectarian inspection" (*shūmon aratamechō*) in both format and content.
16 For a detailed account of the events leading to the crackdown of the revolt in 1638, see *Tokugawa jikki* 3, KT 40, 83–93; Yamamoto 1989, 77–84; Shimura 1989, 108–11.
17 Harufuji 1980, 85.
18 For a comprehensive list of religious inspection experiments in the 1630s, see Ōhashi 2001, 103–06.
19 At the shogunal level, *shūmon aratameyaku* officers simultaneously assumed the office of construction magistrates. But from the Enpō era (1673–80), the task of religious inspection was taken over by the magistrate of temples and shrines, and the *shūmon aratameyaku* was finally discontinued. See Shimizu 1976, 47.
20 See Hōjō 1907, 632.
21 See Shimizu 1981, 193–4.
22 *Buke genseiroku* (1941), 112–13, 120.
23 Kataoka 1972, 710; Shimizu 1994, 63–71.
24 For statistics on the arrests, see Anesaki 1976, 269–70.
25 *Ofuregaki Kanpō shūsei* (first edition, 1934), 8.
26 *Ofuregaki Kanpō shūsei* (first edition, 1934), 8.
27 *Ofuregaki Kanpō shūsei* (first edition, 1934), 633.
28 Narimatsu 2000, 145–8. As Nagura Tetsuzō notes in his examination of Kakudahama village 角田浜村 in Echigo between 1846 and 1866, the head monk of the temple usually had to spend a whole month or more on the road just to carry out the job of "temple stamping" for *danna* patrons who were scattered over a number of villages (Nagura 1999, 63–4).
29 Hōzawa 2015, 30–1.
30 Kinoshita 2002, 4–5; Hirai 2015, 450.
31 Hayami 2001, 72–4.
32 *Ofuregaki Tenmei shūsei*, 684–5.
33 Kinoshita 2002, 4–5. From the late eighteenth century, the Chōshū domain switched to compiling a census register of its own called *tojaku* 戸籍. See Hayami 2001, 50.
34 Hayami 2001, 52–3.
35 Matsuura 2015, 418.
36 Hayami 1997, 63–5.
37 Ōishi 1968, 366–7. Between 1721 and 1846, based on the merging of the *shūmon aratamechō* and *ninbetsu aratamechō*, once every six years the shogunal government was able to conduct a countrywide census.
38 Matsuura 2015, 416–17.
39 Inoue 2008a, 298.
40 Tsuji 1953, 331–6.
41 See Chapter 8 in this volume.
42 *IRR* 1, 324; see also Chapter 4 in this volume.

43 For formats of non-Christian Shinto certificates, see the entry for the fifth day of the eighth month of 1666 in *IMN*, 569; and *IRR* 1, 320–1; see also Chapter 11 in this volume.
44 Tamamuro 1999, 108–09.
45 *IRR* 1, 330.
46 As Stefan Köck shows in this volume (Chapter 11), shrine families in Okayama practiced *shintōuke* throughout the Edo period.
47 See Chapter 9 in this volume.
48 See Chapter 12 in this volume.
49 For details, see Ichimura 1930, 71–4.
50 The *Examples of the Shinto Sect in All Domains* (*Shintō shūmon shokoku ruireisho* 神道宗門諸国類例書), a collection of Shinto documents compiled in 1805, alleges that in many parts of the country Shinto funerals were, although still far from the rule, at least on the rise. It is hard to determine to what extent these documents are reliable, but they cite a rather large number of domains where Shinto funerals were performed. See *Meiji ishin shinbutsu bunri shiryō* 5, 1078–81; and for a detailed discussion of the geographical distribution of Shinto funerals, see Nishida 1979, 77–82.
51 Ōta 1974, 18.
52 *Meiji ishin shinbutsu bunri shiryō* 4, 468–575; Tsuji 1997, 368–79.
53 *Shūkyō kankei hōrei ichiran*, 427.
54 Jaffe 2001, 60; *Oshioki reiruishū*, 123–25.
55 *Shūkyō kankei hōrei ichiran*, 440.
56 It should be noted that the talisman each household was supposed to receive from its parish shrine was associated with the Ise Grand Shrine. Each household was required to enshrine this talisman—the divided spirit of the Ise deities—in its domestic altar for the *kami*. Through this, the state believed that each household would become a "branch shrine" of the Ise Grand Shrine, which would then link the entire populace to the cult center of State Shinto. See Hardacre 1989, 29, 83.
57 Sakamoto 1994, 421–2.
58 Jaffe 2001, 78–87.
59 Hoshino 2014, 241–2; and for a discussion of the passage that led to the eventual removal of the anti-Christian clause, see Breen 1996, 79–89.

Chapter 2

1 This chapter is based on two recent articles of mine: Sonehara 2018a, secs. 1–3; 2018b, sec. 4. My research was supported by a JSPS Grant-in-Aid for Scientific Research (KAKENHI).
2 See, for instance, Rambelli 1996 on *shinkoku*, and Boot 2000 on Ieyasu's apotheosis.
3 Sonehara 1995.
4 *Nihon shoki* 1, Chūai 9/10 (NKBT 67, 338–9); *Nihon sandai jitsuroku* 1, Jōgan 11/12/14.
5 *Hachiman gūji kōmon burui*, 423.
6 Editors' note: In the Japanese context, *nenbutsu* 念仏 (lit. contemplating the Buddha) refers to the practice of reciting the name of Buddha Amida. According to the teachings of Hōnen, this was the (only) appropriate way to pray for Buddhist salvation.
7 *Enryakuji daishūge*, 271.
8 See, e.g., Kaizu 1994 or Nam 1996.
9 On *honji suijaku*, see, e.g., Teeuwen and Rambelli 2003.

10 *Jinnō shōtōki*, 41.
11 Takahashi 1994; Satō 1998.
12 Nishida 1978; Scheid 2001, 243–52.
13 This explanation surfaced in Shingon 真言 texts of the eleventh century and was subsequently taken over by Tendai Esotericism.
14 Taira 2004.
15 On the *danka* system, see, for instance, Hur 2007. See also Nam-lin Hur's contribution to this volume (Chapter 1).
16 Hayashi 1995. See also Hayashi Makoto's contribution to this volume (Chapter 9).
17 Here, I am referring in particular to the work of Hirakawa Arata (2010; 2018).
18 See, e.g., Sonehara 2012.
19 In 1571, trading in Japanese slaves was prohibited by King Sebastian of Portugal (1554–78, *r.* 1557–78), because the increasing number of Japanese slaves in Portugal was perceived as a threat to the Catholic mission in Japan. This prohibition, however, was generally ignored.
20 Shimizu Yūko has discussed the memorandum, which is held at the Jingū Library in Ise (*Jingū bunko* 神宮文庫), and argues that it must be treated as "stately law" (Shimizu 2017).
21 Rich information on European plans to conquer Japan can be found in Takase 1977, pt. 1/3. For a more recent study, see Takahashi 2012.
22 This edict was modeled on the above-mentioned memorandum and issued just one day later. The document is held in the Matsura Monjo 松浦文書 Collection at Matsuura Historical Museum in Hirado, Nagasaki Prefecture. For Japanese originals and translations into English, see also Morris 2018.
23 Translation adopted from Tsunoda, De Bary, and Keene 1958, 317. For a Japanese edition of Hideyoshi's letter, see Murakami 1929, 26–9.
24 In 1602, he prohibited Christian missionary work on Japanese soil and in 1605, in a letter to the Spanish Governor-General of the Philippines, he adopted the same dichotomy of *shinkoku* and Christianity as we saw in Hideshoshi's diplomatic correspondence (Murakami 1929, 91–2).
25 Ieyasu had first edicts against Christianity issued in 1612/4 for the domains under direct Tokugawa control. The quoted edict is the first that pertained to the entire country.
26 *Ikoku nikki*, 33. Translation adopted from Elisonas 2005, 173.
27 Under normal conditions, the choice of a divine title would have involved the head of the Yoshida house, Yoshida Kaneharu 吉田兼治 (1565–1616). At the time, however, the latter was on the verge of dying himself (he actually died on 1616/6/5). Therefore, his uncle Bonshun 梵舜 (1553–1632), a monk affiliated to Sūden's Nanzenji, acted as the *de facto* representative of the Yoshida house, forming a coalition with Sūden.
28 The following analysis of this debate is indebted to Urai Shōmei, who investigated Ieyasu's deification in great depth (Urai 1983). Urai criticized traditional scholarship, which had relied on a comparatively late source, the *Meiryō kōhan* 明良洪範. This is a voluminous history of the Tokugawa by Zōyo 増誉 (?–1707), a resident of the Shingon temple Shōrinji 聖輪寺 in Edo. Based on the more contemporary sources mentioned below, Urai arrived at a new understanding of the motivations that favored the *gongen* title.
29 According to the *Meiryō kōhan*, the debate occurred on 1616/4/18, one day after Ieyasu had died. However, the *Jishō nikki* 慈性日記, a contemporary diary by a Tendai

monk of courtly pedigree covering the period from 1614 to 1643, contains nothing for 4/18 or 4/19, reporting for 4/20: "In Sunpu castle there was a dispute between Tenkai and Sūden regarding Ieyasu's testament" (*Jishō nikki* 1, 48–9). It is thus unclear, on which day the dispute occurred.

30 Hidetada confirmed the *gongen* title on 1616/5/26 (*Jishō nikki* 1, 51).

31 *Honkō kokushi nikki*, 212.

32 Hanging scroll, seventeenth century, colors on silk, 57 x 48 cm; Sakai City Museum.

33 Yoshida Kanetomo famously classified all teachings of Shinto according to their indebtedness to Buddhism. Among these, Kanetomo's own teaching, which he regarded as "the One-and-Only Shinto (*yuiitsu shintō* 唯一神道) as it exists since the beginning of our country," excels as the only pure native tradition (*Yuiitsu shintō myōbō yōshū*, 55–7; Grapard 1992, 137–9). In spite of this anti-Buddhist rhetoric, Yoshida theory and practice was actually heavily influenced by Esoteric Buddhism. This point was criticized by nativist (Kokugaku 国学) scholars in the later Tokugawa period. See, e.g., Chapter 14 in this volume on Hirata Atsutane's 平田篤胤 critique of Yoshida Shinto.

34 See Sonehara 2008.

35 On the relationship between personal *ganmon* and professional *hyōhyaku* in Buddhist ritualism, see, e.g., Watanabe 1995. On the problems of eulogies as historiographical sources, see, e.g., Sone 2009.

36 For details regarding the following examples, see Sonehara 2005. To my knowledge, there exists also one extant eulogy of Tokugawa Hidetada dated 1628, in the possession of the Rinnōji 輪王寺 in Nikkō. It praises Ieyasu both for his military achievements and for his Buddhist erudition and is thus similar to the eulogy of Iemitsu.

37 *Tōshōgū*, 41.

38 Source: *Nikkō-san goshinji ki* 日光山御神事記 (1636).

39 Regarding the *gū* title, its significance and the circumstances of its bestowal have caused heated debates among scholars. See, e.g., Nomura 2015, 132–47.

40 Nomura Gen argues that the marriages between the Tokugawa and Tenno houses "yielded something like objectivity" in the unification of imperial ancestors (Amaterasu, Hachiman) and shogunal ancestors (Tōshō Gongen) (Nomura 2006, 37–8).

41 Since Ietsugu was an infant ruler who died at the age of six, the eulogy was probably drafted by Arai Hakuseki 新井白石 (1657–1725) or another advisor.

42 This theory has been advanced by scholars such as Kitajima Masamoto (1974), Yamasawa Manabu (2012), and Yoshida Atsuhiko (2015).

43 The Tokugawa traced their ancestry back to the Minamoto, who were themselves descendants of Seiwa Tennō 清和天皇 (850–81, *r.* 858–76). On the imaginary family relations of the Tokugawa and the imperial house, see Okano 2018, appendix 2.

44 Letter from Leonard Camps, *opperhoofd* in Hirado 1621–23 (Rekishigaku Kenkyūkai 2013, 128).

45 As a starting point, I would like to mention the apocryphal *Taisei kyō* 大成経 (or *Sendai kuji hongi taisei kyō* 先代旧事本紀大成経), a mythological text attributed to Shōtoku Taishi 聖徳太子, which enjoyed great popularity in the Edo period. This text was probably drafted by several authors who held Tenkai in high esteem and referred to the origin legends of the Tōshōgū contained in *Tōshōsha engi* 東照社縁起. See also Sonehara 2018c, Chap. 6.

Chapter 3

1. On the re-establishment of temples and shrines in Ōmura, see Kudamatsu 2008.
2. Nosco 1994, 573.
3. Tronu 2019.
4. On the prohibition decree of 1614, see also Chapter 1, note 8.
5. *Relación del Reino de Nippon*, 240–2.
6. *Relación del Reino de Nippon*, 240–2. For a more detailed description of the Christian reaction to the 1614 expulsion edict, see Tronu 2012.
7. *Relación del Reino de Nippon*, 250v–2r.
8. Ruiz de Medina 1999, 187.
9. The daimyo of the surrounding domains brought men to Nagasaki as guards. In particular, the daimyo of Kokura 小倉藩 conscripted 500 musketeers (Kataoka 1970, 56).
10. *Relación del Reino de Nippon*, 252r.
11. This brotherhood consisted of local influential citizens, including the four ward heads who administrated the city. See Kataoka 1998 for Misericordia in Nagasaki, and Costa 2007 for Misericordia in all of Japan.
12. Schütte 1968, 746.
13. Álvarez Taladriz 1966a; 1966b.
14. European residents such as Ávila Girón were also forced to sign a declaration in front of the magistrate, but they kept hiding European missionaries. See Lejarza and Schilling 1933, 491.
15. Letter dated March 20, 1620 from the Jesuit Provincial Matheus de Couros, Collection Japonica Sinica 35, ff. 137–8, Archivum Romanum Societatis Iesu, Rome, cited in Pacheco 1977, 69.
16. Pacheco 1977, 69. This might be explained by urban planning and reasons of hygiene, but the timing suggests that it was also intended to eradicate Christianity (Ōhashi 2009, 147–8).
17. Pacheco 1977, 69–70.
18. Pacheco 1977, 69–70.
19. Ramos 2019, 183–4.
20. *Nagasaki-shi shi: chishihen butsuji bu* 1, 83.
21. A Jesuit copy and translation of the document of the donation of the Daidōji 大道寺 was sent to Europe. It has been published in *Documentos del Japón* I.
22. *Cartas* f. 312v.
23. *Documentos del Japón* I, 412.
24. *Nagasaki bugyōjo (Tateyama yakusho) ato* 1998, 9.
25. *Nagasaki-shi shi: chishihen butsuji bu* 1, 352–3.
26. Letter from Mattheus de Couros to Luis Pinheiro, dated February 23, 1619 in Nagasaki, Ms. Legajo 996, Jesuit Archive of the Province of Toledo, Alcala, cited in Álvarez Taladriz 1966a, 257 (98).
27. Letter from Mattheus de Couros in Álvarez Taladriz 1966a, 257 (98).
28. Ōhashi 2001, 100–31.
29. *Shin Nagasaki-shi shi* 2, 41.
30. *Hirado-machi Yokoseura-machi ninzū aratame no chō* 平戸町横瀬浦町人数改之帳 in *Nagasaki Hirado-chō nenbutsuchō*, 1–30.
31. Nakamura 1988, 200.
32. Ōhashi 2009, 137; see Chapter 1 in this volume, p. 25.
33. Most data on temples have been taken from *Nagasaki-shi shi: chishihen butsuji bu*, 2 vols., and *Shin Nagasakishi-shi*.

34 Letter from Mattheus de Couros in Álvarez Taladriz 1966a, 252 (104).
35 Hur 2007, 3–5.
36 *Nagasaki-shi shi: chishihen butsuji bu* 1, 615.
37 *Maruyama Yoriai-machi yuishosho* 丸山寄合町由緒書 cited in *Nagasaki-shi shi: chishihen butsuji bu* 1, 79.
38 *Daionji kiritsudome* 大音寺起立留 cited in *Nagasaki-shi shi: chishihen butsuji bu* 1, 83.
39 *Daionji kiritsudome* cited in *Nagasaki-shi shi: chishihen butsuji bu* 1, 83.
40 *Daionji kiritsudome* cited in *Nagasaki-shi shi: chishihen butsuji bu* 1, 83.
41 Pacheco 1977, 61.
42 *Nagasaki-shi shi: chishihen butsuji bu* 1, 87.
43 *Nagasaki-shi shi: chishihen butsuji bu* 1, 86–7.
44 According to Shimizu Hirokazu, in 1633 100 silver pieces (*gin hyaku mai* 銀百枚) could purchase 141.8 *koku* (21,270 kg) of rice (Shimizu 1981, 180).
45 *Nagasaki-shi shi: chishihen butsuji bu* 1, 88.
46 Most data on shrines have been taken from *Nagasaki-shi shi: chishihen jinja kyōkai bu*, 2 vols., and *Shin Nagasaki-shi shi* 2.
47 Younger brother of Nagasaki Sumikage 長崎純景 (1548?–1622), 14th lord of Nagasaki village, son-in-law of Ōmura Sumitada 大村純忠 (1533–87).
48 *Shin Nagasaki-shi shi* 2, 78.
49 *Cartas*, f. 313r. According to Frois' *Historia*, Vilela had previously led the destruction of shrines and temples in other areas of Kyushu, such as in Hakata (Frois 1976, 1:115). In Ikitsuki 生月, he transformed three temples into churches (*Documentos del Japón* 2, 146–47).
50 *Shin Nagasaki-shi shi* 2, 78.
51 *Nagasaki-shi shi: chishihen jinja kyōkai bu* 1, 25; *Shin Nagasakishi-shi* 2, 78. For more on Aoki, see Nelson 1996, 17–18.
52 *Shin Nagasaki-shi shi* 2, 78.
53 *Shin Nagasaki-shi shi* 2, 78; Nelson 1996, 18.
54 These privileges passed on to his descendants for generations, until the end of the Edo period *Shin Nagasaki-shi shi* 2, 79–80).
55 *Shin Nagasaki-shi shi* 2, 80.
56 In particular, "small dances" (*komai* 小舞, called *komei* in Nagasaki) offered to the *kami* before the procession. Initially these were performed by two reputed geisha of Maruyama-machi and Yoriai-machi, becoming one of the most anticipated parts of the Kunchi. These dances evolved into a full Noh performance by the mid-seventeenth century, and from 1672 a Noh play entitled *Suwa* was established as part of the Kunchi program of events (*Shin Nagasaki-shi shi* 2, 81).
57 Kudamatsu 2004, 107.
58 *Nagasaki-shi shi: chishihen jinja kyōkai bu* 1, 9.
59 *Shin Nagasaki-shi shi* 2, 92.
60 *Shin Nagasaki-shi shi* 2, 90.
61 Kudamatsu 2004, 101.
62 *Shin Nagasaki-shi shi* 2, 90.

Chapter 4

1 At the time, the Nichiren sect was known variously as the Lotus (Hokke 法華) sect or Nichiren-shū. For convenience, I use "Nichiren sect" throughout.

2. For an early example of this argument, see "Hōmon mōsarubekiyō no koto" 法門可被申様之事, *Shōwa teihon Nichiren shōnin ibun* 1:454–5.
3. For the background of *fujufuse* ideas in Nichiren's thought, see Miyazaki 1969, 13–84; Hunter 1989, 19–86.
4. Miyazaki 1969, 159–60; 177–80.
5. Risshō Daigaku Nichiren Kyōgaku Kenkyūjo 1984, 470–93; McMullin 1984, 204–09.
6. Miyazaki 1969, 223.
7. Sakamoto 1956, 57–9; Aiba 1976, 46–8.
8. On "admonishing the state," see Watanabe 1976, 135–40; Stone 1994, 237–40.
9. *Shūgi seihō ron* 宗義制法論 in *Kinsei bukkyō no shisō*, 309–10. *Lotus* references to not begrudging one's life appear at T no. 262, 9:16a15, 36a5, and 43b23.
10. Miyazaki 1969, 230–1; *Honnōji monjo* 本能寺文書, NSZ 20, 273–74.
11. For the petition, see Miyazaki 1969, 237; partially translated in Hunter 1989, 161–3.
12. *Keishi no shinto ni tamau sho* 都師の信徒に賜う書, FFS 1, 285; trans. Hunter 1989, 185–6. For Nichiō's full account of the debate, see FFS 1, 282–5; Hunter 1989, 178–87.
13. Miyazaki 1969, 277–98; Hunter 1989, 200–09.
14. *Shinchi tairon kiroku* 身池対論記録 1, BK 2, 62–4 (*yakubun*), 108–09 (*honbun*).
15. This last charge can be confirmed from Nichiju's personal correspondence (Takagi 1956, 238–9).
16. Hunter (1989) translates this exchange in its entirety.
17. *Ōsaka tairon ki* 大阪対論記, in Miyazaki 1969, 240; Hunter 1989, 175.
18. *Shūgi seihō ron*, in *Kinsei bukkyō no shisō*, 331–32; Hunter 1989, 578–80. Nichiren similarly had spoken of all worldly rulers as holding their lands in fief from Śākyamuni.
19. For Nichiju's response, see *Shinchi tairon kiroku* 2, BK 2, 64–7 (*yakubun*); 109–10 (*honbun*).
20. Allusion to Ieyasu's posthumous title Tōshō Daigongen 東照大権現.
21. For accounts of the debate, see Miyazaki 1969, 384–422; 1959, 159–211.
22. Aiba 1976, 78.
23. *Shinchi tairon kiroku* 10, BK 2, 99–100 (*yakubun*); 129–30 (*honbun*). See also Miyazaki 1959, 3–4.
24. Technically speaking, Fujufuse-ha (Fujufuse faction) seems to be used only after the group was banned and driven underground.
25. For the two factions' relative strength at the time of the debate, see Miyazaki 1959, 27–32.
26. Miyazaki 1959, 6–9, 27–8.
27. See Miyazaki 1959, 81–2, 88–90.
28. Takagi 1956, 246.
29. Tamamuro 1974, 182–3.
30. Takagi 1956, 247.
31. *Honge betsuzu* 19, 413.
32. On Jufuse petitioning, see Takagi 1956, 241–3, 247.
33. Miyazaki 1959, 107–12.
34. "Kanbun no sōmetsu," *s.v.*, NJ, 474b.
35. Miyazaki 1959, 125–9.
36. *Shushō gokoku shō* 守正護国章, BK 2, 222.
37. Hur 2007, 15–16, 95–100. See also Chapter 1 in this volume.
38. Miyazaki 1959, 119–23; Aiba 1976, 85–7, 115; "Hiden kuyō," *s.v.*, NJ, pp. 689c–90a.
39. On the judicial aspects of religious persecution, see Chapter 5 in this volume.

40. *Min'yu mōha ki* 愍諭盲跛記, BK 2, Appendix, 256.
41. Mizuno 1975, 257; see also Chapter 11 in this volume.
42. For these and other examples (including later ones), see *Fujufuse-ha hōnan shiryōshū*, 193-222; Kageyama 1956; Miyazaki 1959, 145; Aiba 1976, 89-137; and Nosco 2018, 69-79.
43. See Miyazaki 1959, 143-56; Aiba 1976, 138-58.
44. See Stone 1994.
45. *Keishi no shinto ni tamau* sho, FFS 1, 282.
46. These factors operated in the 1608-09 "Keichō-era Persecution," the arrest and brutal punishment of Jōrakuin Nichikyō 常楽院日経 (1560-1620) and five of his disciples for aggressively preaching against the Pure Land sect (Aiba 1976, 25-39).
47. Ooms 1985.
48. Ooms 1985, 199.
49. Fabian Fuçan (Fukansai 不干斎, *c*. 1565-1621) writes: "This first commandment, to disobey the command of one's ruler or parents if it goes against the will of Deus, even discarding one's life, conceals an intent [...] to topple and destroy the state" (*Ha Daiusu* 破提宇子 in *Kirishitan sho*, 441).

Chapter 5

1. For a fuller discussion of the judicial procedures summarized here, see Miyazaki, Nakai, and Teeuwen 2020 and the works it cites.
2. The four compilations, known originally by different individual names, were published between 1971 and 1973 in sixteen volumes under the overall title *Oshioki reiruishū*. A fifth collection, that covered up to 1852, was lost in the 1923 Kantō earthquake and is no longer extant.
3. Sanchō-ha, a separate movement that emerged in the 1680s, was the target of concerted repression in the early 1700s. See *Nichirenshū jiten*, 508; *Oshioki reiruishū* 12, 183-91. Thereafter it seems largely to have disappeared, but because it was conjoined with the more persistent Fujufuse in article 52 of the *Rules*, its name was perpetuated as exemplifying banned religious practices.
4. *Tokugawa kinreikō, bekkan* 別巻, 93-4.
5. *Ofuregaki Kanpō shūsei* (1976), 608-10.
6. *Tokugawa kinreikō, bekkan*, 94.
7. Ōhashi Yukihiro has composed a useful chart listing the cases in chronological order and providing brief information about their nature, the precedents cited, and where they may be found in *Precedents* (Ōhashi 2017, 64-9). See also Ōhashi 2014, 60-7.
8. Kataoka, Tamamuro, and Oguri 1974, 264-5, 281.
9. See Kataoka, Tamamuro, and Oguri 1974, 239-80. See also Chilson 2014, 37-45.
10. *Oshioki reiruishū* 1, 471-5.
11. *Oshioki reiruishū* 1, 472-5.
12. *Oshioki reiruishū* 3, 420-1. The Jiun associated with Raigōji should not be confused with the famous Shingon priest of the same name.
13. *Oshioki reiruishū* 3, 421.
14. *Oshioki reiruishū* 3, 424-5.
15. *Oshioki reiruishū* 15, 117-18. The case cited, dating from 1833, is simply mentioned briefly in the context of deliberations over another case; it is thus difficult to reconstruct its specific features.

16 *Oshioki reiruishū* 1, 477–9. For the 1797 case, which followed the precedent of the Raigōji decision, see *Oshioki reiruishū* 1, 483–4.
17 *Oshioki reiruishū* 12, 115–16. The women who cooperated with the schemes by acting as mediums were in both cases sentenced to the lesser punishment of banishment from Edo. *Oshioki reiruishū* 16, 139–40.
18 *Tokugawa kinreikō, bekkan*, 103.
19 *Oshioki reiruishū* 12, 128–9.
20 *Oshioki reiruishū* 12, 121–7; *Tokugawa kinreikō, bekkan*, 111.
21 Kyūi called it the Nehan 涅槃 sect and allowed its priests to marry. The case is included in the section in *Precedents* on warriors and clergy, and the names of the male members of the family mentioned in passing suggest that they may have had some sort of Shinto affiliation or shrine function.
22 *Oshioki reiruishū* 15, 116–18.
23 The official cannot be identified.
24 *Oshioki reiruishū* 6, 267–9. The view today is that the Hida shrine priests did not specifically target the intendant in the rituals they performed. The shrine served as a gathering place for the protestors, and the priests conducted prayers at their request for the protest's success. However, it is now believed that the prayers did not include a curse against the intendant. See *Gifu-ken shi: Tsūshi-hen, kinsei, jō*, 1167–8.
25 *Oshioki reiruishū* 15, 118–19.
26 In the Urakami case, the authorities ultimately accepted the villagers' denial of following a "deviant creed." The Amakusa case was resolved by the villagers admitting they had previously engaged in such practices and promising they would no longer do so (Ōhashi 2001, 147–75, 206–39). See also Nosco 1993, 21–4. *Precedents* contains no reference to either case.
27 The following account draws from Miyazaki, Nakai, and Teeuwen 2020, a complete translation of the largely unpublished records concerning this case. In-text citations below are to this translation. Ōshio Heihachirō is otherwise known for the abortive rebellion he led in 1837, in the aftermath of the Tenpō famine (1833–7).
28 See *Oshioki reiruishū* 11, 492–4; 12, 161–72.
29 For these regulations, see *Ofuregaki Kanpō shūsei* (1976), 634–6; *Kirishitan kankei hōsei shiryō*, 255–7; Hur 2007, 100–02.
30 *Tokugawa kinreikō, bekkan*, 66.
31 *Oshioki reiruishū* 15, 117.

Chapter 6

1 Editors' note: In the Confucian *Book of Rites*, *inshi* (Ch. *yinsi*) is defined as a ceremony performed at an inappropriate place that is inauspicious. In early modern Japan, the term was used for shrines of uncertain pedigree, usually rooted in popular or folk beliefs.
2 A *shikinaisha* is one of the 3,132 shrines listed in the *Engishiki* 延喜式, a legal document on stately rituals compiled by the court in the tenth century.
3 For further details on these reforms, see Chapters 11 and 12 in this volume, as well as the Introduction.
4 Tamamuro 1971, 91–3. Taniguchi even considers the Kanbun policies of Okayama as "unparalleled within the whole of Japan" and as "unique measures" (Taniguchi 1963, 159).

5   Matsudaira Kōekikai 1964, 180–4, 296–303.
6   Inoue 2007b, 4–7.
7   *Kii zoku fudoki furoku*, 351–2.
8   *Matsuyama-shi shi*, 62–5.
9   Cf. Inoue 2009, 162–3.
10 The cases of Ise and Izumo are also discussed by Mark Teeuwen in this volume (Chapter 10).
11 Editors' note: The term *ryōbu* (lit. "both parts") derived from the dual realms of Shingon Buddhism, *vajradhātu* and *garbhakoṣadhātu* (Jp. *kongōkai* 金剛界 and *taizōkai* 胎蔵界), implying the universe of (Esoteric) Buddhism. On the special interpretation of *ryōbu* as Shinto-Buddhist syncretism in contrast to *yuiitsu* as "Shinto only," see Scheid 2003.
12 *Chitose no matsu*, 55–6.
13 *Chitose no matsu*, 55–6.
14 *Buke genseiroku* (revised edition, 1959), 53.
15 Editors' note: *sōgen* or *yuiitsu sōgen* (as below) are common epithets of Yoshida Shinto.
16 *Yuiitsu shintō oyobi Shizu jinja shuinchi haibun ni tsuki jisha bugyō tasshi gaki*, 17.
17 *Shintō shūsei*. The compilation of the *Shintō shūsei* was started by Mitsukuni in 1667. After 1670, more and more was added and it was finally completed in 1730.
18 *Jō shintō shūsei sōkōso* 上神道集成草稿疏 (1670), in *Shintō shūsei*, 4–5.
19 The "heretic teachings" mentioned here clearly refer to Buddhism. This anti-Buddhist gist can be inferred from later passages about paragons of Buddhism such as Shōtoku Taishi 聖徳太子 and Kūkai 空海 (774–835), that contain comments like "they supplanted deities by buddhas" or "they mixed and mingled the purity of the Ancient Source by pouring on it the dirt of the dual parts."
20 *Aizu jinja-shi*, 100–01.
21 *Aizu jinja-shi*, 120.
22 *Aizu jinja-shi*, 120.
23 *Daigaku wakumon*, 435. In this case, as in Okayama, expunged *inshi* were merged into a single shrine.
24 *Jingi hōten*, 3–5.
25 *Jingi hōten*, 3–5.
26 See below, note 41.
27 *Jingi hōten*, 3–5.
28 One example is the criticism of the *honji suijaku* theory in 1662 by the *jisha bugyō* Inoue Masatoshi 井上正利 (1606–75), who contributed to the removal of Buddhist elements from the Ise Shrines and from Kizuki Taisha (Shimaneken Kodai Bunka Sentā 2013, 9–10).
29 *Aizu jinja-shi*, 104.
30 In fact, Hōkō mixes elements from the Five Relations of Confucianism (親, 義, 別, 序, 信) and the Five Constant Virtues (仁, 義, 礼, 智, 信).
31 *Razan Hayashi-sensei bunshū* 48, 114–16.
32 On Mitsumasa's Confucian stance, see also Chapter 8.
33 In his *Shintō taigi* 神道大義 (*Essentials of Shinto*), Banzan speaks about Shinto "virtues," which he sometimes calls "wisdom (智), humaneness (仁) and courage (勇)." Except for "courage," they are clearly derived from the virtues of Confucianism (see above, note 30). Banzan's view of *shinju itchi* is also evident in the following passages: "The Divine Way (*shintō*) of heaven and earth is the same in China and Japan. Those who maintain that the teachings of the Confucian way differ from the teachings of

Shinto do not know the Way" (*Shintō taigi*, 17); "The sages of China and the men of divine wisdom (*shinjin* 神人) of Japan share one virtue, their ways are not different" (*Daigaku wakumon*, 448–9).

34 *Yōfukuki*, 87; 90.
35 *Yōfukuki*, 105–06.
36 See Chapter 2.
37 *Yōfukuki*, 87–8; 100–01.
38 *Jingi hōten*, 3–5.
39 In *Shintō denju* 神道伝授 (*Transmissions of Shinto*, 1644), Razan states that "Shinto is the Way of the just ruler" (*shintō soku ōdō* 神道則王道) (*Shintō denju*, 19), whereas in the preface to *Jingi hōten*, "the Way of the Just Ruler" is equated to the "Confucian Way." In this sense, in Razan's view "Shinto" was Confucianism.
40 *Daigaku wakumon*, 448–9.
41 See, for instance, Teeuwen and Rambelli 2003. *Honji suijaku* is also explained in Chapter 2 of this volume.
42 *Daigaku wakumon*, 448.
43 *Daigaku wakumon*, 449.
44 *Yōfukuki*, 100
45 See also Chapter 7.
46 The legendary first dynasties of Chinese history, Xia, Yin and Zhou, spanning from the third to the first millennium BCE.
47 Editors' note: This seems to be a boastful allusion to the first diplomatic contacts of Tokugawa Japan with Korea in 1607, which in reality did not include formal tributary relations, and with the small kingdom of Ryūkyū (now Okinawa), which was turned into a vassal state by force in 1609.
48 *Razan Hayashi-sensei bunshū* 12, 130–1.
49 *Razan Hayashi-sensei bunshū* 12, 131.
50 *Razan Hayashi-sensei bunshū* 12, 136.
51 We might also mention the kingdom of Ryūkyū. However, it was only after the eighteenth century that Ryūkyū took serious efforts to turn into a Confucian society (Tomiyama 2004, 84–6).
52 Editors' note: The *sekiten* ceremony (Ch. *shidian*) in honor of Confucius originated in ancient China, where it was celebrated twice a year, in spring and autumn. In Japan, it was performed during the Nara period but later almost vanished. The Hayashi family renewed the rite and began to celebrate the *sekiten* ceremony in 1633 with the significant support of Tokugawa Yoshinao. Various domain schools are known to have held these ceremonies as well. See also Chapter 8 in this volume.
53 As a result, however, Japanese society was permeated with Confucianism throughout the Tokugawa period.
54 Inoue 2017, 8–10. See also Kojima 2018.
55 Inoue 2017, 8–10.

Chapter 7

1 See Boot 2015.
2 For details, see Boot 1983.
3 The sources for this story are the preface of a poem Razan wrote at the death of his mother (see *Razan Hayashi-sensei shishū* 2, 23b–24a), his *Nenpu* 年譜 (ibid., *furoku*,

2a–3b), and his *Gyōjō* 行状 (ibid., *furoku*, 35b–36a). *Nenpu* and *Gyōjō* were compiled after his death by his sons.

4 Besides Razan, these include Hori Kyōan 堀杏庵 (1585–1642), Kan Tokuan 菅得庵 (1581–1628), Matsunaga Sekigo 松永尺五 (1592–1657), and others.

5 Only a few insisted on following *Zhu Xi's Family Rituals* (*Zhuzi jiali* 朱子家礼) or even more arcane Chinese rituals. For the egregious examples of Tokugawa Mitsukuni or Ikeda Mitsumasa, see Chapters 8, 9, and 12 in this volume.

6 Paper scroll, 104 x 37 cm, later Edo period. Photo reproduced courtesy of the Kyoto University Museum.

7 A *gongen* is a temporary manifestation of a buddha or bodhisattva. Ieyasu, as Tōshō [Dai]gongen, was regarded as a manifestation of Yakushi Nyorai 薬師如来, the Medicine Buddha. As explained in more detail by Sonehara Satoshi in Chapter 2 of this volume, he was worshipped through a syncretic Buddhist-Shinto ritual called *Sannō ichijitsu shintō* 山王一実神道.

8 Earlier in the same biography, a reference is made to a body of texts called *Honpō shinsho* 本邦神書, which is sufficiently close to Razan's *Honchō jinja kō* to assume that this was the kind of text that Ninchō had in mind.

9 See *Shishigatani Byakurensha Ninchō-oshō gyōgō ki*, 9b. The passage is also quoted in Mitamura 1941, 29.

10 The title clearly refers to the three teachings. The book in four fascicles was prefaced in 1751 and printed 1821 (modern edition NSTS 5).

11 The first part of the text (5 fasc.) was finished in 1707, and the second part (5 fasc.) between 1707 and the author's death in 1721. The book was printed in 1766 (first part) and 1774 (complete text) by Buddhist priests in Kyoto. There is a modern edition in NSTS 2. The author studied medicine and Confucianism in Osaka and Kyoto. In 1684 he entered into the service of Tokugawa Mitsukuni and worked on the compilation of his *History of Great Japan* (*Dai-Nihon shi* 大日本史).

12 NSTS 2, 3.

13 See Ōkuwa and Maeda 2006. The older wood-block copies have no colophons, but the final two lines of the book identify the inquiring Confucian as Razan (or Dōshun 林道春) and the responding Buddhist as Teitoku. Since Razan took the name Dōshun only in 1630, we may assume that the text was put together between this date and 1653, when Teitoku died.

14 *Honchō jinja kō* was first printed between 1645 and 1650 (?). The *Bunshū* and *Shishū* were published in 1662.

15 Translations and transliterations of these texts by M.M.E. Buijnsters (Leiden University) and myself are published on the homepage of the Netherlands Association for Japanese Studies (Boot and Buijnsters 2016; 2019). A late-eighteenth-century text, the anonymous *Discussion in the Hall* (*Denchū mondō* 殿中問答), also belongs to this same strand of adversarial polemics. See Boot 1993; 2011.

16 For more details about the text and its author, see Sonehara 2013.

17 We used the manuscript (3 fasc., 3 vols.) in the possession of Kyoto University.

18 *Bengi* 1:1a–b.

19 *Gobusshin-ron* 0:1a–b.

20 *Taisei kyō* counts 72 fascicles in all. Fascicles 1–38 were printed between 1675 and 1679, but the Ise Shrine protested, and within two years it was banned by the *bakufu*. Blocks and extant copies were ordered to be burned. Of course, they were not; the text remained known and was read and studied during the remainder of the Edo period.

Some fascicles were even re-printed. After the Meiji Restoration, there was less interest. See, however, Kōno 1952, and the modern edition made by Ogasawara Haruo.

21 See *Gobusshin-ron* 1:24b–5a. The story maintains that the *Taisei kyō* was presented to Iemitsu by one Inbe no Tansai 忌部坦斎 (aka. Hirota Tansai 廣田坦斎, active around 1644 to 1648).
22 Jakuhon does not refer to *Taisei kyō* by name, but in *Bengi* 1:7a–b and 2:18b we find references to, respectively, *Taisei kyō* fasc. 1 and 31. In the second book of *Bengi*, nine sections are devoted to Shōtoku.
23 *Bengi* 2:7b–8a.
24 The reference is to *Taisei kyō* 38; this fascicle is part of *Seikō hongi* 聖皇本紀 ("The annals of the holy emperors"), the subtitle given in *Taisei kyō* to the fascicles containing Shōtoku's biography.
25 *Gobusshin-ron* 1:11b–13a.
26 See *Gobusshin-ron* 3:7a–b, 3:14b–15b. The two essays ("disquisitions") are entitled *So Bashi ga ben* 蘇馬子辯; see *Razan Hayashi-sensei bunshū* 1, 293–4.
27 Aka *Kujiki*, a myth-history in ten fascicles, traditionally ascribed to Soga no Umako and Shōtoku Taishi, but in fact a compilation of the early Heian period. It must not be confused with *Taisei kyō*. See Bentley 2006.
28 *Bengi* 2:16a–18a.
29 See *Mengzi* 1B.8.
30 *Gobusshin-ron* 1:13a. Needless to say, the quotation is not from Shōtoku as he is depicted in the old Japanese histories. The simile is found, however, in Yoshida Kanetomo's *Yuiitsu shintō myōbō yōshū*; cf. Scheid 2001, 243–52, and Grapard 1992, 153.
31 *Bengi* 2:18a; *Gobusshin-ron* 1:13b.
32 *Taisei kyō* 31 (*Seikō hongi*, Bidatsu 7/3/19), referenced in *Bengi* 2:18b; *Gobusshin-ron* 1:13b–1:14b.
33 *Bengi* 2:18b–19a.
34 *Gobusshin-ron* 1:14b.
35 Razan's *ritō shinchi shintō* identifies the gods with *li* 理 (Jp. *ri*, principle) and maintains that they are, therefore, all "present in the heart" (*tō shinchi* 当心地), just as is predicated of the *li* in Neo-Confucianism. These ideas found their clearest expression in Razan's *Transmission of Shinto* (*Shintō denju* 神道傳授), but in his own times, this was an obscure text. Razan also mentions his ideas in *Honchō jinja kō* 2 (see NSTS 1, 419) and in an entry in his *Zuihitsu* (*Razan Hayashi-sensei bunshū* 2, 419), where he presents it as a superior alternative to *honji suijaku shintō*, but also remarks that "for most people it is out of ken."
36 See NSTS 1, 365 and also 419.
37 *Bengi* 1:2b.
38 *Bengi* 1:4a–b.
39 *Gobusshin-ron*, 2:1a–10b.
40 *Yamato-hime no mikoto seiki* is one of the five fundamental books of Ise Shinto, *Shintō gobusho* 神道五部書, which probably date from the Kamakura period.
41 *Gobusshin-ron* 2:1b–3a.
42 See *On Emperor Jinmu* (*Jinmu-tennō ron* 神武天皇論) in *Razan Hayashi-sensei bunshū* 1, 280a–82b; Kumazawa Banzan, *Miwa monogatari*, 212–22.
43 *Bengi* 1:11a.
44 *Gobusshin-ron* 1:14b–16a; "disquisition" in *Razan Hayashi-sensei bunshū* 1, 296b–97a.

45 Reference to the emperors Ōjin and Ankan, who are worshipped respectively in Usa 宇佐 and in Yoshino 吉野. Kitano Tenjin 北野天神 in Kyoto is dedicated to the scholar-turned-deity Sugawara Michizane 菅原道真 (845–903).
46 *Gobusshin-ron* 1:16a.
47 *Gobusshin-ron* 1:16a–17a.
48 In the printed edition of *Taisei kyō* of 1679 (4.2a), the "three bodies" are glossed as (*kotowa*)*ri* (*no*) *mi*, *iki* (*no*) *mi*, and *tana* (*no*) *mi*; *tana* is most likely a pseudo-archaic variant of *tane* ("seed"). The terms *li* 理, *qi* 気, and *jing* 精 are three of the Five Pillars (Ch. *wuzhen* 五鎮, Jp. *gochin*), which is an important concept in *Taisei kyō*; it serves as the counterpart of the Confucian concept of Five Agents (Ch. *wuxing* 五行, Jp. *gogyō*).
49 *Gobusshin-ron* 1:17a.
50 For the standard Neo-Confucian interpretation, see Boot 2014.
51 *Bengi* 1:24a, quoting *Honchō jinja kō* 2 (NSTS 1, 419).
52 *Bengi* 2:6a; *Gobusshin-ron* 1:2a–3a. Both are quoting from *Honchō jinja kō* 5 (NSTS 1, 521).
53 *Gobusshin-ron* 1:2b–3a; *Bengi* 2:20b–22b. Razan discusses *tengu* in *Honchō jinja kō* 6 (NSTS 1, 188–91). *Taiheiki* 27 relates an anecdote about a meeting with *tengu*.
54 The figures are based on the number of copies listed in the NIJL catalogue (*Nihon Kotenseki Sōgō Mokuroku*).

Chapter 8

1 Azuma 2008, 79. Tokugawa Yoshinao 徳川義直 (1601–50) may be added to the list.
2 Azuma 2008, 79.
3 *Kaempfer's Japan*, quoted in Bodart-Bailey 2006, 63–4.
4 Hall 1966, 402–03.
5 IMKD 2, 1333; line 4 alludes to *Analects* xv.24 (ii); CC 1, 301; the penultimate line borrows from *Shijing*, Xiaoya 小雅, Xiaowan 小完; CC 4, 335.
6 Gilded bronze statue commissioned by Tsuda Nagatada 津田永忠 (1640–1707). Height 60cm. Shizutani Gakkō, Bizen city, "important cultural property" of Okayama prefecture since Feb. 2020. Image: Wikimedia Commons. Tsuda took care of the Shizutani school and the Ikeda tombs at Waidani (see Figure 8.2). The statue was cast by a Kyoto bronzesmith and placed in the shrine to Mitsumasa in the school's precinct in 1704.
7 Cf. the discussion in IMKD 2, 1175–94.
8 *Wang Yangming quanshu* 王陽明全書, quoted in Ebrey 1991, 178–9.
9 IMN, 143 (1651/1/20).
10 *Yūhiroku* 有斐録 (1749) quoted from Taniguchi 1964, 53; 1961, 87.
11 The Hanabatake community may have been modeled after the Jixia 稷下 gathering of scholar gentlemen (*gakushi* 学士) promoted by King Xuan of Qi 齊宣王 (r. 319-301 BCE). For references, see McMullen 1999, 99, note 100.
12 ZBZ 5, 21.
13 Azuma 2008, 85.
14 IMKD 2, 1458, "Nagatada jihitsu oboegaki" 津田自筆覚書, no. 10.
15 Okayama Kenshi Hensan Iinkai 1984, 735.
16 Ōsawa Sadao 大沢貞雄, *Keifu ryaku* 系譜略 quoted from *Hansui yoha* 泮水余波. In ZBZ 6, appendix (separate pagination), 151.
17 For these revolts and their ideological impact, see McMullen 1999, 117–19.

18 Okumura and Suzuki 1917, 85.
19 IMN, 252.
20 IMN, 246-8 (1654/8/11). Cf. also *The Great Learning*, in CC 1, 370.
21 IMN, 390 (1657/3/2).
22 ZBZ 1, 451-2. For the issues involved in assessment, see Brown 1988.
23 IMN, 252 (1654/8/19).
24 See Mitsumasa's memorandum in Taniguchi 1964, 58, dated by Taniguchi to 1652-55.
25 For a succinct summary of this process, see Taniguchi 1964, 115-24.
26 Tanaka 1979, 44.
27 For this useful term, see Shu 2009, 103, 134, 136.
28 For details of Mitsumasa's Confucian ancestor worship ceremonies, see Azuma 2008.
29 For the text of this announcement, see IMKD 1, 698.
30 IMKD 1, 708-49.
31 Confucian-style tombs of the Ikeda family, Waidani, Bizen city, Okayama prefecture. Image: Wikimedia Commons. The principal graves are those of Mitsumasa's father and grandfather, reinterred here in 1667. Mitsumasa himself, his wife Katsuhime 勝姫 (1618-78), and the eighth Ikeda daimyo of Okayama, Ikeda Yoshimasa 池田慶政 (1823-93), are also buried on this site.
32 Quoted in IMKD 1, 48-9.
33 IMKD 1, 49.
34 IMKD 2, 1144. For a detailed account of the quarrel, see McMullen 1999, 129-45.
35 Kasai 1970, 2:1166.
36 For Mitsumasa's possible awareness of the Mito developments, see IMN, 577 (1667/4/16); Taniguchi 1964, 580. For religious reforms in Mito domain, see Chapter 12 in this volume.
37 For further documentation, see McMullen 1999, 131-6.
38 For the shrines, *Goryōbun yoseyashiro ki* 御領分寄社記, quoted in Taniguchi 1964, 582-3; for Banzan's views, ZBZ 3, 257-8. Banzan's case for reform seems primarily ecological, the predation of forests required for constructing shrines.
39 Further research on Mitsumasa's Shinto beliefs is needed. For Banzan's views on the basic identity of Confucianism and Shinto, see ZBZ 3, 268-9. He interpreted the moral symbolism of the "hard" quality of the sword among the three Shinto regalia to signify that "it settles judgements effectively;" he asserted that "as commentary on the regalia nothing comes up to the *Doctrine of the Mean*" (ZBZ 3, 268; CC 1, 407). Thus, it is questionable whether Banzan's "Confucian Shinto" quite fits the paradigm of "martial Confucianism" described in Inoue Tomokatsu's chapter in this volume. Banzan in fact favored a degree of demilitarization of samurai culture (McMullen 1999, 232-6). He believed that an immediate revival of Shinto was not practicable. "Unless a wise ruler emerges into the world, the revival of Shinto must be difficult" (ZBZ 3, 269).
40 IMKD 1, 839; see also Takeuchi 2017, 127-67 (reverse pagination). This measure is consistent with Banzan's proposal that culturally qualified Kyoto courtiers be invited to disseminate court culture in the provinces (ZBZ 3, 277).
41 Memorandum of Tsuda Nagatada 1673/2 in Taniguchi 1964, 564.
42 Shibata and Hentona 1983, 11: 280-1; *Analects* I, 9; CC 1, 141.
43 Taniguchi 1961, 183.
44 For the text, see Mizuno 1982.
45 De Groot, *The Religious System of China* 3, 832, quoted in Ebrey 1991, xiii.
46 Ebrey 1991, xx.

47 The sense of *kamin* here seems to be the populace as moral and administrative subordinates, recipients of moral guidance from superiors.
48 Mizuno 1982, 289.
49 Text and commentary in Taniguchi 1964, 593–5.
50 Taniguchi 1964, 594.
51 This work has been attributed to Kumazawa Banzan, but dubiously so because he defended cremation under some circumstances and rejected universal post-mortem burial in Japan (ZBZ 2, 285–6; cf. also ZBZ 6, 21).
52 For documentation of this comparison, see McMullen 2020, appendix 7, subsection "Korea."
53 NKSS 2, 585.
54 Takeuchi 2017, 127; IMKD 1, 834–7; the school opened on 1669/12/28.
55 Taniguchi 1961, 159.
56 IMKD 1, 862.
57 Azuma 2008, 95. But the ceremony can only loosely be termed a veneration of Confucius (*sekisai*), since it did not conform with extant *sekisai* directives. It had more in common with Mitsumasa's *yomizome* of 1671/1/2 (see below).
58 IMKD 1, 858.
59 IMKD 1, 858. This school was praised by Banzan (ZBZ 2, 95).
60 For a more detailed account, see McMullen 2020, appendix 6.
61 IMKD 1, 864.
62 IMKD 1, 864. For this gloss on "children," see IMKD 1, 842.
63 Mitsumasa himself had hitherto been in the habit of a personal "first reading" from the Confucian canon at the new year; cf. IMKD 2, appendix 2, 65.
64 Taniguchi 1964, 581.
65 Taniguchi 1964, 581–2. In Taniguchi's opinion, Mitsumasa's policy was "not reckless suppression."
66 *Shusshi kō*, 3a–3b.
67 Taniguchi 1961, 183.
68 Taniguchi 1964, 579–80.
69 ZBZ 6, appendix, 137.
70 ZBZ 2, 156–7.
71 *Analects* I (xi); CC 1, 142.
72 Kaempfer, quoted in Bodart-Bailey 2006, 64.
73 IMKD 2, appendix 2, 126.
74 Hall 1966, 409.
75 IMKD 1, 842; *Biyō kokugaku kiroku*, annual entries for 1672/1/5 to 1679. I am grateful to Stefan Köck for procuring copies of this material.
76 Taniguchi 1964, 565.
77 NKSS 6, 108; IMKD 1, 859–60.
78 NKSS 6, 108.
79 IMKD 1, 865.
80 NKSS 6, 108.
81 Nakai 1980, 159, 199.
82 Watanabe 1997, 73; for Sakai Tadakatsu's attitude to Confucianism, see Taniguchi 1964, 53–7.
83 IMN, 141 (1651/1/16).
84 IMN, 571 (1667/1/29).

85 See e.g. IMKD 2, appendix 2, 61 (1659/1/2): he visits Rikōin 利光院, Taishūji 台崇寺 and Kokuseiji 国清寺.
86 IMN, 523 (1661/2/19). This utterance has canonical resonance. It seems to allude to "The great affairs of state are sacrifice and war" (*Zuo zhuan* 佐傳 Cheng Gong 成公 13 [577 BCE]) CC v, 379, 382), but at the same time reverses the priorities. See also *Sunzi* 孫子, "Warfare is the greatest affair of state" (Sawyer 1993, 63), or the *Analects*, "The things in reference to which the Master exercised the greatest caution were sacrifices (*zhai* 齋), war (*zhan* 戰), and sickness (*ji* 疾)" (*Analects* 7; 12, translation adapted from CC 1, 198).
87 IMN, 143 (1651/1/20).
88 For the history of veneration of Confucius at the Shizutani Sage's Hall, see Shiraki 1931.
89 Shiraki 1931, 18–19. For a striking image of the two juxtaposed shrines, respectively to Confucius himself and to Mitsumasa, see Shizutani Gakkō Shi Hensan Iinkai 1971, 330.

Chapter 9

1 For example, to commemorate Harumi's third centenary, the journal *Kagakushi kenkyū* 276 (2016/1) published a special issue that included articles by six specialists on the history of science, most dealing with Harumi's astronomical methods and his successors (Nakamura and Yoshida 2016, 341–85).
2 Hayashi 2018.
3 See also Bernhard Scheid's Introduction to this volume.
4 Aizu Wakamatsu-shi 2001, 13–23.
5 Koike 2017, 203–37.
6 Aizu Wakamatsu-shi Shuppan Iinkai 1965, 392–413.
7 Aizu Wakamatsu-shi Shuppan Iinkai 1965, 347–62.
8 The original refers to him as Shigemoto 重元. However, this must be a mistake.
9 *Nihon shoki* 1, 76. Aston translates: "spontaneously developed by the operation of the principle of Heaven" (Aston 1972, part I, 4). According to modern interpretations, the sentence explains that the first primordial deities derived from Yang (here *ken* 乾), i.e. Heaven, and were therefore all male (in contrast to Yin /Earth /female). See *Nihon shoki* 1, 547, fn. 12.
10 *Jinzanshū*, fasc. 21, 13.
11 The epithet *meikun* arose in the latter half of the seventeenth century as a designation of daimyo who concerned themselves with Confucian learning and exercised benevolent rule. Representative individuals included daimyo like Tokugawa Yorinobu 徳川頼宣 (1602–71) of Kii 紀伊藩, Ikeda Mitsumasa (1609–82) of Okayama, and Tokugawa Mitsukuni (1628–71) of Mito.
12 *Jinzanshū*, fasc. 21, 13.
13 Hayashi 2018, 41–52.
14 Suinin was a legendary emperor who reigned, according to traditional chronology, from 29 BCE to 70 CE.
15 Hayashi 2018, 37–40.
16 *Shunkai sensei jikki*, sheet 10.
17 The following account is based on *Aizu-han kasei jikki* 2, 648.

18 *Aizu-han kasei jikki* 2, 649–51. See also Scheid's introduction for other quotes from this speech.
19 The following account is based on *Aizu-han kasei jikki* 3, 9–18.
20 The following account is based on Aizu Wakamatsu-shi Shuppan Iinkai 1965, 383–6.
21 Also known as *yorishiro* 依代, the term *katashiro* refers to a ritual object into which a spirit was invited to reside. *Katashiro* were made of materials like paper or wood and often roughly resembled a human shape.
22 Ch. *yu* 虞; for details see Ebrey 1991, 68, 219.
23 According to *Zhu Xi's Family Rituals*, the "first laying out" (Ch. *xiao lian*) is a ceremonial wrapping of the body performed on the first day after someone has died. The corresponding "final laying out" (Ch. *dalian*) occurs one day later (Ebrey 1991, 216–18). In Masayuki's case, these rites were performed on 1672/12/19–20.
24 Ch. *zu ku*; the name of a sacrifice ceremony that marks the end of wailing (Ebrey 1991, 68, 218).
25 Inawashirochō Hensan Iinkai 1982, 318–24.
26 Hanitsu Jinja, Inawashiro, Fukushima-ken.
27 Image: Kokugakuin Daigaku Nihon Bunka Kenkyūjo 1995, 198.
28 Hanitsu Jinja, Inawashiro, Fukushima-ken.
29 Fujii 1991, 29–64.
30 Shimo Goryō Shrine, Kyoto.
31 Katō 1931, 52–4.
32 Tani 2001, 195–9.
33 Two days earlier (1683/9/13), Anzai had entrusted his work *Nakatomi no harae fūsuisō* 中臣祓風水草 in a written note to Ōgimachi Kinmichi 正親町公通 (1653–1733). Kinmichi thus became the successor of Anzai's Suika Shinto.
34 *Ansai sensei ekisaku fujō*, 22–3.
35 *Jinzanshū*, fasc. 15, 6.
36 *Jinzanshū*, fasc. 15, 4.
37 *Jinzanshū*, fasc. 15, 7.
38 *Shinro menmei*, 48–9.
39 *Nebokoro shūi*, 324.
40 Tōkaiji Ōyama Cemetery, Shinagawa-ku, Tokyo.
41 Tani 2001, 77–83.

Chapter 10

1 Hashimoto 2008, 308–09; Hatakama 2008, 332.
2 Hashimoto 2008; Inoue 2005; Takano 2003; Hardacre 2017, 239–43.
3 Inoue 2005, 46.
4 Hashimoto 1997; Scheid 2002, 313–14.
5 For more on policies in Okayama and Mito, see Chapters 11 and 12 in this volume.
6 Inoue 2005, 51.
7 The temple law issued to the Tendai headquarters of Mt. Hiei in 1608 reads: "Mountain monks who fail to exert themselves in the way of learning (*gakudō*) may not reside in the temple quarters."
8 Sueki 2010, 103.
9 On the efforts of Shinto priests to escape from Buddhist affiliation and burial, see Kenney 2000.

10   Nishioka 2002; Inoue 2003; Zhong 2016; the case is also mentioned in Chapter 6 in this volume.
11   Inoue Hiroshi points out that Izumo's concept of *yuiitsu shintō* arose in the context of decades of local competition with the Yoshida, and argues that it was directly inspired by and modeled upon Yoshida Shinto (Inoue 2003). It would appear, however, that the term *yuiitsu* as it was used by the Izumo priesthood was directed primarily against their Buddhist rivals, in spite of possible associations of the term with Yoshida Shinto.
12   Sekisai published an account of his travels in Izumo that includes criticism of the "syncretism" at Izumo Shrine in 1661. Nishioka 2002, 20.
13   The last *seiden* had been built more than four centuries earlier, in 1248. *Honden* was the term for a "temporary" hall of about half the "correct" (*sei*) size. Naomasa gained permission to start preparations for a new *seiden* in 1648, but the project was delayed by the Edo fire of 1657 (Oka 2013, 111).
14   Nishioka 2002, 81–6.
15   On this salon, see Chapter 9 in this volume.
16   Nishioka 2002, 86.
17   Nishioka 2002, 25–9.
18   On these shrines, see Breen and Teeuwen 2010, Chap. 3.
19   Satō 1992, 125.
20   *Sannō ichijitsu shintō* 山王一実神道 was an early modern version of the medieval transmissions of *Sannō shintō*, allegedly based on revelations of Sannō 山王, the "Mountain King" of Mt. Hiei, to Saichō 最澄 (767–822), the patriarch of the Tendai school in Japan. See also Chapter 2 in this volume.
21   Satō 1992, 135.
22   Satō 1992, 108.
23   Satō 1992, 133.
24   Satō 1992, 137.
25   I have earlier made this argument in Teeuwen and Breen 2017, Chap. 6. In the present volume, Inoue Tomokatsu arrives at a similar conclusion (Chapter 6).
26   Ōnishi 1960, 452–3.
27   *Daijingū shintō wakumon jō*, 68.
28   *Daijingū shintō wakumon jō*, 66.
29   For a detailed account of this legal case, see Teeuwen 1996, 264–72.
30   *Tokugawa jikki* 2, ZKT 10, 379; *Tokugawa kinreikō, zenshū* 前集 I.5, 2–3.
31   Teeuwen 1996, 273–89. It was in connection with this conflict that the *oshi* of Yamada and Uji were summoned by the magistrate of temples and shrines Inoue Masatoshi to learn of Izumo's *yuiitsu* restoration (in 1667).
32   Tanido 2011.
33   Ōnishi 1960, 460–1.
34   The incidents mentioned below are described in Tsukamoto 2010. Tsukamoto traces a gradual trend towards more strictness and less flexibility from the mid-eighteenth century onward.
35   Teeuwen 1996, 268.

Chapter 11

1   Inoue 2008b, 276b.
2   Inoue 2008b, 277a.

3   See Chapter 10 in this volume.
4   On Mito and Aizu, see Chapters 9 and 12 in this volume.
5   Kurachi 2012, 129.
6   On Mitsumasa's Confucian mindset and ideas, see also Chapter 8 in this volume.
7   See Chapter 1 in this volume.
8   IMN, 565a.
9   Variant reading: *Gokōkan zakki*. This manuscript is preserved in the Yoshida Family Archive of Tenri University. I have been unable to view the manuscript itself, but the entries I quote have been recently cited independently by two authors: Hatakama 2008, 349–50; Beppu 2013, 142–3.
10 *Ohiroma zakki*, 1667/2/19. Quoted in Hatakama 2008, 349b.
11 *Taisha* as a category of shrines reaches back to the *Engishiki* 延喜式, completed in 927, which categorized shrines as grand shrines and small shrines (*shōsha* 小社) (Toki 1987, 785–9).
12 In the narrow sense, *Yoshida dono* refers to Yoshida Kaneyuki 吉田兼敬 (1653–1717), in 1666 the nominal head of the Yoshida family, whose father Kaneoki 兼起 had died prematurely in 1657. In a broader sense, the Yoshida family as such is being addressed.
13 Compiled by Saitō Kazuoki (斎藤一興; aka Kyūen 九畹) (1758–1823), *bushi* and Confucian scholar of Okayama-han. The work was completed in Kansei 11 (1799) based on documents from the archives of the Ikeda family.
14 IRR 1, 319a.
15 IRR 1, 319a.
16 Tamamuro 1996, 367, 382a. NB: In the English abstract preceding this article, Tamamuro mentions slightly different figures for reasons unknown.
17 Tamamuro 1996, 367a.
18 Hur 2007, 96–9. An outline is also found in Chapter 1 in this volume.
19 Kurachi 1983, 305–07.
20 Kurachi 1983, 309.
21 Hur 2007, 112.
22 IMN, 568b–9a.
23 The decision to allow alternative certification must have been already made on the fourth day of the eighth month. On the fifth day, Mitsumasa sent a letter to the *bakufu* informing its officials about the steps that were planned to be taken in Okayama; cf. IMN, 569a.
24 See also Chapter 8 in this volume. According to McMullen (1999, 133), about two thirds of the *koori bugyō* had been members of a group educated by Banzan in the 1650s.
25 IMKD 1, 560. The volume contains several documents related to the visit of the *junkenshi*, among them the full report of the inspectors regarding their observations in Okayama domain.
26 Fujii has argued that Confucian political ideas were without doubt present among scholars and the ruling class in early modern Japan. The general population, however, would at best have known elements such as social hierarchy, filial piety or loyalty that were derived from Confucianism as a kind of common ethic (Fujii 1975, 136–7).
27 IMN, 569a,b. Also: *Bizen kokushi nichiroku*, TAA-003-572–573.
28 IMN, 569b. Also: *Bizen kokushi nichiroku*, TAA-003-573.
29 See the discussion of this in Chapter 6 of this volume.
30 Cf. also McMullen 1999, 135, fn. 93, where a similar distinction between Confucianism and Shinto is made in a quote from a letter of Mitsumasa of 1667.

31 Okayama Kenshi Hensan Iinkai 1984, 706.
32 IRR 1, 323b.
33 IRR 1, 324a. Also: *Yūhiroku*, 377a.
34 Kurachi 2012, 129–30.
35 According to *Otome-chō: Kanbun 7/1–7/6/10*, TAA-011-505 and IRR 1, 325a. NB: For 1666, the two sources give different figures regarding the total number of monks. The *Otome-chō* has 1,957 whereas IRR offers 1,557 monks. All other figures are identical. Obviously, a scribe or even the compiler of the IRR, Saitō Kazuoki himself, made a mistake when copying their source—probably the very *Otome-chō* of Kanbun 7. This mistake, however, has consequences for scholarly research, because the IRR was published as facsimile in two volumes and is widely available in libraries, unlike the *Otome-chō*, which can only be accessed via microfilm. When taking the mistaken number of 1,557 monks from the IRR as basis one will calculate that only 45.6 percent of the monks remained in Okayama after the purge of 1666/67 instead of 56.7 percent based on the correct numbers, which amounts to a difference of 11 percent. Considering that the number of monks dropped by 43.3 percent, the correct figures are impressive themselves and illustrate the utter consequence by which Mitsumasa's measures were executed.
36 Kurachi 2012, 142. On the general situation of shrine personnel, see also Chapter 13 in this volume.
37 *Satsuyōroku kan* 29, TAE-005-278.
38 Kurachi 2012, 142–3.
39 Kurachi 1983, 209.
40 Kurachi 2012, 142, tbl. 9.
41 *Ōmori Chikugo jōkyō*, TPA-031-353-354.
42 Hatakama 2008, 349b.
43 *Ohiroma zakki*, 1667/2/19. Quoted in Hatakama 2008, 349b.
44 Tamamuro 1991, 127.
45 In 1713, all of the *yosemiya* were merged into one, the Ōdara Yosemiya 大多羅寄宮 in the village of Ōdara 大多羅村 (Chūriki and Kahara 1980, 331–2). Regarding the number of *yosemiya*, cf. Beppu 2013, 142–5.
46 *Ontome-chō hyōjōsho* 1, 100a.
47 The reading *Otome-chō* is given according to the entries in the CiNii catalog. *Ontome-chō* appears to be a variant reading only used for the title of the edited version of the *Ontome-chō hyōjōsho*.
48 *Otome-chō Kanbun* 10, TAA-012-457.
49 *Otome-chō Kanbun* 9, TAA-012-165.
50 *Otome-chō Kanbun* 10, TAA-012-453.
51 *Ōmori Chikugo jōkyō*, TPA-031-352.
52 *Otome-chō Kanbun* 7, TAA-011-700.
53 *Ontome-chō hyōjōsho* 1, 100a.
54 *Gokokuchū jinja ki*, TPA-031-155.
55 Beppu 2013, 148–51.
56 Kurachi 1983, 314.
57 Tamamuro 1991, 138–9.
58 Kurachi 1983, 316–17.
59 Beppu 2013, 157, 225.
60 See the chapters on Confucianism and Shinto in Part 3 of this volume.
61 Beppu 2013, 225.

Chapter 12

1. Research for this paper was funded by the Austrian Science Fund (FWF) under project number P 29231-G24.
2. *Gentō hikki*, 233. 玄桐筆記, (*Notes of Gentō*) is a record of Mitsukuni's words and deeds by Inoue Gentō 井上玄桐 (?–1702), compiled after Mitsukuni's death.
3. See Chapter 10 in this volume.
4. Tamamuro 2003, 3.
5. For more on this subject, see Chapter 1 in this volume.
6. Itō 1968, 813–14.
7. Tamamuro 2001, 262.
8. Tamamuro 1988, 329.
9. Suzuki 2006, 103.
10. Totman 1967, 116–17.
11. Nagoya 1986, iii–iv.
12. Kouamé 2005, 109.
13. I aim to get closer to an answer with my current PhD research on early modern religious policies in Mito.
14. *Hakyakuchō*, 1; my translation is based on the transcription by Natalie Kouamé (2005, 14–59).
15. From 1696, the office was abolished several times before finally becoming a permanent institution from 1750 until the end of the Edo period (Tamamuro 1968, 840).
16. Tamamuro 1968, 839–40.
17. The first two appointed to the office were Yamagata Genshichi 山縣源七 (dates unknown) and Kitagawara Jingoemon 北瓦甚五衛門 (dates unknown). In two letters addressed to domain officials, they complained that the *koori bugyō* Miyake Jūemon 三宅十衛門 (dates unknown) had encroached on their sphere of competence by making decisions about three persons affiliated with abolished temples (*Hakyakuchō*, 20–1).
18. Sasaki 2010, 235–6.
19. Tamamuro 1968, 841–3.
20. Tamamuro 1968, 842–3.
21. Kouamé 2005, 110–11.
22. Tamamuro 1968, 843.
23. Kouamé 2005, 122.
24. As mentioned in note 14, my research is based on Natalie Kouamé's transcription. The original manuscript was compiled by Sugiyama Tadasuke at the end of the Edo period (Kouamé 2005, 100).
25. *Hakyakuchō*, 3.
26. *Hakyakuchō*, 1.
27. *Hakyakuchō*, 2.
28. *Hakyakuchō*, 3.
29. *Hakyakuchō*, 18. Literally "double" (*nijū* 二重). This is not mentioned in the general part of the register, but is derived from a precedence mentioned in an order from 1666/8/22.
30. *Hakyakuchō*, 3.
31. *Hakyakuchō*, 6.
32. *Hakyakuchō*, 3.

33 Sources: Tamamuro 1968, 842, 845; 2003, 6.
34 *Hakyakuchō*, 4.
35 *Hakyakuchō*, 10.
36 Shimonaka 1982, 74.
37 *Hakyakuchō*, 9.
38 *Hakyakuchō*, 21.
39 *Hakyakuchō*, 7.
40 *Hakyakuchō*, 17.
41 *Hakyakuchō*, 11.
42 *Hakyakuchō*, 2.
43 Tamamuro 2003, 6.
44 *Hakyakuchō*, 7.
45 *Hakyakuchō*, 5.
46 *Hakyakuchō*, 17.
47 Tamamuro 1968, 857.
48 Tamamuro 1968, 858.
49 Tamamuro 1968, 858–9.
50 These regulations are taken from *Goyōdome kakinuki* 御用留書抜 (*Excerpt from the lord's regulations*) as cited in Tamamuro 1968, 859.
51 The term *shintō-uke* for certification by shrines was used only in Okayama. See also Chapter 11 in this volume.
52 Itō 1968, 824.
53 This number does not include small wayside shrines.
54 Tamamuro 2003, 2–3.
55 Tamamuro 1968, 869.
56 *Chinjuchō*'s compilation date is often given as 1696 (e.g. Tamamuro 1968, 861; 2003, 2), however, the version printed in ST 18, which I used, must be from a later time, since it contains information about events that happened after 1696, such as the Tokiwa Hachiman Shrine's relocation back to Mito in 1707 (*Chinjuchō*, 171).
57 This number is according to my own count. Tamamuro gives the number as 593 shrines (Tamamuro 2003, 3) and Yoshida, as 555 (Yoshida 1995, 20).
58 *Hakyakuchō*, 3. In the original, these shrines are specified as *yuisho naki ko-hora* 無由緒無小ほら. While *hora* might indeed refer to a small sanctuary, Kouamé deems this most likely a mistake by the copyist (Kouamé 2005, 71).
59 Hikino 2008, 175.
60 Tamamuro 1968, 862.
61 Tamamuro 1968, 861–4. A small number of shrines was administered by laymen.
62 Etō 2014, 44.
63 Tamamuro 2000, 108–10.
64 Source: Tamamuro 2000, 108–10.
65 Tamamuro 2000, 108–10.
66 Tamamuro 1968, 865–6; Etō 2014, 35, 41.
67 Etō 2014, 46–9.
68 Tsutsumi 2001; Etō 2014, 53.
69 See also the Introduction to this volume.
70 Cf. Etō 2014.
71 Etō 2014, 52.
72 *Fuji bunin byōchū sōreijiryaku* 藤夫人病中葬礼事略 as cited in Kondō 1997a, 345.
73 *Fuji bunin byōchū sōreijiryaku*, as cited in Kondō 1997a, 344.

74 Kurakazu 2012, 283–2 as cited in Chard 2013, 328 (41).
75 Kondō 1997b, 48–9.
76 Kurakazu 2012, 283–2, as cited in Chard 2013, 328 (41).
77 One of the cemeteries was located in Fujisan 富士山, a district within the castle town of Mito, east of the castle, another in Tokiwa-mura 常磐村, about 2.5 km to the northwest, and the third in Sakado-mura 酒門村, about 2.5 km to the southeast of Mito castle.
78 *Hakyakuchō*, 8–9.
79 Chard 2013, 327 (42); Ebrey 1991. See also Chapter 8 in this volume.
80 Cited from Tamamuro 1968, 874.
81 See also Chapter 14 in this volume.
82 See the Introduction to this volume, as well as Chapter 9.
83 Inspired by Nariaki's ideas, in 1862 Toda Tadayuki 戸田忠至 (1809–83), a relative of the daimyo of Utsunomiya, initiated the restoration of over one hundred imperial tombs as Shinto sanctuaries (cf. Pickl-Kolaczia 2018, 206–12).
84 Ching 1975, 187.
85 Thal 2002, 385.
86 Tamamuro 1968, 860.

Chapter 13

1 These hamlets were administrative units within the villages and were called differently from place to place. In Izumi province alone, words like *kaito*, *mure*, or even *machi* or *chō* were in use.
2 Inoue 2008b, 279.
3 Bardy 2013, 227–31.
4 Yoshida 2000, 357.
5 Mita 2012, 48–51.
6 Also known as *Law for Shrine Priests* (*Shosha negi kannushi hatto* 諸社禰宜神主法度). See Chapter 10 in this volume.
7 *Yokota Shigeru-shi shozō monjo*, maki 3: Kantō godaidai gojōmoku 関東御代々御條目, 1782/10.
8 *Yokota Shigeru-shi shozō monjo*, sai 1: Shintōsaikyo no jō 神道裁許之状 1718/6/19: 和泉国和泉郡三林村正一位春日明神之祠官横田石見守藤原吉勝恒例之神事参勤之時着風折烏帽子狩衣者神道裁許之状件如 [date and signature].
9 Maeda 2002.
10 Maeda 2002, 337.
11 *Shinshū Izumisano-shi shi*, 371–495.
12 *Shinshū Izumisano-shi shi*, 372–3.
13 This network comprised six shrines, with Hine taking place five in the implicit hierarchy. Their priests were appointed by the court and performed prayers, as courtly representatives, to local gods. Five shrines served individual gods, while the sixth, the "general shrine" (*sōsha* 総社), which was located near the old province government, combined the divinities of the other shrines to be venerated in one place. One founding legend of Hine Shrine is related to the mythical empress Jingū Kōgō 神功皇后, who is said to have buried a boat in this region, at what became Funaoka Hill 船岡山. The figure of Jingū (famous for her Korean conquest) may be related to the Korean

ancestry of the Hine lineage, testified in genealogical records of the Heian period (*Shinsen shōjiroku* 新撰姓氏録, 815).
14. *Shinshū Izumisano-shi shi*, 493–5, a document from the Furuya family dating to 1813. This is an answer by the officials of Hineno and Nagataki villages to an inquiry from the magistracy (*go-bugyō sama* 御奉行様), explaining why the village officials were writing the documents and not the *miyaza* leaders.
15. *Shinshū Izumisano-shi shi*, 390–473.
16. The exact identity of this person, as well as the details (time and name of the fiefdom in the West) are still unclear. According to a Jigen'in document written in 1794, Hine Wakasanokami followed Hideyoshi in the West, made a name for himself and earned a fiefdom (*Shinshū Izumisano-shi shi*, 390–473). Another Jigen'in source states that "there was a priest who followed Nobunaga during the years of the Genki and Tenshō eras (1570–91) and became a feudal lord in the West." (*Shinshū Izumisano-shi shi*, 409). While there were several Hine or Hineno warriors serving both war lords at that time, I was unable to find a Hine Wakasanokami.
17. At the annual festival, which took place on the second day of the fourth month, parishioners carried the divinity's palanquin to a "resting place" (*tabisho* 旅所) located at a branch shrine on Funaoka Hill, outside the territory of the four villages and where the parish elders performed ceremonies. Since these rituals were performed primarily by the villagers, they may have had mundane purposes as well. Besides appealing to the gods, a side-effect of this ritual was the claim of ownership over the *tabisho* and the hill, which was located outside the villages' jurisdiction.
18. *Shinshū Izumisano-shi shi*, 383.
19. Aritōshi Jinja was a shrine with an age-old tradition situated in the territory of Nagataki, one of the four villages of the parish community of the Ōiseki Shrine. We suppose that it had some relationship with the Yoshida and that in this matter, it served as intermediary between them and the community.
20. *Shinshū Izumisano-shi shi*, 372–3.
21. *Shinshū Izumisano-shi shi*, 414–15.
22. *Shinshū Izumisano-shi shi*, 467–8.
23. *Shinshū Izumisano-shi shi*, 429–31.
24. Bardy 2017, 293–5.
25. The map is based on a historical map of Izumi province, commissioned by the government in Genroku 9 (1696) (*Genroku kuni ezu, Izumi no kuni* 元禄国絵図和泉国). It can be accessed via the Digital Archive of the National Archives of Japan (https://www.digital.archives.go.jp).
26. On Yoshida and Kokugaku, see Chapter 14 in this volume.
27. From about the second half of the seventeenth century, the relevant regional authorities included the various ruling houses of the Sekiyado domain 関宿藩, the Tokugawa branch families Hitotsubashi 一橋 and Shimizu 清水, and the *bakufu*.
28. Izumi-shi Shihensan Iinkai 2011, 230.
29. *Yokota Shigeru-shi shozō monjo*, Satsu 1/36. According to the same document, the priesthood was handed over in the following order: from the Jinsaemon branch to the Sajiemon branch and then to Shōbei branch.
30. *Yokota Shigeru-shi shozō monjo*, maki 1–1; maki 1–2; maki 1–3.
31. *Yokota Shigeru-shi shozō monjo*, sai 1.
32. Maeda 2002, 342.
33. *Yokota Shigeru-shi shozō monjo*, satsu 1–36.
34. Bardy 2013, 74–8.

35 *Minami Kiyohiko-shi shozō monjo* 南清彦氏所蔵史, hako 1/55.
36 Jūemon thereby gained the title of Higo-no-kami, but eventually rejected the use of the "*no-kami*" part, which means "governor," claiming that being a farmer he had no merit and no right to use it.
37 See also Chapter 14 in this volume.
38 *Gokyojō to mōsu mono* 御許状と申者 in *Yokota Shigeru-shi shozō monjo*, satsu 1/37.
39 *Gokyojō to mōsu mono* in *Yokota Shigeru-shi shozō monjo*, satsu 1/37.
40 *Takahashi-ke shozō monjo*, Dai 22/73. This document is the complaint of the Renmyōin as it was presented to the village officials. It does not make a distinction between *shasō* and *bettō*, which probably means that the monk of Mt. Kōya was not too well informed about the situation of his subordinate. It also calls the license (*gokyojō*) a "joint letter" (*soegaki* 添書) to the first rank decree.
41 *Takahashi-ke shozō monjo*, dai 22/73. In this document, Jūemon explains clearly that he performed the *sengū* because he was affiliated to the Yoshida, as otherwise he would have called upon a temple to perform such a rite.
42 *Yokota Shigeru-shi shozō monjo*, satsu 1/24.
43 *Yokota Shigeru-shi shozō monjo*, satsu 1/37.
44 *Shinshū Izumisano-shi shi*, 477.
45 *Furuya-ke monjo* 2/38. The source mentions 1,200 *monme* (*ikkan nihyaku me* 一貫弐百目, which equaled twenty *ryō*), but this seems exorbitant. Perhaps it was 1,200 *mon* of bronze money, which is roughly equal to eleven *monme*.
46 *Shinshū Izumisano-shi shi*, 476–7.

Chapter 14

1 See Chapter 10 in this volume.
2 Hashimoto 2008.
3 Breen and Teeuwen 2010, 54.
4 Hardacre 2002, 53.
5 Inoue 2007a, 129–30. See Chapter 13 in this volume.
6 Ishino 2011, 84–5.
7 Ishikawa 2013, 74.
8 Tasaki 1994, 517; Inoue 2007a, 216.
9 Hatakama 2005, 16; Inoue 2007a, 100–06.
10 Endō 2008.
11 Harootunian 1988.
12 McNally 2005, 235.
13 Konkō 2013, 73.
14 Endō 2008, 168.
15 Sugiyama 1980, 83–4, 93–4.
16 Itō 1973, 75; Watanabe 1942, 3.
17 Kondō 1972, 369.
18 Endō 2008, 207.
19 *Jingi hakke gakusoku*, 1; Yamamoto 1911, 426.
20 Nakagawa 2004, 31–2, 36–8.
21 *Zoku shintō taii*, 137–8, 141. The following account is based on this source.

22 Atsutane is wrong here. Yoshida Kanetomo had already reached upper court ranks in the fifteenth century. Other charges leveled by Atsutane, however, have been substantiated by other scholars.
23 Inoue 2007a, 27, 32.
24 It seems that Atsutane had only a vague understanding of the Yoshida shrine precincts, since he conflated the Hasshinden with the octagonal Daigengū 大元宮, at that time the most sacred building in Yoshida Shinto 吉田神道.
25 Atsutane incorporated a number of official documents regarding this dispute into his text, and his understanding of events generally corresponds to modern historiography, except that he has the dispute starting in 1666 when it actually began at the end of 1668. See Hashimoto 2008.
26 See Chapter 9 in this volume. On Koretaru, see also Scheid 2002.
27 Endō 2008, 117.
28 Endō 2008, 178.
29 *Kiyo sōhansho*, 435.
30 *Kiyo sōhansho*, 434.
31 The powerful head temple of the Jōdo Shin 浄土真 sect.
32 For example, Atsutane relied on the Yoshida affiliate Mutobe Yoshika 六人部是香 (1798–1864) and his elder sister to get his writings transmitted to the emperor and the empress dowager. Yoshika became Motoori Ōhira's disciple in 1816, and Atsutane's disciple in 1823.
33 *Miyakawa Danshō kōtatsusho*.
34 Endō 2008, 179; *Kikke keifu den*.
35 Endō 2008, 184–5.
36 Watanabe 1942, 146, 154, 155.
37 *Suzuka Echigo no kami kōtatsusho*.
38 Endō 2008, 189–99.
39 Hatano Takao Kenkyūkai 1994, 63. For the Yoshida price list, see Miyaji 1958, 62–4.
40 Hatano Takao Kenkyūkai 1994, 246.
41 Yoshida 2012, 155–7. The Hōkokutai 報国隊 in Tōtōmi similarly promoted martial arts under the leadership of ten Yoshida affiliated priests, most of whom were Hirata disciples (Inoue 2007a, 305).
42 At that time a detached territory of the Mizuno 水野, the daimyo of Numazu 沼津藩 in the neighboring province of Suruga.
43 Kishino 1980, 57.
44 Kishino 1980, 59.
45 Kishino 1980, 67, 69.
46 Kishino 1979, 27.
47 Mase 1985, 78–85, 92.
48 See, for example, Masaka's discovery of ancient artifacts in 1838 (Kokuritsu Rekishi Minzoku Hakubutsukan, 2007, 368).
49 *Jingihaku shokushō enzetsusho*.
50 Mase 1985, 89.
51 *Jingihaku shokushō enzetsusho*.
52 *Shinshū Hirata Atsutane zenshu* 8, 241.
53 Hatakama 2005, 11, 17.
54 Inoue 2007a, 1–5.
55 Wakabayashi 1991.
56 Quoted in Itō 1973, 169–70.

References

Abbreviations

BK	*Bandai kikyōroku* 万代亀鏡録
CC	*Chinese Classics*
FFS	*Fujufuse shiryō* 不受不施資料
IMKD	*Ikeda Mitsumasa-kō den* 池田光政公伝
IMN	*Ikeda Mitsumasa nikki* 池田光政日記
IRR	*Ikeda-ke rireki ryakki* 池田家履歴略記
KT	*Kokushi taikei* 国史大系
NJ	*Nichirenshū jiten* 日蓮宗事典
NKBT	*Nihon koten bungaku taikei* 日本古典文学大系
NKSS	*Nihon kyōiku shi shiryō* 日本教育史資料
NSTS	*Nihon shisō tōsō shiryō* 日本思想闘諍史料
NST	*Nihon shisō taikei* 日本思想大系
NSZ	*Nichirenshū shūgaku zensho* 日蓮宗宗学全書
ST	*Shintō taikei* 神道大系
T	*Taishō shinshū daizōkyō* 大正新修大蔵経
ZBZ	*Zōtei Banzan zenshū* 増訂蕃山全集
ZKT	*Zoku kokushi taikei* 続国史大系
ZST	*Zoku shintō taikei* 続神道大系

Primary Sources

Aizu jinja-shi 会津神社志. In *Hoshina Masayuki* 保科正之, vol. 1. ZST, ronsetsu-hen 論説編. Tokyo: Shintō Taikei Hensankai, 2002.

Aizu-han kasei jikki 会津藩家世実紀. 15 vols. Edited by Kasei Jikki Kanpon Hensan Iinkai 家世実紀刊本編集委員会. Tokyo: Yoshikawa Kōbunkan, 1973–89.

Ansai sensei ekisaku fujō 闇斎先生易簀訃状. Edited by Ikegami Kōjirō 池上幸二郎. Tokyo: Seishindō, 1939.

Bandai kikyōroku 万代亀鏡録 (BK). 2 vols. Edited by Ōsaki Nichigyō 大崎日行. Tokyo: Bandai Kikyōroku Kankōkai, 1931–3.

Biyō kokugaku kiroku 備陽国学記録. In *Okayama daigaku fuzoku toshokan shozō Ikeda-ke bunko hansei shiryō maikurohan shūsei* 岡山大学附属図書館所蔵池田家文庫藩政史料マイクロ版集成, edited by Okayama Daigaku Ikeda-ke Bunko-ra Kankōkai 岡山大学池田家文庫等刊行会. Microfilm edition: *Kanbun 9/7–12*, reel number: TRA-001-063. *Enpō 1–8*, reel number: TRA-001-363. Okayama: Maruzen, 1992.

Bizen kokushi nichiroku 備陽国史日録. In *Okayama daigaku fuzoku toshokan shozō Ikeda-ke bunko hansei shiryō maikurohan shūsei* 岡山大学附属図書館所蔵池田家文庫藩政史料マイクロ版集成, edited by Okayama Daigaku Ikeda-ke Bunko-ra Kankōkai 岡山大学池田家文庫等刊行会. Microfilm edition: *Kanbun 6/1-6/12* reel number: TAA-003-464. Okayama: Maruzen, 1992.

Buke genseiroku 武家厳制録. In *Kinsei hōsei shiryō sōsho* 近世法制史料叢書, edited by Ishii Ryōsuke 石井良助. Tokyo: Sōbunsha, 1941, revised edition 1959.

Cartas que los padres y hermanos de la Compañia de Jesús que andan en los Reynos de Japón escrivieron a los de la misma Compañia desde el año de mil y quinientos y quarenta y nueve, hasta el de mil y quinientos y setenta y uno. Alcalá: Iñiquez de Lequerica, 1575.

Chinese Classics (CC). 5 vols. Translated by James Legge, 1865–93. Reprint: Hong Kong University Press, 1960.

Chinjuchō 鎮守帳. In *Awa, Kazusa, Shimousa, Hitachi no kuni* 安房・上總・下總・常陸國, edited by Tsuruoka Shizuo 鶴岡静夫 and Iida Mizuho 飯田瑞穂. ST, jinja-hen 神社編 18. Tokyo: Shintō Taikei Hensankai, 1990.

Chitose no matsu 千載之松. In *Ganban shiryō sōsho* 岩磐史料叢書. Vol. 1, edited by Kugimoto Morio 釘本衞雄. Fukushima: Ganban Shiryō Kankōkai, 1916.

Daigaku wakumon 大学或問. In *Kumazawa Banzan* 熊澤蕃山, edited by Gotō Yōichi 後藤陽一 and Tomoeda Ryūtarō 友枝龍太郎. NST 30. Tokyo: Iwanami Shoten, 1971.

Daijingū shintō wakumon jō 大神宮神道或問上, 1666. In *Watarai Shintō taisei zenpen* 度會神道大成 前篇. Zōbo daijingū sōsho 増補大神宮叢書 17. Tokyo: Yoshikawa Kōbunkan, 2008.

Documentos del Japón. 2 vols. Edited by Juan Ruiz de Medina. Rome: Institutum Historicum Societatis Iesu, 1990–5.

Enryakuji daishūge 延暦寺大衆解. In *Kamakura ibun, komonjo-hen* 鎌倉遺文 古文書編, vol. 5. Tokyo: Tōkyōdō Shuppan, 1973.

Fuji bunin byōchū sōreijiryaku 藤夫人病中葬礼事略. Cited in Kondō 1997a.

Fujufuse-ha hōnan shiryōshū 不受不施派法難史料集. Edited by Nagamitsu Norikazu 長光徳和. Okayama: Okayama-ken Chihōshi Kenkyū Renraku Kyōgikai, 1969.

Fujufuse shiryō 不受不施資料 (FFS). 2 vols. Edited by Nichiren Fujufuse-ha Kenkyūjo 日蓮不受不施派研究所. Kyoto: Heirakuji Shoten, 1981–3.

Furuya-ke monjo 古谷家文書. Held by the Rekishikan Izumisano 歴史館泉佐野.

Fusō gobusshin ron 扶桑護仏神論 by Chōon Dōkai 潮音道海, preface 1687. Manuscript held by Kyoto University, signature 1-03-*fu*-1.

Gentō hikki 玄桐筆記 by Inoue Gentō 井上玄. In *Gikō sōsho* 義公叢書, edited by Chiba Shinji 千葉新治. Sendai: Sōkawa Kappansha, 1909.

Gohō shiji ron 護法資治論 by Mori Genjuku 森儼塾, 1766–74. Edited by Washio Junkyō 鷲尾順敬. NSTS 2. Tokyo: Tōhō Shoin, 1930–1.

Gokokuchū jinja ki 御国中神社記. In *Okayama daigaku fuzoku toshokan shozō Ikeda-ke bunko hansei shiryō maikurohan shūsei* 岡山大学附属図書館所蔵池田家文庫藩政史料マイクロ版集成, edited by Okayama Daigaku Ikeda-ke Bunko-ra Kankōkai 岡山大学

池田家文庫等刊行会. Microfilm edition: reel number: TPA-031-143. Okayama: Maruzen, 1992.

Goyōdome kakinuki 御用留書抜. Cited in Tamamuro 1968.

Hachiman gūji kōmon burui 八幡宮寺告文部類. In *Engi, takusen, kōmon* 縁起・託宣・告文. Iwashimizu Hachimangū shiryō sōsho 石清水八幡宮史料叢書, vol. 2. Kyoto: Iwashimizu Hachimangū Shamujo, 1976.

Hakyakuchō 破却帳. In Kouamé 2005. Original MS: National Diet Library, Tokyo, call number わ 081-11; Sugiyama series 杉山叢書 4.

Honge betsuzu busso tōki 本化別頭仏祖統紀. Kyoto: Honmanji, 1973.

Honchō jinja kō 本朝神社考 by Hayashi Razan 林羅山, first printed between 1645 and ca. 1650. NSTS 1. Tokyo: Tōhō Shoin, 1930–1.

Honkō kokushi nikki 本光国師日記 by Konchiin Sūden 金地院崇伝. In *Dainihon bukkyō zensho* 大日本仏教全書 80, *nikkibu* 日記部 6. Tokyo: Suzuki Gakujutsu Zaidan, 1972.

Ikeda Mitsumasa nikki 池田光政日記 (IMN). Edited by Fujii Shun 藤井駿, Mizuno Kyōichirō 水野恭一郎, and Taniguchi Sumio 谷口澄夫. Okayama: San'yō Shuppan, 1967.

Ikeda Mitsumasa-kō den 池田光政公伝 (IMKD). 2 vols. by Nagayama Usaburō 永山卯三郎. Edited by Ishizaka Zenjirō 石坂善次郎. Tokyo: Ishizaka Zenjirō, 1932.

Ikeda-ke rireki ryakki 池田家履歴略記 (IRR). 2 vols. Compiled by Saitō Kazuoki 斎藤一興, 1789–1801. Edited by Yoshida Tokutarō 吉田德太郎. Okayama: Nihon Bunkyō Shuppan, 1963.

Ikoku nikki 異国日記 by Konchiin Sūden 金地院崇伝. In *Ikoku nikki: Konchiin Sūden gaikōbunsho shūsei eiinbon* 異国日記：金地院崇伝外交文書集成 影印本, edited by Ikoku Nikki Kankōkai 異国日記刊行会. Tokyo: Bijutsu, 1989.

Jingi hakke gakusoku 神祇伯家學則, attr. to Hirata Atsutane 平田篤胤. In *Hirata Atsutane kankei shiryō* 平田篤胤関係史料, sōkō 草稿 1–2, held by the National Museum of Japanese History.

Jingi hōten 神祇宝典. In ST, jinja-hen 神社編 3. Tokyo: Shintō Taikei Hensankai, 1983.

Jingihaku shokushō enzetsusho 神祇伯職掌演説書 by Takeo Masatomo 竹尾正韜, 1838. Nishio-shi Iwase Bunko: *Kotenseki shoshi dētabēsu* 西尾市岩瀬文庫／古典籍書誌データベース document no. 52-197.

Jinja-kō bengi 神社考辨疑 by Jakuhon 寂本, 1686, reprint 1716.

Jinnō shōtōki 神皇正統記. In *Jinnō shōtōki/Masukagami* 神皇正統記・増鏡, edited by Iwasa Tadashi 岩佐正, Tokieda Motoki 時枝誠記 and Kifuji Saizō 木藤才蔵. NKBT 87. Tokyo: Iwanami Shoten, 1965.

Jinzanshū 秦山集 by Tani Shigetō 谷重遠. Tokyo: Tani Tateki, 1910.

Jishō nikki 慈性日記 by Sonshōin Jishō 尊勝院慈性. 2 vols. Edited by Hayashi Kanshō 林觀照. Shiryō sōshū 史料纂集 123, 128. Tokyo: Zoku Gunshō Ruijū Kanseikai, 2000.

Kaikichō 開基帳. 1666. Held by the Shōkōkan 彰考館 in Mito.

Kamigoto no uretamigoto 祭事冤論 by Takeo Masatomo 竹尾正韜, 1817. Held by Kokugakuin University, online available through the Database of Pre-Modern Japanese Works (http://kotenseki.nijl.ac.jp).

Kii zoku fudoki furoku 紀伊続風土記附録. Vol. 16. In *Kii zoku fudoki dai 3 shū* 紀伊続風土記 第三輯, edited by Wakayama-ken Shinshoku Torishimarijo 和歌山県神職取締所. Kyoto: Teikoku Chihō Gyōseikai Shuppanbu, 1910.

Kikke keifu den 吉家系譜伝 by Hirata Atsutane 平田篤胤. In *Hirata Atsutane kankei shiryō* 平田篤胤関係史料, sōkō 草稿 1–216, held by the National Museum of Japanese History.

Kinsei bukkyō no shisō 近世仏教の思想. Edited by Kashiwahara Yūsen 柏原祐泉 and Fujii Manabu 藤井学. NST 57. Tokyo: Iwanami Shoten, 1973.

Kirishitan kankei hōsei shiryō キリシタン関係法制史料. Edited by Shimizu Hirokazu 清水紘一, and Shimizu Yūko 清水有子. Tokyo: Sōkyū Shuppan, 2002.

Kirishitan sho, haija sho キリシタン書・排邪書. Edited by Ebisawa Arimichi 海老沢有道. NST 25. Tokyo: Iwanami Shoten, 1970.

Kiyo sōhansho 毀誉相半書 by Hirata Atsutane 平田篤胤. In *Shinshū Hirata Atsutane zenshū, hoi* 5 新修平田篤胤全集 補遺 5, edited by Hirata Atsutane Zenshū Kankōkai 平田篤胤全集刊行会. Tokyo: Meicho Shuppan, 2001.

Kokushi taikei, shintei zōho 国史大系 新訂増補 (KT). 62 vols. Tokyo: Yoshikawa Kōbunkan.

Meiji ishin shinbutsu bunri shiryō 明治維新神仏分離史料. 5 vols. Edited by Murakami Senjō 村上専精, Tsuji Zennosuke 辻善之助, and Washio Junkyō 鷲尾順敬. Tokyo: Meicho Shuppan, 1970.

Meiryō kōhan 明良洪範 by Sanada Zōyo 真田増誉. Tokyo: Kokusho Kankōkai, 1912.

Miwa monogatari 三輪物語 by Kumazawa Banzan 熊沢蕃山. In ZBZ. Tokyo: Meicho Shuppan, 1978.

Minami Kiyohiko-shi shozō monjo 南清彦氏所蔵文書. Held by the Izumi-shi Shihensanjo 和泉市史編纂所.

Miyakawa Danshō kōtatsusho 宮川弾正口達書 by Miyakawa Danshō 宮川弾正. In *Hirata Atsutane kankei shiryō* 平田篤胤関係史料, sasshi 冊子 209-6-1, held by the National Museum of Japanese History.

Nagasaki Hirado-chō ninbetsuchō 長崎平戸町人別帳. Fukuoka: Kyūshū Shiryō Kankōkai, 1965.

Nebokoro shūi 瓊矛拾遺 by Shibukawa Harumi 渋川春海. In *Suika shintō jōkan* 垂加神道 上巻 (Dainihon bunko, shintō hen 大日本文庫 神道篇). Tokyo: Shun'yōsha, 1947.

Nichirenshū shūgaku zensho 日蓮宗宗学全書 (NSZ). 23 vols. Tokyo: Sankibō Busshorin, 1968–78.

Nihon koten bungaku taikei 日本古典文学大系 (NKBT). 102 vols. Tokyo: Iwanami Shoten.

Nihon kyōiku shi shiryō 日本教育史資料 (NKSS). 10 vols. Compiled by Monbushō 文部省. Tokyo: Fuzanbō, 1890–1892.

Nihon sandai jitsuroku 日本三代実録. 2 vols. Tokyo: Yoshikawa Kōbunkan, 1971.

Nihon shisō taikei 日本思想大系 (NST). 67 vols. Iwanami Shoten, 1970–82.

Nihon shisō tōsō shiryō 日本思想闘諍史料 (NSTS). 10 vols., 1930–31, edited by Washio Junkyō 鷲尾順敬. Tokyo: Tōhō Shoin, 1930–1, reprint Meisho Kankōkai, 1971.

Nihon shoki 日本書紀. 2 vols. Edited by Sakamoto Tarō 坂本太郎 et al. NKBT 67–8. Tokyo: Iwanami Shoten, 1965–7.

Ofuregaki Kanpō shūsei 御触書寛保集成. Edited by Takayanagi Shinzō 高柳真三 and Ishii Ryōsuke 石井良助. Tokyo: Iwanami Shoten, 1976, first edition 1934.

Ofuregaki Tenmei shūsei 御触書天明集成. Edited by Takayanagi Shinzō 高柳真三 and Ishii Ryōsuke 石井良助. Tokyo: Iwanami Shoten, 1976.

Ohiroma zakki 御広間雑記. Cited in Hatakama 2008.

Ōmori Chikugo jōkyō tsukamatsuri shake sharyū shintō jōmon mōshiukesōrō ikken 大森筑後上京仕社家者流神道証文申請候一件. In *Okayama daigaku fuzoku toshokan shozō Ikeda-ke bunko hansei shiryō maikurohan shūsei* 岡山大学附属図書館所蔵池田家文庫藩政史料マイクロ版集成, edited by Okayama Daigaku Ikeda-ke Bunko-ra Kankōkai 岡山大学池田家文庫等刊行会. Okayama: Maruzen, 1992. Microfilm edition, reel number: TPA-031-351.

Ontome-chō hyōjōsho 御留帳評定所. 2 vols. Edited by Okayama Daigaku Fuzoku Toshokan Kijū Shiryō Kankō Suishinkai 岡山大学附属図書館貴重史料刊行推進会. Okayama: Okayama Daigaku Shuppankai, 2017.

Oshioki reiruishū 御仕置例類集. 16 vols. Edited by Ishii Ryōsuke 石井良助. Tokyo: Meicho Shuppan, 1971–4.

Otome-chō 御留帳. In *Okayama daigaku fuzoku toshokan shozō Ikeda-ke bunko hansei shiryō maikurohan shūsei* 岡山大学附属図書館所蔵池田家文庫藩政史料マイクロ版集成, edited by Okayama Daigaku Ikeda-ke Bunko-ra Kankōkai 岡山大学池田家文庫等刊行会. Microfilm edition: *Kanbun 7/1–7/6/10*, reel number: TAA-011-408. *Kanbun 7/1–7/12*, reel number: TAA-011-634. *Kanbun 9/8–9/12*, reel number: TAA-012-161. *Kanbun 10/1–10/10*, reel number: TAA-012-447. Okayama: Maruzen, 1992.

Razan Hayashi-sensei bunshū, shishū 羅山林先生文集・詩集. 2 + 2 vols. Compiled by Kyōto Shisekikai 京都史蹟会. Kyoto: Heian Kôko Gakkai, 1918–21.

Relación del Reino de Nippon a que llaman corruptamente Jappon by Bernardino Ávila Girón (1615), manuscript held by Biblioteca Nacional de España, Madrid, signature 19628.

Satsuyōroku kan 29: Hai jisha no bu 撮要録巻29廃寺社之部. In *Okayama daigaku fuzoku toshokan shozō Ikeda-ke bunko hansei shiryō maikurohan shūsei* 岡山大学附属図書館所蔵池田家文庫藩政史料マイクロ版集成, edited by Okayama Daigaku Ikeda-ke Bunko-ra Kankōkai 岡山大学池田家文庫等刊行会. Microfilm edition, reel number: TAE-005-190. Okayama: Maruzen, 1992.

Sendai kuji hongi taisei-kyō 先代旧事本紀大成経. 4 vols. Edited by Ogasawara Haruo 小笠原春夫. ZST ronsetsu-hen 論説編. Tokyo: Shintō Taikei Hensankai, 1999.

Shintō denju 神道伝授 by Hayashi Razan 林羅山, 1644. In *Kinsei shintōron, zenki kokugaku* 近世神道論・前期国学, edited by Taira Shigemichi 平重道 and Abe Akio 阿部秋生. NST 39. Tokyo: Iwanami Shoten, 1972.

Shishigatani byakurensha ninchō-oshō gyōgō ki 獅谷白蓮社忍澂和尚行業記 by Kanen 珂然, 1727. In *Jōdoshū zensho* 浄土宗全書, vol. 18. Tokyo: Jōdoshūten Kankōkai, 1928.

Shinro menmei 新蘆面命 by Tani Shigetō 谷重遠. In *Nihon bunko, dai 4 hen* 日本文庫第四編. Tokyo: Hakubunkan, 1891.

Shinshū Hirata Atsutane zenshu 新修平田篤胤全集. 15 vols. Tokyo: Meicho Shuppan, 2001.

Shinshū Izumisano-shi shi 新修泉佐野市史. Vol. 6. Edited by Izumisano Shihensan Iiinkai 泉佐野史編纂委員会. Osaka: Seibundō, 2005.

Shintō shūsei 神道集成. In ST, shuhen 首編 1. Tokyo: Shintō Taikei Hensankai, 1981.

Shintō taigi 神道大義. In *Banzan zenshū* 蕃山全集, vol. 5, edited by Masamune Atsuo 正宗敦夫. Tokyo: Banzan Zenshū Kankōkai, 1942.

Shintō taikei 神道大系 (ST). 120 vols. Tokyo: Shintō Taikei Hensankai, 1977–2006.

Shōwa teihon Nichiren shōnin ibun 昭和定本日蓮聖人遺文. 4 vols. Edited by Risshō Daigaku Nichiren Kyōgaku Kenkyūjo 立正大学日蓮教学研究所. Minobu-chō, Yamanashi prefecture: Minobusan Kuonji, 1952–9. Revised edition, 1988.

Shūkyō kankei hōrei ichiran 宗教関係法令一覧. In *Shūkyō to kokka* 宗教と国家, edited by Miyachi Masato 宮地正人. Nihon kindai shisō taikei 日本近代思想体系 5: Tokyo: Iwanami Shoten, 1988.

Shunkai sensei jikki 春海先生実記 by Shibukawa Shunsui 渋川春水, 1721. Microfilm manuscript held by the National Diet Library, Tokyo.

Shusshi kō 出思稿 by Matsubara Issei 松原一清. Setsuyō: Hirano Shōzaemon, 1696 (preface 1683). Held by the National Diet Library, Tokyo.

Suzuka Echigo no kami kōtatsusho 鈴鹿越後守口達書 by Suzuka Echigo 鈴鹿越後. In *Hirata Atsutane kankei shiryō* 平田篤胤関係史料, sasshi 冊子 209-6-2, held by the National Museum of Japanese History.

Taishō shinshū daizōkyō 大正新修大蔵経 (T). Edited by Takakusu Junjirō 高楠順次郎 and Watanabe Kaigyoku 渡辺海旭. 100 vols. Tokyo: Taishō Issaikyō Kankōkai, 1924–35.

Takahashi-ke shozō monjō 高橋家所蔵文書. Held by the Izumi-shi Shihensanjo 和泉市史編纂所.

Teisoku-ron 鼎足論 by Taiga 大我, 1821. Edited by Washio Junkyō 鷲尾順敬. NSTS 5. Tokyo: Tōhō Shoin, 1930-1.

Tokugawa jikki 徳川実記. 7 vols. ZKT 9–15. Tokyo: Keizei Zasshisha, 1902–04. Revised edition, 10 vols. KT 38–47.Tokyo: Yoshikawa Kōbunkan, 1964–6.

Tokugawa kinreikō 徳川禁令考. 11 vols. Edited by Shihōshō Daijin Kanbō Shomuka 司法省大臣官房庶務課 and Hōsei Shigakkai 法制史学会, revised by Ishii Ryōsuke 石井良助. Tokyo: Sōbunsha, 1959–61.

Tōshōgū 東照宮. Edited by Sonehara Satoshi 曽根原理. ZST, jinja-hen 神社編. Tokyo: Shintō Taikei Hensankai, 2001.

Tsūkō ichiran 通航一覧. 8 vols. Edited by Hayakawa Junzaburō 早川純三郎. Tokyo: Kokusho Kankōkai, 1912–13.

Yōfukuki 陽復記. In *Kinsei shintōron, zenki kokugaku* 近世神道論・前期国学, edited by Taira Shigemichi 平重道 and Abe Akio 阿部秋生. NST 39. Tokyo: Iwanami Shoten, 1972.

Yokota Shigeru-shi shozō monjo 横田滋氏所蔵文書. Held by the Izumi-shi Shihensanjo 和泉市史編纂所.

Yoshikawa Aremi no ya sensei gyōjō 吉川視吾堂先生行状 by Yoshikawa Yorinaga 吉川従長, 1694. In *Yoshikawa shintō no kisoteki kenkyū* 吉川神道の基礎的研究, by Taira Shigemichi 平重道. Tokyo: Yoshikawa, 1966.

Yuiitsu shintō myōbō yōshū 唯一神道名法要集. In *Urabe shintō* 卜部神道, vol. 1. ST, ronsetsu-hen 論説編 8. Tokyo: Shintō Taikei Hensankai, 1985.

Yuiitsu shintō oyobi Shizu jinja shuinchi haibun ni tsuki jisha bugyō tasshi gaki 唯一神道及び静神社朱印地配分に付寺社奉行達書. In *Hitachi ninomiya Shizu jinja monjo, jō* 常陸二の宮静神社文書 上, edited by Takahashi Hirobumi 高橋裕文. Naka: Shizu Jinja, 2017.

Yūhiroku 有斐録. In *Shiseki zassan* 史籍雑纂, vol. 2, edited by Hayakawa Junsaburō 早川順三郎. Tokyo: Kokusho Kankōkai, 1911.

Zoku kokushi taikei 続国史大系 (ZKT). 15 vols. Tokyo: Keizei Sasshisha, 1902–04.

Zoku shintō taii 俗神道大意 by Hirata Atsutane 平田篤胤, 1809, published 1860. Held by the National Diet Library, Tokyo.

Zoku shintō taikei 続神道大系 (ZST). 50 vols. Tokyo: Shintō Taikei Hensankai, 1995–2007.

Zōtei Banzan zenshū 増訂蕃山全集 (ZBZ), compiled by Masamune Atsuo 正宗敦夫. 7 vols. Edited by Taniguchi Sumio 谷口澄夫 and Miyazaki Michio 宮崎道生. Tokyo: Meicho Shuppan, 1978–80.

Secondary Sources

Aiba, Shin 相葉伸. 1976. *Fujufuse-ha junkyō no rekishi* 不受不施派殉教の歴史. Tokyo: Daizō Shuppan.

Aizu Wakamatsu-shi Shuppan Iinkai 会津若松市出版委員会, ed. 1965. *Aizu Wakamatsu shi 3, kinsei 2* 会津若松史 3, 近世 2. Aizu Wakamatsu: Aizu Wakamatsu-shi.

Aizu Wakamatsu-shi 会津若松市, ed. 2001. *Aizu hansei no hajimari: Hoshina Masayuki kara shidai* 会津藩政の始まり：保科正之から四代. Aizu Wakamatsu-shi shi 5, rekishi-hen 5, kinsei 2 会津若松市史 5, 歴史編 5, 近世 2. Aizu Wakamatsu: Aizu Wakamatsu-shi.

Álvarez Taladriz, José Luis. 1966a. "Fuentes europeas sobre Murayama Toan (1562–1619) I: El pleito de Suetsugu Heizo Juan contra Murayama Toan Antonio (1617–1619), según el Padre Mattheus de Couros, Provincial de la Compañía de Jesús en Japón." *Tenri daigaku gakuhō* 天理大学学報 17 (5): 241–62 (93–114).

Álvarez Taladriz, José Luis. 1966b. "Fuentes europeas sobre Murayama Toan (1562–1619) II: Murayama Toan Antonio según Bernardino de Ávila Girón." *Kobe gaidai ronsō* 神戸外大論叢 17: 395–418.

Anesaki, Masaharu 姉崎正治. 1976. *Anesaki Masaharu chosakushū, dai 1 kan: Kirishitan shūmon no hakugai to senpuku* 姉崎正治著作集 第一巻：切支丹宗門の迫害と潜伏. Tokyo: Kokusho Kankōkai.

Aston, William George. 1972. *Nihongi. Chronicles of Japan from the Earliest Times to A. D. 697*. Rutland, Vt.: Tuttle.

Azuma, Juji 吾妻重二. 2008. "Ikeda Mitsumasa to jukyō sōsai girei" 池田光政と儒教喪祭儀礼. *Higashi Ajia bunka kōshō kenkyū* 東アジア文化交渉研究 1: 79–104.

Bardy, Yannick. 2013. "Sanctuaires Shintō et sociétés locales dans le Japon de l'epoque d'Edo: l'exemple de la province d'Izumi." PhD diss., Paris: Institut National des Langues et Civilisations Orientales. https://tel.archives-ouvertes.fr/tel-00947622.

Bardy, Yannick. 2017. "Patronage d'établissements religieux : stratégies sociales de notables de locaux durant l'époque d'Edo (1600–1868)." *Japon Pluriel* 11: 289–97.

Bentley, John R. 2006. *The Authenticity of Sendai Kuji Hongi: A New Examination of Texts, with a Translation and Commentary*. Leiden and Boston: Brill.

Beppu, Shingo 別府信吾. 2013. *Okayama-han no jisha to shiryō* 岡山藩の寺社と史料. Kinseishi kenkyū sōsho 近世史研究叢書 37. Tokyo: Iwata Shoin.

Bodart-Bailey, Beatrice M. 2006. *The Dog Shogun: The Personality and Policies of Tokugawa Tsunayoshi*. Honolulu: University of Hawai'i Press.

Bodiford, William. 2013. "Myth and Counter-Myth in Early Modern Japan." In *Writing Down the Myths*, edited by Joseph Falaky Nagy. Cursor Mundi, 17 (special issue 2013). Turnhout: Brepols.

Boot, W.J. 1983. "The Adoption and Adaptation of Neo-Confucianism in Japan." Dissertation, Leiden: Leiden. http://www.ngjs.nl → Specialist → Scholarly Publications.

Boot, W.J. 1993. "Shunmuki and Denchū Mondō: Two Instances of Buddhist-Confucian Polemics in the Edo Period." In *Conflict and Accommodation in Early Modern East Asia. Essays in Honour of Erik Zürcher*, edited by Leonard Blussé and Harriet T. Zurndorfer, 38–53. Leiden: Brill.

Boot, W.J. 2000. "The Death of a Shogun: Deification in Early Modern Japan." In *Shinto in History: Ways of the Kami*, edited by John Breen and Mark Teeuwen, 144–66. London: Curzon.

Boot, W.J. 2011. "Kinsei ni okeru ju-butsu ronsō: 'Denchū mondō' o chūshin ni suete (tokushū, Tōshōgū saishi)" 近世における儒仏論争：『殿中問答』を中心にすえて (特集 東照宮祭祀). *Kikan Nihon shisōshi* 季刊日本思想史 78: 88–107.

Boot, W.J. 2014. "Spirits, Gods, and Heaven in Confucian Thought." In *Dao Companion to Japanese Confucian Philosophy* 5, edited by Chun-chieh Huang and John A. Tucker, 69–108. Dordrecht: Springer.

Boot, W.J. 2015. "The Great Learning in Medieval Japan." In *Lectures et usages de la Grande Étude*, edited by Anne Cheng and Damien Mourier-Genoud, 269–97. Paris: Collège de France, Institut des Hautes Études Chinoises.

Boot, W.J., and M.M.E. Buijnsters. 2016. *Jinja-kō bengi. Transcription, Translation, and Introduction*. http://www.ngjs.nl → Specialist → Scholarly Publications.

Boot, W.J., and M.M.E. Buijnsters. 2019. *Fusō gobusshin ron. Transcription, Translation, and Introduction*. http://www.ngjs.nl → Specialist → Scholarly Publications.

Breen, John. 1996. "Beyond the Prohibition: Christianity in Restoration Japan." In *Japan and Christianity: Impacts and Responses*, edited by John Breen and Mark Williams, 75–93. London: Macmillan Press.

Breen, John, and Mark Teeuwen, eds. 2010. *A New History of Shinto*. Oxford: Wiley-Blackwell.

Brown, Philip C. 1988. "Practical Constraints of Early Tokugawa Land Taxation: Annual versus Fixed Assessments in Kaga Domain." *Journal of Japanese Studies* 14 (2): 369–401.

Chard, Robert L. 2013. "Zhu Shunshui's Plans for the Confucian Ancestral Shrines (Zongmiao 宗廟) in Kaga Domain." *Tōyō bunka kenkyūjo kiyō* 東洋文化研究所紀要 164: 348(21)–317(52).

Chilson, Clark. 2014. *Secrecy's Power: Covert Shin Buddhists in Japan and Contradictions of Concealment*. Honolulu: University of Hawai'i Press.

Ching, Julia. 1975. "Chu Shun-Shui, 1600–82: A Chinese Confucian Scholar in Tokugawa Japan." *Monumenta Nipponica* 30 (2): 177–91.

Chūriki, Akira 中力昭, and Kahara Kōsaku 加原耕作. 1980. "Ōdara yosemiya ato" 大多羅寄宮跡. In *Okayama-ken daihyakka jiten* 岡山県大百科事典. Vol. 1, edited by Okayama-ken Daihyakka Jiten Iinkai 岡山県大百科事典委員会, 331–2. Okayama: San'yō Shinbunsha.

Conlan, Thomas. 2016. "When Men Become Gods: Apotheosis, Sacred Space, and Political Authority in Japan 1486–1599." *Questiones Medii Aevi Novae* 21: 89–106.

Costa, João Paulo Oliveira. 2007. "The Brotherhoods (Confrarias) and Lay Support for the Early Christian Church in Japan." *Japanese Journal of Religious Studies* 34 (1): 67–84.

Ebrey, Patricia Buckley. 1991. *Confucian and Family Rituals in Imperial China*. Princeton: Princeton University Press.

Elisonas, J.S.A. 2005. "Statement on the Expulsion of the Bateren." In *Sources of Japanese Tradition, Vol. 2: 1600 to 2000*, edited by Wm. Theodore de Bary, Carol Gluck, and Arthur E. Tiedemann, 171–4. New York: Columbia University Press.

Endō, Jun 遠藤潤. 2008. *Hirata kokugaku to kinsei shakai* 平田国学と近世社会. Tokyo: Perikansha.

Endō, Shūsaku 遠藤周作. 1992. *Kirishitan jidai: junkyō to kikyō no rekishi* 切支丹時代：殉教と棄教の歴史. Tokyo: Shōgakkan.

Etō, Yoshinobu 江頭慶宣. 2014. "Tokugawa Mitsukuni no Hachiman shinkō: Hachiman aratame no mondai o tōshite" 徳川光圀の八幡信仰：八幡改の問題を通して. *Shintō-shi kenkyū* 神道史研究 62 (2): 35–77 (233–75).

Frois, Luis. 1976. *Historia de Japam*. Edited by Joseph Wicki. 5 vols. Lisbon: Biblioteca Nacional de España.

Fujii, Manabu 藤井学. 1975. "Kinsei shoki no seiji shisō to kokka ishiki" 近世初期の政治思想と国家意識. In *Kinsei* 近世 2. Iwanami kōza, Nihon rekishi 岩波講座日本 歴史 10, 135–72. Tokyo: Iwanami Shoten.

Fujii, Naomasa 藤井直正. 1991. "Kifu o motsu sekihi no keifu" 亀趺をもつ石碑の系譜. *Otemae Joshi Daigaku ronshū* 大手前女子大学論集 25: 29–64.

Gifu-ken shi: Tsūshi-hen, kinsei, jō 岐阜県史：通史編 近世 上. Gifu-ken, 1968.

Gonoi, Takashi 五野井隆史. 1990. *Nihon kurisuto kyōshi* 日本キリスト教史. Tokyo: Yoshikawa Kōbunkan.

Grapard, Alan G., trans. 1992. "'Yuiitsu Shintō Myōbō Yōshū' by Yoshida Kanetomo." *Monumenta Nipponica* 47 (2): 137–61.
Haga, Shōji 羽賀祥二. 1998. *Shisekiron: 19 seiki Nihon no chiiki shakai to rekishi ishiki* 史蹟論 : 19 世紀日本の地域社会と歴史意識. Nagoya: Nagoya Daigaku Shuppan.
Hall, John Whitney. 1966. *Government and Local Power in Japan, 500–1700: A Study Based on Bizen Province*. Princeton, NJ: Princeton University Press.
Hardacre, Helen. 1989. *Shintō and the State, 1868–1988*. Princeton, NJ: Princeton University Press.
Hardacre, Helen. 2002. *Religion and Society in Nineteenth-Century Japan: A Study of the Southern Kantō Region, Using Late Edo and Eary Meiji Gazetteers*. Ann Arbor: Center for Japanese Studies, The University of Michigan.
Hardacre, Helen. 2017. *Shinto: A History*. New York: Oxford University Press.
Harootunian, Harry. 1988. *Things Seen and Unseen: Discourse and Ideology in Tokugawa Nativism*. Chicago: Univ. of Chicago Press.
Harufuji, Hiroshi 服藤弘司. 1980. *Bakuhan taisei kokka no hō to kenryoku 1: bakufuhō to hanpō* 幕藩体制国家の法と権力 1 : 幕府法と藩法. Tokyo: Sōbunsha.
Hashimoto, Masanobu 橋本政宣. 1997. "Kanbun 5 nen 'Jinja jōmoku' no kinō" 寛文 5 年「神社条目」の機能. *Shintō shūkyō* 神道宗教 168-9: 271–9.
Hashimoto, Masanobu 橋本政宣. 2008. "Yoshida-ke no shoshake kan'i shissō undō: Kanbun 9 nen Yoshida shissō ikken sōron o chūshin ni" 吉田家の諸社家官位執奏運動 : 寛文 9 年吉田執奏一件争論を中心に. *Kokuritsu rekishi minzoku hakubutsukan kenkyū hōkoku* 国立歴史民俗博物館研究報告 148: 289–329.
Hatakama, Kazuhiro 幡鎌一弘. 2005. "Tokugawa jidai kōki no shintō to Shirakawa-ke" 徳川時代後期の神道と白川家." *Tenri daigaku oyasato kenkyūjo nenpō* 天理大学おやさと研究所年報 12: 11–19.
Hatakama, Kazuhiro 幡鎌一弘. 2008. "17 seiki chūyō ni okeru Yoshida-ke no katsudō: kakuritsuki to shite no Kanbun-ki 十七世紀中葉における吉田家の活動 : 確立期としての寛文期." *Kokuritsu rekishi minzoku hakubutsukan kenkyū hōkoku* 国立歴史民俗博物館研究報告 148: 331–56.
Hatano Takao Kenkyūkai 羽田野敬雄研究会, ed. 1994. *Bakumatsu Mikawa-kuni kannushi kiroku: Hatano Takao mansai kakidome hikae* 幕末三河国神主記録 : 羽田野敬雄萬歳書留控. Osaka: Seibundō.
Hayami, Akira 速水融. 1997. *Rekishi jinkōgaku no sekai* 歴史人口学の世界. Tokyo: Iwanami Shoten.
Hayami, Akira 速水融. 2001. *Rekishi jinkōgaku de mita Nihon* 歴史人口学で見た日本. Tokyo: Bungei Shunjū.
Hayashi, Makoto 林淳. 1995. "Kinsei tenkanki ni okeru shūkyō hendō" 近世転換期における宗教変動. In *Kinsei, kindai to bukkyō* 近世・近代と仏教, Nihon no bukkyō 日本の仏教 4, edited by Nihon Bukkyō Kenkyūkai 日本仏教研究会, 2–28. Kyoto: Hōzōkan.
Hayashi, Makoto 林淳. 2018. *Shibukawa Harumi* 渋川春海. Nihonshi riburetto, hito 日本史リブレット人 50. Tokyo: Yamakawa.
Hickman, Money L. 1996. *Japan's Golden Age: Momoyama*. New Haven and London: Yale University Press.
Hikino, Kyōsuke 引野亨輔. 2008. "Kinsei gōki no chiiki shakai ni okeru 'shinbutsu bunri' sōdō" 近世後期の地域社会における「神仏分離」騒動. In *Minshū no 'chi' to shūkyō* 民衆の〈知〉と宗教, Kinsei no shūkyō to shakai 近世の宗教と社会 3, 160–85. Tokyo: Yoshikawa Kōbunkan.
Hirai, Shōko 平井昌子. 2015. "Shūmon ninbetsu aratamechō no kisai keishiki: kisai sareta kazoku o yomu" 宗門人別改帳の記載形式 : 記載された家族を読む. In *Tokugawa*

Nihon no kazoku to chiikisei: rekishi jinkōgaku to no taiwa 徳川日本の家族と地域性：歴史人口学との対話, edited by Ochiai Emiko 落合恵美子, 435–59. Kyoto: Minerva Shobō.

Hirakawa, Arata 平川新. 2010. "Spein no tainichi senryaku to Ieyasu, Masamune no gaikō" スペインの対日戦略と家康・政宗の外交. *Kokushi danwakai zasshi* 国史談話会雑誌 50: 193–209.

Hirakawa, Arata 平川新. 2018. "Spein to Porutogaru no Nihon seifukuron o megutte" スペインとポルトガルの日本征服論をめぐって. *Rekishi hōron* 歴史評論 815: 70–87.

Hōjō, Ujinaga 北条氏長. 1907. "Kirishitoki" 契利斯督記. In *Zokuzoku gunsho ruijū, dai 12: Shūkyōbu* 続々群書類従 第十二：宗教部, edited by Ichijima Kenkichi 市島謙吉, 626–68. Tokyo: Kokusho Kankōkai.

Hoshino, Seiji 星野靖二. 2014. "Meiji kokka to Kirisutokyō" 明治国家とキリスト教. In *Shōgun to tennō* 将軍と天皇, Shirīzu Nihonjin to shūkyō: kinsei kara kindai e シリーズ日本人と宗教：近世から近代へ 1, edited by Shimazono Susumu 島薗進 et al, 237–67. Tokyo: Shunjūsha.

Hōzawa, Naohide 朴澤直秀. 2015. "Jidan kankei to sōsai bukkyō" 寺檀関係と葬祭仏教. In *Sei to shi* 生と死, Shirīzu Nihonjin to shūkyō: kinsei kara kindai e シリーズ日本人と宗教：近世から近代へ 3, edited by Shimazono Susumu 島薗進 et al, 25–51. Tokyo: Shunjūsha.

Hunter, Jeffrey. 1989. "The *Fuju Fuse* Controversy in Nichiren Buddhism. The Debate between Busshōin Nichiō and Jakushōin Nichiken." PhD diss., University of Wisconsin.

Hur, Nam-lin. 2007. *Death and Social Order in Tokugawa Japan: Buddhism, Anti-Christianity, and the Danka System*. Cambridge, Mass: Harvard University Asia Center.

Ichimura, Kisaburō 市村其三郎. 1930. "Shinsōsai mondai to sono hatten" 神葬祭問題とその発展. *Shigaku zasshi* 史学雑誌 41 (9): 70–85.

Inawashirochō Hensan Iinkai 猪苗代町史編纂委員会, ed. 1982. *Inawashiro chōshi, rekishihen* 猪苗代町史 歴史編. Inawashiro: Inawashirochō.

Inoue, Hiroshi 井上寛司. 2003. "Kinsei ni okeru Izumo taisha no 'shinbutsu bunri'" 近世における出雲大社の「神仏分離」. *Kokugakuin zasshi* 国学院雑誌 104 (11): 164–76.

Inoue, Tomokatsu 井上智勝. 2005. "Jingi kanrei chōjō Yoshida-ke to shosha negi kannushi hatto 神祇管領長上吉田家と諸社禰宜神主法度." *Shikyō* 史境 50: 38–57.

Inoue, Tomokatsu 井上智勝. 2007a. *Kinsei no jinja to chōtei ken'i* 近世の神社と朝廷権威. Tokyo: Yoshikawa Kōbunkan.

Inoue, Tomokatsu 井上智勝. 2007b. "17 seiki chūkōki no ryōshu kenryoku to ichinomiya, shikinaisha: sono hogo, kenshō seisaku to seitōsei" 一七世紀中後期の領主権力と一宮・式内社：その保護・顕彰政策と正当性. *Nihon shūkyō bunkashi kenkyū* 日本宗教文化史研究 11 (2): 1–18.

Inoue, Tomokatsu 井上智勝. 2008a. "Kinsei kokka kenryoku to shūkyō: kenkyū no shinten o mezashite" 近世国家権力と宗教：研究の進展をめざして. In *Kokka kenryoku to shūkyō* 国家権力と宗教, Kinsei no shūkyō to shakai 近世の宗教と社会 2, edited by Takano Toshihiko 高埜利彦 and Inoue Tomokatsu 井上智勝, 297–310. Tokyo: Yoshikawa Kōbunkan.

Inoue, Tomokatsu 井上智勝. 2008b. "Kinsei jinja tsūshi kō 近世神社通史稿." *Kokuritsu rekishi minzoku hakubutsukan kenkyū hōkoku* 国立歴史民俗博物館研究報告 148: 269–87.

Inoue, Tomokatsu 井上智勝. 2009. "Kanbun 9 nen shikinen sengū: jingū ni okeru shinbutsu bunri to bakuhan kenryokusha no shisō" 寛文九年式年遷宮：神宮における神仏分離と幕藩権力者の思想. In *Dai 62 kai shikinen sengū kinen (tokubetsu ten): Ise jingū to kamigami no bijutsu* 第 62 回式年遷宮記念 特別展：伊勢神宮と神々の美術, 162–4. Tokyo: Kasumi Kaikan.

Inoue, Tomokatsu 井上智勝. 2013. *Yoshida shintō no 400 nen: Kami to aoi no kinsei-shi* 吉田神道の四百年：神と葵の近世史. Tokyo: Kōdansha.

Inoue, Tomokatsu 井上智勝. 2017. "Shinkoku to chūka: enbu e no dōtei to kunkai" 神国と中華：偃武への道程と訓戒. *Nihon shisō-shi kenkyūkai kaihō* 日本思想史研究会会報 33: 1–11.

Ishikawa, Tatsuya 石川達也. 2013. "Shirakawa-ke no shashi kansen to ikai shissō" 白川家の社祠勧遷と位階執奏. *Shūkyō kenkyū* 宗教研究 86 (4): 74–6.

Ishino, Kōji 石野浩司. 2011. "Shirakawa hakke 'maiasa godaihai' no seiritsu: saishi daikōken o meguru 'Hasshinden' no tenkai 白川伯家「毎朝御代拝」の成立：祭祀代行権をめぐる「八神殿」の展開." *Kōgakkan daigaku shintō kenkyūjo kiyō* 皇学館大学神道研究所紀要 27: 61–93.

Itō, Hiroshi 伊藤裕. 1973. *Taigaku Hirata Atsutane den* 大壑平田篤胤伝. Tokyo: Kinshōsha.

Itō, Tasaburō 伊東多三郎. 1968. "Shūkyō no tōsei to kirishitan" 宗教の統制と切支丹. In *Mito-shi shi, chūkan* 水戸市史　中巻 1, edited by Itō Tasaburō 伊東多三郎, 807–35. Mito: Mito-shiyakusho.

Izumi-shi Shihensan Iinkai 和泉市史編纂委員会, ed. 2011. *Ikedadani no rekishi to kaihatsu* 池田谷の歴史と開発. Izumi-shi no rekishi 和泉市の歴史 3. Izumi: Izumi-shi.

Jaffe, Richard M. 2001. *Neither Monk nor Layman: Clerical Marriage in Modern Japanese Buddhism*. Princeton, NJ: Princeton University Press.

Kageyama, Gyōō 影山堯雄. 1956. "Fujufuse no hōnan narabi ni ryūsō seikatsu ni tsuite" 不受不施の法難並びに流僧生活について. In *Nichiren fujufuse-ha no kenkyū* 日蓮不受不施派の研究, edited by Kageyama Gyōō, 142–98. Kyoto: Heirakuji Shoten.

Kaizu, Ichirō 海津一朗. 1994. *Chūsei no henkaku to tokusei* 中世の変革と徳政. Tokyo: Yoshikawa Kōbunkan.

Kasahara, Kazuo, ed. 2001. *A History of Japanese Religion*. First edition. Tokyo: Kosei Publishing Company.

Kasai, Sukeharu 笠井助治. 1970. *Kinsei hankō ni okeru gakutō gakuha no kenkyū* 近世藩校に於ける学統学派の研究. Vol. 2. Tokyo: Yoshikawa Kōbunkan.

Kataoka, Rumiko. 1998. "Fundação e organização da Misericordia de Nagasáqui." In *Misericordias: cinco Séculos*, 111–20. Oceanos 35. Lisbon: Comissão Nacional para as Comemorações dos Descobrimentos Portugueses.

Kataoka, Yakichi 片岡弥吉. 1970. *Nagasaki no junkyōsha* 長崎の殉教者. Tokyo: Kadokawa Shoten.

Kataoka, Yakichi 片岡弥吉. 1972. "Ōmura-han Koori kuzure ikken kaidai" 大村藩郡崩れ一件解題. In *Nihon shomin seikatsu shiryō shūsei* 日本庶民生活史料集成, 18: 709–59. Tokyo: San'ichi Shobō.

Kataoka, Yakichi 片岡弥吉, Tamamuro Fumio 圭室文雄, and Oguri Junko 小栗純子. 1974. *Kinsei no chika shinkō: Kakure kirishitan, kakure daimoku, kakure nenbutsu* 近世の地下信仰：かくれキリシタン・かくれ題目・かくれ念仏. Tokyo: Hyōronsha

Katō, Genchi 加藤玄智. 1931. *Honpō seishi no kenkyū: seishi no shijitsu to sono shinri bunseki* 本邦生祠の研究：生祠の史実と其心理分析. Tokyo: Meiji Seitoku Kinen Gakkai.

Kenney, Elizabeth. 2000. "Shinto Funerals in the Edo Period." *Japanese Journal of Religious Studies* 27 (3–4): 239–71.

Kinoshita, Futoshi 木下太志. 2002. *Kindaika izen no Nihon no jinkō to kazoku: Ushinawareta sekai kara no tegami* 近代化以前の日本の人口と家族：失われた世界からの手紙. Kyoto: Minerva Shobō.

Kishino, Toshihiko 岸野俊彦. 1979. "Mikawa Hirata-ha kokugakusha: Takeo Masatomo, Masahiro, Masatane oboegaki" 三河平田は国学者：竹尾正韜・正寛・正胤覚書.

Nagoya jiyū gakuin tanki daigaku kenkyū kiyō 名古屋自由学院短期大学研究紀要 11: 22–58.

Kishino, Toshihiko 岸野俊彦. 1980. "Watanabe Masaka oboegaki: Kasei-ki o chūshin ni 渡辺政香覚書：化政期を中心に." *Nagoya jiyū gakuin tanki daigaku kenkyū kiyō* 名古屋自由学院短期大学研究紀要 12: 53–76.

Kitajima, Masamoto 北島正元. 1974. "Tokugawa Ieyasu no shinkakuka ni tsuite" 徳川家康の神格化について. Kokushigaku 国史学 94: 1–13.

Kojima, Tsuyoshi 小島毅. 2018. *Tennō to jukyō shisō: dentō wa ika ni tsukurareta no ka?* 天皇と儒教思想：伝統はいかに創られたのか？ Tokyo: Kōbunsha.

Koike, Susumu 小池進. 2017. *Hoshina Masayuki* 保科正之. Tokyo: Yoshikawa Kōbunkan.

Kokugakuin Daigaku Nihon Bunka Kenkyūjo 國學院大学日本文化研究所, ed. 1995. *Shinsōsai shiryō shūsei* 神葬祭資料集成. Tokyo: Perikan.

Kokuritsu Rekishi Minzoku Hakubutsukan 国立歴史民俗博物館, ed. 2007. *Hirata Atsutane kankei shiryō mokuroku* 平田篤胤関係資料目録. Sakura-shi: Rekishi Minzoku Hakubutsukan Shinkōkai.

Kondō, Keigo 近藤啓吾. 1997a. "Mito no sōrei: Mito Tokugawa-ke no sōgi shidai to funbo no sei" 水戸の葬礼：水戸徳川家の葬儀次第と墳墓の制. In *Shinsōsai daijiten* 神葬祭大事典, edited by Katō Takahisa 加藤隆久, 344–63. Tokyo: Ebisu Kōshō Shuppan.

Kondō, Keigo 近藤啓吾. 1997b. "Tokugawa Mitsukuni no sōrei 徳川光圀の葬礼." In *Shinsōsai daijiten* 神葬祭大事典, edited by Katō Takahisa 加藤隆久, 46–9. Tokyo: Ebisu Kōshō Shuppan.

Kondō, Yoshihiro 近藤喜博. 1972. *Shirakawa-ke monjinchō* 白川家門人帳. Osaka: Seibundō.

Konkō, Hideko 金光英子. 2013. "Shokoku monjin-chō ni miru Shirakawa-ke no monjin" 諸国門人帳に見る白川家の門人. *Shūkyō kenkyū* 宗教研究 86 (4): 72–4.

Kōno, Seizō 河野省三. 1952. *Kuji taisei-kyō ni kan-suru kenkyū* 旧事大成経に関する研究. Tokyo: Geiensha.

Kouamé, Nathalie. 2005. *Le sabre et l'encens. Ou comment les fonctionnaires du fief de Mito présentent dans un «Registre des destructions» daté de l'an 1666 l'audacieuse politique religieuse de leur seigneur Tokugawa Mitsukuni*. Paris: Collège de France, Bibliothèque de l'Institut des Hautes Études Japonaises.

Kudamatsu, Kazunori 久田松和則. 2004. *Ise oshi to danna: Ise shinkō no kaitakusha-tachi* 伊勢御師と旦那：伊勢信仰の開拓者たち. Tokyo: Kōbundō.

Kudamatsu, Kazunori 久田松和則. 2008. *Kirishitan denraichi no jinja to shinkō: Hizen no kuni Ōmura-ryō no baai* キリシタン伝来地の神社と信仰：肥前国大村領の場合. Ōmura: Tomatsu Jinja Saiko Yonhyakunen Jigyō Iinkai.

Kurachi, Katsunao 倉地克直. 1983. "Okayama-han ni okeru shūmon aratame ni tsuite: shinshoku-uke kara tera-uke e" 岡山藩における宗門改について：神職請から寺請へ. In *Okayama no rekishi to bunka* 岡山の歴史と文化, edited by Fujii Shun Sensei Kiju Kinenkai 藤井駿先生喜寿記念会, 304–31. Okayama: Fukutake Shoten.

Kurachi, Katsunao 倉地克直. 2012. *Ikeda Mitsumasa: gakumonsha to shite jinseigyō mo naku sōraeba* 池田光政：学問者として仁政行もなく候へば. Kyoto: Minerva Shobō.

Kurakazu, Masae 倉員正江. 2012. "Mito-han ni okeru sōsai girei ni tsuite ichi kōsatsu: Tokugawa Mitsukuni no sōsai, byōsei o chūshin ni" 水戸藩における葬祭儀礼についての一考察：徳川光圀の葬祭・廟制を中心に. *Ningen kagaku kenkyū* 人間科学研究 9: 287–271.

Lejarza, F., and D. Schilling. 1933. "Relación del reino de Nippon por Bernardino de Avila Girón (C.1618)." *Archivo Ibero-Americano* 36: 481–531.

Maeda, Hiromi. 2002. "Court Rank for Village Shrines: The Yoshida House's Interactions with Local Shrines during the Mid-Tokugawa Period." *Japanese Journal of Religious Studies* 29 (3/4): 325–58.

Mase, Kumiko 間瀬久美子. 1985. "Bakuhansei kokka ni okeru jinja sōron to chōbaku kankei: Yoshida, Shirakawa sōron o chūshin ni" 幕藩制国家における神社争論と朝幕関係：吉田・白川争論を中心に. *Nihonshi kenkyū* 日本史研究 277.

Matsudaira Kōekikai 松平公益会, ed. 1964. *Takamatsu-hanso Matsudaira Yorishige-den* 高松藩祖松平頼重傳. Takamatsu: Matsudaira Kōekikai.

Matsuura, Akira 松浦昭. 2015. "Shihai keitai to shūmon aratamechō kisai: Echizen no kuni o chūshin toshite" 支配形態と宗門改帳記載：越前の国を中心として. In *Tokugawa Nihon no kazoku to chiikisei: rekishi jinkōgaku to no daiwa* 徳川日本の家族と地域性：歴史人口学との対話, edited by Ochiai Emiko 落合恵美子, 411–33. Kyoto: Minerva Shobō.

Matsuyama-shi shi 松山市史. Vol. 2. Matsuyama: Matsuyama-shi.

McMullen, James. 1999. *Idealism, Protest, and the Tale of Genji: The Confucianism of Kumazawa Banzan (1619–91)*. Oxford: Clarendon Press.

McMullen, James. 2020. *The Worship of Confucius in Japan*. Cambridge, Massachusetts: Harvard University Asia Center. Appendices online via https://ora.ox.ac.uk/objects/uuid:a9f555ec-2e47-4db9-8841-e0bd95602da3.

McMullin, Neil. 1984. *Buddhism and the State in Sixteenth-Century Japan*. Princeton: Princeton University Press.

McNally, Mark. 2005. *Proving the Way: Conflict and Practice in the History of Japanese Nativism*. Cambridge, MA: Harvard University Asia Center.

Mita, Satoko 三田智子. 2012. "Shinoda myōjinsha to Shinoda-gō: Hōreki-ki no shasō, shake, ujiko kan sōron" 信太明神社と信太郷：宝暦期の社僧・社家・氏子間争論. *Shidai Nihonshi* 市大日本史 15: 43–65.

Mitamura, Engyo 三田村鳶魚. 1941. "Taisei-kyō gaku no dentō" 大成経学の伝統. *Dainichi* 大日 239: 26–31.

Miyaji, Harukuni 宮地治邦. 1958. "Yoshida shintō saikyojō no juju ni tsuite" 吉田神道裁許状の授受について. *Shintōgaku* 神道学 19: 58–65.

Miyazaki, Eishū 宮崎英修. 1959. *Kinsei fujufuse-ha no kenkyū* 禁制不受不施派の研究. Kyoto: Heirakuji Shoten.

Miyazaki, Eishū 宮崎英修. 1969. *Fujufuse-ha no genryū to tenkai* 不受不施派の源流と展開. Kyoto: Heirakuji Shoten.

Miyazaki, Fumiko, Kate Wildman Nakai, and Mark Teeuwen. 2020. *Christian Sorcerers on Trial: Records of the 1827 Osaka Incident*. New York: Columbia University Press.

Mizuno, Kyōichirō 水野恭一郎. 1975. "Bizen-han ni okeru shinshoku-uke seido ni tsuite" 備前藩における神職請制度について. In *Buke jidai no seiji to bunka* 武家時代の政治と文化, 242–71. Osaka: Sōgensha.

Mizuno, Kyōichirō 水野恭一郎. 1982. "Okayama-han shinshoku-uke seido hokō" 岡山藩神請制度補考. *Ōryō shigaku* 鷹陵史学 8: 236–92.

Morris, James Harry. 2018. "Rethinking the History of Conversion to Christianity in Japan: 1549–1644." PhD diss., University of St. Andrews. http://hdl.handle.net/10023/15875.

Murai, Sanae 村井早苗. 1991. "Bakufu wa naze Kanbun-ki ni shūmon aratamechō o seidoka shita ka" 幕府はなぜ寛文期に宗門改帳を制度化したか. In *Sōten Nihon no rekishi, 5: kinsei hen* 争点日本の歴史：第五巻 近世編, edited by Aoki Michio 青木美智男 and Hosaka Satoru 保坂智, 80–7. Tokyo: Shinjinbutsu Ōraisha.

Murai, Sanae 村井早苗. 2002. *Kirishitan kinsei to minshū no shūkyō* キリシタン禁制と民衆の宗教. Nihonshi riburetto 日本史リブレット 37. Tokyo: Yamakawa Shuppansha.

Murakami, Naojirō 村上直次郎, ed. 1929. *Ikoku ōfuku shokanshū, zōtei ikoku nikkishō* 異国往復書翰集・増訂異国日記抄. Ikoku sōsho 異国叢書 11. Tokyo: Sunnansha.

Nagura, Tetsuzō 奈倉哲三. 1999. *Bakumatsu minshū bunka ibun: Shinshū monto no shiki* 幕末民衆文化異聞：真宗門徒の四季. Rekishi bunka raiburarī 歴史文化ライブラリー 79. Tokyo: Yoshikawa Kōbunkan.

Nagasaki bugyōjo (Tateyama yakusho) ato 長崎奉行所（立山役所）跡. 1998. Nagasaki-ken bunkazai chōsa hōkokusho 長崎県文化財調査報告書 146. Nagasaki: Nagasaki-ken Kyōiku Iinkai.

Nagasaki-shi shi: chishihen butsuji bu 長崎市史：地誌編仏寺部. 1923. 2 vols. Nagasaki: Nagasaki Shiyakusho.

Nagasaki-shi shi: chishihen jinja kyōkai bu 長崎市史：地誌編神社教會部. 1929. 2 vols. Nagasaki: Nagasaki Shiyakusho.

Nagoya, Tokimasa 名越時正. 1986. *Mito Mitsukuni* 水戸光圀. Tokyo: Kinseisha.

Nakai, Kate Wildman. 1980. "The Naturalization of Confucianism in Tokugawa Japan: The Problem of Sinocentrism." *Harvard Journal of Asiatic Studies* 40 (1): 157–99.

Nakamura, Kōya 中村孝也. 1960. *Tokugawa Ieyasu monjo no kenkyū, gekan no ichi* 徳川家康文書の研究・下巻の一. Tokyo: Nihon Gakujutsu Shinkōkai.

Nakamura, Tadashi 中村質. 1988. *Kinsei Nagasakishi bōeki no kenkyū* 近世長崎貿易史の研究. Tokyo: Yoshikawa Kōbunkan.

Nakamura, Tsukō 中村士, and Yoshida Tadashi 吉田忠, eds. 2016. "Shōtokushū, Shibukawa Harumi botsugo 300 shūnen: Shibukawa Harumi kenkyū no shintenkai ni mukete" 小特集、渋川春海没後300周年：渋川春海研究の新展開に向けて. *Kagakushi kenkyū* 科学史研究 276.

Nakagawa, Kazuaki 中川和明. 2004. "Hirata Atsutane no 'Zoku shintō taii' no keisei to kankō" 平田篤胤の『俗神道大意』の形成と刊行. *Tōyō bunka* 東洋文化 93: 30–42.

Nam, Gi-hak 南基鶴. 1996. *Mōko shūrai to Kamakura bakufu* 蒙古襲来と鎌倉幕府. Kyoto: Rinsen Shoten.

Narimatsu, Saeko 成松佐恵子. 2000. *Shōya nikki ni miru Edo no sesō to kurashi* 庄屋日記にみる江戸の世相と暮らし. Kyoto: Minerva Shobō.

Nelson, John K. 1996. *A Year in the Life of a Shinto Shrine*. Seattle: University of Washington Press.

Nichirenshū jiten 日蓮宗事典 (NJ), 1981. Tokyo: Nichirenshū Shūmuin.

Nishida, Nagao 西田長男. 1978. "Sankyō shiyō kajitsu setsu no seiritsu" 三教枝葉花実説の成立. In *Nihon shintōshi kenkyū* 日本神道史研究 4, by Nishida Nagao 西田長男. Tokyo: Kōdansha.

Nishida, Nagao 西田長男. 1979. *Nihon shintōshi kenkyū 6, kinsei-hen, jō* 日本神道史研究6 近世編 上. Tokyo: Kōdansha.

Nishioka, Kazuhiko 西岡和彦. 2002. *Kinsei Izumo-taisha no kisoteki kenkyū* 近世出雲大社の基礎的研究. Tōkyō: Taimeidō.

Nomura, Gen 野村玄. 2006. *Nihon kinsei kokka no kakuritsu to tennō* 日本近世国家の確立と天皇. Osaka: Seibundo.

Nomura, Gen 野村玄. 2015. *Tenkabito no shinkakuka to tennō* 天下人の神格化と天皇. Kyoto: Shibunkaku.

Nosco, Peter. 1993. "Secrecy and the Transmission of Tradition: Issues in the Study of the 'Underground' Christians." *Japanese Journal of Religious Studies* 20 (1): 3–29.

Nosco, Peter. 1994. "Japanese Policy toward Religions in the 'Christian' Century." In *O Século Cristão Do Japão. Actas Co Colóquio Internacional Comemorativo Dos 450 Anos de Amizade Portugal-Japão (1543–1993)*, edited by Roberto Carneiro and Teodore de

Matos, 569–73. Lisbon: Instituto de Historia de Além-mar, Universidade Nova de Lisboa.

Nosco, Peter. 2018. "Secrecy and Privacy in Religious Faith and Practice." In *Individuality in Early Modern Japan*, edited by Peter Nosco, 61–79. New York: Routledge.

Ōhashi, Yukihiro. 2009. "Orthodoxie, Hétérodoxie et Kirishitan: Maintien de l'ordre et prohibition du christianisme dans le Japon moderne." Translated by Nathalie Kouamé. *Histoire et missions chrétiennes* 11: 131–60.

Ōhashi, Yukihiro 大橋幸泰. 2001. *Kirishitan minshūshi no kenkyū* キリシタン民衆史の研究. Tokyo: Tōkyōdō Shuppan.

Ōhashi, Yukihiro 大橋幸泰. 2014. *Senpuku kirishitan: Edo jidai no kinkyō seisaku to minshū* 潜伏キリシタン：江戸時代の禁教政策と民衆. Tokyo: Kōdansha.

Ōhashi, Yukihiro 大橋幸泰. 2016. "16–17 seiki Nihon ni okeru Kirishitan no juyō, kinsei, senpuku" 16–17世紀日本におけるキリシタンの受容・禁制・潜伏. *Kokubungaku kenkyū shiryōkan kiyō, ākaibuzu, kenkyūhen* 国文学研究資料館紀要　アーカイブズ研究編 12: 123–34.

Ōhashi, Yukihiro 大橋幸泰. 2017. *Kinsei senpuku shūkyō ron: Kirishitan to kakushi nenbutsu* 近世潜伏宗教論：キリシタンと隠し念仏. Tokyo: Azekura Shobō.

Ōishi, Shinzaburō 大石慎三郎. 1968. *Kinsei sonraku kōzō to ieseido* 近世村落構造と家制度. Tokyo: Ochanomizu Shobō.

Oka, Kōzō 岡宏三. 2013. "Fukko zōei no kunō" 復古造営の苦悩. In *Heisei no daisengū: Izumo taisha ten* 平成の大遷宮：出雲大社展, edited by Shimane Kenritsu Kodai Izumo Rekishi Hakubutsukan 島根県立古代出雲歴史博物館, 110–13. Matsue: Hābesuto.

Okano, Tomohiko 岡野友彦. 2018. *Genji chōja: buke seiken no keibu* 源氏長者：武家政権の系譜. Tokyo: Yoshikawa Kōbunkan.

Okayama Kenshi Hensan Iinkai 岡山県史編纂委員会. 1984. *Okayama kenshi dai 6 kan, kinsei 1* 岡山県史第6巻　近世1. Okayama: San'yō Shinbunsha.

Okumura, Yasuyuki 奥村保之, and Seishō Suzuki 鈴木政証, eds. 1917. *Jigo keishi roku* 事語継志録. Nihon ijin genkō shiryō 日本偉人言行資料 2. Tokyo: Kokushi Kenkyūkai.

Ōkuwa, Hitoshi 大桑斉, and Maeda Ichirō 前田一郎. 2006. *Razan, Teitoku Ju-butsu mondō: chūkai to kenkyū* 羅山・貞徳『儒仏問答』：註解と研究. Tokyo: Perikansha.

Ōnishi, Gen'ichi 大西源一. 1960. *Daijingū shiyō* 大神宮史要. Tokyo: Heibonsha.

Ooms, Herman. 1985. *Tokugawa Ideology: Early Constructs, 1570–1680*. Princeton: Princeton University Press.

Ōta, Masahiro 太田正弘. 1974. "Atsuta daigūji Senshū-ke ridan no keika ni tsuite" 熱田大宮司千秋家離檀の経過について. *Kokugakuin zasshi* 国学院雑誌 75 (7): 13–19.

Pacheco, Diego. 1977. "Iglesias de Nagasaki durante el siglo cristiano 1568–1620." *Boletín de la asociación Española de Orientalistas* 13: 49–70.

Pickl-Kolaczia, Brigitte. 2018. "The Bunkyū Restoration: The Restoration of Imperial Tombs and Re-Design of Imperial Ancestor Worship." *Vienna Journal of East Asian Studies* 9 (1): 201–34. https://doi.org/10.2478/vjeas-2017-0007.

Rambelli, Fabio. 1996. "Religion, Ideology of Domination, and Nationalism: Kuroda Toshio on the Discourse of Shinkoku." *Japanese Journal of Religious Studies* 23 (3/4): 387–426.

Ramos, Martin Nogueira. 2019. "Renier sa foi sans perdre son âme. Les catholiques japonais au début de la proscription (XVIIe s.)." *Cahiers d'études des cultures Ibériques et Latino-Américaines* 5: 177–204.

Rekishigaku Kenkyūkai 歴史学研究会, ed. 2013. *21 seiki no sekai e: Nihon to sekai, 16 seiki igo* 21世紀の世界へ：日本と世界　16世紀以後. Sekaishi shiryō 世界史史料 12. Tokyo: Iwanami Shoten.

Risshō Daigaku Nichiren Kyōgaku Kenkyūjo 立正大学日蓮教学研究所, ed. 1984. *Nichiren kyōdan zenshi* 日蓮教団全史. Kyoto: Heirakuji Shoten.

Roberts, Luke Shepherd. 2012. *Performing the Great Peace: Political Space and Open Secrets in Tokugawa Japan*. Honolulu, University of Hawai'i Press.

Ruiz de Medina, Juan, ed. 1999. *Martiriologio De Japón*. Rome: Institutum Historicum Societatis Iesu.

Sakamoto, Koremaru 阪本是丸. 1994. *Kokka shintō keisei katei no kenkyū* 国家神道形成過程の研究. Tokyo: Iwanami Shoten.

Sakamoto, Yukio 坂本幸男. 1956. "Bukkyōgaku yori mitaru Ōshi no shisō" 仏教学より見たる奥師の思想. In *Nichiren fujufuse-ha no kenkyū* 日蓮不受不施派の研究, edited by Kageyama Gyōō 影山堯雄, 57–76. Kyoto: Heirakuji Shoten.

Sasaki, Shokaku 佐々木章格. 2010. "Mito kaikichō ni miru Sōtōshū jiin ni tsuite" 水戸開基帳にみる曹洞宗寺院について. *Indogaku bukkyōgaku kenkyū* 印度学仏教学研究 30 (1): 235–37.

Satō, Hiroo 佐藤弘夫. 1998. *Kami, hotoke, ōken no chūsei* 神・仏・王権の中世. Kyoto: Hōzōkan.

Satō, Masato 佐藤真人. 1992. "Kinsei shake no Yoshida shintō juyō: Hie shashi no jirei o megutte" 近世社家の吉田神道受容：日吉社司の事例をめぐって. *Ōkurayama ronsō* 大倉山論叢 33: 107–52.

Sawyer, Ralph D., trans. 1993. *The Seven Military Classics of Ancient China*. Boulder, CO: Westview Press.

Scheid, Bernhard. 2001. *Der eine und einzige Weg der Götter: Yoshida Kanetomo und die Erfindung des Shinto*. Vienna: Verlag der Österreichischen Akademie der Wissenschaften.

Scheid, Bernhard. 2002. "Shinto as a Religion for the Warrior Class: The Case of Yoshikawa Koretaru." *Japanese Journal of Religious Studies* 29 (3/4): 299–324.

Scheid, Bernhard. 2003. "'Both Parts' or 'Only One'? Challenges to the Honji Suijaku Paradigm in the Edo Period." In *Buddhas and Kami in Japan: Honji Suijaku as a Combinatory Paradigm*, edited by Mark Teeuwen and Fabio Rambelli, 204–21. London: Routledge.

Scheid, Bernhard. 2004. "Overcoming Taboos on Death: The Limited Possibilities of Discourse on the Afterlife in Shinto." In *Practicing the Afterlife: Perspectives from Japan*, edited by Susanne Formanek and William LaFleur, 205–30. Vienna: Verlag der Österreichischen Akademie der Wissenschaften.

Schütte, Franz Josef. 1968. *Introductio ad Historiam Societatis Iesu in Iaponia 1549–1650*. Rome: Institutum Historicum Societatis Iesu.

Schweizer, Anton. 2016. *Ōsaki Hachiman: Architecture, Materiality, and Samurai Power*. Berlin: Reimer.

Shibata, Atsushi 柴田篤, and Hentona Tomokuni 辺土名朝邦, eds. 1983. *Nakamura Tekisai, Muro Kyūsō* 中村惕斎・室鳩巣. Sōsho, Nihon no shisōka, jugaku-hen 叢書・日本の思想家，儒学篇 11. Tokyo: Meitoku Shuppan.

Shimane-ken Kodai Bunka Sentā 島根県古代文化センター, ed. 2013. *Izumo-taisha no Kanbun zōei ni tsuite: taisha go-zōei nikki no kenkyū* 出雲大社の寛文造営について：大社御造営日記の研究. Matsue: Shimane-ken Kodai Bunka Sentā.

Shimizu, Hirokazu 清水紘一. 1976. "Shūmon aratameyaku nōto" 宗門改役ノート. *Kirisutokyō shigaku* キリスト教史学 30: 42–56.

Shimizu, Hirokazu 清水紘一. 1981. *Kirishitan kinseishi* キリシタン禁制史. Kyōikusha rekishi shinsho. Nihonshi 教育社歴史新書．日本史 109. Tokyo: Kyōikusha.

Shimizu, Hirokazu 清水紘一. 1994. "Koori kuzure kō: Kanbun-ki shūmon aratame-sei e no tenbō" 郡崩れ考：寛文期宗門改制への展望. *Nihon rekishi* 日本歴史 554: 62–78.

Shimizu, Yūko 清水有子. 2017. "Toyotomi Hideyoshi seiken no shinkoku sengen: bateren tsuihōrei no kihonteki seikaku to Hideyoshi no shūkyō seisaku o fumaete" 豊臣秀吉政権の神国宣言：伴天連追放令の基本的性格と秀吉の宗教政策を踏まえて. *Rekishigaku kenkyū* 歴史学研究 958: 2–13.

Shimura, Kunihiro 志村有弘, annot. 1989. *Shimabara gassen ki* 島原合戦記. Kyōikusha shinsho, genpon gendaiyaku 教育社新書，原本現代訳 37. Tokyo: Kyōikusha.

Shimonaka, Kunihiko 下中邦彦, ed. 1982. *Ibaraki-ken no chimei* 茨城県の地名. Nihon reikishi chimei taikei 日本歴史地名大系 8. Tokyo: Heibonsha.

Shin Nagasaki-shi shi 新長崎市史. 2012–14. 4 vols. Nagasaki: Nagasaki-shi Shihensan Iinkai.

Shiraki, Yutaka 白木豊. 1931. *Shizutani seidō sekisai no gi ni tsukite* 閑谷聖堂釋菜之儀に就きて. Okayama-ken, Wake-gun: Shiraki Yutaka.

Shizutani Gakkō Shihensan Iinkai 閑谷学校史編纂委員会, ed. 1971. *Shizutani gakkō shi* 閑谷学校史. Bizen: Shizutani Gakkō Shi Kankōkai.

Shu, Zenan. 2009. "Cultural and Political Encounters with Chinese Language in Early Modern Japan: The Case of Kinoshita Jun'an." D.Phil. thesis, Oxford: University of Oxford.

Sone, Masato 曽根正人. 2009. "Review of Heianki no gammon to bukkyōteki sekaikan" 平安期の願文と仏教的世界観 by Kudō Miwako 工藤美和子. *Nihonshi kenkyū* 日本史研究 567: 48–54.

Sonehara, Satoshi 曽根原理. 1995. "Shinkoku shisō" 神国思想. In *Nihon chūsei kenkyū jiten* 日本中世史研究事典, 148. Tokyo: Tōkyōdō Shuppan.

Sonehara, Satoshi 曽根原理. 2005. "Tokugawa Ieyasu nenki gyōji ni arawareta shinkoku ishiki" 徳川家康年忌行事にあらわれた神国意識. *Nihonshi kenkyū* 日本史研究 510: 92–119.

Sonehara, Satoshi 曽根原理. 2008. *Shinkun Ieyasu no tanjō: Tōshōgū to gongensama* 神君家康の誕生：東照宮と権現様. Rekishi bunka raiburarī 歴史文化ライブラリー 256. Tokyo: Yoshikawa Kōbunkan.

Sonehara, Satoshi 曽根原理. 2012. "Kirishitan, Tōshō shinkun, tennō" キリシタン・東照神君・天皇. In *Nihon shisō kōza 3, kinsei* 日本思想史講座 3, 近世, edited by Karube Takashi 苅部直, Kurozumi Makoto 黒住真, Satō Hiroo 佐藤弘夫, Sueki Fumihiko 末木文美士, and Tajiri Yūichirō 田尻祐一郎, 33–66. Tokyo: Perikan.

Sonehara, Satoshi 曽根原理. 2013. "Edo-jidai no shūgō shisō: Chōon Dōkai no shintōsetsu o megutte" 江戸時代の習合思想：潮音道海の神道説をめぐって. In *"Shinbutsu shūgō" saikō* 「神仏習合」再考 = *Rethinking 'Syncretism' in Japanese Religion*, edited by Lucia Dolce and Mitsuhashi Tadashi 三橋正, 317–37. Tokyo: Bensei Shuppan.

Sonehara, Satoshi 曽根原理. 2018a. "Gongen-sama no 'bukkoku', 'shinkoku'" 権現様の「仏国」「神国」. *Gendai shisō* 現代思想 46 (16): 198–206.

Sonehara, Satoshi 曽根原理. 2018b. "Tōshōgū saishi kara miru Nihon kinsei shūkyō" 東照宮祭祀から見る日本近世宗教. *Shichō* 史潮 83: 17–35.

Sonehara, Satoshi 曽根原理. 2018c. *Tokugawa jidai no itanteki shūkyō: Togakushi-san bettō Jōin no chōsen to zasetsu* 徳川時代の異端的宗教：戸隠山別当乗因の挑戦と挫折. Tokyo: Iwata Shoin.

Stone, Jacqueline I. 1994. "Rebuking the Enemies of the Lotus Sutra: Nichirenist Exclusivism in Historical Perspective." *Japanese Journal of Religious Studies* 21 (2-3): 231–59.

Sueki, Fumihiko 末木文美士. 2010. *Kinsei no bukkyō: hana hiraku shisō to bunka* 近世の仏教：華ひらく思想と文化. Tokyo: Yoshikawa Kōbunkan.

Sugiyama, Shigetsugu 椙山林繼. 1980. "Yoshida-ke Kantō yakusho no sōritsu to shoki no katsudō" 吉田家関東役所の創立と初期の活動. *Kokugakuin daigaku Nihon bunka kenkyūjo kiyō* 國學院大學日本文化研究所紀要 45: 59–106.

Suzuki, Eiichi 鈴木暎一. 2006. *Tokugawa Mitsukuni* 徳川光圀. Tokyo: Yoshikawa Kōbunkan.

Taira, Masayuki 平雅行. 2004. "Shinbutsu to chūsei bunka" 神仏と中世文化. In *Chūsei shakai no kōzō* 中世社会の構造, edited by Rekishigaku kenkyūkai 歴史学研究会 and Nihonshi kenkyūkai 日本史研究会, 167–95. Nihonshi kōza 日本史講座 4. Tokyo: Tōkyō Daigaku Shuppankai.

Taira, Shigemichi 平重道. 1983. "Kaidai" 解題. In *Yoshikawa shintō* 吉川神道, edited by Taira Shigemichi, 5–91. ST, ronsetsu-hen 論説編 10. Tokyo: Iwanami Shoten.

Takagi, Shōsaku 高木昭作. 1992. "Hideyoshi, Ieyasu no shinkokukan to sono keifu: Keichō 18 nen 'Bateren tsuihō no bun' o tegakari toshite" 秀吉・家康の神国観とその系譜：慶長十八年「伴天連追放之文」を手がかりとして. *Shigaku zasshi* 史学雑誌 101 (10): 1–26.

Takagi, Yutaka 高木豊. 1956. "Kanbun hōnan zengo: Fujufuse-shi kenkyū danshō" 寛文法難前後：不受不施史研究断章. In *Nichiren fujufuse-ha no kenkyū* 日蓮不受不施派の研究, edited by Kageyama Gyōō 影山堯雄, 236–67. Kyoto: Heirakuji Shoten.

Takahashi, Hiroshi 高橋裕史. 2012. *Buki, jūjika to sengoku Nihon: Iezusukai senkyōshi to 'tainichi buryoku seifuku keikaku' no shinsō* 武器・十字架と戦国日本：イエズス会宣教師と「対日武力征服計画」の真相. Tokyo: Yōsensha.

Takahashi, Miyuki 高橋美由紀. 1994. *Ise shintō no seiritsu to tenkai* 伊勢神道の成立と展開. Tokyo: Taimeidō.

Takano, Nobuharu 高野信治. 2018. *Bushi shinkakuka no kenkyū* 武士神格化の研究. Tokyo: Yoshikawa Kōbunkan.

Takano, Toshihiko 高埜利彦. 2003. "Edo jidai no jinja seido" 江戸時代の神社制度. In *Genroku no shakai to bunka* 元禄の社会と文化, edited by Takano Toshihiko 高埜利彦, 268–309. Tokyo: Yoshikawa Kōbunkan.

Takase, Kōichirō 高瀬弘一郎. 1977. *Kirishitan jidai no kenkyū* キリシタン時代の研究. Tokyo: Iwanami Shoten.

Takeuchi, Emiko 武内恵美子. 2017. "Okayama han gakkō to Urakami Gyokudō no gagaku chishiki 岡山藩学校と浦上玉堂の雅楽知識." *Nihon dentō ongaku kenkyū* 日本伝統音楽研究 14: 114–30.

Tamamuro, Fumio. 2001. "Local Society and the Temple-Parishioner Relationship within the Bakufu's Governance Structure." Translated by Holly Sanders. *Japanese Journal of Religious Studies* 28 (3/4): 261–92.

Tamamuro, Fumio 圭室文雄. 1968. "Kanbun, Genroku no shaji kaikaku" 寛文・元禄の社寺改革. In *Mito-shi shi, chūkan* 水戸市史 中巻 1, edited by Itō Tasaburō 伊東多三郎, 836–76. Mito: Mito-shiyakusho.

Tamamuro, Fumio 圭室文雄. 1971. *Edo bakufu no shūkyō tōsei* 江戸幕府の宗教統制. Tokyo: Hyōronsha.

Tamamuro, Fumio 圭室文雄. 1974. "Kakure daimoku" かくれ題目. In *Kinsei no chika shinkō: Kakure kirishitan, kakure daimoku, kakure nenbutsu* 近世の地下信仰：かくれキリシタン・かくれ題目・かくれ念仏, edited by Kataoka Yakichi 片岡弥吉, Tamamuro Fumio 圭室文雄, and Oguri Junko 小栗純子, 115–205. Tokyo: Hyōronsha.

Tamamuro, Fumio 圭室文雄. 1988. "Danka seido" だんかせいど. In *Kokushi daijiten* 国史大辞典, 9:329. Tōkyō: Yoshikawa Kōbunkan.

Tamamuro, Fumio 圭室文雄. 1991. "Okayama-han no shintō-uke seido" 岡山藩の神道請制度. In *Shintō no tenkai* 神道の展開, edited by Shimode Sekiyo 下出積与, 125–39. Kōza shintō 講座神道 2. Tokyo: Ōfūsha.

Tamamuro, Fumio 圭室文雄. 1996. "Okayama-han no jisha seiri seisaku ni tsuite" 岡山藩の寺社整理政策について. *Meiji Daigaku jinbun kagaku kenkyūjo kiyo* 明治大学人文科学研究所紀要 40: 363–82.

Tamamuro, Fumio 圭室文雄. 1998. "Keichō 19 nen no terauke shōmon ni tsuite" 慶長十九年の寺請証文について. *Fūzoku shigaku* 風俗史学 2: 2–27.

Tamamuro, Fumio 圭室文雄. 1999. *Sōshiki to danka* 葬式と檀家. Tokyo: Yoshikawa Kōbunkan.

Tamamuro, Fumio 圭室文雄. 2000. "Mito-han ni okeru Hachiman-sha no hakyaku" 水戸藩における八幡社の破却. In *Nihon no fū to zoku* 日本の風と俗, edited by Nihon Fūzokushi Kenkyūkai 日本風俗史研究会, 98–115. Tokyo: Tsukubane-sha.

Tamamuro, Fumio 圭室文雄. 2003. "Edo-jidai no mura chinju no jittai: Mito-hanryō mura chinju no sūryōteki kentō" 江戸時代の村鎮守の実態：水戸藩領村鎮守の数量的検討 *Meiji Daigaku kyōyōronshū* 明治大学教養論集 368: 1–27.

Tanaka, Seiji 田中誠二. 1979. "Kanbun-ki no Okayama hansei: Ikeda Mistsumasa no shūkyō seisaku to chishi no gen'in" 寛文期文の岡山藩政：池田光政の宗教政策と致仕の原因. *Nihonshi kenkyū* 日本史研究 202: 33–67.

Tani, Seigo 谷省吾. 2001. *Suika shintō no seiritsu to tenkai* 垂加神道の成立と展開. Tokyo: Kokusho Kankōkai.

Tanido, Yūki 谷戸佑紀. 2011. "Jingū oshi no rentai ishiki no hōga ni tsuite: Kinsei zenki 'Naikū rokubō deiri' o sozai ni 神宮御師の連帯意識の萌芽について：近世前期「内宮六坊出入」を素材に. *Kōgakkan ronsō* 皇学館論叢 44 (3): 24–45.

Taniguchi, Sumio 谷口澄夫. 1961. *Ikeda Mitsumasa* 池田光政. Tokyo: Yoshikawa Kōbunkan.

Taniguchi, Sumio 谷口澄夫. 1963. "Okayama hansei kakuritsuki ni okeru jisha seisaku" 岡山藩政確立期における寺社政策. In *Chiiki shakai to shukyō no shiteki kenkyū* 地域社会と宗教の史的研究, edited by Ogura Toyofumi 小倉豊文, 157–80. Kyoto: Yanagihara Shoten.

Taniguchi, Sumio 谷口澄夫. 1964. *Okayama hansei-shi no kenkyū* 岡山藩政史の研究. Tokyo: Hanawa Shobō.

Tasaki, Tetsurō 田崎哲郎. 1994. "Kaisetsu" 解説. In *Bakumatsu Mikawa no kuni kannushi kiroku: Hatano Takao mansai kakidome hikae* 幕末三河国神主記録：羽田野敬雄萬歳書留控, edited by Hatano Takao Kenkyūkai 羽田野敬雄研究会, Osaka: Seibundō.

Teeuwen, Mark. 1996. *Watarai Shintō: An Intellectual History of the Outer Shrine of Ise*. Leiden: Research School CNWS.

Teeuwen, Mark, and John Breen. 2017. *A Social History of the Ise Shrines: Divine Capital*. London: Bloomsbury.

Teeuwen, Mark, and Fabio Rambelli, eds. 2003. *Buddhas and Kami in Japan: Honji Suijaku as a Combinatory Paradigm*. London: Routledge.

Thal, Sarah. 2002. "Redefining the Gods: Politics and Survival in the Creation of Modern Kami." *Japanese Journal of Religious Studies* 29 (3/4): 379–404.

Toki, Masanori 土岐昌訓. 1987. "Taisha, shōsha" 大社・小社. In *Kokushi daijiten* 国史大辞典 8: 758–9. Tokyo: Yoshikawa Kōbunkan.

Tomiyama, Kazuyuki 豊見山和行. 2004. *Ryūkyū ōkoku no gaikō to ōken* 琉球王国の外交と王権. Tokyo: Yoshikawa Kōbunkan.

Totman, Conrad D. 1967. *Politics in the Tokugawa Bakufu, 1600–1843*. Cambridge, Mass: Harvard UnivPress.

Tronu, Carla. 2012. "Sacred Space and Ritual in Early Modern Japan: The Christian Community of Nagasaki (1569–1643)." PhD diss., Department of History, School of Oriental & African Studies, University of London.

Tronu, Carla. 2019. "The Post-Tridentine Parish System in the Port City of Nagasaki." In *Catholic Missionaries in Early Modern Asia: Patterns of Localization*, edited by Nadine Amsler, Andreea Badea, Bernard Heyberger, and Christian Windler. London: Routledge.

Tsuji, Zennosuke 辻善之助. 1953. *Nihon bukkyōshi, kinsei-hen* 日本仏教史 近世編 2. Tokyo: Iwanami Shoten.

Tsuji, Zennosuke 辻善之助. 1997. "Shinshoku no ridan mondai ni tsuite" 神職の離檀問題について. In *Shinsōsai daijiten* 神葬祭大事典, edited by Katō Takahisa 加藤隆久, 364–80. Tokyo: Ebisu Kōshō Shuppan.

Tsukamoto, Akira 塚本明. 2010. "Kinsei Ise jingūryō ni okeru shinbutsu kankei ni tsuite" 近世伊勢神宮領における神仏関係について. *Jinbun ronsō* 人文論叢 27: 15–34.

Tsunoda, Ryusaku, William Theodore De Bary, and Donald Keene. 1958. *Sources of Japanese tradition*. New York: Columbia University Press.

Tsutsumi, Teiko 堤禎子. 2001. "Satake-shi to Hachiman shinkō" 佐竹氏と八幡信仰. *Ibaraki rekishikan hō* 茨城県立歴史館報 28: 55–74.

Urai, Shōmei 浦井正明. 1983. *Mō hitotsu no Tokugawa monogatari: shōgunke reibyō no nazo* もうひとつの徳川物語：将軍家霊廟の謎. Tokyo: Seibundō Shinkōsha.

Wakabayashi, Bob Tadashi. 1991. "In Name Only: Imperial Sovereignty in Early Modern Japan." *Journal of Japanese Studies* 17 (1): 25–37.

Watanabe, Hideo 渡辺秀夫. 1995. "Ganmon" 願文. In *Shōdō no bungaku* 唱導の文学, Bukkyō bungaku kōza 仏教文学講座 8, edited by Itō Hiroyuki 伊藤博之, Imanari Genshō 今成元昭, and Yamada Shōzen 山田昭全, 132–59. Tokyo: Bensei Shuppan.

Watanabe, Hōyō 渡辺宝陽. 1976. *Nichirenshū shingyōron no kenkyū* 日蓮宗信行論の研究. Kyoto: Heirakuji Shoten.

Watanabe, Kenji 渡辺憲司. 1997. *Kinsei daimyō bungeiken kenkyū* 近世大名文芸圏研究. Tokyo: Yagi Shoten.

Watanabe, Kinzō 渡邊金造. 1942. *Hirata Atsutane no kenkyū* 平田篤胤の研究. Tokyo: Rokkaku Shobō.

Yamamoto, Hirofumi 山本博文. 1989. *Kan'ei jidai* 寛永時代. Nihon rekishi sōsha 日本歴史叢書 39. Tokyo: Yoshikawa Kōbunkan.

Yamamoto, Nobuki 山本信哉. 1911. *Shintō sōsetsu* 神道叢説. Tokyo: Kokushi Kankōkai.

Yamasawa, Manabu 山澤学. 2012. *Nikkō Tōshōgū no seiritsu: kinsei Nikkōsan no 'shōgon' to saishi, soshiki* 日光東照宮の成立：近世日光山の「荘厳」と祭祀・組織. Kyoto: Shibunkaku Shuppan.

Yokota, Fuyuhiko 横田冬彦. 2014. "Kinsei no mibunsei" 近世の身分制. In *Kinsei* 近世 1. Iwanami kōza, Nihon rekishi 岩波講座 日本歴史 10, edited by Fuji Jōji 藤井讓治 et al., 277–312. Tokyo: Iwanami Shoten.

Yoshida, Asako 吉田麻子. 2012. *Chi no kyōmei: Hirata Atsutane o meguru shobutsu no shakaishi* 知の共鳴：平田篤胤をめぐる書物の社会史. Tokyo: Perikansha.

Yoshida, Atsuhiko 吉田昌彦. 2015. "Tōshōgū shinkō ni kansuru ikkōsatsu: ōkenron ni kanren sasete" 東照宮信仰に関する一考察：王権論に関連させて. *Kyūshū bunkashi kenkyūjo kiyō* 九州文化史研究所紀要 58: 1–79.

Yoshida, Toshizumi 吉田俊純. 1995. "Tokugawa Mitsukuni no jisha seiri to sonraku" 徳川光圀の寺社整理と村落. *Chihōshi kenkyū* 地方史研究 45 (1): 20–39.

Yoshida, Yuriko 吉田ゆり子. 2000. *Heinō bunri to chiiki shakai* 兵農分離と地域社会. Tokyo: Asekura Shobō.

Zhong, Yijiang. 2016. *The Origin of Modern Shinto in Japan: The Vanquished Gods of Izumo*. London: Bloomsbury.

Contributors

Dr. Yannick Bardy (University of Lille)

Prof. emer. W.J. Boot (Leiden University)

Prof. Hayashi Makoto (Aichi Gakuin University, Nagoya)

Prof. Nam-lin Hur (University of British Columbia)

Prof. Inoue Tomokatsu (Saitama University)

Dr. Stefan Köck (Austrian Academy of Sciences)

Prof. emer. James McMullen (University of Oxford)

Prof. emer. Kate Wildman Nakai (Sophia University, Tokyo)

Brigitte Pickl-Kolaczia, MA (Austrian Academy of Sciences)

Dr. Bernhard Scheid (Austrian Academy of Sciences)

Dr. Sonehara Satoshi (Tohoku University, Sendai)

Prof. emer. Jacqueline I. Stone (Princeton University)

Prof. Mark Teeuwen (University of Oslo)

Dr. Carla Tronu (Kyoto University)

Prof. emer. Anne Walthall (University of California, Irvine)

Index

abandoned temple; see haidera
Age of the Gods; see jindai
aidono 相殿 (associate deity) 144
Aizu 会津 (domain) 4–5, 11–5, 29–30, 91–6, 117, 133–48, 152, 157, 161–2, 163, 173, 178
Aizu jinja-shi 会津神社志 13, 95–8
Aizuhan kasei jikki 会津藩家世実紀 218
Aizu-Wakamatsu 会津若松 (castle) 139–40
Akita 秋田 (domain) 23, 205
All Saints (church; Todos os Santos) 49, 54
amagoi 雨乞 (rain prayer) 192, 194, 197
Amakusa 天草 (region) 84, 227
Amaterasu 天照 (Tenshō Daijin) 14, 40, 111, 137–8, 143, 209, 217, 222
Ame no Futodama 天太玉 113
Ame no Koyane 天兒屋根 113, 203, 208, 210–1
Ame no Minakanushi 天御中主 206
Amida 阿弥陀 54, 78–80, 94, 155, 220
Anahobe 穴穂部 (prince) 109
Analects 235
ancestor temple; see bodaiji
Andō Yūeki 安藤有益 135–6
Anjūin Nichinen 安住院日念; see Taguchi Heiroku
Ankan Tennō 安閑天皇 111, 232
Ankokuin Nichikō 安国院日講 69, 71
anshitsu 庵室; see hermitage
anshu 庵主 54
Aoki 青木 (family) 57
　　Katakiyo 堅清 57
　　Kensei 賢清 56–57
Aoyama Cemetery 青山墓地 144
apostate (see also korobi) 51, 53, 87
aragaki 荒垣 (fence) 184
Arai Hakuseki 新井白石 106, 222
Arima 有馬 (family) 47, 49, 59
　　Naozumi 直純 50
Aritōshi 蟻通 (shrine) 194–7, 243

Asai Rin'an 浅井琳庵 143
ascetic (see also Shugendō, yamabushi) 58, 69, 85, 88, 180
Ashiarai 足洗 (village) 182
Asukai Masaaki 飛鳥井雅章 209
Atsuta 熱田 (shrine) 30–1, 172
Augustinians 47, 51
Avatar Illuminating the East; see Tōshō Daigongen
Avīci Hell 66
Ávila Girón, Bernardino de 48, 223
Awa (province) 68
Azuchi 安土 (castle) 62
Azuchi shūron 安土宗論 (Azuchi debate) 62, 64

Bhaiṣajyaguru; see Yakushi Nyorai
bakufu 幕府 (shogunate) passim
bakuhan 幕藩 16, 22, 31
Bandai 磐梯 (Mt.) 138
banishment (see exile)
barbarian 97, 100–1, 136, 159
Batavia 42
Bateren tsuihō no bun 伴天連追放之文; see also Hai kirishitan no fumi 218
Bateren tsuihō rei バテレン追放令 36
benevolence; see nin
Betsuki Shōsaemon 別木庄左衛門 120
bettō 別当 (Buddhist supervisor) 10, 185, 192, 195–9, 244
　　bettōji 別当寺 (supervisory temple) 42, 92, 185, 195
Bidatsu Tennō 敏達天皇 109
Bitchū (province) 71
Bizen (province) 71, 169, 172–3
Bo Yi 伯夷 66
bodaiji 菩提寺 (ancestor temple) 39, 42
Bonshun 梵舜 221
bon 盆 festival 125
Book of Rites 227
branch temple; see matsuji

buddha country; see bukkoku
Buddhism passim
   funerary Buddhism; see sōsai bukkyō
   Buddhist icons 9, 191
   Buddhist monk/priest passim
   Buddhist Shinto (see also ryōbu [shūgō] shintō; honji suijaku shintō) 3, 5
   Buddhist supervisor; see bettō
   Buddhist temple patron; see danna, danka
   Buddhists shrine monk; see shasō
budō 武道 (Way of the Warrior) 206–7
bugyō 奉行 (magistrate) 51, 126, 166, 214, 219, 243
buke 武家 186
buke tensō 武家伝奏 209
bukkoku 仏国 (buddha country) 35
Bungo (province) 24
Bungo-machi 豊後町 57
bushi 武士 (warrior nobility) 34, 41, 114, 134–5, 138, 180, 238
Busshō-in Nichiō 仏性院日奥 63–8, 70, 72, 169, 225

Calendar 6, 48, 133–138, 146–147
Carvalho, Diego 23
castle town 59, 120, 156, 180, 183, 187, 212, 242
census register of sectarian inspection (nayosechō; ninbetsuchō; ninjuchō; shūmon ninbetsuchō; shūmon ninbetsu aratamechō) 23–32, 52–3, 69–70, 72, 81–2, 154, 165, 166–71, 178, 219
certificate of sectarian inspection; see shūmon tegata
certification of religious affiliation; see shūmon aratame
cessation of wailing; see sokkoku
Chiken'in Nissen 智見院日暹 65–8
Chikugo (province) 54
China 35–7, 42–3, 59, 95–102, 104–12, 120, 124, 136, 142, 228–9
chinju 鎮守 see tutelary shrine
Chinjuchō 鎮守帳 184–5, 241
chinkonsai 鎮魂祭 204
Chinzei-ha 鎮西派 (branch sect) 80
Chion'in 知恩院 55, 142

chokuganji 勅願持 (imperial prayer temple) 62
Chōon Dōkai 潮音道海 5, 107
Chōon'in Nichiju 長遠院日樹 65–8, 225
Chōshōji 長照寺 56
Chōshū 長州 (domain) 27, 219
Christianity (see also Kirishitan) 1–4, 21–32, 35–7, 43, 47–60, 61, 73, 78, 84–7, 153, 166–7, 177, 218, 221, 223
Chunqiu 春秋 109
civil certification; see zoku-uke
Classic of Filial Piety 125–6
Coelho, Gaspar 36
compassion; see jihi
Confucianism passim
   Confucian funeral; see funeral
   Confucian tutor; see hanju
Confucius 98, 109, 117–31, 229, 234–5
Couros, Matheus de 223
Criminal Judgment Precedents Organized by Category; see Oshioki reiruishū
crypto Christians; see Kirishitan

Daidōji 大道寺 223
Daigakuin 大学院 56
Daigengū 大元宮 245
Daigo Tennō 醍醐天皇 97
Daigoji Sanbōin 醍醐寺三宝院 152
daihonji 大本寺 (superior head temple) 183
daikan 代官 (shogunal intendant; local deputy) 84, 121, 165, 172
daikan gashira 代官頭 164–6,
Daikoin Tōun Shōtetsu Koji 大虚院透雲紹徹居士 146
daimoku 題目 (title of the Lotus Sūtra) 71
daimyo ([domain] lord) passim
   daimyō shōnin seido 大名証人制度 134
Dainichi honkoku 大日本国 (Dainichi's original country) 35
Dainichi Nyorai 大日如来 (Mahāvairocana) 35
Dai-Nihon shi 大日本史 230
Dai-Nihonkoku 大日本国 (Great Japan) 35
Daionji 大音寺 51–5
dairen 大斂 (final laying out; dalian) 140, 236
Daitake 大嶽 (Mt.) 82
Daizōkyō 大蔵経 (Tripiṭaka) 41

dalian 大斂; see dairen
dance 57, 184, 206, 224
danka 檀家; see danna
  danka seido 檀家制度 32, 36
danna 檀那/旦那 (Buddhist temple patron; danka) 10, 26, 31, 154, 159–62, 165, 219
  danna dera 檀那寺 27, 30–2, 178
danrin 檀林 68
Date Masamune 伊達政宗 15, 218
Datong li 大統暦 137
Deguchi Nobuyoshi 出口延佳 98, 100, 159
deification (see also funeral) 1–2, 9, 13–17, 142, 218, 221
deities of heaven and earth; see jingi
deliberative council; see hyōjōsho
Den'yo Kantetsu 伝誉関徹 54–5
Denchū mondō 殿中問答 114, 230
destruction/reduction (of religious buildings; see also haidera) 6–7, 11, 29–30, 47–51, 54, 59, 91, 96, 152, 164, 169–70, 177–83, 186, 189, 224
deviant practice (ihō; ishū) 4, 75–88, 227
deviant theses; see isetsu
display of heads; see gokumon
district magistrate; see koori bugyō
divination 85, 208
divine country; see shinkoku
Doi Toshikatsu 土井利勝 129
domain official in charge of religious matters; see jishakata
domain school; see hankō
Domain Shinto (hanryō shintō) 1–17, 151–62, 163–75, 177–89, 218
Dominicans 47, 51
dōri 道理 135
dōshi 導師 (Buddhist supervisor) 41
Dosui kuyō rei 土水供養令 (Land and Water Offerings Edict) 69
Dutch East Indian Company 42

ebumi 絵踏; see fumie
Echigo (province) 219
Edo-machi 江戸町 (Nagasaki) 51, 57
eight imperial tutelary deities; see Hasshinden
Eitatsu Nittai 叡達日体 68
emperor; see tenno
Engishiki 延喜式 94, 97, 193, 227, 238

Enryakuji 延暦寺 34, 42
eulogy (ganmon; hyōhyaku) 39–42, 222
exile (banishment; see also ontō) 4, 48, 62–71, 76–86, 157, 170, 182–3, 195, 205–7, 211, 227

Fabian Fuçan (Fukansai 不干斎) 226
fields of compassion; see hiden
final laying out; see dairen
first laying out; see shōren
first reading (ritual); see yomizome
first sacrifice of repose; see shogu
Five Agents; see wuxing
Five Constant Virtues (wuchang 五常) 228
five-man group; see goningumi
Five Pillars; see wuzhen
Five Relations (wulun 五倫) 228
Four Books 104, 124
Franciscans 23, 47
Fujian (province) 100–1
Fujinami Ujitomi 藤波氏富 93
Fujisan 富士山 (Mito) 242
Fujiwara Seika 藤原惺窩 104
Fujufuse 不受不施 (branch sect) 3–4, 7, 10, 29, 61–73, 76–87, 123, 169–71, 217, 225–6
fujufuse 不受不施 (no receiving, no giving) 3, 61–73, 169–70, 225
Fukuda 福田 (village) 71
fukuden 福田 (merit fields) 70
Fukuoka 36
fumie 踏絵 (ebumi) 23, 53
Funai 府内 51
Funaoka 船岡 (hill) 242–3
fundraising; see kanjin
funeral 6, 9–10, 14–16, 60, 68, 125, 133–5, 138–40, 143–4
  Confucian funeral 15, 98, 101, 118, 124–5, 127, 140, 142–5
  Shinto funeral (shinsōsai; see also deification) 6–7, 13–5, 30–2, 139–40
Furukawa Mitsura 古川躬行 206
Furukawa-machi 古河町 51
Furu-machi 古町 54
Furuya 古谷 (family) 193, 196, 243
  Rokuemon 六右衛門 196, 200
Fushimi Inari 伏見稲荷 (shrine) 204

Fusō gobusshin ron 扶桑護仏神論 107–14
Futaarayama 二荒山 (shrine) 94
Futamata 二俣 (shrine) 92

gakudō 学道 153, 236
Gakuenji 鰐淵寺 155, 158
gakushi 学士 (scholar gentleman) 232
gakushi 学師 (scholar teacher) 205, 206, 210, 211
ganmon 願文; see eulogy
Gantan shihitsu 元旦試筆 117
Gentō hikki 玄桐筆記 240
Gion 祇園 (village) 171
Goa 36–7
gōbyō bugyō 御廟奉行 121
gōgaku 郷学 (rural commoners' school) 130
gohei 御幣 (ritual wand) 185, 195, 199, 200
Gohō shiji ron 護法資治論 106
gokumon 獄門 (display of heads) 82, 86
goma 護摩 159, 209
gongen 権現 3, 8, 11, 38–9, 43, 111, 221–2, 230
  Gongen-sama 権現様 67
goningumi 五人組 (five-man group) 24–5
Goryōbun yoseyashiro ki 御領分寄社記 233
Goryōbunchū miya yurai 御領分中宮由来 92
gosanke 御三家 (Three Great Houses [of the Tokugawa]) 11, 178, 217
gōsha 郷社 (communal shrine) 191
gōshi 合祀 (merging of shrines) 185–6
Goyōdome kakinuki 御用留書抜 241
Goyōzei Tennō 後陽成天皇 64
great councilor (*tairō*) 16, 128, 137
Great Learning (*Daxue* 大學) 104
gū 宮 (palace) 40, 222
guishen 鬼神 (spirits of the dead) 110, 206
gundai 郡代 (district official) 166, 177
gunjin 軍陣 130
Gyokusen'in 宝泉院 56
gyōnin 行人 179–81

Hachiman 八幡 (deity) 15, 40, 143, 178, 185–7, 212, 218, 222

Hachiman 八幡 (shrine; Hachimangū) 7, 177, 185–7, 212–3, 215
  Arakawa Wakamiya 安良川若宮 185
  Baba 馬場 185
  Iwashimizu 石清水 34
  Maigi 舞木 212–3
  Ōsaki 大崎 15, 218
  Ōta 太田 185
  Terazu 寺津 212
  Tokiwa 常葉 185–6, 241
  Yuzuki 湯月 92
Hachiman aratame 八幡改 (Hachiman reform) 185–6
Hada Shinmeisha 羽田神明社 (shrine) 212
Hagiwara Kaneyori 萩原兼従 13
Hai kirishitan no fumi 排吉利支丹文; see also *Bateren tsuihō no bun* 37, 218
haibutsu kōju 廃仏興儒 (persecute Buddhism and raise Confucianism) 163
haidera 廃寺 (abandoned temple) 51
Hakata 博多 (town) 36, 224
Hakke gakusoku 伯家学則 (*Principles of Study for the Shirakawa House*) 206
hakuchō 白張 192
Hakyakuchō 破却帳 179, 180, 182, 184, 187
Hall, John Whitney 117
Hamada 浜田 (domain) 31
Hanabatake 花畠 (Flower Meadow; New Brigade) 119, 121, 232
Hanitsu 土津 (shrine) 15, 140, 142
  Hanitsu Reishin 土津霊神 (Hanitsu Divine Spirit) 15, 140
  Hanitsushinfun shizume ishi 土津神墳鎮石 140–1
hanju 藩儒 (Confucian tutor) 13, 93, 98, 115
hankō 藩校 (domain school) 115, 126, 128, 229
hanryō shintō 藩領神道; see Domain Shinto
Hasegawa Fujihiro 長谷川藤広 48
Hasegawa Gonroku 長谷川権六 49, 54–7
Hasshinden 八神殿 (shrine) 203–4, 208, 245
hatamoto 旗本 (shogunal liege vassal) 25
Hatano Takao 羽田野敬雄 211–2, 215
Hattori Ankyū 服部安休 13, 135, 140

Hattori Nakatsune 服部中庸 210
Hayashi 林 (family) 98, 104, 128, 229
    Gahō 鵞峯 95, 98, 104, 135
    Hōkō 鳳岡 97–8, 135
    Razan 羅山 (Dōshun 道春) 5, 98, 101, 104–7, 135, 155, 159, 187
head temple; *see* honji
hermitage (*anshitsu*) 54, 67, 68
heterodoxy (*see also* pernicious creed; deviant practice) 3, 4, 22, 69, 79, 107, 127, 169, 180
Hida (province) 79, 84–6, 227
hiden 悲田 (fields of compassion) 70
    Hiden Fujufuse 悲田不受不施 (branch sect) 70
Hie 日吉 (shrine) 6, 157–8, 161
Hieizan 比叡山 (Mt. Hiei) 1, 34, 157–8, 236–7
Higashi Honganji 東本願寺 79
Higashiebe 東江部 (village) 29
Hiji Hōmon 秘事法門 (sect) 78–81, 85
Hiki Samon 日置左門 126
Hine 日根 (shrine); *see* Ōiseki Shrine
Hineno 日根野 (village) 193–4, 243
Hine Wakasanokami 日根若狭守 194, 243
Hinoe 日野江 (domain) 50
Hirado 平戸 (domain) 42, 55, 92, 222
Hirado-machi 平戸町 23, 53
Hirado-machi Yokoseura-machi ninzū aratame no chō 平戸町横瀬浦町人数改之帳 23
Hiramaro; *see* Urabe Hiramaro
Hirata 平田 (family) 204–6
    Atsutane 篤胤 8, 203–16, 222
    Kanetane 銕胤 205–6
    Kaneya 鉄弥 206
Hirata 平田 (school) 8, 211–6, 245
Hirata Shinto 平田神道 216
Hiroshima 広島 (domain) 24
Hirota Tansai 廣田坦斎; *see* Inbe no Tansai
hissoku 逼塞 (strict seclusion) 77
Hitachi (province) 94, 183
Hitorigoto 独言 (*Soliloquy*) 209–10, 215
Hitotsubashi 一橋 (family) 243
hitsuki 比都器 140
Hizen (province) 54, 56, 92
Ho no Inazuchi no kami ben 火雷神辯 112

hōbō 謗法 (slandering the dharma) 62
hōji 法事 (Buddhist memorial service) 60, 63–4, 185, 187
Hōjō Ujinaga 北条氏長 25
Hokke 法華 (sect); *see* Nichiren sect
Hōkōji 方広寺 63
hokora 祠 (*see also* shōsha) 191
holder of the realm; *see* tenkabito
Honchō jinja kō 本朝神社考 5, 107, 110–1, 114, 230–2
honden 本殿 (Izumo) 155, 237
Hōnen 法然 34, 220
Honganji 本願寺 1, 210
hongan 本願 mendicant 155–8, 161
Honhakata-machi 本博多町 55
honji 本地; *see* honji suijaku
honji 本寺 (head temple) 1, 55, 64–5, 69, 78, 80–3, 152–3, 179, 183, 245
honji suijaku 本地垂迹 (origin and trace; honji; suijaku) 34–5, 97, 99, 111–2, 186, 228
    honji suijaku shintō 本地垂迹神道 231
Honkō kokushi nikki 本光国師日記 38
Honkuji 本久寺 71
Honpō shinsho 本邦神書 230
Honrenji 本蓮寺 51
Hori Kyōan 堀杏庵 230
Hōrinbō 宝林坊 182
hōryū 法立 72
Hoshina 保科 (family)
    Masatsune 正経 139–40
    Masayuki 正之 5–6, 10–6, 24, 29–30, 91–8, 117, 133–48, 152, 156–7, 161, 178, 188, 217–8, 236
Hosokawa Tadaoki 細川忠興 22
hotchū 法中 72
hyōhyaku 表白; *see* eulogy
hyōjōsho 評定所 (deliberative council) 4, 76, 79–88, 159–62, 172

Ichijō Kanera 一条兼良 104
ichiko 市子 (female shrine dancer) 184
ichinomiya 一之宮 30, 173
Ichiura Kisai 市浦毅斎 122–3, 128
Ihara Ōkura 井原大内蔵 195
Ihara Shikibu 井原式部 195
ihō 異法; *see* deviant practice
ijutsu 異術 (strange arts) 86, 88

Ikeda 池田 (family) 119, 121, 122, 130, 165, 232–3, 238
  Mitsumasa 光政 5, 7, 11, 15, 29–30, 71, 92, 98, 115, 117–31, 163–75, 178, 217–8, 230, 232–5, 238–9
  Terumasa 輝政 121
  Toshitaka 利隆 121
  Tsunamasa 綱政 30, 126, 128, 173
  Yoshimasa 慶政 233
  Yoshiyasu 吉泰 41
Ikeda-ke rireki ryakki 池田家履歴略記 165, 169
Ikegami Honmonji 池上本門寺 65, 67
Iki 壱岐 (island) 92
ikigami 生神 (living gods) 112–3
Ikkō 一向 (sect) 1, 51, 54, 78–9, 153, 179, 181, 245
Ikōbyō 威公廟 187
Ikuta Yorozu 生田萬 (Michimaro 道満) 211
illustrious lords; *see* meikun
Imai Tōken 今井桐軒 (Ujun 有順) 95–8
imperial court 6–13, 22, 34, 36, 41–2, 100, 104–5, 109, 123, 137, 151–3, 192–9, 203–16, 221, 227, 233, 242, 245
Inaba Masanori 稲葉正則 (Mino no kami 美濃守) 14, 135, 139, 217
Inaba Masayuki 稲葉正往 139
Inakawa Jurōemon 稲川十郎右衛門 172
Inari 稲荷 (shrine) 56, 204
Inari myōjin sage 稲荷明神下げ (Inari medium) 85
Inawashiro 猪苗代 (town) 134
Inawashiro-ko 猪苗代湖 (lake) 138
Inbe no Tansai 忌部坦斎 (Hirota Tansai 廣田坦斎) 231
ingō 院号 179
Inner Shrine (Ise) 93, 137–8, 158–62, 184
Inoue Gentō 井上玄桐 240
Inoue Masakane 井上正鉄 206
Inoue Masashige 井上政重 24, 53
Inoue Masatoshi 井上正利 69, 135, 156–7, 228, 237
insei 院政 (rule of retired emperors) 34
inshi 淫祠 (illicit shrine; *yinshi*) 5, 6, 11, 13, 91–102, 123, 151–2, 163, 228

inspection of temples and shrines; *see* jisha junken
Isahaya 諫早 (family) 56
Ise (province) 158
Ise 伊勢 (shrine) 6, 10, 58–9, 92–3, 111, 138, 152, 156–62, 201, 208, 220, 228, 230
Ise-machi 伊勢町 (Nagasaki) 58
Ise-no-miya 伊勢宮 (shrine, Nagasaki) 56–9
Ise Shinto 98, 231
isetsu 異説 (deviant theses) 75–88
Iseya Dennojō 伊勢屋傳之丞 54
ishū 異宗; *see* deviant practice
isson issha seido 一村一社制度 (system of one tutelary shrine per village) 174, 184
Itakura Katsushige 板倉勝重 65
Iwahashi 磐椅 (shrine) 138
Iwaki-taira 磐城平 (domain) 92, 163
Iwami (province) 31
Iwanashi 磐梨 (district) 71
Iyo (province) 92
Izu (province) 208
Izu islands 70
Izumi (province) 8, 83, 191–9, 242
Izumo 出雲 (shrine; *see also* Kizuki Shrine) 6, 10, 93, 154–8, 161, 201, 237
Izumoji Nobunao 出雲路信直 143, 144

jahō 邪法 169
Jakuhon 寂本 5, 107–14, 231
Jakushōin Nichiken 寂照院日乾 65–7
jakyō 邪教; *see* pernicious creed
jashūmon 邪宗門; *see* pernicious creed
Jesuits (Society of Jesus) 21–3, 36, 47–51, 54–6, 136, 223
Ji 時 (sect) 179, 181
ji'nin 神人 (shrine servant) 196, 200
Jie 桀 109
Jigen'in 慈眼院 193–6, 243
jihi 慈悲 (compassion) 70
jiin hatto 寺院法度 (temple laws) 10, 69, 152, 177
jiin seiri 寺院整理 29

Jikū 慈空 80–81, 85
jindai 神代 (Age of the Gods) 10, 135, 145, 147, 206, 208, 214–5
jindai moji 神代文字 (ancient script of the gods) 212
jingi 神祇 (deities of heaven and earth) 97
　jingi hakuō 神祇伯王 (kingly councilor of divinities) 204
　jingidō 神祇道 94, 151, 153–4, 161, 163
　jingikan 神祇官 (Office of Deities) 92, 211, 214–5
Jingi hōten 神祇宝典 (Treasure Books of the Deities of Heaven and Earth) 96–9, 228–9
jingū 神宮 (divine palace) 40
Jingū Kōgō 神功皇后 242
Jingūji 神宮寺 (Nagasaki) 56
jingūji 神宮寺 (shrine temple) 160
jinja aratame 神社改 (shrine reform) 13, 183
Jinja jōmoku 神社条目 (Shrine Clauses; Shosha negi kannushi hatto; Law for Shrine Priests) 6–7, 10, 14, 134, 145, 151–63, 171–4, 177, 179, 192–4, 197, 201, 203–4, 209, 242
Jinja-kō bengi 神社考辨疑 107, 109, 113–4, 230–2
Jinja sōroku 神社総録 95
Jinmu Tennō 神武天皇 6, 97, 110–1, 137–8, 146–7, 207–8, 231
jinnō 神皇 (divine ruler) 97
Jinnō shōtōki 神皇正統記 35, 221
Jinshin koseki 壬申戸籍 (Family register of the year of Jinshin) 32
Jinzanshū 秦山集 135
jisha bugyō 寺社奉行 (magistrate of temples and shrines) 24, 27, 30, 65, 68–9, 82, 94, 155–7, 160, 178–9, 206, 213, 219, 228
jisha junken 寺社巡見 (inspection of temples and shrines) 179
jishakata 寺社方 195
jisha o-aratamechō 寺社御改帳 (register of temples and shrines) 179
jisha yaku 寺社役 179
Jishō nikki 慈性日記 221–2
Jitsujōin Nichiden 実成院日典 63

Jiun 慈雲 80
Jixia 稷下 232
Jōdo 浄土 (sect) 55, 62, 80, 106, 142, 179, 181
Jōdo Shin 浄土真 (sect; see Ikkō sect)
Jōin 乗因 217
Jōkyō reki 貞享暦 (Jōkyō calendar) 133, 136
Jōrakuin Nichikyō 常楽院日経 226
Ju-butsu mondō 儒仏問答 107, 114
Jufuse 受不施 (sect) 67, 70, 72, 225
jui 儒医 (physician) 104
junkenshi 巡見使 (itinerant inspector of the bakufu) 166, 238
junshi 殉死 11, 134
Jurchen 136
jusha 儒者 (teacher of Confucianism) 104

Kachi 加知 143
Kaempfer, Engelbert 117, 128
kagami 鏡 (mirror) 185
Kagatsume Naozumi 加々爪直澄 69
Kagoshima 鹿児島 41
kagura 神楽 (Shinto ceremonial dancing) 184
Kai (province) 65, 82
kaieki 改易 134
ka'i hentai 華夷変態 136
Kaikichō 開基帳 179–181
kaji 加持 (ritual) 159
kajitsu 花実 35
Kajiya-machi 鍛治屋町 55
kaku 額 (shrine tablet) 140
Kakudahama 角田浜 (village) 219
Kamakura 34, 62, 197, 207, 231
kami 神 (Shinto deity) passim
Kamigoto no uretamigoto 祭事冤論 (Treatise on Wrongs in Sacred Affairs) 214
Kaminogō 上之郷 (village) 193
Kamumusubi 神皇産 (deity) 206
Kan Tokuan 菅得庵 230
Kan'eiji 寛永寺 37
Kanazawa 金沢 (domain) 24
Kanbun era (1661–73) 2, 8, 61, 68, 71, 73, 91–4, 96, 134, 164, 174, 227
　Kanbun inchi 寛文印知 134
　Kanbun no sōmetsu 寛文の惣滅 225
kanjin 勧進 (fundraising) 62, 158–60

kanjin bikuni 勧進比丘尼 (fundraising nun) 93
kannamesai 神嘗祭 (harvest festival) 138
kannushi 神主 6, 84, 134, 151, 177, 184, 186, 192, 194, 203, 242
   zoku kannushi 俗神主 171
   kannushi sōtō 神主惣頭 (general superior of Shintō priests) 172–4
Karatsu 唐津 56
karidono 仮殿 (provisional shrine hall) 140
kari gakkan 仮学館 (temporary school) 125
kariya 仮屋 (temporary shelter) 140
Kasama 笠間 (domain) 135
Kasuga 春日 (shrine, Ikeda valley) 192–3, 196–9, 200–1
Kataoka Tomonori 片岡友謙 143
katashiro 形代 140, 236
Katsuhime 勝姫 233
Katsuragi 葛城 (mountains) 194
Katsuyama-machi 勝山町 51
Kawachi (province) 80
Kawamura Heitaibei 川村平太兵衛 165
Kazagashira 風頭 (Mt.) 55–56
Kazan Tennō 花山天皇 204
kazeori eboshi 風折烏帽子 192
Kazusa (province) 68, 71
Keijuin 慶寿院 182
Keikōin 慶光院 93, 159–60
kenchichō 検地帳 (cadastral register) 27
Kenjūin Nissei 堅住院日勢 71
Kenninji 建仁寺 104
Kibe Pedoro 岐部ペドロ 22
Kibitsu no miya 吉備津宮 173
kifu 亀砆 (turtle stone) 142
kiganji 祈願寺 ([imperial or *bakufu*] prayer temple) 62
Kii (province; Kishū) 42, 92, 163, 173, 194
Kii 紀伊 (domain; Kishū 紀州藩) 13, 178, 217, 235
kikai 奇怪 (strange acts) 75, 77–78, 81–5
kikyū 気躬 112
Kinmei Tennō 欽明天皇 110
Kirishitan 切支丹 (*see also* Christianity) 21–7, 37, 73, 84–8, 218
   Kakure Kirishitan 隠れキリシタン (crypto Christians) 71–2
   kirishitan ruizoku 切支丹類族 87
   Kirishitan shūmon osame sōrō rui 切支丹宗門修候類 85

Kishiwada 岸和田藩 (domain) 194
kishōmon 起請文 (*see also* oath) 34, 218
Kishū; *see* Kii province
Kishū 紀州藩 (domain); *see* Kii domain
Kisshōin 吉祥院 182
Kitabatake Chikafusa 北畠親房 35
Kitagawara Jingoemon 北瓦甚五衛門 240
Kitajima 北島 (family) 155
Kitano Tenjin 北野天神 (shrine) 112, 232
kitō 祈祷 10, 172, 189
kitōji 祈祷寺 (temple for everyday rituals) 39
Kiyohara 清原 (family) 104
Kizuki 杵築 (shrine; *see also* Izumo Shrine) 93, 104, 228
Kizuki shohatto 杵築諸法度 155
Kōchi 高知 (domain) 92, 163
Kōeiji 光永寺 51
Kōfukuji sōjō 興福寺奏状 34
kofun 古墳 71
Kogo shūi 古語拾遺 108
Koizumi 小泉 64
Kojiki 古事記 108, 147, 206
Kojima 小島 (village) 56
Kōkai 公海 41
Kōkaku Tennō 光格天皇 214
kokka kangyō 国家諫暁 (admonishing the state) 63, 225
kokudaka 石高 27
Kokugaku 国学 (National Learning) 6, 8, 17, 188, 197, 203, 222, 243
Kokura 小倉 (domain) 22, 10, 223
Kokuseiji 国清寺 235
kokushu 国主 63
komai 小舞 (*komei*; *see also* dance) 56
Konchiin Sūden 金地院崇伝 (*see* Sūden)
Konkōmyō kyō 金光明経 217
konpon 根本 35, 37, 109
Koori 郡 (village) 24, 53, 60
   Koori kuzure 郡崩れ (crushing of Koori) 24
koori bugyō 郡奉行 (district magistrate) 166, 178–9, 238, 240
Korea 35–6, 49, 58, 100–1, 125, 136, 229, 234, 242
korekihō 古暦法 137
korobi 転 (*see also* apostate) 22–3
Kōtaiji 皓台寺 50
Kōyasan 高野山 (Mt. Kōya) 199–200, 244

Kujikata osadamegaki 公事方御定書 (*Rules for Deciding Judicial Matters*) 76–87
Kujiki 旧事記; *see Sendai kuji hongi*
Kūkai 空海 109, 208, 228
Kumamoto 熊本 (domain) 24, 53
Kumazawa Banzan 熊沢蕃山 96–100, 104, 106, 111, 119–27, 130, 166–7, 228, 231, 233–4, 238
kumigashira 組頭 183
Kumon Kurōzaemon 公文黒郎左衛門 56
Kunchi くんち (festival) 57–8, 60, 224
Kuroda Toshio 黒田俊雄 33
Kurodani 黒谷 142–3
Kurosawa Sekisai 黒澤石斎 155–6, 237
Kuwayama Sadamasa 桑山貞政 93
kuyō 供養 (Buddhist offerings) 66
kyōden 敬田 (fields of reverence) 70
Kyōto machibugyō 京都町奉行 (Kyoto magistrate) 157
Kyūi 及意 83, 87, 227

Law for Shrine Priests; *see Jinja jōmoku*
Law for Temples of all Buddhist Sects; *see Shoshū jiin hatto*
Lesser Learning 124
li 理 (principle; *ri*) 112–3, 231–2
local deputy; *see daikan*
Lord of Heaven; *see Tentei*
Lotus sect; *see Nichiren sect*
Lotus Sūtra 42, 61–3, 66, 70–2

Macao 48
machi bugyō 町奉行 (town magistrate) 183
machidoshiyori 町年寄 (municipal administrator [Nagasaki]) 55
Maeda Toshiie 前田利家 15
Maeda Tsunanori 前田綱紀 117, 135
magistrate; *see bugyō*
magistrate of temples and shrines; *see jisha bugyō*
Maigi 舞木 (village) 212–3
Maitreya 111
Makassar (King of ~) 42
Mandate of Heaven (*tianming*; *tenmei*) 41, 43
Manila 36, 48
mappō 末法 (Final Dharma age) 62

Maruyama 丸山 (Mt.) 56
Maruyama-machi 丸山町 57, 224
Masumida 真清田 (shrine) 30
Matsubara Issei 松原一清 127
Matsudaira 松平 (family)
　Naomasa 直政 93, 155–6, 157, 237
　Nobutsuna 信綱 55, 120, 123, 129
　Yorishige 頼重 92
Matsue 松江 (domain) 155–7, 161
matsuji 末寺 (branch temple) 55, 64–9, 153, 183, 199
Matsukura Katsuie 松倉勝家 23
Matsukura Shigemasa 松倉重政 50
Matsunaga Sekigo 松永尺五 230
Matsunaga Teitoku 松永貞徳 107, 230
Matsunomori 松森 (shrine) 56
Matsuoka Ichinosuke 松岡市之助 (Ichidayū 市太夫) 165, 172–4
Matsuoka Sanai 松岡左内 (Motoatsu 帰厚) 211
Matsura 松浦 (family) 56
matsuri 祭 (Shinto festival) 57–8, 60, 138, 192, 194, 243
Matsuyama 松山 (domain) 92
Meiji Restoration 32, 115, 178, 231
meikun 名君 (illustrious lords) 11, 117, 135, 235
Meiryō kōhan 明良洪範 221
Meishō Tennō 明正天皇 41
memorial service (*see also hōji*) 63, 185
mendicant 47–8, 51, 155–8
Mibayashi 三林 (village) 192, 197
mibun 身分 (social rank) 100
middle ages (*chūyō*) 95–6, 102, 114, 209
Migaki 見垣 (family) 173
Mikawa (province) 8, 203, 205, 211–6
Miki Hirotaka 三木広隆 211
miko 巫女 183–5, 204
mikoshi 神輿 57
Mimasaka (province) 71
Mineyama 見禰山 (Mt.) 138, 140
Ming 明 (dynasty) 100, 119, 136–7
Mino (province) 24
Minobu 身延 (Mt.) 65–9,
Minobu-Ikegami debate; *see Shinchi tairon*
Minobu-san Kuonji 身延山久遠寺 65–6
mirror; *see kagami*
Misake 味酒 (shrine) 92
Misericordia brotherhood 49, 51, 55, 223

Misogi-kyō 禊教 206
mitama matsuri 御魂祭
Mito 水戸 (castle) 180, 183, 187, 242
Mito 水戸 (domain) *passim*
Mito-ryōbun murawari 水戸領分村割 184
Miwa (god) 111
Miyagawa Danshō 宮川弾正 210–1, 245
Miyake Jūemon 三宅十衛門 240
miyaza 宮座 (shrine assembly) 191–6, 243
Mizuno Gunki 水野軍記 85
Mizuno Morinobu 水野守信 23, 53, 56
Mizuno Tadakuni 水野忠邦 205
Momozono Tennō 桃園天皇 204
Mon'yō 文養 155–6
Mongol invasions 34, 62
Mononobe no Moriya 物部守屋 108–9
monto 門徒 63, 65, 179
monzeki dera 門跡寺 105
Mori Genjuku 森儼塾 106
Morisaki 森崎 (cape) 56
Morisaki 森崎 (shrine) 56
 Morisaki Gongen 森崎権現 56
Motoori Norinaga 本居宣長 210, 214
Motoori Ōhira 本居大平 210, 245
mountain ascetic; *see yamabushi*
munefuda 棟札 195
murakiri 村切 191
Murayama 村山 (family) 49, 51
 Murayama Tōan 村山当安 49
Murodō 室堂 (village) 193, 197, 199
Musashi (province) 65
mushuku 無宿 (unregistered person) 70, 81–2
Mutobe Yoshika 六人部是香 245
Mutsu (province) 92, 163, 173
myōjin 明神 38–9
Myōkakuin Nichikan 妙覚院日閑 71
Myōkakuji 妙覚寺 63, 67, 169
Myōshinji 妙心寺 121

nagarō 永牢 (indefinite incarceration) 79–80
Nagasaki (town) 3, 22–3, 36, 47–60, 207, 219, 223–4
Nagasaki 長崎 (village) 50, 56, 224
Nagasaki bugyō 長崎奉行 (Nagasaki magistrate) 24, 48–59

Nagasaki daikan 長崎代官 (magistrate of Nagasaki's outer wards) 49, 51, 54, 57, 59
Nagasaki Sumikage 長崎純景 50, 224
Nagasaki Tamehide 長崎為英 56
Nagasaki zushi 長崎図志 56
Nagataki 長滝 (village) 193, 243
Nagura Hanzaemon 名倉半左衛門 139–40
naidaijin 内大臣 64
naijin 内陣 (inner sanctum) 195
Naikū chinza koki 内宮鎮座古記 137
naishin 内心 72
naishinji 内心寺 72
Nakae Tōju 中江藤樹 5, 104, 119, 121, 125–6, 128
Nakae Yasaburō 中江弥三郎 126
Nakamura Tekisai 中村惕斎 122–4, 130
Nakasai 那珂西 (village) 185
Nakatomi 中臣 (family) 109, 208, 211
 Chijimaro 智治麿 211
 Kamatari 鎌足 208
Nakatomi no harae fūsuisō 中臣祓風水草 236
Nakatomi no harae hongi 中臣祓本義 211
Nankōbō Tenkai 南光坊天海 (*see* Tenkai)
Nanzenji 南禅寺 37, 221
Naruse Kazue 成瀬主計 139–40
Nashinoki Sukeyuki 梨木祐之 143
National Learning; *see* Kokugaku
nayosechō 名寄帳 (*see also* census register of sectarian inspection) 27–28, 178
Nebokoro shūi 瓊矛拾遺 147, 236
negi 禰宜 6, 134, 151, 177, 184, 203, 242
Negoroji 根来寺 193–4
Nehan 涅槃 (sect) 227
nenbutsu 念仏 (contemplating the Buddha) 34, 78, 81, 161, 220
Nenbutsu 念仏 (sect) 73
nenshu kaigyō shiki 年首開業式 126
Nether World; see *yomotsukuni*
New Brigade (Shingumi); *see* Hanabatake
Nichiden 日典; *see* Jitsujōin Nichiden
Nichiju 日樹; *see* Chōon'in Nichiju
Nichikan 日閑; *see* Myōkakuin Nichikan
Nichiken 日乾; *see* Jakushōin Nichiken
Nichikō 日講; *see* Ankokuin Nichikō
Nichikyō 日経; *see* Jōrakuin Nichikyō
Nichinen 日念; *see* Taguchi Heiroku
Nichiō 日奥; *see* Busshō-in Nichiō

Nichion 日遠; see Shinshōin Nichion
Nichiren 日蓮 61–6, 70, 72, 82, 225
Nichiren 日蓮 (sect; Lotus sect; Hokke sect) 3–4, 7, 10, 29, 51, 61–9, 71–3, 76, 82, 86, 123, 169–70, 179, 180–1, 224
Nihon chōreki 日本長暦 (Comprehensive Calendar of Japan) 137–8, 146–7
Nihon sandai jitsuroku 日本三代実録 220
Nihon shoki 日本書紀 34, 108, 135–7, 147, 220, 235
Nikkō 日光 9, 39, 43, 222
Nikkyō 日境; see Tsūshin'in Nikkyō
nin 仁 (benevolence) 66, 110, 134, 228
ninbetsuchō 人別帳 (see also census register of sectarian inspection) 27–28, 178
Ninchō 忍澂 106, 114, 230
ningi no michi 仁義の道 (Way of benevolence and righteousness) 37
Ninigi 瓊々杵 111
ninjuchō 人数帳 (see also census register of sectarian inspection) 27–28
ninnon 任恩 (worldly benevolence)
ninomiya 二之宮 66
Nishi Honganji 西本願寺 78–9
Nishimura Gengorō 西村源五郎 165, 172
Nishiyama 西山 (village) 56–7
Nissen 日暹; see Chiken'in Nissen
Nittai 日体; see Eitatsu Nittai
no receiving, no giving; see fujufuse
Nōbi kuzure 濃尾崩れ 24
Nobo 野母 (village) 54
Noguchi Tosa 野口土佐 198
Nonaka 野中 (family) 145
  Nonaka Kenzan 野中兼山 127
Numazu 沼津 (domain) 245

oath (see also kishōmon) 34, 77, 81, 218
Ōbaku 黄檗 (sect) 5, 107
Obama 小浜 (domain) 24, 52
obusuna 産土; see ubusuna
Oda Nobunaga 織田信長 1, 36, 62, 64, 99–100, 158, 194, 243
Ōdara 大多羅 (village) 239
Ōdara Yosemiya 大多羅寄宮 239
Odawara 小田原 (domain) 135, 217
ōdō 王道 (Royal Way; Way of the Just Ruler) 99, 110, 229

offerings (see also kuyō) 57, 61–3, 66–73, 83, 121, 124–6, 131, 140, 147, 155
Office of Deities; see jingikan
Ōgimachi Kinmichi 正親町公通 236
Ōhama 大浜 213
  Ōhama Jinya 大浜陣屋 212
Ōhato 大波止 57
Ohiroma zakki (Gokōkan zakki) 御広間雑記 164, 172, 238–9
ohoto 於保止 140–1
Ōiseki 大井関 (shrine; Hine Shrine) 193–201, 243
Ōjin Tennō 応神天皇 110, 185–6, 232
ōjō 往生 (transition to paradise) 78, 80
Oka 岡 (family) 173
Okamoto Daihachi 岡本大八 (incident) 37
Okayama 岡山 (castle) 120–1, 125, 129, 172
Okayama 岡山 (domain) passim
Okazaki 岡崎 (domain) 212, 214
Oman no kata お万の方; see Yōjūin.
Ōmori Chikugo 大森筑後 173
Ōmura 大村 (domain) 24, 53–4, 223
Ōmura 大村 (family) 47, 49, 54, 59
  Sumitada 純忠 224
onden 恩田 (fields of obligation) 70
One-and-Only Shinto; see yuiitsu shintō
Ōnin 応仁 (war) 207
onmyō no kami 陰陽頭 (head of the Yin Yang Bureau) 137
onmyōji 陰陽師 (Yin Yang diviner) 82, 85
ontō 遠島 (see also exile) 76
Ontome-chō hyōjōsho 御留帳評定所 172, 239
opperhoofd 42, 222
origin and trace; see honji suijaku
origin story; see yuisho
original form (of the kami); see honji suijaku
orthodoxy 37, 72, 75, 162
Osaka 4, 22, 24, 48, 64, 71, 78, 80, 83–8, 191, 230
Osaka magistrate 80–1, 84–7
Ōsawa Sadao 大沢貞夫 119, 232
oshi 御師 (pilgrimage entrepreneur) 159–62, 204, 237
Oshiage 押上 144

Ōshio Heihachirō 大塩平八郎 84, 227
Oshioki reiruishū 御仕置例類集 (*Criminal Judgment Precedents Organized by Category*) 75–9, 81–7, 220, 226–7
otegata お手形 69–70
Otome-chō 御留帳 170–2, 239
otona 乙名 (ward head) 23–6, 48–9, 51, 53, 57, 59, 223
Otone 乙子 (village) 31
Ōuchi Norihiro 大内教弘 9
Ōuchi Yoshitaka 大内義隆 50
Outer Shrine (Ise) 58, 98, 138, 156, 159–62
Outline of Vulgar Shinto; see Zoku shintō taii
Owari 尾張 (domain) 13, 15, 30–1, 139, 178, 217
Owari (province) 24, 30, 172
Ōyama Tameoki 大山為起 143

pernicious creed (*jakyō*; *jashūmon*) 1–4, 81, 85–6, 152–4
pilgrimage entrepreneur; *see oshi*
Pinheiro, Luis 223
Principles of Study for the Shirakawa House; *see Hakke gakusoku*

Raigōji 来迎寺 80–1, 226–7
rain prayer; *see amagoi*
receiving, but not giving; *see Jufuse*
register of sectarian inspection (*shūmon aratamechō*; *shūshi aratamechō*) 25–8, 32, 52–3, 178, 219
Reigen Tennō 霊元天皇 137
reiji 霊璽 (Shinto tablet) 140, 143
Renmyōin 蓮明院 199–200, 244
resting place; *see tabisho*
Ricci, Matteo 85, 136
rigaku shintō 理学神道 (Shinto of the study of principles) 13
righteousness 37
Rikkokushi 六国史 33
Rikōin 利光院 235
Rinnōji 輪王寺 157–8, 222
Rinzai 臨済 (sect) 54, 179, 181, 183
ritō shinchi shintō 理当心地神道 (Shinto of principles present in the heart) 13, 110, 113, 231
rōjū 老中 (senior councilor) 14, 30, 55, 76, 84, 86, 88, 93, 120, 126, 139, 205, 217

rōnin 浪人 119–20, 124, 134, 178
Royal Way; *see ōdō*
rule of retired emperors; *see insei*
Rules for Deciding Judicial Matters; *see Kujikata osadamegaki*
rural commoners' school; *see gōgaku*
ryōbu 両部 (both parts; dual parts) 93, 155, 159, 197, 228
   ryōbu [shūgō] shintō 両部[習合]神道 98, 158, 208
Ryōkai 亮海 42
Ryūkoku 龍谷 (branch sect) 78
Ryūkyū 229

sacred 1, 33, 42–3, 50, 73, 95, 140, 161, 182, 201, 206, 245
   sacralization 3, 11, 43, 73, 124, 236
   sacred treasures 208, 99
sacrifice (*sai*) 97, 113, 121, 124–6, 235
   first sacrifice of repose (*shogu*) 140
Sada 佐太 (shrine) 156–7
Saeki 佐伯 (village) 71
Saga 佐賀 (domain) 24
Sahimeyama 佐毘売山 (shrine) 31
sai 祭 (*see* sacrifice)
Saichō 最澄 158, 237
Saigen 齋源 (school) 113
Saitō Kazuoki 斎藤一興 (Kyūen 九畹) 238–9
Sakado 酒門 (village) 188, 242
Sakai 堺 (town) 62, 198
Sakai Tadakatsu 酒井忠勝 24, 123, 129, 234
Sakai Tadakiyo 酒井忠清 16, 128, 137
Sakura-machi 桜町 51
Sakusa Yorikiyo 佐草自清 156
Śākyamuni 66, 95, 225
Samakumine 佐麻久嶺 (shrine) 92
Sanchō-ha 三鳥派 (branch sect) 77, 81, 83, 226
sandō 参道 (procession road) 140
sangō 山号 179
sanja takusen 三社託宣 (scroll) 143
sankyō itchi 三教一致 (unity of the three teachings) 35, 103, 110
Sannō 山王 237
   Sannō ichijitsu shintō 山王一実神道 (Shinto of the All-Encompassing Truth of Sannō) 38–9, 158, 230, 237

sannomiya 三之宮 183
Sanuki (province) 71, 92
Sanzai 三才 (village) 182
sarcophagus; *see sekkan*
Sarutahiko 猿田彦 (shrine, Kyoto) 144
Sasutahiko 刺田比古 (shrine) 92
Satake (family) 佐竹 186
    Yoshinobu 義信 185
Satsuma 薩摩 (domain) 27, 41
Satsuyōroku 撮要録 171, 239
Sebastian of Portugal 221
sect (*see also shūmon*) *passim*
Segidera 世義寺 93
seiden 正殿 155, 237
seijin 聖人 (Confucian Holy One) 108
Seikō hongi 聖皇本紀 109, 231
seikyū 精躬 (seed body) 112
seisaku o hōjiru 正朔を奉じる (follow the legitimate rule)
seishin ōmyō no michi 聖神奧妙之道 (Way of sacred divine mystery) 95
Seiwa Tennō 清和天皇 185, 222
Seizan-ha 西山派 (branch sect) 80
Sekigahara 関ヶ原 23, 37
sekisai 釈菜 126, 128, 234
sekiten 釈奠 (*shidian*) 101, 126, 229
Sekiyado 関宿 (domain) 199, 243
sekkan 石棺 (sarcophagus) 140
Sendai 仙台 (domain) 15, 23
Sendai kuji hongi 先代旧事本紀 (*Kujiki*) 109, 231
Sendai kuji hongi taisei kyō 先代旧事本紀大成経 (*Taisei kyō*) 108, 222, 231
sendatsu yaku 先達役 57
Sengoku (period) 9, 11, 100, 134,
sengū 遷宮 (*see also shikinen sengū*) 142, 192, 199, 244
senior councilor; *see rōjū*
Senke 千家 (family) 155
Seonji 施音寺 199
separation of Shinto and Buddhism (*shinbutsu bunri*) 2, 6–7, 16, 93–4, 100, 154, 163, 185, 189
sewanin 世話人 196
shaden 社殿 (shrine building) 184, 194
shake 社家 192
    shake no hō 社家の法 100
shakubuku 折伏 62–3, 73
shanin/shajin 社人 184, 196

shasō 社僧 (see also *bettō*) 92, 94, 171, 183, 185, 192–5, 199, 200, 244
shenyi 深衣 104
Shibukawa (family) 渋川 146
    Harumi 春海 5, 16, 133–8, 144–8, 235
    Hisatada 昔尹 147
shidian 釈奠; *see sekiten*
Shihsan jing jusu 十三経注疎 117
shijū sōden no hiden 四重相伝の秘伝 (secret initiation of the fourfold transmission) 139
shikinaisha 式内社 11, 13, 92–5, 217, 227
shikinen sengū 式年遷宮 (*see also sengū*) 93
Shima Ichinojō 島市之丞 156
Shimabara 島原 (domain) 23, 50
    Shimabara rebellion 21, 23, 41, 51–7, 60, 177
Shimada Kakuemon 島田覚右衛門 136
Shimazu Yoshitaka 島津吉貴 41
Shimizu 清水 (family) 243
Shimo Goryō 下御霊 (shrine) 143–4, 236
Shimonomiya 下宮 (Lower Shrine of Futaarayama Shrine) 94
Shimōsa (province) 68, 71
Shimotsuke Utsunomiya 下野宇都 (shrine) 94
Shin Daijin 新大神 (shrine) 56, 59
Shin Korai-machi 新高麗町 49
Shinano (province) 26, 29
shinbutsu bunri 神仏分離; *see* separation of Shinto and Buddhism
shinbutsu shūgō 神仏習合; *see* syncretism
Shinchi tairon 身池対論 (Minobu-Ikegami debate) 66, 225
shinchi 神地 (shrine estate) 93
Shingaku 心学 5, 118–123, 128–9
Shingon 真言 (sect) 5, 56, 105, 167–72, 179–182, 185, 193, 209, 221, 226, 228
Shingon Ritsu 真言律 (sect) 83–5
Shingumi 新組 (New Brigade); *see* Hanabatake
shinji 神事 57
shinjin 信心 (faith) 160, 162
shinjin 神人 229
shinjin shijin 真人至人 108
shinju itchi 神儒一致 (unity of Shinto and Confucianism; *see also* syncretism) 98, 228

shinkoku 神国 (divine country; *see also* *shinmei no kuni*) 2–3, 21–22, 33–43, 97–99, 102, 147, 220–1
shinkon 心魂 (soul) 80
shinmei no kuni 神明の国 (Land of the Gods; *see also shinkoku*) 14
Shinobugaoka 忍ヶ丘 (shrine) 128
shinpan 親藩 1, 217
shinryō 神領; *see* shrine domain
shinsho 神書 (writings of Shinto) 98, 230
Shinshōin Nichion 心性院日遠 66–7
shinshoku 神職 (*see also* Shinto priest) 163, 168–9, 171–4, 185, 192
shinshoku-uke 神職請; *see* Shinto certification
shinsōsai 神葬祭; *see* funeral
shintai 神体 94, 172, 185, 208
Shinto *passim*
 Shinto-Buddhist syncretism; *see* syncretism
 Shinto certification (*shintō-uke*; *shinshoku-uke*) 2, 7, 10, 13, 30, 32, 98, 123, 163–164, 167–75, 184, 238, 241
 Shinto festival; *see matsuri*
 Shinto priest (shrine priest; *see also kannushi*; *negi*; *shake*; *shinshoku*) *passim*
shintō 神道 (Way of the Gods) 95, 97–8, 161, 207, 228–9
 shintō chōjō 神道長上 (*see* superintendent of Shinto)
 shintōgata 神道方 135, 144
 shintōsai kyojō 神道裁許状 (licence of Yoshida Shinto) 192–3, 196–201
 shintōsha 神道者 204
 shintō-uke 神道請; *see* Shinto, certification
Shintō denju 神道伝授 229, 231
Shintō gobusho 神道五部書 231
Shintō shūmon shokoku ruireisho 神道宗門諸国類例書 220
Shintō shūsei 神道集成 94–7, 228
Shintō taigi 神道大義 228–9
Shirakawa 白川 (family) 8, 10, 151, 199, 201, 203–216
 Sukenobu 資延 214
Shirakawa-in 白河院 (retired emperor) 34
Shiratori 白鳥 (shrine) 92

shisso 執奏 (court ranks) 203
Shixian li 時憲暦 136
Shizu 静 (shrine) 94, 183–4
shizume ishi 鎮石 (pacifying stone) 140
Shizutani 閑谷 130, 232, 235
Shōfukuin 正福院 182
shogu 初虞 *see* sacrifice of repose
shogun 1, 14, 16, 22, 39–42, 58–9, 63, 93, 101, 105, 121, 126, 134, 159, 178, 191, 217
 seii taishōgun 征夷大将軍 101
 shogunal intendant; *see daikan*
 shogunate (*bakufu*) *passim*
shōju 摂受 62
Shōkakuji 正覚寺 50, 56
shōren 小斂 (first laying out; *xiaolian*) 140
Shōrinji 聖輪寺 221
shōsha 小社 238
Shosha negi kannushi hatto 諸社禰宜神主法度 (*Law for Shrine Priests*); *see Jinja jōmoku*
Shoshū jiin hatto 諸宗寺院法度 (*Law for Temples of all Buddhist Sects*) 10, 152, 177
Shōtoku Taishi 聖徳太子 5, 108–10, 114, 222, 228, 231
Shōtokuin 照徳院 182
Shoushi li 授時暦 136–7
shōya 庄屋 (village-head) 124, 165–6, 197
Shrine Clauses; *see Jinja jōmoku*
shrine *passim*
 collective shrine; *see yosemiya*
 communal shrine; *see gōsha*
 grand shrine; *see taisha*
 illicit shrine; *see inshi*
 merging of shrines; *see gōshi*
 shrine domain (*shinryō*) 93, 161
 shrine estate; *see shinchi*
 shrine maiden; *see miko*
 shrine parishioner; *see ujiko*
 shrine priest; *see* Shinto priest
 shrine temple; *see jingūji*
 small shrine; *see shōsha*
Shu Qi 叔齊 66
Shugendō 修験道 (*see also yamabushi*) 69, 82, 152, 158, 215
shugi nō 祝儀能 58

shuin 朱印 (vermillion seal) 54
  shuinchi 朱印地 (vermillion-seal land) 58, 69
  shuindera 朱印寺 (vermillion-seal temple) 54
  shuinjō 朱印状 (vermillion-seal decree) 93, 159–60, 194, 212–5
shukke 出家 77
shūmon (sect, religion) 宗門 168
  shūmon aratame 宗門改 (certification of religious affiliation, religious inspection) 24, 52, 69, 165–6, 170–4, 177–8, 184, 238, 241
  shūmon aratamechō 宗門改帳; see register of sectarian inspection
  shūmon aratameyaku 宗門改役 (Office of Sectarian Inspection) 24, 53, 219
  shūmon ikki 宗門一揆 (sectarian revolt) 23
  shūmon ninbetsu aratamechō 宗門人別改帳; see ninbetsuchō
  shūmon ninbetsuchō 宗門人別帳; see ninbetsuchō
  shūmon tegata 宗門手形 (certificate of sectarian inspection) 178
Shun 舜 108
Shuntokuji 春徳寺 54
shūshi aratamechō 宗旨改帳; see register of sectarian inspection
shūshi 宗旨 (creed) 159, 162
Shusshi kō 出思稿 127
Soga no Umako 蘇我馬子 108–9, 231
sōgen 宗源 (Ancient Source) 94–6
Sōgen 宗源 (school; see also Yoshida Shinto) 113
sōgen senji 宗源宣旨 (rank certificate of Yoshida Shinto) 192, 198, 200
Sōja Myōjin 惣社明神 (shrine) 171
sokkoku 卒哭 (cessation of wailing; zuku) 140
Soliloquy; see Hitorigoto
Sōsai benron 葬祭辨論 125
sōsai bukkyō 葬祭仏教 (funerary Buddhism) 36
Sōsai giryaku 喪祭儀略 188
Sōsai no gi 葬祭の儀 124
Sōtō 曹洞 (sect) 179, 181, 183
spirits 82, 97, 113, 206
St. Francis (church) 51

St. Isabel (church) 49, 55
St. John (church) 51
St. Laurence (church; San Lorenzo) 49, 58
St. Mary (church) 51
St. Mary of the Assumption (Cathedral) 48
St. Michael (church; San Miguel) 49
strange acts; see kikai
Sūden 崇伝 (Konchiin Sūden) 2, 37–8, 66, 218, 221–2
Suetsugu Heizō 末次平蔵 49, 51, 54
Sugawara Michizane 菅原道真 232
suijaku 垂迹; see honji suijaku
Suika Reisha 垂加霊社 143–4
Suika Shinto 垂加神道 135, 137, 236
Suiko Tennō 推古天皇 108
Suinin Tennō 垂仁天皇 138, 235
Sulawesi Island 42
Sumiyoshi 住吉 (shrine, Nagasaki) 56
Sumiyoshi Myōjin 住吉明神 56
Sunpu 駿府 (castle) 38, 222
Sunzi 孫子 235
Suruga (province) 245
sutra 14–5, 64, 113, 129, 138–9, 155
superintendent of Shinto (~ of the office of deities; shintō chōjō) 92, 203, 211
Sushun Tennō 崇峻天皇 108–9
Suwa 諏訪 (shrine) 56–60
Suwa jinja engi 諏訪神社縁起 56
syncretism 142, 237
  Shinto-Buddhist syncretism (shinbutsu shūgō; see also ryōbu) 5, 7–9, 43, 129, 164, 173, 183, 209, 228, 230
  Shinto-Confucian syncretism 98, 129

tabisho 旅所 (resting place) 57
Taguchi Heiroku 田口平六 (Nichinen 日念) 70–71
Taibo 太伯 111–2
Taiga 大我 106
Taiheiki 太平記 114, 232
Taihime 泰姫 187
tairō 大老 see great councilor
Taisei kyō 大成経; see Sendai kuji hongi taisei kyō
taisha 大社 (grand shrine) 164, 238
Taishōji 体性寺 56
Taishūji 台崇寺 235
Takada 高田 (domain) 24
Takai Sanenori 高井実徳 84–6

Takai 高井 (district) 29
Takamatsu 高松 (domain) 92
Takamimusubi 高皇産霊 (deity) 206
Takayama Ukon 高山右近 22, 48
Takeo Masatomo 竹尾正靹 212-5
Tamura Enchō 田村圓澄 33
Ta-mura 田村 (village) 182
Tanba (province) 64
Tang (period) 135, 142
Tang 湯 (King ~ of Shang) 42, 108
Tani Jinzan 谷秦山 133, 144-5
Taniguchi Sumio 谷口澄夫 127-8, 227, 233-4
Tateyama 立山 (Mt.) 49, 51, 54
Teisoku-ron 鼎足論 106
temple *passim*
    temple certification; *see terauke*
    temple district; *see teramachi*
    temple school; *see terakoya*
Temple Laws; *see Shoshū jiin hatto*
temporary school; *see kari gakkan*
Ten'yōji 天曜寺 42
tenaraisho 手習所 (literacy school) 123-4, 130
Tendai 天台 (sect) 3, 9, 26, 34, 37, 42, 56, 58, 61, 70, 80, 83, 155-8, 169-71, 179-812, 187, 217, 221, 236-7
tengu 天狗 82, 113, 232
Tenjin 天神 (shrine, Izumi) 198
tenkabito 天下人 (holder of the realm) 36-7
Tenkai 天海 (Nankōbō Tenkai) 3, 37-42, 66, 217, 222
Tenkaiban daizōkyō 天海版大藏経 41
Tenmangū 天満宮 (shrine) 56
tenno (emperor; *see also* Way of the Emperor) 13, 17, 33-4, 41-2, 63, 101, 104, 109, 112-3, 136, 137, 156, 178, 185, 203-9, 212, 214, 216, 222, 231, 245
Tenshō Daijin 天照大神; *see* Amaterasu
Tentei 天帝 (Lord of Heaven) 85
terakoya 寺子屋 (temple school) 170
teramachi 寺町 (temple district) 58
terauke 寺請 (temple certification) 2, 7, 10, 21-32, 53, 60, 69, 101, 105, 122-3, 147, 152-3, 161-2, 164-75, 184
    terauke shōmon 寺請証文 (temple certificate) 26, 153

Terazu 寺津 (village) 212
three bodies 112, 232
Three Dynasties (China) 101, 229
Three Great Houses of the Tokugawa; *see gosanke*
Three Sacred Treasures (*see* sacred treasures)
Toda Tadamasa 戸田忠昌 30
Toda Tadayuki 戸田忠至 242
Toeda Hikogorō 戸枝彦五郎 138-42
tojaku 戸籍 (census register) 219
Tōkai Zenji (Tōkaiji) 東海禅寺 146-7, 236
Tōkaku-bō 東覚坊 171
Toki Nagamoto 土岐長元 135
Tokiwa 常磐 (village) 185-8
Tōkōji 東光寺 182
tokorobarai 所払 (*see also* exile) 77
tokoyo no kuni 常世国 (Eternal World) 113
Tokugawa 徳川 (family) *passim*
    Hidetada 秀忠 22, 38, 55, 57, 159, 222
    Ieharu 家治 204
    Iemitsu 家光 11, 23-5, 40-1, 68, 108, 120, 222, 231
    Ietsugu 家継 41, 222
    Ietsuna 家綱 11, 24-5, 41, 57, 93, 120, 134, 137
    Ieyasu 家康 *passim*
    Kishū Tokugawa 紀州徳川 13, 42
    Mitsukuni 徳川光圀 7, 11, 15, 29-30, 92-98, 115, 117, 123, 135, 137, 152, 177-89, 218, 228, 230, 235, 240
    Nariaki 斉昭 188, 242
    Tsunaeda 綱條 178, 184-7
    Tsunayoshi 綱吉 16, 133, 137, 208
    Yorifusa 頼房 186-7
    Yorinobu 頼宣 13, 235
    Yoshimune 吉宗 76
    Yoshinao 義直 13, 15, 97-8, 101, 139, 229, 238
Tomomatsu Ujioki 友松氏興 134-5, 138-42, 145
Torigoe 鳥越 (shrine) 206
torii 鳥居 184
Tosa (province) 92, 127, 145, 163, 173
Tosa 土佐 (domain) 15, 27
toshiyori 年寄 192, 196-7

Tōshō Daigongen 東照大権現 (Avatar Illuminating the East; Tōshō Gongen) 3, 39–43, 129, 217, 222, 225, 230
Tōshōgū 東照宮 (shrine)
    Kagoshima 鹿児島 41
    Mito 水戸 189
    Nikkō 日光 9, 38–43, 222
    Nagoya 名古屋 208
    Tottori 鳥取 42
    Wakayama 和歌山 42
Tōshōsha 東照社 40
Tōshōsha engi 東照社縁起 222
Tottori 鳥取 (domain) 41
Toyokuni 豊国 (shrine) 9, 38, 218
Toyotomi (family) 9, 49, 91, 218
    Hideyori 秀頼 194
    Hideyoshi 秀吉 1–2, 9, 13, 15, 35–8, 47–8, 58, 63–6, 72, 99–100, 155, 158, 169, 191, 193–4, 218, 221, 243
Toyouke 豊受 (deity) 138
Tozaki 戸崎 (village) 182
tozama daimyō 外様大名 23, 119
Tōzenji 東漸寺 26
transition to paradise; see ōjō
Treasure Books of the Deities of Heaven and Earth; see Jingi hōten
Treatise on Wrongs in Divine Affairs; see Kamigoto no uretamigoto
Tripiṭaka; see Daizōkyō
Tsuchimikado Yasutomi 土御門泰福 137
Tsuchiura 土浦 (domain) 30
Tsuda Nagatada 津田永忠 124, 126, 232–3
Tsugaru 津軽 (domain) 14
Tsushi Gen'emon 都志源右衛門 165
Tsushima 対馬 (island) 64, 67
Tsūshin'in Nikkyō 通心院日境 68
turtle stone; see kifu
tutelary shrine/deity (chinju; see also ujigami) 32, 56, 164–7, 171, 174, 179, 184–6, 189, 191, 193, 197, 203
    one tutelary shrine per village; see isson issha seido

ubusuna 産土 (obusuna; see also ujigami; chinju) 56, 164–5
uchi 内 15
Uji 宇治 93, 158–60, 237
ujigami 氏神 (see also tutelary deity; ubusuna) 164, 186

ujiko 氏子 (shrine parishioner) 32, 57, 167–8, 174, 191,
    ujiko shirabe 氏子調 (ujiko aratame 氏子改) 32
Ukon 右近 194
unity of Shinto and Confucianism; see shinju itchi
unity of the three teachings; see sankyō itchi
unregistered person; see mushuku
Urabe 卜部 (family) 109, 208–9
    Urabe Hiramaro 卜部平麿 211
Urakami 浦上 (village) 84
Usa 宇佐 112, 232
Usaida 兎田 (village) 193
Ushimado 牛窓 (village) 127
Usuki 臼杵 (domain) 22
Utsunomiya 94, 242

vermillion-seal; see shuin
Vietnam 101
Vilela, Gaspar 56, 224
village head; see shōya
village official 26, 29, 182, 193–8, 243–4
village tutelary shrine; see chinju

Waidani 和意谷 121–2, 232–3
Waita 脇田 (village)
Wakayama 和歌山 (domain)
Wang Yangming 王陽明 119, 122, 129
Watanabe Masaka 渡辺政香 212–6
Way of the Emperor (Imperial Way) 113, 207, 209, 214
Way of the Gods; see shintō
Way of the Warrior; see budō
Wen 文 (King ~) 111
Wu 武 (King ~) 42, 108
wuxing 五行 (Five Agents; gogyō) 232
wuzhen 五鎮 (Five Pillars; gochin) 232

xiaolian 小斂; see shōren
Xuan 宣 (King ~) 232
Xuanming li 宣明暦 133, 136

yabusame 流鏑馬 (horse-back archery) 57
Yakuōin 薬王院 187
Yakushiji Kuzaemon 薬師寺久左衛門 57

Yakushi Nyorai 薬師如来 (Tathāgata Bhaiṣajyaguru) 42, 230
yamabushi 山伏 (see also Shugendō) 56, 179–82
Yamada 山田 (town) 93, 158–60, 237
   Yamada bugyō 山田奉行 (Yamada magistrate) 93, 158, 160
Yamada Yoshio 山田孝雄 216
Yamaga Sokō 山鹿素行 104
Yamagata Genshichi 山縣源七 240
Yamaguchi 山口 (town) 50
Yamaguchi Naotomo 山口直友 48
Yamato-hime 倭姫 111
Yamato-hime no mikoto seiki 倭姫命世記 111, 231
Yamazaki Ansai 山崎闇斎 5, 13, 104, 133–8, 142–7, 156
Yanagita Kunio 柳田国男 147
Yao 堯 108
Yasuda Muneyuki 保田宗雪 (Yasuda Wakasa no Kami) 25
Yatabe 矢田部 (village) 71
Yin Yang diviner; see onmyōji
yinsi 淫祠; see inshi
yōhaisho 遥拝所 (place for worshipping from afar) 140, 161
Yō senji 永宣旨 (Edict of Eternal [Priestly Office]) 156
Yojūin 養珠院 (Oman no kata お万の方) 65, 67
Yokoseura-machi 横瀬浦町 53
Yokota 横田 (family) 193, 197
   Iwami-no-kami 石見守 192, 198–9
   Jinsaemon 仁左衛門 197–8, 243
   Sajiemon 左二右衛門 197, 243
   Shōbei 庄兵衛 197–9, 243
Yokota Shun'eki 横田俊益 135
yomizome 読初 (first reading ritual) 125–6, 128, 234
yomotsukuni 黄泉国 (Nether World) 113
Yonezawa 米沢 (domain) 24
Yoriai-machi 寄合町 57, 224
yoriki 与力 84
yorishiro 依代 236
yosemiya 寄宮 (collective shrine) 92, 96, 165, 172, 239
Yoshida 吉田 (domain) 212
Yoshida 吉田 (family) 6–16, 30, 35, 92, 145, 151–3, 156–9, 161, 164–5, 172–4, 177, 184–8, 191–201, 203–16, 221, 237–8, 243–5
   Kaneharu 兼治 221
   Kanemi 兼見 9
   Kaneoki 兼起 238
   Kanetomo 兼倶 9–10, 35, 100, 155, 203, 208, 211, 222, 231, 245
   Kanetsura 兼連 140
   Kaneyuki 兼敬 238
Yoshida 吉田 (shrine, Kyoto) 208, 245
Yoshida 吉田 (shrine, Mito) 183–4
Yoshidaji 吉田寺 187
Yoshida-Ōuchi cult 9
Yoshida Shinto 吉田神道 9–10, 13–6, 37, 39, 100, 139, 142, 144–5, 147, 152, 155–8, 161, 165, 172–3, 184, 195, 197, 200, 208–9, 222, 228, 237, 245
   licence of Yoshida Shinto; see shintōsai kyojō
   rank certificate of Yoshida Shinto; see sōgen senji
Yoshikawa Aremi no ya sensei gyōjō 吉川視吾堂先生行状 144, 218
Yoshikawa 吉川 (family) 144–5
   Koretaru 惟足 5, 13–5, 96, 134–47, 152, 209, 218
   Yorinaga 従長 145, 218
Yoshikawa Shinto 吉川神道 137
Yoshimi Yoshikazu 吉見幸和 208
Yoshino 吉野 112, 232
Yoshino Gongen 吉野権現 111
yudate 湯立 (ritual) 57
Yui Shōsetsu 由井正雪 120
yuiitsu shintō 唯一神道 (One-and-Only Shinto) 10, 139, 155–8, 203, 208, 222, 237
Yuiitsu shintō myōbō yōshū 唯一神道妙法要集 155, 231
yuisho 由緒 (origin story) 185, 194, 241
Yūryaku Tennō 雄略天皇 111–2
Yūzū Dainenbutsu 融通大念仏 (sect) 80, 85

Zen 禅 (sect) 37, 100, 103–4, 107, 146–7, 179
Zenda 善田 (village) 26
Zhongyong 中庸 113

Zhou 紂 109
Zhou 周 (dynasty) 42, 66, 95–8, 111, 229
Zhu Shunsui 朱舜水 189
Zhu Xi 朱熹 5, 101, 104, 122–30, 134–5, 147
Zhu Xi's Family Rituals; see *Zhuzi jiali*
Zhuzi jiali 朱子家礼 7, 124–7, 188, 230, 236
Zōjōji 増上寺 39

Zoku shintō taii 俗神道大意 (*Outline of Vulgar Shinto*) 244
zoku-uke 俗請 (civil certification) 53
Zōtokuji 蔵徳寺 54
Zōyo 増誉 221
Zuirinji 瑞輪寺 68
Zuiryūsan 瑞龍山 (cemetery) 187
zuku 卒哭; see *sokkoku*

www.ingramcontent.com/pod-product-compliance
Lightning Source LLC
Chambersburg PA
CBHW072126290426
44111CB00012B/1788